Sisters and Strangers

Patricia Duncker is hereby identified as author of this work in
accordance with Section 77 of the Copyright, Designs and Patents
Act 1988.

First published 1992

Blackwell Publishers
108 Cowley Road, Oxford, OX4 1JF, UK

Three Cambridge Center
Cambridge, Massachusetts 02142, USA

Library of Congress Cataloging in Publication Data

Duncker, Patricia, 1951–
Sisters and strangers: an introduction to contemporary feminist
fiction/Patricia Duncker.
p. cm.
Includes bibliographical references and index.
ISBN 0–631–14492–7: $55.00. — ISBN 0–631–14493–5 : $19.95
1. English fiction—Women authors—History and criticism.
2. Feminism and literature—Great Britain—History—20th century.
3. Women and literature—Great Britain—History—20th century.
4. English fiction—Black authors—History and criticism.
5. English fiction—20th century—History and criticism.
6. Lesbians' writings, English—History and criticism. 7. Lesbians
in literature. 8. Blacks in literature. I.–Title.
PR88.F45D86 1991
823'.914099287—dc20
91–12053
CIP

British Library Cataloguing in Publication Data

A CIP catalogue record for this book is available from the British Library.

Typeset in 10 on 11 pt Ehrhardt
by TecSet Ltd, Wallington, Surrey
Printed in Great Britain by T. J. Press Ltd, Padstow, Cornwall

This book is printed on acid-free paper.

Sisters and Strangers

An Introduction to Contemporary Feminist Fiction

PATRICIA DUNCKER

BLACKWELL

Oxford UK & Cambridge USA

For S.J.D.

At home, my mother said, 'Remember to be sisters in the presence of strangers.' She meant white people, like the woman who tried to make me get up and give her my seat on the Number 4 bus, and who smelled like cleaning fluid. At St. Catherine's they said, 'Be sisters in the presence of strangers,' and they meant non-catholics. In high school, the girls said, 'Be sisters in the presence of strangers,' and they meant men. My friends said, 'Be sisters in the presence of strangers,' and they meant the squares.

But in high school, my real sisters were strangers; my teachers were racists; and my friends were that color I was never supposed to trust.

Audre Lorde, *Zami: A New Spelling of My Name*

Contents

Preface

The decision to write a critical account of my reading was made while I was active in many feminist groups and campaigns within the British women's movement. I was involved with the Greenham peace actions and taught feminist writing both in an academic context and to groups of women, many of whom would not describe themselves as feminists. I therefore make no apologies for the bias in this book towards British writing and British experience. Certainly there have been many American texts published in Britain – theory, fiction, and writing that breaks down the distinction between the two. I have written about these American books when they have been widely read and influential within British feminism and when I myself was influenced by them, but we all have our own battles to fight, because we have all been shaped by different histories, and the women's liberation movement in Britain has been significantly different from the women's movement in America.

I have concentrated on fiction, in the broadest sense, because that is the genre which interests me most as a writer and as a reader. However, in the chapter 'Writing Against Racism' I have referred, at length, to poetry written by Blackwomen. This is because a good deal of Black feminist – or Black Womanist – political theory is written as poetry, for reasons I have tried to describe in that chapter. Writing by Lesbians, Blackwomen (both Asian and Afro-Caribbean) and Blacklesbians who live and work in Britain has never received careful critical attention, even within the political frontiers of feminist literary criticism. This is a project that is just beginning and of which this book is a part. I do not believe that the sexual or racial identity of a writer constitutes a theoretical category or even necessarily marks a certain kind of writing; but the experience of being forced into a particular marginal position does have implications for a woman who finds herself writing from the rim of the circle. Her relationship to the languages she uses, to the forms she inhabits, will be different from that of the acknowledged legislators of literary traditions. Her position will affect how she is published or why she remains unpublished – and how she is read. The knowledge that her work will be judged by an audience, some part, or even the majority, of which will certainly be both racist and anti-Lesbian does affect how a woman writes. And I, as a white woman, am faced with the inescapable, insoluble difficulty of how I should discuss writing by Blackwomen. Not to make Black writing central to my arguments, which is where that writing so clearly belongs, on the grounds that whatever approach I choose will be racist, would be to silence and obliterate Blackwomen's work and energy. White culture in Britain must be prepared to address the emerging Black writers in this country – and be prepared for the inevitable, and long overdue, transformation and change. I wish to be part of that process. I have tried to write honestly.

I have addressed myself to all these difficulties in chapters 6 and 7, 'Writing Lesbian' and 'Writing Against Racism'; but I have also discussed work by women who might wish to define themselves as Blackwomen writers, or Lesbian, elsewhere in the book, wherever it was appropriate to do so. In other words, I have refused to transform chapters into ghettos.

Ideas are always produced collectively and so I have many women to thank: Caro Marsh, Lizzie Batten and Rose Buxton – whoever they are and wherever they are now; and the women who read some of the books with me in my feminist fiction classes and women's writing tutorials, and shared their responses and ideas. I would also like to thank my teachers, Jean Gooder, Sita Narasimhan, Hilda Brown and Marilyn Butler, while making it perfectly clear that they are in no way responsible for what follows. The men's corner in radical feminist acknowledgements is never very large, but I would like to thank James Read.

Blackwell asked three readers to comment on the typescript. Kath Burlinson and Kathleen Wheeler read the book critically, helpfully and honestly. I have tried to profit from their advice. The third reader clearly found this book both a painful and unpleasant read and therefore decided to remain anonymous.

To the women who have been both on my side and by my side in difficult times a simple word of thanks is hopelessly inadequate; but here it is anyway. Thank you to Dominique Rondi and Noëmi Neumann for writing to me and ringing me up. Noëmi Neumann died on 25 April 1988; she was and is very much loved. My most inarticulate thanks – as always – to Nasim Kassam and Sheila Duncker.

P. D.
France, 1991

Acknowledgements

The author and publisher are grateful to the following for permission to reprint copyright material.

To Elizabeth Wilson for excerpts from *Mirror Writing*, © Elizabeth Wilson, published by Virago Press, 1982. To Frauenoffensive Verlag and The Women's Press for excerpts from Verena Stefan, *Shedding*, © The Women's Press 1979. To Van Gennep, Amsterdam and The Women's Press for Anja Meulenbelt, *The Shame is Over*, © English translation, The Women's Press, 1980. To The Women's Press for permission to reprint excerpts from: Gillian Slovo, *Death by Analysis*, 1984; Jen Green and Sarah Lefanu, *Despatches from the Frontiers of the Female Mind*, 1985; Michèle Roberts, *The Visitation*, 1983; Mary Wings, *She Came too Late*, 1986; Merle Collins, *Angel*, 1987; excerpts from Merle Collins's poem 'No Dialects Please' and Meiling Jin, 'Hurt', both printed in *Watchers and Seekers*, 1987; Marion Molteno, *A Language in Common*, 1987; Ravinder Randhawa, *A Wicked Old Woman*, 1987; Sistren, *Lionheart Gal*, 1986; Jane Palmer, *The Planet Dweller*, 1985; Ellen Galford, *The Fires of Bride*, 1987; Anna Livia, *Accommodation Offered*, 1985; Caeia March, *Three Ply Yarn*, 1986; Suniti Namjoshi, *The Conversations of Cow*, 1985, and *The Blue Donkey Fables*, 1988; Isabel Miller, *Patience and Sarah*, 1979; Valerie Miner, *Murder in the English Department*, 1984; Jill Miller, *Happy as a Dead Cat*, 1983; Nicky Edwards, *Mud*, 1986; Sharan-Jeet Shan, *In My Own Name*, 1985. Copyright in the above is held by the individual authors, The Women's Press, London. To David Higham Associates for permission to print excerpts from Alice Walker, *Meridian*, © Alice Walker, published by The Women's Press, 1982. To The Charlotte Sheedy Literary Agency, New York for excerpts from Audre Lorde, *Sister Outsider*, © Audre Lorde, published by The Crossing Press, 1984. To Sara Maitland for excerpts from *Telling Tales*, © Sara Maitland, published by Journeyman Press, 1983. To Judith McDaniel, literary executor of The Estate of Barbara Deming, for permission to use excerpts from *A Humming Under my Feet*, © The Estate of Barbara Deming, published by The Women's Press. To Wallace Literary Agency for excerpts from Marge Piercy, *Woman on the Edge of Time*, © 1976, Marge Piercy and Middlemarsh Inc. Published by Alfred A.

Knopf and The Women's Press. To Rebecca O'Rourke for excerpts from *Jumping the Cracks*, © Rebecca O'Rourke, published by Virago Press, 1987. To Lis Whitelaw for excerpts from Rosemary Manning, *A Corridor of Mirrors*, © The Estate of Rosemary Manning, published by The Women's Press, 1987. To Rachel Barton and Sita for excerpts from *The Scarlet Thread*, © Rachel Barton, published by Virago Press, 1987. To W. W. Norton and Company Inc., for excerpts from May Sarton, *Recovering: A Journal*, © 1980 May Sarton. To Suzette Haden Elgin for excerpts from *Native Tongue*, 1985 and *The Judas Rose*, 1988, © Suzette Haden Elgin, published by Daw Books Inc. New York, and The Women's Press, London. To Curtis Brown Group Ltd for excerpts from Joan Riley, *The Unbelonging*, 1985, *Waiting in the Twilight*, 1987, and *Romance*, 1988 © Joan Riley, published by The Women's Press. To Routledge for excerpts from Elizabeth Wilson, *Hidden Agendas*, © Elizabeth Wilson, published by Tavistock, 1986. To Karnak House for excerpts from Grace Nichols, *i is a long-memoried woman*, © Grace Nichols, published by Karnak House, 1983. To Gower Publishing Group for excerpts from Jack Zipes, *Don't Bet on The Prince*, © Jack Zipes, 1986. To Barbara Wilson of The Seal Press, Seattle for excerpts from *Murder in the Collective*, © Barbara Wilson, published by The Women's Press, 1984, and Becky Birtha, *Lover's Choice*, © Becky Birtha, published by The Women's Press, 1988. To Judy Holland and Sarah Burton for excerpts from Hannah Wakefield, *The Price You Pay*, © Hannah Wakefield, published by The Women's Press, 1987. To Fyna Dowé for permission to reprint in full her poem 'The Word', © Fyna Dowé, originally published in *Watchers and Seekers*, The Women's Press, 1987. To Savi Hensman for her poem 'Black is Not a Skin Colour', originally published in her collection *Flood at the Door*, with illustrations by Sarah Moriarty, Centerprise Trust Ltd, 1979. To Bloomsbury for excerpts taken from *Mothers and Lovers* by Elizabeth Wood, published by Bloomsbury Publishing Ltd (1988). To Pluto Press for excerpts from Lauretta Ngcobo (ed.), *Let it be Told*, © individual authors, Pluto Press, 1987. To Alyson Publications for excerpts from Sally Miller Gearhart, *The Wanderground*, © Sally Miller Gearhart, published by The Women's Press, 1985. To Simon & Schuster for excerpts from Hélène Cixous, 'The Laugh of the Medusa', in Elaine Marks and Isabelle de Courtivron (eds), *New French Feminisms*, © each individual author, published by Harvester-Wheatsheaf (now part of the Simon & Schuster International Group), 1981. To A. M. Heath & Company Ltd for excerpts from Darcia Maraini, *Letters to Marina*, © Darcia Maraini, © translation by Dick Kitto and Elspeth Spottiswood, published by Camden Press Ltd, 1987. Extracts taken from Jeanette Winterson, *Oranges Are Not the Only Fruit*, © Jeanette Winterson, published by Pandora Press, 1985, and Jane Rule, *This is not for You*, © Jane Rule, published by Pandora Press, 1987, are reproduced by kind permission of Unwin Hyman. To Chatto and Windus for excerpts taken from Toni Morrison, *Beloved*, © Toni Morrison, published by Chatto and Windus, 1987. To Posy Simmonds for permission to reproduce her cartoon, 'The World Turned Upside Down', first published in *The Guardian* and reprinted in *Pure Posy*, Jonathan Cape, 1987. To Alison Ward for permission to use excerpts from *The Glass Boat*, published by Brilliance Books, 1983. To Éditions Gallimard for excerpts from *Moi Rigoberta*

Menchú, edited and narrated by Elisabeth Burgos-Debray, 1983, © English translation by Ann Wright, published by Verso, 1984. To Prism Press for excerpts from Gail Chester and Julienne Dickey (eds), *Feminism and Censorship: The Current Debate*, 1988. To Virago Press for permission to include excerpts from the following publications: Christina Roche, *I'm not a feminist, but. . .*, 1985; Carolyn Steedman, *Landscape for a Good Woman*, 1986; Grace Nichols, *Whole of a Morning Sky*, 1986; Aileen La Tourette, *Cry Wolf*, 1986; Zoë Fairbairns, *Stand We at Last*, 1983; Maureen Duffy, *That's How It Was*, published by Virago, 1983; Beatrix Campbell, *Wigan Pier Revisited*, 1984, copyright held by the individual authors; Violette Leduc, *La Bâtarde*, © Editions Gallimard, translated by Derek Coltman, first published in Great Britain by Peter Owen Ltd in 1965, published by Virago Press, 1985. To Sheba Feminist Publishers for excerpts from Audre Lorde, *The Cancer Journals*, 1980; *Zami*, 1984; *Our Dead Behind Us*, 1986; Suniti Namjoshi, *Feminist Fables*, 1981; Barbara Burford, *The Threshing Floor*, 1986 (© held by individual authors). To Naiad Press for excerpts from Claire Morgan (Patricia Highsmith), *The Price of Salt*, published by Naiad Press in 1984. To Blackwomantalk for an excerpt from 'I'd also like to say. . .' by Adjoa Andoh in *Black Women Talk Poetry*, © Blackwomantalk, 1987. To Onlywomen Press for excerpts from Lilian Mohin (ed.), *One Foot on The Mountain*, 1979; Anna Wilson, *Cactus*, 1980; and *Altogether Elsewhere*, 1985; Anna Livia, *Relatively Norma*, 1982, and *Bulldozer Rising*, 1988; Caroline Forbes, *The Needle on Full*, 1985; and Lilian Mohin and Sheila Shulman (eds), *The Reach*, 1984 (© held by the individual authors). To Methuen for excerpts from Toril Moi, *Textual/Sexual Politics*, 1985; Elizabeth Wilson, *Prisons of Glass*, 1986; Gayatri Spivak, *In Other Worlds*, 1987; Sara Maitland, *A Book of Spells*, 1987; and Michèle Roberts, *The Wild Girl*, 1984, and *The Book of Mrs Noah*, 1987 (© held by the individual authors).

1

On Writing and Roaring

'. . . a woman's power and charm resides in mystery, not in muscular rant. But possibly rant is a sign of vitality: it mars the beautiful creature, but shows that she is alive.'

E. M. Forster, *A Room With A View*

This book is an autobiography of reading. It is about the books, written by women to women, which I have read; books which gave me good cause for anger, recognition and pain, books which changed the way I saw the world and the way I lived my life. It is therefore impossible for me to write an impartial survey of feminist achievements in the Great Field of Literature; that is not how these books were written, nor how they were received. I have watched the extraordinary explosion of feminist writing in every part of the world since the late 1960s. In these years we have been able again to write for one another, to write assuming that there is a political community there to be addressed, to write knowing that there is a women's liberation movement. I must necessarily tell the story of my own reading, reveal my particular politics of reading, and offer my perspective on the politics of the British women's movement over the past years. What I have to say will therefore be partial, opinionated and unfinished. We have only just begun to make up our own culture, invent our own stories. Feminism is a raw politics, still being shaped and made by the communities of women who are the divisive edge of revolutionary change.

I first called myself a feminist in 1970, though I must have had visible nascent tendencies before then: one of the boys in my year at school used to call me The Suffragette. But it was in 1970, when I first went up to Newnham College, Cambridge to study literature, that I first joined a women's group, Scarlet Women, and first read Germaine Greer's *The Female Eunuch*, which I reviewed for the first and only issue of our feminist magazine, *Bloody Women*. I took good care not to read Kate Millett's *Sexual Politics* because, at that time, I was wedded to a politics of literature which embraced the Great Tradition. This consisted of a long string of supposedly lonely, isolated geniuses, creating order out of chaos, shaping the world in their own image, and in the course of their heroic struggles coming up with Eternal Truths and Everlasting Values. The lonely genius was more or less always male and usually a poet, but there were good fellows like Henry Fielding who wrote jolly fiction about equally good fellows enjoying the roast beef of old England and wenches in taverns. Kate Millett turned on my heroes, the gods of the sexual revolution of the 1960s, and made them out to be a pack of violent misogynists. I was very anxious that I might have to stop reading – or at least stop enjoying reading – D. H. Lawrence.

I am white and middle-class, but not entirely English. My father is Jamaican, and I was born and brought up in a woman-dominated household on an island which has been exploited by the British for over a hundred years. I was educated largely in England. My parents bought me an expensive education at public school where I learned how to sound like one of the ruling class even if I never had the money to back up the accent. This background is very important to me and my writing. I am implicated in the political structures of white, racist Britain, but I am also an observer. I still have my Jamaican passport; I had to apply for British nationality and resident status. There were no difficulties, of course, because the British immigration laws are overtly racist, and I am white. But I was not born here. This is not my country. When I first read Wordsworth I had never seen a daffodil. In St Andrew's High School for Girls, Kingston, Jamaica, we looked at a picture. 'This is a daffodil,' said the teacher. English literature was an alien culture, one that I was anxious to acquire. I wanted to belong. It was therefore not surprising that I put up a good fight when asked to be savagely critical of a tradition within which I had taken such pains to find a place.

A psychological and political split ensued. I was involved daily in various feminist campaigns: against the Cambridge League for the Preservation of Gentlemen's Colleges (now, I believe, defunct); in support of a woman in town whose supplementary benefit had been cut off and whose children had been taken into care because she had indulged herself with the occasional boyfriend; demanding a women's bar in College; buying the bread, cheese and Branston pickle for the Women's Lunch. But for the rest of my time I studied the Grand March of Great White Male Writers, subconsciously convinced that if I started asking questions it would all end in tears. So I studied my Great Tradition: Chaucer, Spenser, Shakespeare, Milton, Wordsworth, George Eliot, Henry James, D. H. Lawrence. I did notice that there was something wrong with the list. But George Eliot, surely, only gave herself a man's name because she had to keep quiet about not being adequately married. Or perhaps she thought that it would get her a better reception from the critics and a more serious response from her publishers and other writers. I took great care not to ask the next question: Why were women writers not taken seriously? Of course they were. Look how seriously everybody takes Jane Austen. And I wrote essays about how Jane Austen might be narrow and limited in scope, but, after all, she was drawing on a woman's experience. And yet, what depth! Ah, what penetration! What an ear for dialogue! What insight into women's psychology! The critical significance of their little concerns with match-making, materials, stuff, jams, bonnets, balls, soldiers, visits. Admirable. And how wise to concern herself with courtship rather than marriage, of which, as a spinster, she would have had no experience. Such is the power of literary ideology and the anxious desire of a young student to do well that I never appreciated the matrimonial relationship of Mr and Mrs Bennett, nor saw beyond the end of Jane Austen's final sentences to the inevitable woe that there is in marriage.

I did ask myself why there were not any female Shakespeares. And Virginia Woolf told me why.[1] How could there be? Women were not taught to read. If Miss Shakespeare had set off to make her fortune in London she would certainly have been raped and murdered. In any case, she would not have been able to earn her living as an actress. Boys played women on Shakespeare's stage.[2] And so the rationalizing went on. I never asked the second set of questions in my literature supervisions. I kept my feminist sexual politics and my literary studies in two separate boxes. The women's liberation movement meant to me then what it means to me now: feminism is a political analysis of women's oppression by men and a political response to the conditions of that oppression. And I take women's oppression to mean the suffering, disadvantage and deprivation women endure precisely because of their sex. Which is not to say that women do not suffer other disadvantages and other oppressions; but all women are oppressed as women. There are, notoriously, many feminisms. The women's liberation movement was then, and still is, a broad and heterogeneous movement. But it is grounded in a struggle that is not solitary, but collective. And that collective struggle has a common aim: to transform society, all societies, so that the accident of sex is not oppressive to women. In *Gossip: A Journal of Lesbian Feminist Ethics* Kris, a Blackwoman, movingly describes her experience of sexual abuse and the racism she encountered among white feminists while trying to come to terms with her own grief within the Lesbian community.[3] Kris's response was brave, practical and politically acute. She set up a phone line and support group for other black women who were child abuse survivors. And she dedicated her testimony to the women who did not survive. This response – a critical political analysis of her own experience and, in the light of that analysis, an astute, loving commitment to other women – is at the core of feminist theory and feminist practice at their very best.[4]

Feminism is therefore about the forging of bonds between women, even across our differences. It is about challenging the assumptions and expectations which bolster up male power and male privilege and cluster like barnacles around the fact of sexual difference. Even to speak of sexual difference masks the facts of privilege; it is nonsense to discuss sexual difference without confronting male power.

Sex is a biological fact. Some of us are irrefutably women and some of us are men.[5] But that is not the end of the story. Upon that fact we have built the most peculiar edifice of social expectations and constructed a host of institutions, which as often as not confine women to the kitchens, the caring professions, the service industries and the ranks of the wickedly low-paid or unemployed. A key word deployed in the process is 'natural'; and the concept of nature, is, I find, usually mobilized to end the discussion. You must have heard it said: it's only natural for women to want children. Women are natural wives and mothers. Women are naturally passive, or naturally emotional, intuitive, irrational. Women are naturally faithless and fickle: or, oddly enough, naturally devoted, loyal and faithful. Women are naturally lustful and lascivious. Women are naturally frigid. Feminists have always challenged this unstable concept of nature, because the social and cultural norms which suit the status quo often

Figure 1 'The world turned upside-down': Posy Simmonds in The Guardian, 1987

masquerade as eternal, immutable differences. But we are not locked into biological prisons and the breaking point of nature is human being itself.[6]

Gerd Brantenberg's *The Daughters of Egalia* is a fantastical allegorical novel which reverses the biological mirror of Nature.[7] Menwim, crushed by and dependent upon the powerful, violent wim, are kept in their place by the demonstrably ridiculous assertion that 'after all, it is menwim who beget and receive children'. Brantenberg is a Norwegian Lesbian feminist. She knows that there is nothing natural about heterosexuality, nor about the system of sexual oppression. It is man-made. Brantenberg's text has moments of high comedy as the lordies, beards in anxious curlers, cultivate their rolls of fat to attract the heartless, magnificent wim. The sexual encounters she describes, revealing her whole-hearted political commitment to the clitoral (as opposed, of course, to the vaginal) orgasm, blow the whistle on any natural aspects we might have imagined inherent in current heterosexual practice. There is no natural expression of sexuality, and we would be wise to remember that. But the book becomes alarming and uncanny when it does affirm the apparently unchangeable: that is, the superior physical strength of men. One of the menwim, Spinnerman Owlman, smashes his desk to pieces in front of his mixed class. The menwim's liberation movement begins with an act of violence. Violence is often glamorized and eroticized in popular novels by men. Brantenberg herself has worked in refuges for women who have been battered by men. Violence usually has a very different political meaning in feminist writing: it becomes a sinister force for social control. Brantenberg's novel polarizes her readers into women and men, or in this case wim and menwim; this is a characteristic tactic within feminist fiction.

Men seldom challenge the social construction of masculinity, which is also often trumpeted forth as a natural fact, because they do not perceive it as being in their interest to do so. But masculinity too is fraught with contradictions. Here is John Bowen, writing in the *New Statesman*:

> The experience of masculinity for all men is one of violence, of heterogeneous groupings and alliances against ourselves, other men, women. Our task is first to make clear what these contradictions are, to celebrate that they exist and then to exploit them. It is perhaps here that a politics of masculinity differs from a feminist politics. A feminist politics is often concerned with the forging of alliances, of stressing the common experience of oppression, of uniting women in that common knowledge. A progressive politics of masculinity has to be primarily concerned with destroying alliances between men against others, and founding other alliances, both within and more importantly outside the traditional forms of male organisation, from the sports club to the trade union.[8]

Men who read or study literature are in an interesting position with respect to the debates of sexual politics, because literature is inescapably concerned with the relations between the sexes – indeed, this is the classic territory of fiction – with the construction of gender and with what it means to be of one sex or the other within particular social circumstances. But in those first years as a professional student of literature I made, as I say, an absolute separation between my sexual politics and my textual sexual politics.[9] I must have fused brain cells in the process.

I had my doubts, of course, and these suddenly surfaced when I was studying John Donne. I knew Donne was wonderful. T. S. Eliot said he was. I even knew why. One of his contemporaries, Thomas Carew, wrote an elegy on his death in 1631, in which he praised Donne's 'line of masculine expression'. The garden of Elizabethan poetry, was, according to Carew, 'with Pedantique weeds o'erspred'; but Donne had changed all that. Like a gigantic phallic mower he had put poetry in good order; and many of the metaphors used to describe him doing just that were couched in terms of masculine sexual aggression. Donne, apparently, 'committed Holy Rapes upon our Will'. Rape has a radically different meaning for a woman reader than for a man, and it was disconcerting to move from the streets, where I was busy taking direct action in defence of a woman's right to control her own body, into the library, to use 'bold Rape' and 'ravishment' as terms of critical approbation.

But I persevered. I knew most of Donne's remorselessly heterosexual love poems off by heart. One in particular used to haunt me: 'The Sunne Rising'. This is a rant against the sun for coming into the room while the poet and his mistress are still making love. In the last verse he supposedly celebrates the woman.

> She is all States, and all Princes, I,
> Nothing else is.

I wrote cautious essays about how the poet–lover's arrogance carries absolute conviction. What I did not challenge then was the assumption in the poem that the man was an absolute sexual ruler and that the woman was the ruled subordinate; or that Donne was praising a system of sexual oppression that actually existed in seventeenth-century England, and still exists in England now. The topical metaphors of imperialism and conquest applied to sexual love litter his love poems. Here is a passage from 'Elegie: To His Mistress Going to Bed' (Donne speaking, of course):

> O my America, my new founde lande
> My kingdome, safeliest when with one man mann'd
> My myne of precious stones, my Empiree
> How blest I am in this discovering thee.

So, imperialism was a legitimate metaphor for the ownership and control of women's bodies. I noticed that the women never answered back in Donne's poems. Occasionally they did things – slept with someone else, died or killed fleas in the bed – but Donne got all the good lines and he did all the talking. One of his poems opened with a great shout: 'For Godsake hold your tongue and let me love . . . ' Then Donne became a priest and started telling God what to do. I gave up writing about John Donne and wrote about George Herbert instead.

Herbert was also a priest. He didn't talk to women. He only talked to God. And, interestingly, God was given lines in the poems. He was even allowed to argue back. So the men were willing to talk to invisible Gods and even to let them answer: but they rendered present women invisible and denied them speech. Aristotle said that silence was a woman's glory, and obviously a lot of men took that seriously.

But why were women poets not writing back? Were we educated? Would we have been published? Could we write? Would the forms, genres, styles – even the words men had constructed – hold what we wanted to say? Or had our masters realized the link between literacy and revolution? John Donne's love poetry was full of invisible, silent women. Many contemporary feminist books are about breaking silences: Tillie Olsen's *Silences* for example, and Adrienne Rich's *On Lies, Secrets and Silence*.[10] I started to listen to silences and I learned that silence is not absence, it is not even necessarily complicit acquiescence. Silence is not consent. And I learned that education was as much about withholding information as imparting it; I learned that reading is a profoundly political process. In my hot youth I heard the silence of women become a wonderful, unrelenting roar.

The radical basis of feminism is story-telling: sitting in circles, listening to one another, valuing one another's words, telling one another stories. For feminism rises not out of every woman's solitary experience, but out of a political analysis of women's collective experience. And of course we all start from different places. The diversity of feminism should be a virtue and a strength, and it is in our interest to be committed to dialogue, discussion and solidarity across our differences, for there is no party line and no monolithic dogma. The fact of feminism which makes it both difficult and unpopular to swallow is that we are required, as individuals, to ask ourselves where we stand with respect to an extraordinary system of social relations, roles and expectations based on the biological accident of sex. What do we think about sexual politics? Where are we placed within that system? And in what ways has that sexual system made us what we are? None of these questions is comfortable to ask. But it does matter to ask, not just: is this a woman or a man writing, talking? but: what is the significance of the fact that it is a woman, and a feminist woman, who writes?

A feminist approach to writing by women should also be a commitment to dialogue, and to a community of writers and readers. Patriarchal criticism subsumes all other texts within its own, like a scavenger: feminist criticism should refuse that process of disintegration and digestion. I am not an arbiter of taste; I speak for myself. And this book is the story of a dialogue, the story of all the women who wrote down their stories and who spoke to me.

I perceive three strands within the project of feminist literary criticism. The first is the feminist critique of sexist literary ideology, which questions the deep structures of the text, whether written by a woman or a man, questions what has been assumed to be natural, challenges cliché, prejudice, woman-hating, the existing structures of power in the world which have been endorsed on the page. Kate Millett's missile *Sexual Politics* was a bravura performance which has never really been equalled: this and Germaine Greer's *The Female Eunuch*, even seen against the immense flood of sophisticated thinking which has poured off the presses, feminist and otherwise, to make our revolution, or to make the careers of individual women, still read like Jeremiahs with a new vision for Israel.[11] Both books present a still largely unanswered – indeed, an unanswerable – case for a women's revolution.

Elaine Showalter coined the term 'gynocritics' from the French, '*la gynocritique*', to name a discourse within feminist criticism which concerns itself with

> *woman as writer* – with woman as the producer of textual meaning, with the history, themes, genres and structures of literature by women. Its subjects include the psychodynamics of female creativity; linguistics and the problem of a female language; the true trajectory of the individual or collective female literary career; literary history; and of course studies of particular writers and works.[12]

This critical project, crucial to our understanding of our own history as literary women, women writing, is the second thread; and it overlaps with the third, of feminist speculative critical writing in the French intellectual tradition which adopts and develops themes from psychoanalysis and linguistics.[13]

There was one brief and glorious moment when I did imagine that psychoanalysis would be an immensely powerful and suggestive theory for the study of literature. An account of the creation of psycho-sexual identity and the construction of gender is, of course, of critical importance to the reading and writing of fiction. All fiction – fairy-tales, short stories, novels – necessarily places sexual politics and sexual difference at the core of the text, so that a theoretical challenge to the supposedly natural categories of male and female in the splintering of masculinity and femininity would indeed be revolutionary in its implications. The insistence in modern post-Freudian theory that there is a *linguistic* basis for the construction of sexual difference and that the human subject, masculine or feminine, comes into being only through language, is an idea of extreme relevance for every kind of feminist writing; we do, after all, construct our fictions and polemics through language.

Freudian theory denies the notion that there is any stable human personality. There is no unified perceiving subject; we are a mass of conscious and unconscious drives, sexual and otherwise, processes and desires about which we know little and over which we have even less control. We do not become who we are by what we experience, but are unknown, even to ourselves. Freud's theories on psycho-sexual development shatter the notion of any kind of natural sexuality and, in particular, any notion of heterosexuality as a natural preference. But this contention, on the face of it extraordinarily pertinent for feminism, loses its radical edge in the mire of the Oedipus myth.

> For Freud there is no sexual difference in the pre-Oedipal stage: through the oral, anal and phallic phases, the little girl is no different from the little boy. It is at the moment of the Oedipal crisis that the crucial change in the little girl's orientation occurs: whereas the little boy continues to take his mother as his object, the little girl has to turn from her pre-Oedipal attachment to the mother and take her father as love-object instead. This shift is not only hard to explain; it is also

difficult to accomplish: it is even dubious, as Freud freely admits, whether most women really manage wholly to relinquish their pre-Oedipal attachment and develop a fully 'mature' femininity.[14]

The implication for Lesbians is clear: we are remorselessly stuck in the pre-Oedipal phase and fixated on our mothers.

The turn-of-the-century sexologists, Freud included, do need to be read within their historical context and in relation to the feminist campaigns of the period. In her account of the struggles on these issues conducted by the women's movement in the early twentieth century, Sheila Jeffreys make it clear that homosexuality among women was irresistibly connected with feminism.[15] A woman who refused to adopt a feminine sex role, who refused to marry and reproduce, was in herself unnatural. And it is during this earlier period of feminism that the Lesbian becomes a marked clinical category, and that the stereotype of the short-haired mannish Lesbian is invented and portrayed in fiction. Elizabeth Wilson's scepticism on the value of psychoanalysis for feminism, which I share, proves particularly acute on the question of Lesbianism. She writes:

> ... feminist theoretical writings drawing on psychoanalysis have had remarkably little to say about homosexuality and lesbianism. If anything, psychoanalysis seems to have been used implicitly to justify heterosexual relationships at a period in the women's movement when women who wanted to relate to men sexually felt under pressure from feminists who were lesbians.[16]

Wilson's central objection to psychoanalysis is the way in which it has been used to shut down debate around the construction of gender. We learn our psycho-sexual roles and that's that: if we don't learn them properly we end up neurotic, psychotic and hysterical. Freud's theory, fragmented, speculative, contradictory, becomes dogmatically prescriptive. Few commentators make much of the fact that the theory is also very clearly ethnocentric. Oedipus may have something to say to white, western, capitalist Vienna, but the familial structures in Jamaica surrounding me in my childhood were very different. That tense neurotic triangle of mother–father–child hardly existed. Most Jamaican children are brought up by older female relatives, often their grandmothers.[17] In my family this role was taken by my godmother, Aunt Vi, then well into her sixties, whom I adored, and still do, and who was my most constant companion. I had a nurse too, but Miss Vi was the supervisor. Advocates of psychoanalytic theory as a tool for feminist analysis rarely point this out, but I would have thought that, since Freud is describing the neuroses of western capitalism, it is unlikely that a universal theory of sexual difference, gender construction or the acquisition of language could ever be derived from his work. And Freud would certainly have agreed. So far as he was concerned, his 'observations stood or fell by the quality of clinical evidence he was able to produce in support of them'.[18]

My own experience of psychoanalysis is instructive here. In 1978 I became seriously depressed and retreated to the bottom of my sleeping bag. A wealthy member of my family suggested that I should be handed over to an analyst who was enormously expensive and quite wonderful. He could, apparently, have cured Virginia Woolf.[19] Try anything once, I thought, and agreed. The analyst was a white man who lived in a beautiful flat, full of handsome furniture. When I arrived at 7.30 in the morning, still almost asleep, he did not ask me who I was or what seemed to be the trouble. Instead, he sat down and looked at me. I avoided the couch and sat down in an armchair. We sat in silence for an hour. This cost £55. The same thing happened again the following week. I sat there wondering if I should tell him my dreams. I couldn't remember them. Had transference taken place? Would I notice if it had? At the end of that session I wrote him a letter saying that I was abandoning the analysis as it didn't seem to be getting anywhere. He wrote back and told me that analysis takes a long time. I decided to go on holiday in France with a friend and returned very cheerful and completely cured.

Upon hearing this sorry tale one feminist friend shrieked, 'Patricia, you nerd! You were supposed to freely associate!' With what, I wondered? And an American woman, herself a Freudian psychoanalyst, jumped up and down with hilarity and rage. 'What an idiot! He should have said something. Your silence was resistance. A rebellion! He should have talked about why it was that you were silent. The analysis had already begun.' Now no one comes to analysis innocent of Freud's supporting theories. Both the women who commented upon my experience of analysis, although neither was entirely serious, made one common assumption: that I was somehow in the wrong.[20] I had failed to perform. I had rebelled. I had refused the terms of the engagement. (I had also saved myself and my relatives a lot of money.) My own view of Freud, for I think I should come clean here, is that of an admiring enthusiast. He is an extraordinary writer. But I think that we should read his work as speculative or detective fiction, the Tales of the Old Vienna Woods, which would encourage a healthy suspicion and irreverence.

I am dubious about the easy shift from analysing people to analysing texts. I acknowledge the similarities: a memory, dream or fragment, gnomic or enigmatic, can resemble the psychic structure of a lyric poem; the sequential narration of a life history might well have the characteristic features of a realist novel, the disruption and displacement of that sequence might read like a modernist text. Both written texts and human beings are marked by gaps, omissions, evasions, silences; that the gaps and the blanks are as critical, as significant as what is actually said is certainly true. Like the space between musical notes, the blank silences set the terms for what can be heard. Women's silences are particularly significant; very often we ourselves – our bodies, our voices – are the silences, the censored spaces in the texts, as I found reading John Donne's love poems. We must be there to be loved, but we must hold our tongues. Hélène Cixous, advocate *extraordinaire* of *l'écriture féminine*, answers back.

> . . . my desires have invented new desires, my body knows unheard-of songs . . .
> And why don't you write? Write! Writing is for you, you are for you; your body is yours, take it . . .

By writing her self, woman will return to the body which has been more than
confiscated from her . . .
Write your self. Your body must be heard . . .
It is by writing, from and toward women, and by taking up the challenge of
speech which has been governed by the phallus, that women will confirm women
in a place other than that which is reserved in and by the symbolic, that is in a
place other than silence.
Women should break out of the snare of silence.[21]

Speak! Write! And we are then confronted with the problems of language – the
phallic language, the signs, systems, meanings, even modes of thought that are
not of our own making.

In December 1984 I drove up to North Yorkshire to discuss a book project
on feminist spirituality with a woman I had never met before. I received a very
warm welcome. We had a vegetarian lunch. As we settled down in front of the
fire to talk she said, smiling, 'I must make it quite clear that I don't accept any
form of rationality and that I cannot use patriarchal reasoning of any kind in
discussion.' I turned very pale, as the hierarchy of subject, verb, object and the
phallic march of patriarchal logical thinking in which I was thoroughly drilled
faded away with fife and drum into the distance. This was, of course, a
statement of intent on the part of my friend. She was warning me that my usual
assumptions need not apply. I hastily agreed that if the arms race was rational I
was for lunacy every time.

Until that afternoon I had always, without being aware that I did so, assumed
that rationality and logic were gender-neutral; that thinking, in a reasoned
conventional mode, was not oppressive to women. I was convinced that what
mattered was *what* we thought, not so much *how* we thought it. And was it
possible to think without language? And if we do only think in language, it is
true that 'men control language . . . and that women are alienated from
language to a degree that men are not'?[22]

My friend argued that there was an indivisible link between *logic* and *force*. I
spent many hours pondering that statement. We cannot separate language, or
indeed rational argument, from the institutions they create or the uses to which
they are put. Let me explain. I was always rendered uneasy by love poetry, the
literary purpose of which was to argue the textual woman concerned into bed. I
did not like John Donne's 'The Exstasie' when we first read it at school. The
two souls of the lovers are compared to 'two equall Armies' negotiating; I wasn't
too sure about the soul, but I knew that when it came to bodies women were
never in an equal negotiating position.[23] Donne argued that his mistress's soul
and his own united to form a third element.

Wee then, who are this new soule, know,
    Of what we are compos'd, and made,
For, th'Atomies of which we grow,
    Are soules, whom no change can invade.

Fair enough, but the very next stanza utterly changed the terms of the engagement:

> But O alas, so long, so farre
> Our bodies why doe we forbeare?

At this point I puffed myself up with all the feminist righteousness a sixteen-year-old can muster and pointed that women's bodies and men's bodies were not at all the same, whatever their souls were like, and that what he said could not happen; change and invasion were precisely what were going to happen to the woman in the poem. She, as usual, had not said anything at all, other than what Donne said she said. My teacher (a man) tried to reassure me and pointed out that Donne was perfectly aware of what I had said and that he was redefining sexuality. 'The Exstasie' was a mutual consummation, not a long-winded seduction. I was not convinced.

We all found Andrew Marvell's 'To His Coy Mistress', which we read next, much more convincing, because he made no bones about the terms of the encounter. 'Deserts of vast Eternity' do indeed lie before us all. Marvell, too, speaks of 'we' all the way through, but it is the propositional we; she can dissent at any time. And the woman too has strength and sweetness, she too is an 'am'rous bird of prey'. The poem is utterly open-ended. Marvell does not tell her what is happening; he simply makes out a case for bed at once. She could have listened to the argument – a very good one – and still refused.[24]

Rational, logical argument is always linear thinking which arrives at a resolution. Logic posits a single correct answer. Even a paradox suggests that the right answer has been deferred, that the solution exists somewhere else. But I do not think that men have a monopoly on logic any more than that they have absolute control over meaning; if they had, neither I nor any of the other women whose work I have read would have written at all. We would be unable to express any meanings of our own. I think that there is a link between logic and force, but it is not a necessary one. We can produce our own arguments and present them, if we wish to, in non-linear ways. We can and should write for each other in innovative, flexible, creative forms. We are not subject to language or thinking as if we were abject serfs within systems outside or even inside ourselves. We can think, speak and write differently if we choose to do so – and if we have the economic and political power to put that decision into action. But we can also keep a different kind of silence.

The problem with any deterministic theory of language which maintains that we are constructed as thinking beings entirely within and through language is that we then lose touch with the fact that it is perfectly possible to have an experience for which there are no words. Linguistic determinism always denies or subverts a politics of experience, and feminism is based upon the collective experience of women,[25] which is the experience of being sexually oppressed by men, an oppression which has many forms, many faces and many languages.

For the French intellectual feminists the unstable distinction between woman and text, analyst and analysand, is re-drawn in the blurred frontiers between literary and critical writing, between author and critic. I think that the disintegration of the latter category is particularly useful. A critic judges writing, sets up her own standards of taste, and chooses between the good, the bad and the ugly. I also think that this power should not be underestimated. May Sarton's bitter distress about the bad review of her novel *A Reckoning* is not an oversensitive artist's neurosis. Here are her reasons.

> Every writer is too aware of his [sic] own defects, too filled with anxiety about his work, too full of self doubt to be able blithely to cast aside a bad review. It is a drop of poison and slowly gets into the system, day by day . . . You can rise above one or two public humiliations such as this, but finally after ten or more it gets to you. I felt finished . . . Here one must face the fact that my livelihood as well as my talent as a writer are involved. A bad review keeps readers from buying a book, it is as simple as that. When a major work near the end of a long life is 'wasted' in this way, it means that the writer must set to at once and produce another in order to keep afloat financially.[26]

All criticism is opinion – and political opinion too. A critic will usually argue for the kind of writing she wants to read, and to see written; which is why the faceless magisterial authority invested in criticism is so pernicious. Every critic has a vested interest, so it is only good manners to say what that interest is, and to make your politics utterly, explicitly clear; also to make visible the political process through which you are moving, for only the arrogant and the mad ever arrive at a fixed and static position. Reading with suspicion gives each one of us the power and the liberty to disagree with every book we read. Yet we must desire to be drawn in, engaged, persuaded, convinced. My reading is an active, somewhat aggressive experience. I never borrow books because I like to write back in the margins, which is what we, as women, have always done. If we could write, we did so in the margins of the patriarchal text.

It was, and is, very important for us to tell and to read the stories of each other's lives, of our own lives, of our conversions to feminism. But we must subject our own stories to a rigorous political questioning. Most of our social behaviour, including our sexual codes, even our most apparently private fantasies and desires, are in fact experienced as if we were acting out prescribed roles. And we often interpret our experiences as we have been told to do. A raped woman often really does feel that it was her fault. The politics of consciousness-raising aims not to deny that experience, but to look carefully at the reasons why it suits men that we should feel shame and guilt, at why we should take the blame for their violence. We should not therefore be surprised if, in telling our stories, we uncover unknown acres of pain, grief, frustration and rage. In Elizabeth Wilson's *Prisons of Glass* a somewhat valedictory, elegiac chord sounds throughout.[27] The novel tells, in a sequence of fragmented scenes, like an old film, the story of the women's liberation movement and the politics which accompanied its emergence. The central figure, Crystal, ends up retreating into convention, about to be married, involved in psychoanalysis, finally collecting the stories of the women she once knew while she was an activist of sorts in the women's movement. She ends up doing the research for *Prisons of Glass*. There is one dreadful, accurate chapter, 'The Lost Weekend', where sisterhood strains at the seams. The editorial collective of *Termagant*, barricaded into a country cottage, harangue each other in underhand ways for a whole weekend and depart on Sunday evening with all the wounds unhealed. All of us have probably been through nightmares like this one, where torrents of egotism and need, interspersed with outbursts of tears and bids for power, make a family Christmas discussing some dead relative's will look like a pushover. But common political ground can never be assumed; I cannot remember ever thinking that it could be, and I do not think so now.

> Yet they were here, sitting round in a circle, revealing themselves in order to affirm their sameness, mutual identification was the purpose . . . the sameness they wanted was of women oppressed and in struggle, forging a common identity to brandish against the world . . . It hadn't been as easy as they'd expected to work together all year. You couldn't explore your differences because the constant imperative of sisterhood stifled dissent.[28]

I was surprised reading this. Presumably the *Termagant* collective did all actually think that they were 'women oppressed and in struggle' or they would not have been there in the first place. Wilson chooses to emphasize frustration, difference, enmity and division. Certainly, working in any group, we do all experience these things; but in my life, oddly enough, where women gather, the sense of community is always there too. I was recently in hospital, and experienced the same solidarity and understanding, even across our differences, in the gynaecology ward that I also found in a rural women's discussion group. There I was the odd. one out, the unmarried woman without small children. There was disagreement, certainly; sisterhood never stifled quite significant dissent; but there was a more overpowering feeling that we were all on the same side. I was as surprised to feel this there as were the rest of the group. Intriguingly, in Wilson's narrative, it is the political alliances with men, outside the *Termagant* collective, which really cause the trouble: who is in the Communist Party, who is part of a Trotskyist group, who is stuck in a truly awful heterosexual relationship. It is part of the malaise of the women's liberation movement in the recent years that we bewail our divisions, insist on our differences, fragment ourselves into ever smaller groups, without looking hard at the reasons why.[29] The common cause of women is a product of our oppression. So are the reasons why sisterhood, much lamented as prematurely dead by many defeated feminists, is so difficult to apprehend and to achieve. It is not in the interests of men for women to give that common cause a political shape; but that is the project of feminism, and it lies within our power to do so.

How does the writing of fiction connect with shaping a new world? 'Literature is a "discursive practice" . . . whose conventions encode social conventions and are ideologically complicit. Moreover, since each invocation of a code is also its reinforcement or reinscription, literature does more than transmit ideology: it actually creates it . . . '[30] Here, Greene and Kahn make the point, with their somewhat comic and impenetrable turn of phrase, that an act of writing is an act of faith, rather like saying the Mass. The Word becomes flesh; write it and it becomes a fact, an ideological fact at least. And because feminism is the refusal to endorse the existing state of affairs between women and men and the resulting divisions between women, feminism points out a new way of seeing and a new way of being. Feminist writing will therefore always be oppositional. We must always write polemic, until we have written our new world into being. And in this sense our writing is always utopian, speculative writing. We are not only writing against the grain of every structure, every timber which upholds our world; we are writing the future. Which is what the Lesbian feminist science fiction writer Joanna Russ means when she says: 'It's all science fiction.'[31]

But is it all simply a matter of content? Of what we choose to write about? Does it simply mean that we have to depict men as monsters and women as wonderful? Well, this is much-disputed territory. What is women's writing? And what is feminist fiction? Indeed, we are not always on secure ground if we ask: What is a woman? But as Elizabeth Wilson, in her role as internal critic of socialist feminism, points out: 'I believe we can – and should – judge theory in terms of its political results.'[32] The writing – fiction, autobiography, poetry, broadsheets, leaflets, enraged polemics – which made so radical a difference to our lives actually asks all these questions. Moreover, it asks them of women. I think this is an important aspect of feminist writing: the audience to whom the fiction is addressed is assumed to be female and mutinous. The 'we' of Verena Stefan's *Shedding* are angry women:

> Do I find it more stimulating to appeal to a man than a woman? They have *broken our spirits*. This inadequate term, socialization! This prettifying concept, conditioning.
> We can move only if we move towards the opposite sex, and even then only in the choreographed movements they taught us when they broke us to harness.[33]

We – the women; they – the men; the reader is always constructed as a woman, and as a particular sort of woman with a particular sort of politics. This is what makes feminist writing often infuriating or exhilarating to read: our assent is savagely commandeered or assumed.

One woman reading my writing – an earlier draft of this book – and trying to tone me down, asked: 'Why are you always so angry?' I promptly lost my temper. I think that rage is an important aspect of feminism and of feminist writing. As women we are not free. I am not free until all women, of whatever colour, age, class, race and sexuality are free too. And we have a lot to be angry about. Anger is not considered an appropriate emotion for women. I think that this is also an important point for feminist fiction. For women, writing itself becomes an act of transgression, an articulation of all the things we should not feel or think, a deliberate conscious refusal to be nice girls.

Germaine Greer said that women have very little idea of how much men hate them. Well, to read Jill Miller's *Happy as a Dead Cat* is to discover that the sentiment is entirely reciprocal.[34] The narrator is an unnamed working-class woman trapped in a conventional marriage with five children. She is very angry and she is not a nice girl. What the book makes painfully visible is the sheer exhaustion and physical labour involved in being a wife and mother. The master–slave relationship is precisely drawn. The master has no access to the slave's mind. But we have – we women, we readers. The husband is given no name other than Shitface; and the woman's fantasies are all the desires fuelled by rage, savage, fantastical revenge.

> I dreamed one night I'd cut twenty penises off, and fed them to a pack of wild dogs. He wanted to know why I woke that morning with a grin on my face. Never did tell him . . . 'Apple tart in the fridge love' . . . Been there a fortnight, might choke or poison you with a bit of luck . . . As far as I can see, the way to a man's heart is with a pissing pick-axe . . . (pp. 7, 11, 51).

Her hatred flows like an underground stream. Two things liberate the heroine: another woman and a book. The woman is her friend Jane. ('It was Jane who had made me aware of sexism'; p. 24) and Jane has read the book, Marilyn French's *The Women's Room*. 'There was a time, gal, when I bowed and scraped, and touched my forelock to his every whim. Then a well-meaning friend lent me *The Women's Room*. I felt so angry that I had to challenge him. That's when the shit really hit the fan' (pp. 25–6). Jane pitches her rebellion in class terms, with her husband as the boss and herself as the forelock-tugging proletariat. But the book is the political instrument that sets women free. Miller's *Happy as a Dead Cat* is about silence and subversion, about thinking differently and finding new words to say it. The real action of the novel takes place inside the narrator's mind, although the decisive move comes when Shitface insists on adding his anti-social father to the household: the heroine, with her five children, moves out, and sets up a business with Jane. It is a happy ending, women together, taking care of each other's children; as Jane says, 'Here I am, a working mother, free, and as happy as a pig in shit' (p. 26). A working mother's life is never easy or simple, but, as Miller makes perfectly clear, having Shitface in the house was to land herself with not five children, but six.

Feminist writing does not respect the boundaries, categories and genres which men have made. We are deliberately indecorous in our conceptions and in the execution of our work. Adrienne Rich's study of motherhood, *Of Woman Born: Motherhood as Experience and Institution*, contains autobiography, poetry, myth, literary criticism, hearsay, historical analysis, anecdotes, gossip, old wives' tales.[35] In feminist fiction, theory, polemic, narrative, fantasy, verismo soap opera and good advice often intertwine. This informality, urgency and irreverence result in the revelatory intimacy of women together, talking. Feminist writing often narrates the events of the contemporary women's liberation movement, taking as its theatre contemporary political events. Thus fiction becomes historical documentary. Nicky Edwards' *Mud* takes as its points of reference the two big gatherings at USAF Greenham Common in December 1982 and December 1983.[36] I was there on both days. I saw what she describes. The effect of this is curious. As I read the novel, a meditation on peace and the politics of peace and war by an ex-Greenham dyke, I am implicated in a whole community of writers and readers. The heroine of *Mud*, which is written as a confessional first-person narrative, is writing a play about the Great War. Any woman who has ever spent any time sleeping in the mud at Greenham will have noticed the relevance of a comparison between Greenham and the trenches: mud and fires on both sides and the wire between us. The women-only peace camps emphasize the sexual polarization which is our social reality in particularly naked terms. The men are on the inside, the powerful under siege, planning their next war. In Edwards' novel, the heroine, a Lesbian called Jo, meets 83-year-old Ada in the course of her research. The connections between the women are the only significant connections; the men's story and the story of the Great War is still told, but ambivalently blurred by aggression, pushed aside by the writer and her heroine while Ada's life and memories take precedence. Feminist fiction challenges the heterosexual norms of fiction; the centre of significant exchange no longer lies between women and men, but between the women.

Radical feminist opposition to the peace politics of Greenham speaks in the form of Beryl's Lesbian separatist household. Peace is not a women's issue, so the argument goes; to save the world for our husbands, families and children is to save a world where women are raped, abused, exploited and underpaid. The point is not to save the world but to change it. I find this argument greatly persuasive. A Blackwoman whom I met in June 1983 heard that I had just returned from the two-day blockade at USAF Upper Heyford. 'Oh,' she said cheerfully, 'are you against the bomb? I'm all for it. Drop it at once!' 'What?' I answered incredulously, filled with political zeal and conscious virtue at having grappled with scores of policemen. 'Look,' she said, 'You've got to be living a life worth saving to bother banning the bomb. And if you're Black, quite often you're not.' Point taken.[37] Peace is of course a word without meaning if it is not coupled with justice.

Edwards' *Mud* both addresses and contributes to contemporary feminist debate. Fiction engages directly with practical politics. The 'other woman' in the story is Ada, old and open-minded. Jo comes out, or rather, is forced out of the closet during the last long scene in the pub where the two women get drunk together and All is Revealed. Ada simply says, ' "Each to his own. Or her own." And that was Ada's last comment on the unplanned pronouncement' (p. 177). Ada is the teacher, the wise woman. ' "You're stuck in the past, girl. That's your trouble." I was shocked, though she only spoke lightly. "When you get to see as much history as I've done, on the hoof as it were, you realise it's not much cop" ' (p. 192). A new, somewhat romantic image of the sprightly, vivid, open-minded old woman is emerging in feminist writing. I wondered if Edwards was influenced by the American Lesbian writer May Sarton, who writes about old women, old age and the persecution of the old. In *Mrs Stevens Hears the Mermaids Singing* F. Hilary Stevens, the poet whose memories form the action of the book, is seventy, and has, as she says, earned every year. *As We Are Now* tells the story of Caro, seventy-six, and her courageous insistence on her own power, dignity and identity in the face of her gradual extinction by systematic humiliation in an old people's home. Laura in *A Reckoning* visits her very ancient mother, Sybille, who may be senile, but who is still frustrated, angry, alive.[38] Other American Lesbian writers who have been published in Britain make old women central to their narratives: Jane Rule's Amelia Larsen in *Against the Season* is the pivot of all the other characters. Jan Clausen (*The*

Proserpine Papers) and British working-class writer Caeia March (*Three Ply Yarn* and *The Hide and Seek Files*) both use the experience of fictional old women as a device to uncover a lost Lesbian history, to make the eternally invisible tradition of Lesbian life part of a contemporary Lesbian perspective.[39] The contemporary women's movement has been dominated by young women; this was not true of the suffragettes, many of whom were mothers and grandmothers. There are now networks for older Lesbians and older feminist women. The fictional writing both reflects and creates this political shift.

Feminist writing is both produced from within and addressed to the community of women. Edwards' heroine Jo is a writer, living and working alone; but she is vulnerable to the opinions of the Lesbian women who challenge her Greenham politics. She feels herself answerable to her community. The open-ended debate in the book is a real dialogue. Edwards and her writer are knowingly 'dissecting the contemporary lifestyle of [their] kind' (p. 176). The image of the artist as a lonely genius, wresting form from chaos and creating meanings in isolation, still has its adherents. Michèle Roberts' Helen in *The Visitation* writes feminist novels, just as her author does; she has writer's blocks, comes out in rashes when she touches the pen, is silenced by her social conscience. 'I can't write anything at the moment,' she admits: 'I can't do anything. I can't think about anything but the horrors of international politics. It seems obscene to bother about writing.'[40] This seems to assume that writing has nothing whatever to do with international politics. The criticism Helen anticipates usually comes from 'the mocking male reviewer', but does also come from 'the correct feminist' – whoever she is. She recognizes her friend Beth as 'scornful of anything smacking of self-indulgence, so prone to criticise the elitist, individual nature of artists' style of work . . . ' (p. 81). Not all artists work in that way, and in fact Helen sets herself a task which would, I think, be possible to achieve only within the community of women: 'now define *self*, now define *woman* . . . Start to write' (p. 173). We cannot discover what a woman is in isolation; we need each other.

One Foot on the Mountain, the first anthology of British feminist poetry, from 1969 to 1979, stresses the collective enterprise.[41] Many contributors thank their writers' groups for criticism, encouragement and support. All feminist writing becomes politics rather than literature if the writer is forced to choose: to be either for or against the propositions set out. It says a great deal about the British literary establishment that politics and literature are so hard to imagine hand in hand.[42] Propaganda is still a term of dismissive critical abuse. Thalia Doukas, one of the contributors to *One Foot on the Mountain*, says cautiously of her own work: ' . . . I am not so much trying to create literature; I am trying to speak' (p. 229). Here is the old politics of literature at work: poets – men – create art in isolation; feminist women have begun the difficult task of simply trying to speak to one another. Ann Oosthuizen's celebration of her writers' group in 'Bulletins from the Front Line', 'We read the latest bulletins from the front line/Carefully we study the terrain together' (p. 26), echoes across to the last lines in Michèle Roberts' first novel *A Piece of the Night*: 'The women sit in circles talking. They are passing telegrams along battle-lines, telling each other stories that will not put them to sleep, recognising allies under the disguise of femininity, no longer smuggling ammunition over back garden walls, no longer corpses in the church and mouths of men.'[43] Oosthuizen and Roberts talk to each other, as writing women have always done, telling each other stories. That is the central enterprise of feminist fiction; and in Roberts' words also rests the acknowledgement that all the stories we have been told, the stories that are not of our own making, are lies to silence us. And so we cannot primarily create ART. Art, literature, fiction, poetry, all these things have not been made in our image. Art aspires to permanence. Ambitious we certainly are; but we also know that much of our work is provisional. We must be suspicious writers, as well as suspicious readers; we must interrogate traditions, forms, the very notions of inspiration and craft. We can take nothing on trust.

Within the writers' groups of the feminist movement the practice of writing often becomes a collective project. Zoë Fairbairns, in her introduction to *Tales I Tell My Mother*, makes the source of the writing visible: 'this is how we define ourselves . . . ' and tells us how they did it. The process becomes as critical as the product.

> We met in each other's homes to produce this book, at intervals of between one and three weeks. Stories were circulated amongst us in the intervals, and were then fully discussed. Changes were usually made in the light of the discussions, and no story has been included that does not have the unanimous agreement of the group that it should be included; nevertheless we believe that collectivity has its limits, and each story is ultimately the work of its individual author, and is signed as such.[44]

Most writers do, in fact, have writers' groups, and always have done. For the Brontës it was the entire family; for Wordsworth it was Coleridge, his adoring sister Dorothy, his wife Mary and his sister-in-law Sara. Dorothy copied William's poems, learned them by heart and recited them to order: she wrote defending his methods to those who disagreed. She provided her 'wild eyes' as his source of seeing; he copied passages verbatim from her journals into his own notebooks.[45] Dorothy and Coleridge were often with him when he encountered the subjects of his poetry; in the final draft he usually writes them out and we see the solitary Romantic genius experiencing the visionary landscape on his own. Dorothy always acknowledges her companions: 'walked with Coleridge over the hills.'[46] Dorothy, too, was a writer; like many other women she used informal genres, letters and journals. Shelley's household was his writer's group; Byron enlisted his doctor, his publisher and, indeed, Shelley's entourage. During a wet summer in 1816 they all sat round the fire by Lake Geneva encouraging each other to write ghost stories; only Mary Shelley completed her story – *Frankenstein*. But the writers' groups of literary tradition were not often acknowledged or given public praise. Very often, as in the case of the Wordsworth family, the authors were men and the groups were admiring women.

A feminist writers' group comes together as a political cell, in which each member is equal to every other. Writing itself becomes a political act. Here is

Valerie Miner: 'Writing stories is activism . . . art and activism are not contradictory, but mutually inclusive.'[47] The pattern is not that of genius and
accompanying invisible support group, but that of an egalitarian commitment to
a common politics and mutual respect. No one perspective, no one achievement
is to be privileged over any other. Sara Maitland, of the the group working on
Tales I Tell My Mother, argues in the third discussion piece (consisting of brief
pieces of polemic which provide some of the theoretical, aesthetic and political
ideas of the group) that 'This is not an anthology, it is a book, a single entity, an
accumulation of points of view' (p. 114). Feminist fiction is usually prefaced by
generous acknowledgements to the women who typed, hunted for books, read
the drafts. Nicky Edwards thanks the woman who lent her the room with the
typewriter. But in the end the limits of collectivity are soon reached; each piece
of writing is signed – with one name. Apart from Somerville and Ross, who
even continued to write together with the aid of supernatural assistance after
one of them had died, I know of few women who wrote fiction jointly.
Katherine Bradley and Edith Cooper wrote under the name of 'Michael Field'
in the late nineteenth century; Hannah Wakefield is the pen-name for two
anonymous American women who wrote *The Price You Pay*, a racy political
thriller.[48] In the fields of theory, history and biography, of course, it is a
different question and many women collaborate on research and the production
of ideas. Has fiction become too closely associated with the idea of individual
expression? Should prose fiction and the characters in the landscape of the
novel become public property? Should we be able to help ourselves to another
writer's characters and scenarios, improve upon them or recycle the ideas
without fears of copyright lawsuits? Feminist writers have not challenged the
ownership of ideas so much as the construction of genius. And there remains a
great difference between writing with the support of a group, and writing as a
group.

Writers have also usually written from within and for a distinct community, or
at least a known culture: for patrons, for the courts of kings and queens, for the
white, middle-class, heterosexual world. Feminist writing – or at least, the
writing produced by western, white, heterosexual, middle-class feminists – is
not the only oppositional culture struggling, if not to become literature, then
simply to speak. Lesbian and Gay writing becomes the Other of normative
heterosexual assumptions in the making of fiction. Black and Asian writing
within Britain defines itself against white, racist culture. Proletarian or
working-class writing is the Other of bourgeois culture. But, as Sigrid Weigel
argues, 'It cannot make sense to use the category of "outsiders" to describe
women's culture because of the sheer numbers of those concerned.'[49] Weigel
develops the point, with which I agree, that women 'are both participants in the
existing culture, but also excluded from and oppressed in it' (p. 63). It is this
uncanny contradiction which is the source of Weigel's necessary literary
'double focus' and of Barbara Deming's political 'double-vision'. Deming
writes,

> Feminists, it seems to me, for a certain period of time now must expect to have to
> live with what amounts to *political* double vision. When we look at any man who

would classically be termed oppressed, we are now going to see *two* men: one an oppressed person, and so a comrade, but the other a person who oppresses us. More grotesquely still, if we are, as I am, white and from the middle-class, we are going to see: one person who oppresses me, another who sees me as *his* oppressor.[50]

The oppressor is also our father, our lover, our brother, our friend. And we must see him as both. We must learn to read the literary forms under patriarchy as structures which have excluded us and yet which we have also helped to build. There are no easy answers. There is only a multiplying sequence of complexities. Weigel states that 'unlike the colonised, women cannot resist by drawing on memories of an autonomous prepatriarchal culture. They do not have any collective memory of a mode of existence independent of the patriarch/coloniser.'[51] Well, this is not altogether true. Lesbian writing and Lesbian memory refuses to honour the patriarchs and challenges, in however veiled and warped a way, the coercive structures of heterosexuality.[52]

But what is Lesbian writing? Alison Hennegan's brief, perceptive article in the first issue of *Women's Review*, 'What Lesbian Novel?' asks all the difficult questions. 'Does it mean by lesbians, for lesbians, about lesbians? All three, any two or just one?'[53] Can heterosexual women write Lesbian novels? Could men? Hennegan eventually opts for a conservative definition of the Lesbian novel: 'A lesbian novel for me has become one in which a lesbian author's experience and necessarily oblique vision of the world (which continues to marginalise her) informs her work, regardless of the gender or sexuality of her characters' (p. 12). This is true so far as it goes. But then what is a Lesbian? Obviously, she is someone who suffers as an outsider in heteropatriarchy and whose sexual love for other women renders her lived experience less valid, less central, less significant than that of the heterosexual women of our culture. This definition must be provisional. I would not want to presuppose a heterosexual world in which Lesbian women were always forced into oblique and marginal positions in their writing and in their lives. And many Lesbians who are writers still resist the label 'Lesbian writer'; sometimes because they are firmly in the closet and sometimes because they are not feminists and have internalized a substantial helping of institutional homophobia. May Sarton's *A Reckoning* is a book which Hennegan cheerfully describes as a Lesbian novel, 'because Sarton's own lesbianism informs and deepens her understanding and perception of women together' (p. 12). Sarton, however, spent a year getting over a review of the same novel which accused her of writing 'a Lesbian novel in disguise.'[54] She felt belittled and persecuted by the label, 'Lesbian'. 'Guilt by association will make a reviewer accuse me of cowardice if all my characters are not Lesbians, apparently . . . I have wished to be thought of in human terms. The vision of life in my work is not limited to one segment of humanity or another and it has little to do with sexual proclivity' (pp. 80–1). Sarton's problem is bound up with her politics of literature. Human experience is not a common, universal constant, there to be addressed and explored by every writer; the enterprise of feminism has proved precisely that. Women's experience is radically different from that of men; to be Lesbian, Gay or heterosexual, Black or white, is to inhabit an utterly different world. And so long as writers like Sarton hysterically disdain the label 'Lesbian', Lesbians will be regarded as less than human.

If the practice of writing is irrevocably and unavoidably political in implication – and, indeed, intent – we must unmask our own political positions and investments, in criticism and in fiction. The political dimensions of each woman's feminism, the point from which she starts, will be influenced by the political situation in which she already finds herself. Reformist feminists usually place faith in the liberal rhetoric of rights and the transformation of existing structures: all we have to do is write the women back into the stories, institutions, hierarchies. But this necessarily involves women in the acceptance of male values, procedures, structures and methods. Parity, equality, justice for women. It sounds convincing. But equality on what terms? Or rather, whose? The gains can of course be considerable; I am thinking of the rise of the women's committees on local councils and the festival of municipal feminism made possible during the early 1980s by the Women's Committee of the now defunct and lamented GLC. Socialist feminists have offered a just critique of the contemporary women's liberation movement. Back in the early days of the 1970s western feminism was indeed largely white, visibly heterosexual and middle-class. The campaigns and issues around which the movement was organized were middle-class demands. But no divisions are static; not only class, but also race, ethnic origin, disability and sexuality divide women from one another. The internal critiques within the women's liberation movement during the 1980s tended to focus on minority group rights and on making visible more dimensions of women's experience of oppression. The central problem with a socialist feminist critique of class oppression is that it divides women one from another, middle-class from working-class, without acknowledging the fact that definitions of class are largely male definitions. Beatrix Campbell, in *Wigan Pier Revisited*, tells how her voyage to Orwell's white working-class hinterland transformed her socialist perspectives:

> . . . being a feminist puts a woman both inside and outside the mainstream of working-class politics; which are stewed in sexual prejudice and privilege. I began as the kind of feminist who said, 'It's not the men, it's the system': but this journey convinced me that men and masculinity in their everyday individual manifestations, constitute a systematic block of resistance to the women of their own community and class. Both individual men and the political movements men have made within the working class are culpable.[55]

I agree that both men and their systems are in need of a radical overhaul – and a radical feminist critique.

Radical and revolutionary feminism specifically emphasizes the facts of sexual oppression and of male violence against women, which *all* women suffer, regardless of age, race or class. Ironically, violence against women is one of the most central and abiding themes of our literary culture, from the rape of Helen and the sack of Troy, through Othello's murder of Desdemona to the ritual slaughter of D. H. Lawrence's *The Woman Who Rode Away*.[56] The political campaigns around which radical feminists organize are committed to making visible and countering that violence: protests against pornography, attacks on porn shops, supporting and working in Women's Aid refuges for the survivors of domestic violence by men, staffing the Rape Crisis lines. When women or men accuse feminists of being too extreme, bullying and divisive, they usually mean radical feminists. The reason is easy to understand: it is that women who are radical feminists name men as the oppressors of women. Here is a passage from the editorial manifesto of *Trouble and Strife*, a radical feminist magazine:

> Men oppress women but not because of their (or our) biology – not because men are physically stronger, nor because men have phalluses and women bear children and may breast feed, nor because men are innately more aggressive. We consider men oppress women because they benefit from doing so. All men, even those at the very bottom of male hierarchies, have advantages that flow from belonging to the category male. Even the most sympathetic to women's liberation derive benefits from women's subordination.[57]

This is disturbing to read because it addresses the roots of the divisions between women and men, and the fact of their separation. Yet it is the idea of separatism as a political strategy which arouses the the most rapid and pervasive alarm. The prospect of women's withdrawal from men, throwing them out of our beds and out of our heads, usually fills the room with enraged cries. I find this most interesting, simply because separatism, total separatism for women, is very rarely possible. Men own and run all the institutions, all the positions of power and influence. They don't do all the work – far from it; we do – but they do have most of the jobs. Until the beginning of this century women in Britain did not have the vote, nor access to Parliament, the law, the professions; our hold on higher education was tenuous. Working-class women, unsurprisingly, were not however excluded from the factories or the mills. My point here is simply this; separatism is bound up with power.[58] Men can and have practised their own separatism by excluding women. Women's exclusion of men is a radical reclamation of space and power for ourselves.

It is not necessary to be a socialist feminist to incorporate an analysis of class and race into a political reading of feminist fiction. My first feminist group, 'Scarlet Women', would now be regarded as radical feminist. I was the only one of us studying literature; the other women were economists, anthropologists, historians. Marxist and anti-racist politics informed our first feminist analyses. The books we read were impenetrably theoretical; but we were committed to direct action. I do not think that our crude insistence on the material basis of our oppression, or our blunt slogans, were an isolated phenomenon confined to university groups of young women; our politics certainly did come 'from this tension between men's power and women's resistance'.[59] A woman in one of my adult classes on feminist fiction held in autumn 1985 told us all about her first consciousness-raising session in 1970. Each of the women in her group was either married or living together with one man. Armed with the politics of women's resistance, all of them made sorties home and took their stand upon the domestic hearth with revolutionary statements, such as 'From now on you will clean the lavatory and make the breakfast.' Murky scenes followed. But their, and our, sexual politics was about resisting male oppression on every level.

Black power and feminism have a historical relationship in the nineteenth century and a more particular connection during the 1960s when white, western feminism emerged out of the male-dominated revolutionary left. That historical inheritance of revolutionary Marxism and post-imperial political struggle is of critical importance for radical feminism. Kate Millett, Shulamith Firestone, Andrea Dworkin, Barbara Deming – all American radical feminists of the 1970s and 1980s – all old guard, old left. My own political history is similar, although the revolutionary left in England, or at least the bit of it I was in, operated in an odd atmosphere of drugs and muddle. I can remember organizing a jumble sale to buy guns, undermining capitalism by fly-posting the Cowley works in Oxford at one in the morning and affirming my commitment to Black Power by pouring red paint over a racist cricket wicket. I used to be a revolutionary socialist who espoused everybody's cause – except her own. I would now describe myself as a radical feminist.

I stress this connection between radical feminism and revolutionary socialism because many socialist feminists – and I am now thinking of Cora Kaplan in her essay in the anthology *Making a Difference* – construct radical feminism as the misguided demon at the bottom of Pandora's box. Radical feminism, so she says, 'wholly vindicates women's psyche, but sees it as quite separate from men's, often in direct opposition'; it defends 'female sexuality as independent and virtuous between women, but degrading in a heterosexual context'.[60] The critique of heterosexuality as one of the key institutions through which patriarchy is organized and men given direct access to women's bodies, women's labour and women's strength is certainly central to radical feminism. But it is not an automatic correlative, and I know of no woman who would claim that it was, that sexuality is therefore independent and virtuous between women. Virtuous is rather a wonderful Victorian word, and certainly does away with the sinful and mysterious connotations of Lesbianism. Well, in some ways I'm all for sin, but it is self-evidently not the case that sexuality between women presents no problems; as the Leeds Revolutionary Feminists tartly put it, 'We never promised you a rose garden.'[61] Indeed, it is precisely because heterosexuality is so pervasively oppressive, even within the Lesbian and Gay community, both to those who never bought the whole package deal of home, marriage and babies anyway and to those who have given it up in disgust, that heterosexuality, both as sexual practice and as state institution, remains such a central focus for argument, criticism and analysis. Nor do I like Kaplan's heterosexist assumption that female sexuality is expressed in exactly the same way between women as it is between women and men. And it seems very odd to imagine, as Kaplan does here, anybody's sexuality existing outside class, race and cultural structures.

Kaplan offers a brief reading of Charlotte Brontë's *Jane Eyre*. This novel has been central for some practitioners of contemporary feminist literary criticism; it has been read as a classic text for feminist fiction.[62] *Jane Eyre* is structured as a quest romance, the story of a solitary, spirited woman, written as a passionate first-person confessional narrative. Jane seeks personal happiness, personal fulfilment. Manifestos such as 'I care for myself' and 'We were born to strive and to endure' are bound to go down well among the downtrodden and the rebellious. Jane's outburst on the leads is famous:

> It is in vain to say that human beings ought to be satisfied with tranquillity: they must have action; and they will make it if they cannot find it . . . Millions are condemned to a stiller doom than mine, and millions are in silent revolt against their lot. Nobody knows how many rebellions besides political rebellions ferment in the masses of life which people earth. Women are supposed to be very calm generally: but women feel just as men feel . . . [63]

Kaplan argues that here, in talking about 'human beings' and 'millions' Brontë is advocating proletarian revolution. I would have thought that it was perfectly clear that she meant women, all women, women as a class. She explicitly suggests that women's rebellions are something other than political rebellions. Kaplan goes on to say that the difference between women 'is at least as important an element as the difference between the sexes, as a way of representing both class and gender'.[64] I do not actually think that this is true, but my point here is that in either socialist feminist politics or socialist feminist criticism an emphasis on class difference deepens the divisions among women – as indeed they are divided in the text of *Jane Eyre*: mad Creole whore, pale plain virgin, unsavoury society fortune-hunter and quite unspeakably immoral French dancer. Kaplan ticks off the radical feminists for seeking out 'a "hidden" sympathy between women'[65] and points to the hostile and denigrating representations of women in women's writing, even in writing which, like *Jane Eyre*, has been claimed as feminist fiction. So, women beware women, we are our own worst enemies. But what do the women above have in common? They all either are, or want to be, Mrs Rochester. That is precisely how patriarchy works, either on the page or in the world: by dividing the women. So the maggot at the core of the carcass of Thornfield is Edward Fairfax Rochester. It is not enough to say that women belittle and abuse other women without saying why. And I question any political approach that privileges and emphasizes the differences among women. In whose interest will that be? Not ours.

It is odd, given her stated concern with race[66] as a category, that Kaplan does not emphasize Bertha Rochester's inheritance. Bertha is huge, tall as a man. Jane sees her fearful, *blackened*, savage face in the glass, wearing the bridal veil. Bertha looms out of the page as the West Indian Other, the Creole, not just the madwoman, but the Blackwoman, in the attic.[67] Kaplan states that Bertha turns violently upon her rival.[68] This is not true. She does not. She appears in Jane's room on her wedding night, like Frankenstein's monster, as her psychic double, as a warning, as the real Mrs Rochester. And her symbolic gesture is utterly clear. She tears the wedding veil and tramples upon it. So long as passion unchecked by reason runs mad upstairs, Jane cannot marry the obscene object of her desire. But why is passion out of control represented by a Blackwoman? On a more literal textual level Rochester is still married, he is Bluebeard, Bertha is his secret, and this is what happens to his wives. Bertha is one of the millions condemned to a stiller doom than Jane Eyre. She must have action, and she makes it when she cannot find it; she burns down the rotten edifice of patriarchy.

A Jamaican Blackwoman, reading *Jane Eyre* as a schoolgirl, narrates her distress and rage at the betrayal of Bertha Mason/Rochester.

> In third form, they gave us *Jane Eyre* to read. It was the only piece of literature in which there was any mention of the Caribbean. It was also the only book by a woman which they had given us to read. We liked the bits about school and then we came upon the mad heiress from Spanish Town locked up in the attic. At first we giggled, knowing that it was Jane we were supposed to identify with and her quest for independence and dignity. Then we got to the part where this masterpiece of English Literature describes Bertha Mason as 'inferior, blue skinned . . . etc.'. Someone was reading it out loud in the class as was the custom. Gradually the mumbling and whispering in the class room crescendoed into an open revolt with loud choruses of 'It's not fair, Miss!' Miss admitted it seemed unfair, but she went on to do nothing with that insight . . . I couldn't put it down . . . anxiously looking for a chapter, a paragraph or a sentence that might redeem the insane animal inferiority of the Caribbean. It was a women's novel and I had liked so much of the earlier part, but I couldn't stomach the way I had been relegated to the attic. I felt betrayed. Dimly, a few pages in the novel had spoken to my life in a way which most of the nonsense we wasted our lives on at school did not.[69]

This Caribbean reader saw her sister, not the stranger, in Bertha Rochester. Already obliterated within the peculiar British education she was receiving at St Andrew's High School for Girls, Kingston, Jamaica (which is, incidentally, where I too was being educated at exactly the same time in some other classroom), she suddenly saw a crack in the slab of nonsense – which raises the complicated relationship between representation and experience. That literature should 'speak to life' is anathema in some quarters. But fictional discourse is much more versatile, imaginative and sophisticated than many other forms of writing. The Caribbean woman who justly felt betrayed learned a political lesson from Charlotte Brontë, a lesson about racism and denial, which she never forgot. She saw that the sign, Bertha Rochester, madwoman, whore, Blackwoman, was overdetermined by bitter meanings; that Blackwomen are often represented as treacherous, lascivious, dangerous. For her *Jane Eyre* could never be a celebratory feminist text. Nor could it ever be so for any woman who makes anti-racist politics crucial to her politics of reading.

Equally damaging to a celebratory reading of *Jane Eyre* as feminist fiction as the differences and divisions among women are the sexual politics articulated in the relationship betwen Rochester and Jane. Yes, it is a power struggle, yes, Rochester's mutilation and subsequent dependency are the only terms upon which Jane, armed with a Victorian fictional legacy, can return. But it is also a passion thoroughly saturated with the mythologies of rape and sexual violence. Read on.

> 'Jane! will you hear reason?' . . . (he stopped and approached his lips to my ear); 'because, if you won't, I'll try violence.' His voice was hoarse; his look that of a

man just about to burst an insufferable bond and plunge headlong into wild licence. I saw that in another moment, and with one impetus of frenzy more, I should be able to do nothing with him. The present – the passing second of time – was all I had in which to control and restrain him: a movement of repulsion, flight, fear would have sealed my doom – and his. But I was not afraid: not in the least. I felt an inward power; a sense of influence, which supported me. The crisis was perilous; but not without its charm.[70]

Brontë is interested in unequal relationships; Rochester is Jane's employer, master, old enough to be her father, sexually experienced and not too particular on the matter of morals and mistresses. But it is precisely this imbalance of power which Brontë perceives as erotic. Wild licence, so she says, is not without its charm. Rochester can only be controlled and restrained by soothing duplicity and floods of tears. The heterosexual nexus of passion, power and force is the sexist basis of rapist ideology and this is, in the end, all the action Jane ever finds. Significantly, the book ends not with Jane and Rochester but with the apocalyptic imperialism of St John Rivers struggling for the heathen soul of India. Jane Eyre's feminist credo – 'We were born to strive and to endure' – has passed to him. The racist enterprise of colonial force achieves heroic status.

What would happen to the text of *Jane Eyre* if we really did elaborate an analysis of racism and read Bertha Rochester as the heroine? Well, we would have to write another book, articulating the experience and destruction of Bertha Rochester. Jean Rhys did: *Wide Sargasso Sea* (1966). And this is what we should do – write the gaps in each other's texts, and in each other's contributions to feminist theory.

Any theoretical thinking which attempts to build on systems that are not of our own making runs the risk of incorporating their institutional woman-hating. I use the term woman-hating rather than misogyny simply because the latter term has status, authority and respectability. Woman-hating is a raw, blunt term which means what it says.[71] British feminism has historical and deeply-rooted bonds with British traditions of revolutionary socialist thought.[72] All the women who contributed to *Tales I Tell My Mother* defined themselves as socialists. *Feminist Review* is produced by a socialist feminist collective.[73] The 1980s phenomenon of municipal feminism emerged from the work of socialist feminists in the Labour Party and on the left. The women's sections within the Labour Party encouraged women to organize autonomously and yet to remain part of the party structures. These were often set up amidst nasty scenes and furious diatribes from women and men committed to mixed groups. Black sections were even more furiously resisted. But socialist feminist politics should be both a radical searching analysis and a force for social change. This has not always been the case. From a radical feminist perspective, feminists who identify their political interests as socialist have often seemed to subscribe to the most damaging kinds of reformist compromise: the politics of collaboration and co-operation in the continuing sexual subordination of women to men.[74] Even the powerful presence of women on the picket line during the National Union of Miners' strike of 1984–5, a development which was warmly applauded by the socialist press, has its ambiguous political aspect. I may be a cantankerous cynic, but I was not wholly convinced by the arguments *Feminist Review* produced to appropriate Women Against Pit Closures for socialist feminism: 'That this mobilisation was done from a traditional basis in family and community and in relation ultimately to men does not, we believe, gainsay the feminist forms of action within that movement.'[75] But the family and the local community are precisely the places where our oppression is situated and reproduced. This fact is rendered more problematic and complex with Black or Asian communities, where the family is also the source of support, strength and resistance to white racism. The miners' wives' actions may have mobilized women as women, but not for women. And that makes all the difference. But of course, the women's struggle did not end with the strike; much of the energy and political experience gained on the picket lines has gone into the creation of women's centres, women's projects, an autonomous women's movement. Many of the women who were involved in the strike are now organizing for themselves and for other women. Once we begin, there's no turning back.

The idea that women constitute a class is not new.

> Women, whether seamstresses, factory hands, servants, authoresses, count-esses . . . do form one common class. There may be every variety of education, of thought, of habit . . . but so long as there is 'class' legislation, so long as the law makes an insurmountable difference between men and women, women must be spoken of as a separate class.[76]

Does a Marxist analysis of class provide a useful political language in which to discuss the subordination and oppression of women by men when they are not being considered in relation to men? Women are very often regarded as inheriting the class position of their husbands or nearest male relatives. If that is the case then the gulf between the Colonel's Lady and Judy O'Grady becomes wider still. I would like to believe that we are all sisters under the skin, but I think that still has to be imagined and fought for. A lot of white racist privilege has to be dismantled. There is a myth that women can slide from one class to another much more easily than men are able to do. We can marry up. For women, class is a matter of surfaces: manner, voice, clothes. *My Fair Lady* turns Eliza Doolittle into a Hungarian princess; and she gets away with it. Men cannot rise so easily, because they have to produce property, wealth, contacts, education, substance, some tangible evidence of status.[77] A woman, so says the fairy-tale, need only be visually and verbally presentable. But Eliza Doolittle is herself the creation of a middle-class male mind. Her story is a myth to keep working-class women in their place. Here is Marlene Packwood. 'Working class women virtually never break out of the trapping of family life to become directors of companies, lecturers, surgeons, literary critics, journalists, photo-graphers, artists, dancers . . . Our confidence is weak, our voices quiet and our demands ignored against those who have had the benefits of a university education.'[78] The reality of the economic divide between middle-class and working-class women, and the still deeper financial chasm which separates Black from white, cannot be disentangled from the privilege attached to articulacy, education, knowledge. Packwood points out the alienation from their own language experienced by some working-class women. English is a language that is more strongly class-marked than other European languages.[79] 'We at times experience the English language as alien, full of subtleties and nuances which are available to the middle classes. Certain worlds are totally out of our area of experience . . . The most basic need, language itself, almost as basic as breathing, is still not yet ours for the asking.'[80] In her autobiographical and political analysis of her own life and that of her mother, Carolyn Steedman states a savage fact. 'We are divided: a hundred years ago I'd have been cleaning your shoes. I know this and you don't.'[81] Well, middle-class women must make it their business to know.

But what of the other dimension, racism, which is thrown up by the text of *Jane Eyre*? Gloria Joseph, in her contribution to a collection of essays edited by Lydia Sargent, *Women and Revolution*, refuses to endorse either the idea that women constitute a class, or Hartmann's definition of patriarchy. Racism, she says, institutional racism, has (at least in the USA) created two separate societies – 'one white, one Black'.[82] The categories of Marxism are sex-blind and race-blind. And the psychological dynamics that function between Black men and Black women 'are qualitatively and culturally different from those of whites' (p. 93). Joseph's analysis is contradictory and problematic. She constructs a powerful case for the way in which the shared experience of slavery proved a terrible equalizer in the lives of American Blacks, women and men, in that both sexes are victims of violence. The enemy is the whites. 'The rape of Black women and the lynching and castration of Black men are equally heinous in their nature' (p. 94). So, for Joseph, a simple analysis of patriarchy can never be acceptable, because the basic assertion that the original division is between the sexes cannot apply to Black women. She declares: 'Writers must recognise . . . the Black women in American society have at least as much in common with Black men as with white women' (p. 95). This assertion is extremely problematic for feminism, or at least for radical feminism. But Joseph shifts her ground; she does not claim that Black men do not oppress Black women, which would, in any case, be disproven by the evidence. There is too painful a testimony by too many Blackwomen to the contrary. Maya Angelou, in the first volume of her autobiography *I Know Why The Caged Bird Sings*, describes how, as a child, she was raped by her mother's lover. Alice Walker in *The Color Purple* narrates a catalogue of child rape and domestic battery which makes quite harrowing reading.[83] But Joseph, Angelou and Walker all insist that the political meaning of this violence cannot be read in the same way as the violence between the sexes in the white ruling group. These women share a powerful common concern to build a potent solidarity between Blackwomen and Black men in their common struggle against a racist world. The happy ending of *The Color Purple* is a case in point: the batterers learn to sew pants and be gentle. They become, in fiction at any rate, fit companions for Blackwomen.

What fuels Joseph's rage is the more than legitimate demand of the white women's movement that we should extend and deepen our analysis and give full consideration to Blackwomen's voices, needs and demands. 'White feminists have to learn to deal adequately with the fact that by virtue of their whiteness they are oppressors as well as oppressed persons' (p. 105). Joseph makes one interesting exception in the general denunciation. Some Lesbian radical feminists, she observes, do not support white racism. 'They alone as a group of women will more readily offer aid or come to the defense of a Black woman' (p. 101). But is this really so surprising? What have Lesbian radical feminists, who refuse to pass themselves off as heterosexual, to gain from white patriarchy? They too are outsiders. And a woman whose political position identifies women, all women, as a species under threat, will see a Blackwoman as herself.

In her dialogue with Jill Lewis, *Common Differences*, Joseph analyses the political meanings of Black homophobia at some length. She points out that 'Black feminists and/or lesbians are seen as identifying with white culture, despite references in many accounts of life in African cultures to women identifying with or relating to other women.'[84] This resistance from within Black communities both to heterosexual feminism and to Lesbian feminism is not justifiable, but it is understandable. As Joseph tartly admits, 'Many Black males refrain from examining lesbian politics in fear of having to relinquish some of their treasured male privileges' (p. 192). And those few privileges would be all the more savagely guarded within a community that is under threat.

Into the midst of this problematic analysis roars Audre Lorde – Lesbian, feminist, Caribbean/American, poet, theorist, biomythographer, mother, lover, woman: fat, Black and magnificent. Lorde gave me the title for this book. I named this book after her not only because she has influenced my thinking a great deal, which she has, but because the moment in her biomythography *Zami* where she points out the contradictions of who is our sister and who the stranger, cited as the epigraph to this book, seems to me to speak directly to the problems of racism and feminist theory.[85] We form our alliances as sisters by creating a group who are strangers; but each group shifts and intersects with others, refuses to remain constant or reliable. We need Lorde's awareness of complexity as well as Barbara Deming's 'double-vision'. Lorde is a wise woman, who can teach us how to love our own bodies and each other, how to fight racism, oppression, injustice, how to face death. Lorde's essays in *Sister/Outsider*, another title which gestures towards the separations between sisters and strangers, are full of candour, intelligence and rage.[86] She has no use whatever for guilt when she challenges white feminists: 'Guilt and defensiveness are bricks in a wall against which we all flounder; they serve none of our futures.'[87] Guilt shifts the attention back from the Blackwoman who suffers injustice to the white woman who, though she may not have created the structures of white racism, certainly benefits from them and from the institutions of white privilege. Our business should be to dismantle those structures and institutions which endorse our privilege rather than settle into abject paralysis at our guilt. We do not unmask racism in a political vacuum, Lorde insists, but 'in the teeth of a system for which racism and sexism are primary'. Lorde's political position is always on the perimeter. 'I have often wondered why the farthest-out position always feels so right to me; why extremes, although difficult and sometimes painful to maintain, are always more comfortable . . .'[88] Only on the edge is there no room for compromise or intellectual dishonesty. And this woman on the edge, Black, Lesbian, feminist, is able to watch the power structures which bind us back to the rich, white men at the core. This enables her to speak hard words which none of us can afford to ignore.

> I am a lesbian woman of Color whose children eat regularly because I work in a university. If their full bellies make me fail to recognize my commonality with a woman of Color whose children do not eat because she cannot find work, or who has not children because her insides are rotted from home abortions and sterilization; if I fail to recognize the lesbian who chooses not to have children, the woman who remains closeted because her homophobic community is her only life support, the woman who chooses silence instead of another death, the woman who is terrified lest my anger triggers the explosion of hers; if I fail to recognize them as other faces of myself, then I am contributing not only to each of their oppressions but also to my own, and the anger which stands between us then must be used for clarity and mutual empowerment, not for evasion by guilt or for further separation. I am not free while any woman is unfree, even when her shackles are very different from my own. And I am not free as long as one person of Color remains chained. Nor is any one of you.[89]

Lorde starts from very hard facts: freedom lies not only in the womb and in the mind but in the stomach and the bank. The freedom of women is about having enough to eat. Our own political compromises with the system which destroys our sisters and ourselves might become clearer to us if we asked each other outright: How much do you earn? Who pays you? What do you have to do to earn that money? But the main enemy for Lorde is silence. Her experience of breast cancer and the political meaning of that cancer are anatomized in *The Cancer Journals*. 'Death . . . is the final silence . . . I was going to die, if not sooner then later, whether or not I had ever spoken myself. My silences had not protected me. Your silence will not protect you . . . it is not difference which immobilizes us, but silence.'[90]

Speaking or writing silences is our theme; and to do this is to uncover the hidden sympathy between women of whatever colour, age, creed and sexuality. For this sympathy is the woodworm of patriarchy. A woman's revolution would both free Bertha Rochester, the Blackwoman in the attic, and free Jane Eyre from the bewitching mythology of rape embedded in romance. As for the men: they have a hell of a lot more to lose than their chains.[91]

I am not unaware of the many developing threads in feminist literary theory and criticism. Nor am I being perversely obstinate and irreverent when I refuse to engage head-on with those complicated debates over French feminism, psychoanalysis, Marxist dialectic,[92] the class struggle,[93] structuralism, signs, signifiers, post-structuralism, deconstruction, intertextuality, *langue, parole*, the split subject, semiotics, femiotics, marginal discourses and gaseous abstractions.[94] I love it all. To wallow in theory is to indulge in a bout of intellectual press-ups before returning, covered in the sweat of secret languages, to the academic arena. All those debates inform my reading and my writing, they inform this book. And I am not an advocate of the plain-woman-looks-at-a-piece-of-prose approach to writing. We always come to fiction with a shopping basket full of preconceptions, prejudices and assumptions. I remember an editor's comment on a piece of my own work: 'It's too obviously a piece of writing. I can't forget I'm reading prose and just enjoy the story.' I was about to mention modernism, but stopped myself in time – as I was myself stopped by another writer in a workshop on style at the Lesbian Writers Conference in February 1984: 'When you use the word sonnet,' she interrupted, 'I begin to feel the cold sweat of panic. We can't write sonnets. We're in them.' Which beings me to the central political dilemma of this book: the twisted knot of politics, style and practice of writing.

We are not utterly absent from the traditions of literature and we are not completely silenced and confined to the margins of patriarchal culture. Christina Rossetti and Elizabeth Barrett Browning wrote sonnets: magnificent, extraordinary love poems. And it is arguable that the novel is our form; that the loose baggy monster is in our own image. It took a mere hundred years – from around 1740 to around 1840 – for women to establish themselves as the main consumers and producers of prose fiction. The novel was a new form which deliberately cultivated the 'plain style'. You didn't have to have a classical education to write novels. When the epistolary novel was all the rage in the eighteenth century, all that was necessary was the ability to dash off an exciting letter. Letters, traditionally, are a private form of writing. A woman's form. But they do, of course, have a classical heritage – in Cicero's letters and in those of the Renaissance humanists – and an impeccable moral ancestry, in the letters of St Paul. Thus women could write, using an informal style, but still claim that the form was irreproachable. By the end of the nineteenth century there was no longer any need to defend either the novel as a form, or the quality of work from the women who wrote.[95] But whatever the potential of the novel as a woman's form it is as well to remember here that the novel has not always been used to convey progressive meanings – even when the pen has been in the woman's hand.

The woman who told me to shut up about sonnets was displaying 'a healthy distrust of all conceptual and methodological tools which are of non-feminist origin'.[96] It is a distrust I share. But what is the answer? Do we junk all our literary traditions within patriarchy, all aesthetic theory, all the history of writing, from ruling-class epic to ballads and tavern songs, all love poetry, epics not written by the ruling class, on the grounds that it is not our culture, despite the fact that women have contributed to and shaped that culture, in small, ruthlessly censored, but significant ways? Do we ignore the relationship between our own submerged traditions and those of the ruling culture? And even if we were tempted to throw the lot down the lavatory, would that be possible? We cannot make words in a void; languages are systems, games, forms with a history. And all languages, all psychological structures, all literary forms carry meanings stuck like limpets to the bottom of the ship, meanings which we did not independently create and which we cannot always control. Can we transform the traditional meanings of fiction? And what other meanings do we want to create for ourselves?

Feminist fiction is about the reclamation of power and control, the invasion of space both on the page and in the imagination that is ours by right and from which we have been systematically exiled and excluded by men who have set themselves up as the arbiters of taste and culture.[97] Feminists write against received opinions, against accepted norms. If a woman perceives herself as she is perceived within our culture, she has already capitulated. Thus, even the process of making the self who writes, of constructing our selves, is an embattled, oppositional struggle. For even the form of the novel is not neutral. Feminism is neither a pious utopian hope for a better world, nor the sum of every woman's experience. It is a political analysis of the ways in which women are oppressed by men and the structures men have made. Feminism is a response to male power and male privilege. We are, therefore, in all our writing, necessarily confrontational, in opposition. We will always write polemic. And polemic can never be objective or disinterested. Polemic argues a case. Feminist writers are necessarily polemicists and will take up the page to harangue, bully and persuade. Roaring is undiluted polemic; the just rage of women who have been smothered, frustrated, destroyed. Writing, even women's writing, has too often worn the straitjacket of art – male art, male ideology. And so we must learn to craft our roaring with subtlety and cunning, and learn to be artful, in every sense of the word.

Notes

1 See Virginia Woolf, *A Room of One's Own* (1928; London, Penguin, 1972). When I read Ellen Galford's *Moll Cutpurse: Her True History* (Edinburgh, Stramullion, 1984), I was delighted to hear Judith Shakespeare tell her own story.

2 The homoerotic implications of this are thoroughly explored in Lisa Jardine's *Still Harping on Daughters: Women and Drama in the Age of Shakespeare* (Brighton, Harvester, 1983), esp. ch. 1.

3 Kris, 'Another Kind of Coming Out', *Gossip: A Journal of Lesbian Feminist Ethics*, no. 2 (1986), pp. 80–9.

4 If this sound hopelessly idealistic then I suggest you ask the cynic in your brain how she intends to change the world.

5 Well, fairly irrefutably. The transsexuals in our midst seem to me to claim more space than they deserve. As a gay librarian I knew once said, speaking of a male colleague who had undergone the operation, 'Some people will do anything to get a man into bed.' I find myself broadly in sympathy with Janice Raymond's views, expressed in her book *The Transsexual Empire* (London, Women's Press, 1980). Any man or woman who is unhappy with the codes and definitions which circumscribe us as women or men has my sympathy, but the answers are political, not surgical.

6 I am indebted here to Jon Ward's brilliant essay 'The Nature of Heterosexuality', in Gillian Hanscombe and Martin Humphries (eds), *Heterosexuality* (London, GMP, 1987).

7 Gerd Brantenberg, *The Daughters of Egalia* (1977; London, Journeyman, 1985).

8 John Bowen, 'Speaking of Men', *New Statesman*, 24 May 1985. See also Rowena Chapman and Jonathan Rutherford (eds), *Male Order: Unwrapping Masculinity* (London, Lawrence & Wishart, 1988).

9 Please see Mary Jacobus, 'Is there a Woman in this Text?', *New Literary History*, vol. 14, no. 1 (1982), pp. 117–41, and Toril Moi, *Sexual/Textual Politics* (London, Methuen, 1985), for further information on why it is not actually possible to perform these kinds of intellectual self-delusion.

10 Tillie Olsen, *Silences* (London, Virago, 1980); Adrienne Rich, *On Lies, Secrets and Silence* (New York, Norton, 1979).

11 Kate Millett, *Sexual Politics* (1970; London, Virago, 1977); Germaine Greer, *The Female Eunuch* (London, MacGibbon & Kee, 1970).

12 See Elaine Showalter, 'Towards a Feminist Poetics', in Mary Jacobus (ed.), *Women Writing and Writing about Women* (London, Croom Helm, 1979), p. 25. I also liked Showalter's point about 'the connection between feminist consciousness and conversion narratives'. I absolutely agree.

13 See Deborah Cameron, *Feminism and Linguistic Theory* (London, Macmillan, 1985) for an iconoclastic and demystifying approach to the subject, and Moi, *Sexual/ Textual Politics*, for a more respectful version.

14 Moi, *Sexual/Textual Politics*, pp. 132–3.

15 Sheila Jeffreys, *The Spinster and Her Enemies: Feminism and Sexuality 1880–1930* (London, Pandora, 1985), pp. 107ff. and esp. ch. 6.

16 Elizabeth Wilson, 'Psychoanalysis: Psychic Law and Order?', in *Hidden Agendas: Theory, Politics and Experience in the Women's Movement* (London, Tavistock, 1986), p. 164.

17 See Sistren, *Lionheart Gal: Life Stories of Jamaican Women* (London, Women's Press, 1986).

18 Cameron, *Feminism and Linguistic Theory*, p. 131.

19 Whether Woolf needed curing is a matter for some dispute. See Roger Poole's suggestive study, *The Unknown Virginia Woolf* (1978; Brighton, Harvester, 1982). However, in all his speculations about her relationship to her own body, he fails to confront her lesbianism.

20 I am indebted to Sheila Shulman for this point.

21 Hélène Cixous, 'The Laugh of the Medusa', in Elaine Marks and Isabelle de Courtivron (eds), *New French Feminisms: An Anthology* (Brighton, Harvester, 1981), pp. 246, 250, 251.

22 Cameron, *Feminism and Linguistic Theory*, p. 133. See also her reader on feminism and language, which I would regard as essential reading on this debate (her introductory essay is particularly illuminating): Deborah Cameron (ed.), *The Feminist Critique of Language: A Reader* (London, Routledge, 1990).

23 But Rosemary Manning, imagining both lovers as women, utterly changes the meaning of the poem. She comments: 'Nothing was ever said by any poet or philosopher which analysed so powerfully and truthfully both the consummation of love and the strange moment of pause before it.' Rosemary Manning, *A Time and a Time: An Autobiography* (1971; London, Marion Boyars, 1986), p. 83.

24 I am willingly persuaded by the argument that Marvell was probably a gay writer. There is a playful self-contained intensity in poems like 'The Definition of Love' which recognizes a genuine equality; and a willingness to be undone, to be vanquished (see 'The Fair Singer') which is very different from Donne's aggressive masculinity.

25 See Deborah Cameron's cogent and lucid analysis of this point in her *Feminism and Linguistic Theory*, pp. 129–33.

26 May Sarton, *Recovering: A Journal* (New York, Norton, 1980), pp. 20–1; *A Reckoning* (1978; London, Women's Press, 1984).

27 Elizabeth Wilson, *Prisons of Glass* (London, Methuen, 1986).

28 Ibid., p. 111.

29 Julia Penelope looks very hard at the reasons why in a long three-part article, 'The Mystery of Lesbians', which discusses the liberal takeover of the women's liberation movement. The article is republished from the American journal *Lesbian Ethics* in

Gossip: A Journal of Lesbian Feminist Ethics, nos. 1, 2, 3 (London, Onlywomen, 1986). Every woman who defines herself as a feminist should read this article; it is a disturbing and necessary piece of polemic.

30 Gayle Greene and Coppélia Kahn, 'Feminist Scholarship and the Social Construction of Woman', in Greene and Kahn (eds), *Making a Difference: Feminist Literary Criticism* (London, Methuen, 1985), pp. 4–5. Illuminating in flashes and occasionally unreadable, this book is an all-American collection, which is therefore informed by American critical issues and concerns.

31 Joanna Russ, *Extra(Ordinary) People* (New York, St Martin's, 1984), p. 147. The phrase is an epigraph by Carol Emshwiller at the head of the last piece in the book.

32 Elizabeth Wilson, 'Thoughts on *Beyond the Fragments*', in *Hidden Agendas*, p. 70.

33 Verena Stefan, *Shedding* (1975; London, Women's Press, 1979), p. 72.

34 Jill Miller, *Happy as a Dead Cat* (London, Women's Press, 1983).

35 Adrienne Rich, *Of Woman Born: Motherhood as Experience and Institution* (1976; London, Virago, 1977).

36 Nicky Edwards, *Mud* (London, Women's Press, 1986).

37 For a closer discussion of this debate see three pamphlets: *Breaching the Peace: A Collection of Radical Feminist Papers* (London, Onlywomen, 1983); a reply by Jean Freer, *Raging Womyn: In Reply to* Breaching the Peace. *A Comment on the Women's Liberation Movement and the Common Womyn's Peace Camp at Greenham* (free publication, 1984; donations to The Womyn's Land Fund, PO Box 51, 190 Upper Street, Islington, London N1); and Wilmette Brown, *Black Women and the Peace Movement* (published July 1983 by the International Women's Day Convention with part of a grant from the GLC Women's Committee; available from King's Cross Women's Centre).

38 May Sarton, *Mrs Stevens Hears the Mermaids Singing* (1965; New York, Norton, 1975); *As We Are Now* (1973; London, Women's Press, 1983); *A Reckoning*. See also Barbara Macdonald with Cynthia Rich, *Look Me in the Eye: Old Women, Aging and Ageism* (London, Women's Press, 1984). Macdonald, whose wonderful seamed face stares out of the cover of this edition, has written a powerful review of Sarton's *As We Are Now*: see her essay in the collection *The Power of the Old Woman*.

39 Jane Rule, *Against the Season* (1971; London, Pandora, 1988); Jan Clausen, *The Proserpine Papers* (1988; London, Women's Press, 1989); Caeia March, *Three Ply Yarn* (London, Women's Press, 1986) and *The Hide and Seek Files* (London, Women's Press, 1989).

40 Michèle Roberts, *The Visitation* (London, Women's Press, 1983), p. 81.

41 Lilian Mohin (ed.), *One Foot on the Mountain* (London, Onlywomen, 1979).

42 In 1986 the men had a fight about it: Tom Paulin and Craig Raine disagreed at some length in the literary columns of the patriarchal press about what political poetry is, and what should be included in Paulin's anthology *The Faber Book of Political Verse*. I didn't bother to follow their arguments terribly closely as it was quite clear that they were not talking to me.

43 Michèle Roberts, *A Piece of the Night* (London, Women's Press, 1978), p. 186.

44 Zoe Fairbairns et al., *Tales I Tell My Mother* (London, Journeyman, 1978), pp. 1, 2–3.

45 See Dorothy's description of the daffodils at Ullswater and compare William's poem; notice also her description of the leech-gatherer, which became Wordsworth's 'Resolution and Independence' some four years later. In *The Journals of Dorothy Wordsworth*, ed. Mary Moorman (Oxford, Oxford Paperbacks, 1971), the poems are reprinted at the end and cross-referenced to the text.

46 *Journals of Dorothy Wordsworth*, p. 4.

47 Valerie Miner, 'Feminist Fiction and Politics', in Fairbairns et al., *Tales I Tell My Mother*, p. 61.
48 Hannah Wakefield, *The Price You Pay* (London, Women's Press, 1987).
49 Sigrid Weigel, 'Double Focus: On the History of Women's Writing', in Gisela Ecker (ed.), *Feminist Aesthetics* (London, Women's Press, 1985), p. 62.
50 Barbara Deming, 'To Fear Jane Alpert is to Fear Ourselves', *Remembering Who We Are* (Pagoda–Temple of Love, 1981; distributed by Naiad, Tallahassee, Fla), p. 112.
51 Weigel, 'Double Focus', p. 63. The Matriarchy Network in Britain would certainly disagree. See their journal *Arachne*, available to women only from Arachne Collective, Matriarchy Research and Reclaim Network (if it still exists). I do not have any firm opinions on this point. There certainly was a goddess-religion that preceded Jehovah; but whether the societies in which that religion was practised really were egalitarian and did indeed honour women is matter for dispute. Goddess-worshipping cultures are not now warm supporters of women's autonomy and power. Wherever the Blessed Virgin Mary is worshipped women are even more savagely policed and controlled. There are many possible explanations for this; perhaps where women's power is acknowledged men's fear of that power increases accordingly. For a depressing read see Gerda Lerner, *The Creation of Patriarchy* (Oxford, Oxford University Press, 1986).
52 See Lillian Faderman, *Surpassing the Love of Men: Romantic Friendship and Love Between Women from the Renaissance to the Present* (1981; London, Women's Press, 1985) and Sheila Jeffreys' review article on her work, 'Does It Matter If They Did It?: Lillian Faderman and Lesbian History', *Trouble and Strife*, no. 3 (Summer 1984), pp. 25–9.
53 Alison Hennegan, 'What Lesbian Novel?', *Women's Review*, no. 1 (November 1985), p. 10–12. The *Women's Review* ran from November 1985 to July 1987 – then went bankrupt.
54 Sarton, *Recovering*, p. 20.
55 Beatrix Campbell, *Wigan Pier Revisited: Poverty and Politics in the 1980s* (London, Virago, 1984), p. 14.
56 This offensive short novel is carefully analysed by Kate Millett, *Sexual Politics* (1970; London, Virago, 1977), pp. 285–93.
57 Editorial, *Trouble and Strife*, no. 1 (Winter 1983).
58 See also Marilyn Frye, 'Some Reflections on Separatism and Power', in *The Politics of Reality* (Trumansburg, NY, Crossing Press, 1983), pp. 95–109.
59 The continuing justification for *Trouble and Strife*, printed on the inside cover of every issue. Still going strong.
60 Cora Kaplan, 'Pandora's Box: Subjectivity, Class and Sexuality in Socialist Feminist Criticism', in Greene and Kahn, *Making a Difference*, p. 151. For a socialist feminist analysis of the women's liberation movement see also Lynne Segal, *Is the Future Female? Troubled Thoughts on Contemporary Feminism* (London, Virago, 1987), which takes the same line as Kaplan.
61 See the paper by the Leeds Revolutionary Feminists – much disputed, debated, endorsed, reviled – in *Love Your Enemy? The Debate between Heterosexual Feminism and Political Lesbianism* (London, Onlywomen, 1981), p. 8.
62 See Sandra M. Gilbert and Susan Gubar, *The Madwoman in the Attic: The Woman Writer and the Nineteenth Century Literary Imagination* (New Haven, Yale University Press, 1979), ch. 10.
63 Brontë, *Jane Eyre*, ch. 12. This passage is cited and discussed by Kaplan in 'Pandora's Box'; read it yourself and see what you think.
64 Kaplan, 'Pandora's Box', p. 166.

65 Ibid.

66 'Race' is in itself a dubious term which masks the real problem. We are all of different races. It is not race which should bother us, it is *racism*: the deliberate discrimination practised by the powerful against the powerless on the basis of racial categories.

67 See the superb essay by Chikwenye Okonjo Ogunyemi, 'Womanism: The Dynamics of the Contemporary Black Novel in English', *Signs*, vol. 11, no. 1 (Autumn 1985), pp. 63–80. I am greatly indebted to her insights on *Jane Eyre*.

68 Kaplan, 'Pandora's Box', p. 172.

69 Sistren, *Lionheart Gal: Life Stories of Jamaican Women* (London, Women's Press, 1986), p. 185.

70 Brontë, *Jane Eyre*, ch. 27.

71 See Andrea Dworkin's early analysis *Woman Hating* (New York, Dutton, 1974).

72 See Barbara Taylor, *Eve and the New Jerusalem: Socialism and Feminism in the Nineteenth Century* (London, Virago, 1983).

73 See special issue of *Feminist Review* on 'Socialist Feminism: Out of the Blue', no. 23 (Summer 1986).

74 Elizabeth Wilson and Angela Weir, both socialists and feminists, provide a searching and critical analysis in their article, 'The British Women's Movement' (1984), reprinted in Wilson, *Hidden Agendas*, pp. 93–133.

75 *Feminist Review*, no. 23 (Summer 1986), p. 10.

76 'Women as a Class', editorial, *Englishwomen's Review*, May 1876, cited in Patricia Hollis, *Women in Public: The Women's Movement 1850–1900. Documents of the Victorian Women's Movement* (London, Allen & Unwin, 1979), p. 336.

77 Representing the phallus in the symbolic order does seem to require goods and credit cards, certainly not just the correct genital equipment. Does the phallus have a material basis, rather than a purely symbolic function as a sign of difference? I think we should be told.

78 Marlene Packwood, 'The Colonel's Lady and Judy O'Grady – Sisters Under the Skin?', *Trouble and Strife*, no. 1 (Winter 1983), p. 8.

79 French carries a strong regional marking; but as one French woman told me (in conversation, July 1986), so far as class is concerned it is hard to decipher from accent or language. 'One can make the most awful mistakes,' she said. I don't pretend to understand the French class system, but this comment reveals the obvious fact that how we treat one another is strongly dependent on class. If one woman simply addresses another woman *as a woman*, what would constitute an awful mistake?

80 Packwood, 'The Colonel's Lady and Judy O'Grady', p. 12.

81 Carolyn Steedman, *Landscape for a Good Woman: A Story of Two Lives* (London, Virago, 1986), p. 2.

82 Gloria Joseph, 'The Incompatible Ménage à Trois: Marxism, Feminism and Racism', in Lydia Sargent (ed.), *Women and Revolution: The Unhappy Marriage of Marxism and Feminism* (London, Pluto, 1981), p. 92. See also her book written with Jill Lewis, a British socialist feminist, *Common Differences: Conflicts in Black and White Feminist Perspectives* (New York, Anchor/Doubleday, 1981).

83 Maya Angelou, *I Know Why the Caged Bird Sings* (1969; London, Virago, 1984); Alice Walker, *The Color Purple* (1982; London, Women's Press, 1983).

84 Joseph and Lewis, *Common Differences*, p. 191.

85 Audre Lorde; *Zami: A New Spelling of My Name* (1982; London, Sheba, 1984).

86 Audre Lorde, *Sister/Outsider: Essays and Speeches* (Trumansberg, NY, Crossing Press, 1984).

87 Lorde, 'The Uses of Anger: Women Responding to Racism', in *Sister/Outsider*, p. 124.

88 Lorde, *Zami*, p. 15.

89 Lorde, 'The Uses of Anger', pp. 132–3.

90 Lorde, *The Cancer Journals* (San Francisco, Spinsters, Ink, 1980), pp. 20–3. (There is now also an English edition: London, Sheba, 1985.) See also Lorde's essays, *A Burst of Light* (Ithaca, NY: Firebrand, 1988; also published in Britain by Sheba).

91 Thank you to Heidi Hartmann for this phrase. See her contribution to Sargent, *Women and Revolution*, p. 33.

92 I have spoken fairly critically of both the theory and the practice of psychoanalysis and revolutionary socialism in this introductory polemic; but I have not discussed their enormous and important contribution to feminist theory, I have just outlined why I do not find either very helpful in my reading, writing, living. Other women do.

93 'Much better to write the class struggle than the class war,' as my aunt used to advise me: 'struggle denotes heaving bodies.' 'That's right,' shouted my uncle, a Trotskyist, 'reduce everything to sex.' This anecdote is germane to my political position; the struggle that is sexual politics is the point where I began.

94 For further help with the gaseous abstractions, see Moi, *Sexual/Textual Politics* and Elaine Showalter (ed.), *The New Feminist Criticism: Essays on Women, Literature and Theory* (London, Virago, 1986); for an excellent critique of the problems of theorizing women's poetry, Jan Montefiore's *Feminism and Poetry: Language, Experience, Identity in Women's Writing* (London, Pandora, 1987); and for the fiction Paulina Palmer's *Contemporary Women's Fiction: Feminist Theory and Narrative Practice* (Brighton, Harvester, 1989). I owe a good deal to Paulina Palmer's intelligence and generosity as both colleague and friend. We don't agree – and have had many creative disagreements. I am grateful for them, and for her support.

95 See Jane Spencer, *The Rise of the Woman Novelist: From Aphra Behn to Jane Austen* (Oxford, Blackwell, 1986). For a brief and convincing explanation as to why women emerged so strongly as the makers of the novel, see also Josephine Donovan, 'The Silence is Broken' (1980), reprinted in Deborah Cameron (ed.), *The Feminist Critique of Language: A Reader* (London, Routledge, 1990), pp. 41–56.

96 Weigel, 'Double Focus', p. 63.

97 I find myself warmly in agreement here with Suzanne Kappeler. See her study *The Pornography of Representation* (Cambridge, Polity, 1986) and her article, 'What is a Feminist Publishing Policy?', in Gail Chester and Julienne Dickey (eds), *Feminism and Censorship: The Current Debate* (London, Prism, 1988), pp. 233–7. See also Christina Battersby, *Gender and Genius: Towards a Feminist Aesthetics* (London, Women's Press, 1989).

2

A Note on the Politics of Publishing

The suppression of feminist ideas in western capitalist patriarchies is achieved not through legislation, but through control of the market. Access to public opinion has been managed, historically and structurally, by men, and in the private sector is moreover determined by profit. Women's contributions have been excluded on a massive scale, rejected for publication or republication and preservation; they have not been censored as such.

Suzanne Kappeler, 'What is a Feminist Publishing Policy?'

Female printers did exist. There were, in fact, the immediate material conditions for all-female production of pamphlets. There were some women authors and a larger number of women printers. But the female printers did not print the work of female writers. Why not? Possibly because the articulate shared consciousness of womanhood was missing? There was no shared objective, no common movement, to draw together the separate female producers.[1]

There were women who wrote and women who printed writing in the Renaissance; but probably not enough women who could read or buy books to produce a movement that could have been recorded on the page. Unlike Mr Shepherd, I am quite sure that there was a 'shared consciousness of womanhood' among the women of the period, but it was probably articulated in the kitchens and the fields. In the early 1970s there were women writing, printing and publishing their own work, not for the approval of men – although the books are, of course, available to the general public – but for one another. Onlywomen Press, then called The Women's Press, grew from a revolutionary movement, publishing poetry, pamphlets and posters.[2] The Press has retained that early commitment to radicalism, which is reflected in what it publishes. In 1985 it published the papers from three conferences on sexual violence held in the 1980s: 'Sexual Violence Against Women' (Leeds, 1980); 'Women Against Violence Against Women' (London, 1981); and 'Male Power and the Sexual Abuse of Girls' (Manchester, 1982).[3] These papers are not written in elegant, conventional prose. They have the raw immediacy of the movement; the smell of the streets. They taste of all the necessary anger that is still there despite the efforts on the part of middle-class academics to turn women's liberation into women's studies. And in the meantime, over the past ten years, feminist books have become big business.

In 1988 the first two feminist publishing houses in Britain to address mainstream society, Virago and The Women's Press, came officially of age. Virago had been publishing women's books for fifteen years. The Women's Press was ten years old. Both were products of the women's liberation movement and the 1970s. Virago began by reprinting lost women's writing in its enormously successful series, Virago Modern Classics. It now prints new fiction as well as explicitly Lesbian fiction and Lesbian anthologies. The Women's Press has never been an independent publishing house, but has always had close links with the Namara Group. Both these presses now have an annual turnover of over a million pounds. On the back of their success the straight, male-dominated presses began to produce their own feminist lists. This book is an example of precisely this phenomenon: I was asked to write an essay on feminist writing by Julia Mosse, then the feminist editor at Basil Blackwell.

Another example of the straight male presses getting in on the act is the women writers' list at Methuen, run by Elsbeth Linder. She wrote an article about Methuen's editorial policy and working methods in *Women's Review*. 'The company is not run as a collective – editorial decisions are reached through discussion with fellow editors and sales people and are ratified at a weekly editorial meeting . . . Then come the conversations, to reach a perception of the book's sales potential . . . there is also a shared belief that success comes from being rigorously selective.'[4] Editors and sales people work together: this is, after all, a business, not a charity, and the point is to make money, if not for the authors then at least for the publishers. At no point does Linder say what 'rigorously selective' actually means, or what her criteria are, although she does say that 'manuscripts arriving via agents tend usually to receive the quickest attention, the assumption being that anything which has survived the initial hurdle of the agent's scrutiny must have some potential'. Potential here must mean marketing potential. When Methuen launched its first women's writing list in 1984 it published already established names: Caryl Churchill, Michelene Wandor, Michèle Roberts, Marina Warner. Linder calmly states what she has in common with the feminist presses. 'All of us have a commitment to women's writing. All our lists need to be financially profitable in order to survive.' She gives no indication that there might be any contradiction between or difficulty in reconciling these two statements. Is a market created by a political movement? Does the one vanish if the other is suppressed? We all know that the fragile gains women have made are easily reversible.

My fear for women's work, in whatever genre, is simply this: the straight male presses only produced their feminist lists when women had proved themselves to be profitable. They let the women take the risks, then climbed aboard the financial bandwagon. So far as radical Lesbian writing is concerned, Only-women Press is the only publisher with an exclusive commitment to radical Lesbian politics. But if the straight male presses buy off well-known women writers – and I don't blame the authors: I do think that women should be well paid – the women-run presses are left with the risks rather than the best-sellers. And if they go out of business, feminist innovation, ambition and radical politics will surely go too. We are not in the majority; and I fear the political effects of majority taste.

Let me explain what I mean by the political effects of majority taste. Once, during a Black Hour in the publishing industry, I was trying to hawk some of my work round the male presses. I found a sympathetic male ear. 'Look,' he said, 'I like your work. But it's much too serious and much too worrying. I can sell books on Gardening, Orchids, Nazis, Cats, Golf and the Royal Family. So if you can write me a story about a Nazi who takes to golf, gardening and orchids to get over the guilt, has a fetish about the Royal Family and eventually strangles his cat, I can sell it.' He was only just joking; and this was certainly the first time I had ever heard it implied that the Nazis were neither worrying nor serious but, apparently, a commercial product. But these are the laws of the market-place. They have nothing to do with feminism, nor with quality. Publishers print what sells.

Ironically, a new Lesbian publishing house has taken that point to heart. Silver Moon Books, an offshoot of Silver Moon Bookshop in Charing Cross Road, began publishing in 1990, their first two titles both reprints from America's Lesbian-Easy-Reads publishers, Naiad Press. It was a conscious decision on the part of Silver Moon's publishers, Jane Cholmeley and Sue Butterworth, to 'do "fun" lesbian books'. Interviewed by The Women's Press Bookclub news reporter, Sue had this to say: 'Of course other feminist publishers do Lesbian detective fiction, for example. But I think they do perceive themselves, quite rightly, as more serious presses, whereas what we're looking for is just to provide "the Friday night read" . . . We don't think other presses are doing that.'[5] Their editorial policy reflects the field research they have done during their years as Lesbian and feminist booksellers. They know what sells. Not surprisingly, this is the lowest common denominator – easy cliché genres, romance, thrillers and detective stories. Whether these genres can be so easily transformed into interesting writing by an added Lesbian presence remains to be proven. Irene Coffey read one of Silver Moon Books' first titles, Claire McNab's *Lessons in Murder*[6] and had this to say about Lesbian detectives.

> The detective is in a morally powerful position, and is working dangerously and dramatically to expunge the immediate world of evil. And this moral question is of crucial importance to the lesbian reader as an outsider of mainstream society, all too often condemned as an immoral and evil influence. In this kind of lesbian crime fiction there is a re-alignment of lesbian identity into the side of the law, the side of righteousness.[7]

In contemporary Britain, where we now live with Section 28, any hopes of abandoning our outlaw status and re-aligning ourselves with the law seem like cosy fantasies. But the question goes deeper than that: what is the side of righteousness in a racist, sexist and violent society? Fun reads cannot afford to ask this kind of question.

How can we dismantle those racist and sexist structures in our fiction if we continue to endorse them through the means by which we produce our books? This is not easy, because we need money and power to maintain our independence. The women-run presses which insist on collective ways of working will not command either the finance or the expertise to expand into major capitalist enterprises. Democracy is appallingly time-consuming, often gory, and incredibly frustrating, as every feminist who has ever worked in a collective well knows. But the refusal to separate the process and the product is a wise one. Sheba Feminist Publishers are now run by Black and white women together. This has not been an easy political process and has meant rethinking methods of working. They gave an interview to *Spare Rib* in July 1986.

> *Sue O'Sullivan*: For instance we do have certain things which we follow: when we edit a book we try and have two women working on it; a black and a white woman. It's a small thing but it's there as a kind of check.
> *Pratibha Parmar*: Also things around publicity. For example when we're promoting a black woman's book we try and make sure that a black woman and a white woman are involved. This is because black women are often promoted by the mainstream media in ways that are racist. We want to avoid that. Of course we want all the reviews and interviews we can get but we don't want them at the expense of what we stand for.[8]

Sheba have published fine writing by British Blackwomen; among their publications are *A Dangerous Knowing: Four Black Women Poets* (1984) and Barbara Burford's *The Threshing Floor* (1986). The two best-selling Black-women writers published by The Women's Press and Virago, Alice Walker and Maya Angelou respectively, are both Americans. Racism is more unsettling when it comes closer to home. Tales of the Deep South, over the seas and far away, are less disturbing to read and more conducive to righteous white indignation. Sheba are to be congratulated for publishing Black writers who live here in Britain, and for tackling racist issues on our doorstep.

Both Sheba and Onlywomen Press have an editorial support group of other women. This support group is unpaid and will usually advise on what is to be published. The members' jobs are not advertised; the problem here is that while it is perfectly understandable that women will want to work with other women whom they find sympathetic and co-operative it does mean that what is actually published will be chosen by a tiny group of like-minded women. The answer here is not to undermine or abandon what we have, but to extend the tentacles of feminist practice into the straight presses. Any woman who has had her work processed by every single member of a collective will have a horror story to tell. Books and essays written by committee or collective are usually neither contentious, coherent nor interesting; but Sheba's idea of having a Blackwoman and a white woman working together on every text, in effect an anti-racist collective method of working, is excellent and if adopted more widely would certainly challenge some of the institutional racism of Britain. At the very least, that practice would ensure jobs for Blackwomen.

A significant number of the books I shall discuss are published by Onlywomen Press and The Women's Press. I went to see them both and asked about their publishing policies and methods of working. It is not my intention here to provide a history of all the feminist presses in Britain, nor even a detailed study of Onlywomen and The Women's Press.[9] I simply wish to raise some of the problems involved in publishing feminist writing, because these affect the writers, the texts, how they are marketed – and, crucially, who gets published in the first place. Nevertheless, Onlywomen and The Women's Press have, in my opinion, published the best and most interesting feminist texts of the past fifteen years.

I talked about Onlywomen Press with Lilian Mohin, one of the founders of the Press, one of its present directors and editor of many of its collections. The women who know Lilian Mohin would all agree that it is her tenacity and energy that have given the Press its shape and distinctive style. Onlywomen offers a brief history of its enterprise in every copy of the catalogue.

In 1984 the Press altered the text on its logo, which originally read as follows: 'A Women's Liberation publishing and printing group, producing work by and for women as part of creating a feminist communication network, and ultimately, a feminist revolution.' They now describe themselves, with crisp and savage brevity, as 'Radical feminist and Lesbian publishers'. The design of the logo has also changed. Lilian explains the transformation. 'We felt that the picture on the old one is much too racially specific to be consistent with our anti-racist position. The new one implies a bit of our history (as printers) through resemblance to a printer's block as well as stating exactly who we are.'

I asked Lilian about the politics of the Press and its original aim, the assertion and illumination of Lesbian radical feminism. She explained that all the women who set up the press were both Lesbians and radical feminists, and she argues forcefully for a necessary connection between the two. The firmness with which the Press wishes to be known as 'exactly who we are' is, I think, characteristic of its politics, which are nothing if not courageous and uncompromising. The much-publicized and much-discussed malaise and fragmentation of the women's liberation movement, the co-option of feminism as a liberal ideology of equal rights, and the Labour Party's creeping socialism of the early 1980s fired the women at Onlywomen Press with the conviction that they should take an even firmer, clearer stand. *The Observer*, seeing the word 'Lesbian', subsequently refused to take their advertising on the grounds that it would be noticed. There have been problems with other reviews; but one interesting exception has been the fearless *Times Literary Supplement*, which agreed to review their anthology of Lesbian feminist poetry *Beautiful Barbarians* (1986). Lilian points out that no one could accuse the *TLS* of being Lesbian. Other reviews might have to be more careful. The effect of declaring themselves to be radical feminist and Lesbian publishers has produced universal alarm among the straight presses; but they have been 'selling books hand over fist'. The reason is simple: 'Put Lesbian in large print on the front of the books and Lesbians will buy them.'

The Press has had to be exceedingly cautious concerning the printing and production of its books. Three of the original collective went to Camberwell Printing College to learn how to print: they were the first women whom the College had ever accepted for training. Knowing how to print has been a critical issue; their experience with their anthology of British feminist poetry, *One Foot On The Mountain*, was instructive.[10] Lilian describes this anthology as 'a movement book', indicating that the book both grew out of and reflects the women's liberation movement of the 1970s. Many of the poems are outspoken, very radical, consciously breaking taboos. When the text came back from the first (male) printer to whom it was given, it was very badly done, and printed on different kinds of paper. The second printer, a radical left (male) press, sent it back covered in coffee stains. Onlywomen Press demanded that the edition be

In 1974 several radical feminist lesbians in London formed a group to print and publish work from the women's liberation movement. In order to control the processes involved, three of us went to a technical college to learn to print. As the Women's Press we published six books of poetry, the first British Women's Liberation Movement calendar and a collection of posters. In 1977 we set up the first British conference on women in printing and publishing. Just before this event we were obliged to change our name to ONLYWOMEN PRESS because a commercial publisher had taken our name, registering it officially where we had not. We chose ONLYWOMEN PRESS to keep a name close to our original one, making a clear connection with the ground-breaking work we had already done.

In 1978 we set up as commercial printers as well as publishers, equipped with antiquated presses and backed by small loans from women in the movement. We trained several new women as printers and managed also to pay the rent and subsidise our publishing.

In mid-1984 we gave up printing to concentrate exclusively on publishing. Some of us miss the logical charms of the printing presses. All of us miss the certainty of a printer for lesbian and radical feminist work. The transition concentrates all our efforts toward the assertion and illumination of lesbian radical feminism — our original aim.

 (a)

(b)

Figure 2   *Onlywomen Press: (a) the original logo and (b) the revised version, with the press's brief history of itself*

pulped and the work done again. The printer then turned very nasty and held the artwork to ransom. When the women had themselves set up a business as jobbing printers they took the printed text of the pamphlet produced by the Matriarchy Study Group, *Menstrual Taboos*, to the binders. It didn't come back. They went round to ask for it and found it in the bin. Apparently, the men do read the texts. Now the women always demand a letter from their printers, stating that they undertake to print the work according to the Trade Standards, every time they deliver a manuscript. 'But,' says Lilian, 'it's easier to deal with printers and binders if you know how to print. As printers we did a lot of work for other feminist groups and continually had to intercede between these groups and print finishers, as well as offer design and print production education.'

Lilian maintains that knowing how to print has made a difference to how she judges writing, and to the values in writing which she is prepared to champion and defend. She demands 'a kind of clarity', and, as she puts it most succinctly, 'no bullshit'. The Press wants the books to be beautiful. There is no standard format for the texts, although since 1987 it has developed a basic blue cover design. Each cover illustration is original, and consistent with the contents of the book, not the Press. They are convinced that they can sell the books they believe in. 'And even if you don't believe in it, you can sell 2,000 of anything. In the case of feminist books women want them and will buy them.' They print what they want to see in print and do very little market research.

I asked about their periodical venture, *Gossip: A Journal of Lesbian Feminist Ethics*. *Gossip* ran for six issues from 1986 to 1988 and then suddenly ceased publication when, as the editors admitted in the last issue, ' . . . the production, public meetings schedule and financial worries (exacerbated by those who only borrow or photocopy rather than subscribe) have become too large a task for us to shoulder alongside our other commitments and responsibilities'.[11] Lilian said that they had started *Gossip* ' . . . because we wanted it. Because we needed it.' The journal was a brief but telling success. Most of the subscribers were British; but there were subscriptions from abroad: women in the United States, Australia, Japan, France, Holland, Belgium. *Gossip* generated plenty of discussion. A 'Lesbian Ethics Day' was held in Bristol on 15 April 1989. Thus the Press initiated and generated a debate within Lesbian feminism.

Gossip's subscription list reflects the international character of the Lesbian community and also demonstrates the need for the journal. The subscriptions were often accompanied by warm messages of support. Lilian comments: 'From the first we intended our work to be sold to everyone, everywhere; and to be drawn from radical feminist lesbian writers everywhere. We would pull no punches, but address ourselves very publicly to lesbians only, remaining as oblivious as possible to the presence of men.'

I asked how *Gossip* began. In 1983–4 Onlywomen Press held a series of meetings at Sisterwrite Bookshop in London on the topic of Lesbian Ethics. The GLC had supported the Press with a subsidy and they liked their beneficiaries to hold events. The meetings were packed, and the seriousness with which the topics were discussed – Lesbian sexuality, motherhood, friendship between women, anti-Lesbianism in the women's liberation movement, racism and anti-racism – convinced the Press that there was a need for a permanent forum where serious issues could be raised. This group generated the initial energy. Then, early in 1985 while flying back from the United States, Lilian read Julia Penelope's article on the liberal takeover of the women's movement, entitled 'The Mystery of Lesbians', which was first published in the American journal *Lesbian Ethics*.[12] She determined to make this long, three-part analysis easily available to a British audience: and Penelope's defence of separatism was duly published in the first three issues of *Gossip*.

The Press's support group of women read the manuscripts which come in. Unpaid members of Onlywomen Press are also full members so far as publishing decisions are concerned. Initially, all of them read all the manuscripts: yet they still try to keep the waiting time for expectant writers down to a minimum. Their long, understanding, committed rejection letters are famous – and time-consuming. Lilian makes the point that they spend a lot of time working on manuscripts which they do not publish. Many of the authors they do print are known to the collective. This is probably inevitable, given the politics of the Press; but only five of the authors who contributed work to the first Lesbian fiction anthology *The Reach* were invited to submit stories.[13] The rest arrived through the letter-box in response to advertising.

Onlywomen Press uses the Writer's Guild model contract, so their authors do rather better than they do with other commercial publishers. This is because at the beginning, as Lilian says simply, 'We were all writers.' Their royalties start at 10 per cent, rising to 12 per cent after the first 2,000 copies, and eventually to 15 per cent after 5,000 copies. Lilian comments:

> If we had more money we'd plough it into advertising – not as hype or promotion but simply to let women know that our books are available. Whenever someone hears of us or requests a catalogue, they order nearly all our books. All our novels are printed in initial runs of 5,000 and most of them are in their second printing. With titles from abroad we print 3,000 initially since we are thereby excluded from certain foreign markets. All our books sell, and sell well. In our case, absence of profit is more closely linked to our low prices, minute profit margins and political intentions.

They are committed to keeping their books in print whenever possible.

Onlywomen Press has never abandoned its engagement with radical and contemporary issues. In 1983 it published *Breaching the Peace*, a critical and cogent response to the women's peace movement and the phenomenon of Greenham.[14] Their pamphlet series provide radical essays and practical guides such as *Down There: An Illustrated Guide to Self-Examination* by Sophie Laws, in a cheap format. And the Press has remained unwavering in its commitment to its original politics. Funding has always been precarious. It began in 1974 as a voluntary group. The ILEA gave grants to the individual women who studied printing at Camberwell, knowing when it did so that the women intended to set up a women's press. While three of them were learning to be printers they used the equipment at Camberwell to print feminist material. Around 1977–8 they moved into a Dickensian basement in Hackney where they rented space and a printing machine for £10 a week. Here they printed commercial work and with those funds subsidized the women's work. The Press survived on small gifts from women in the movement; anything between £2.50 and £100. It received tiny grants from the Arts Council, for individual books, which did not in fact cover the production costs.

When the now deceased GLC was offering subsidies to radical causes the Press applied for a small grant, largely for the printing side, which they used to buy equipment. Onlywomen were not happy with the strings attached to GLC money, which was in any case more readily given to socialist causes than to enterprises such as radical feminist and Lesbian publishing. While the printing business was still operating it consisted of a collective of up to eight, with four full-time workers. No one earned more than £30 per week. In 1984 Onlywomen Press finally ceased printing to concentrate on publishing work. A Greater London Arts Grant at last enabled a living wage to be paid – after ten years of printing, publishing and radical feminist activity. Until 1989 there were only two full-time workers, Anna Livia and Lilian Mohin; they earned £8,580 apiece, less if the money was tight. The Press relied on voluntary help, part-time workers and unpaid outside support. Onlywomen has always been a limited company, but members have never had contracts as workers.

Some of the women who have worked with the Onlywomen Press collective, including Mohin herself, are Americans, long-term residents in Britain; this has meant that the Press has always had strong transatlantic connections. *For Lesbians Only: A Separatist Anthology* is a political/theoretical history book of Lesbian separatism; primarily American, with a substantial section from French-speaking Lesbian separatists, it remained unpublished in America.[15] Onlywomen Press is now reassessing its position and hoping to publish more books every year on a broader range of subjects – theology, history, theory and Lesbian radical feminist criticism – along with regular anthologies of short fiction and poetry collections. But the present economic climate is of course very far from favourable. Editorial independence is astonishingly expensive. Small may be beautiful, but it is often economically impossible.

Onlywomen Press has remained unwavering in its commitment to its original politics, partly because some of the women who were involved in the project at the beginning are still there. But the survival of the Press is also due to an obstinate integrity, a refusal to be hijacked, co-opted, bought out or otherwise silenced. We need hard words in hard times.

The commercial press which took and registered the original name of Onlywomen Press is, of course, The Women's Press Ltd. And The Women's Press has marketed feminism with immense financial success. Right from the start, it had more conventional funding, from a male-dominated group of companies. Its original founder had worked in straight publishing. Its politics have always been more broadly based than those of Onlywomen Press, and certainly never explicitly Lesbian. The Women's Press was hard to pin down for interview or discussion and, irritatingly, never answered my letters. But I finally managed to speak to Katy Nicholson, who was then the publicity manger (she has now left the Press). I asked her to tell me all she could about the history of the Press, its publishing policies and its methods of working.

The woman who had the original enthusiasm for The Women's Press was Stephanie Dowrick, an editor at Triad. The Press has always been a limited company and originally had close links with another publishing house, Quartet, also part of the Namara Group. Namara, owned by Naim Attulah, guarantees the Women's Press overdraft. Initially, Quartet did all its sales and marketing but it has gradually become progressively less dependent on Quartet, ever since it began trading. The Press published its first five titles in 1978: *Aurora Leigh* by Elizabeth Barrett Browning, *The Awakening* by Kate Chopin, *Lives of Girls and Women* by Alice Munroe, *Lolly Willowes* by Sylvia Townsend Warner and *Love and Freindship* (sic) by Jane Austen. This last text was illustrated by Suzanne Perkins, who eventually became the Press's art director. All the first titles were reprints: at that time there was still a huge body of fine writing which was out of print. Virago has since remedied the situation and The Women's Press has subsequently concentrated on publishing new work, as indicated by its slogan: 'Live authors, live issues'. The Press has expanded every year since 1978 and now publishes over sixty titles a year. Katy was employed in 1983 to deal with publicity. Now all their services are in-house. They still share their warehousing and their 'reps' (representatives), who sell the books to the booksellers, with Quartet; and their funding is still guaranteed by Namara, who keep an eye on The Women's Press financially. But I was assured that Namara had no editorial control whatsoever over what is published and that the profits are fed back into the Press and not creamed off.

The Women's Press is not, and never has been, a collective. But it does not employ secretaries or a receptionist and there is some ideal of regular communication among the staff. This is what Katy describes as 'a whiff of collectivity in the wind'. As the Press has grown it has evolved a more formal structure, with a member of staff in each department. There is a formal hierarchy: Ros de Lanerolle is the managing director and she has the last word. But there is a weekly meeting of all the full-time workers in the Press, held at present on Tuesday afternoons during working hours, where the week's reading is handed out and the books to be published are discussed. I asked if they gave the books written by Blackwomen to the Blackwomen on the staff to read and the books by Lesbians to the Lesbians. Katy said they did.

The Press receives around thirty manuscripts every week, plus around ten poetry collections and some eight non-fiction proposals; 25 per cent of the work it receives comes through literary agents. The Press does not have a poetry list, so the poetry collections are usually returned fairly swiftly. (It publishes Alice Walker's poetry simply because she is one of their best-selling authors, and it does publish various anthologies, such as the collections performed by The Raving Beauties, *In The Pink* and *No Holds Barred* – but not, at present, individual collections.) It is, however, interested in fiction, especially in new fiction by British women. What, then, are its criteria for deciding that a text is suitable material for the Women's Press? This proved difficult to explain precisely: 'The book must be woman-centred in some way . . . perhaps with a woman as the central character . . . ' It was easier to indicate what the Press looks for by examples. With the present volume of work it is simply not possible for every member of staff to read everything, but where there is a doubt or a difficult decision to be made, then most of them will read the book. Much of the reading is done in-house, but outside readers are employed to comment on specialist texts. The standard Press letter to a reader asking her to comment on a manuscript contains the following paragraph:

> To give you an idea of what to 'read' for we would generally suggest that we'd like you to speculate in your report why you think the enclosed title should or should not be published by TWP, and to identify any 'original' aspects (or lack of them) of the work considered. In general we ask readers to look for feminist/cultural perspectives in the work, as well as writing skill and relevance to our market. In terms of fiction, we are looking for novels that feature central female protagonists who initiate action and who are presented in a very positive way. (This is a very general statement so please use your judgement where these comments seem unclear or irrelevant to the specific title you are reading for us.)

And the comments sheet also asks the question: 'Are there any political/ editorial problems with this title?' The women at the Press do have a very definite idea of what they are looking for; but it is never too clearly defined.

When Katy first came to the Press in 1983 there were three women working in the office and one woman working from home. They were all white. Katy had come from straight publishing; she had worked at Cassell and Souvenir. As the Press expanded and began to publish the work of Blackwomen writers, including Alice Walker, the political contradictions inherent in a team of white women publishing Blackwomen's work became more starkly evident. It now employs Blackwomen and all vacancies are automatically advertised in the Black press. There are very few Blackwomen in publishing; Allison and Busby, The Women's Press, Virago and Women in Publishing are now jointly involved in setting up a proposed training scheme for Blackwomen in publishing.

There are, of course, inevitably problems for Blackwomen who come to work with a previously all-white team. Katy pointed out: 'I would hope that it's made us more aware of the issues surrounding what we are publshing.' The example she gave was Sharan-Jeet Shan's autobiography *In My Own Name* (1985).[16] The book received extensive media attention, but the coverage was uncomprehend- ing and racist. The media read the book as an attack on the supposedly barbarous South Asian custom of arranged marriage, despite Shan's careful disclaimer and explanation in her preface. Shan herself received threats from the Sikh community, who felt threatened and betrayed. Katy was of the opinion that the Press should have been more sensitive to the possibility that this would happen, and that they should have done more to protect their author. The problem remains that whatever we write can be used against us. For Black- women and South Asian women who wish to be critical of sexism and prejudice in their communities there is always the additional danger that white racists will pick on what they write and use it to confirm damaging racist stereotypes. Joan Riley's first novel, *The Unbelonging* (1985), was also published by The Women's Press; and here there arose the problems caused by the complex intersection of racism and sexism. A Blackwoman who publishes her work with The Women's Press rather than a Black press is seen to be affirming her loyalties with white feminists rather than with Black and Asian women and men, and therefore betraying her race. *The Unbelonging* is an important publication: the first novel by a Black British Caribbean woman to be published in this country. It is the first of several books by Riley published by The Women's Press.[17] The irony in all this is pinpointed by the fact that Caryl Phillips, a Black male writer whose work lies in the same territory and historical area of experience as that of Joan Riley, publishes with Faber. His *The Final Passage*, a novel set in the Caribbean and in England, was also published in 1985. To publish with Faber is not regarded as a political statement; publishing with The Women's Press is. Despite these problems The Women's Press intends to publish more work by South Asian and Black Afro-Caribbean women. Katy was quite certain that the women had been writing for years: their work had simply remained unpublished.

There is also a big market for Lesbian fiction, especially since there is, in Britain at least, less competition from the straight press, which tends to take up less radical and less controversial feminist material. Katy Nicholson felt that Lesbian writers were now able to take a Lesbian perspective for granted and not to feel that they were betraying The Cause if they presented a Lesbian character who was not ideal in every respect. The Women's Press has had problems with distribution because the reps who take their books round to the booksellers are not, as a group, card-carrying feminists. Moreover, most of them are men. The Press has discovered that it is not a selling point to have the word 'Lesbian' in the first or second line of the blurb on the back on the back of the book. The bookshop managers are usually men and may refuse to take the book, arguing that it is a 'specialist interest'.[18] The reps are of the opinion that if the word appears further down the blurb it will sell the book, and the managers don't usually read it all. The Deadly Word, Katy maintained, does not usually appear at all on Virago covers: instead, there is a closet code; 'constant companion', 'life partner', 'great friend'. Close inspection of the Virago blurbs reveals that this is in fact not the case. Aileen La Tourette's *Nuns and Mothers* (Virago, 1984) says of its heroine: 'One foot in straight domesticity with husband and children in England, the other in America in wild, wonderful lesbian love with Georgia'. In fact, since I spoke to Katy, Virago has taken the plunge into Lesbian writing.[19] The fact is that women who might not, in any other circumstances, read either poetry or difficult fiction will buy and read Lesbian writing. Yet despite the richness of the writing being published now, these books are still a whisper in a giant silence. Katy said that she believed that there was a heterosexual market for Lesbian fiction, and offered herself as an example. 'I'm a heterosexual woman who likes reading Lesbian fiction. It's a sort of touchstone.'

I asked about the feminist politics of the Press, which has, in the past, published pioneer texts of radical feminist theory from the United States.[20] Katy said that the women on the staff would define themselves as both radical feminist and socialist feminist. They were all active in various campaigns, both in left-wing politics and in the women's movement. Ros de Lanerolle is involved in the anti-apartheid movement; Sarah Lefanu has also written for *Marxism Today*; Jan Green had worked at the Brighton Rape Crisis Centre and had been part of an all-women rock band, Devil's Dykes; Jan Broom had been involved in setting up a radical bookshop in Bristol; Mary Hemming had worked for Scottish and Northern Distributors. Katy agreed that the women of the Press did see their politics are being well to the left of their colleagues at Virago; they saw themselves as having a sharper, more radical edge. The Women's Press slogan, 'Live authors, live issues', was also intended to suggest contemporary, controversial writing.

It is conscious political policy on the part of The Women's Press to give a voice to women who hitherto have not had access to print. It will not – and this is also conscious policy – publish the work of a woman of one culture writing about women of another culture. And its publishing scope is decidedly international. My question about their best-sellers was easy to answer. Alice Walker's *The Color Purple* sold well, even initially, with no reviews at all, and since Spielberg's film has sold over half a million. Marge Piercy's *Woman on the Edge of Time* has already sold well over 70,000 copies. Among non-fiction best-sellers are Walker's essays *In Search of Our Mothers' Gardens* and Ellen Kuzwayo's *Call Me Woman*, which is the autobiography of a Blackwoman from South Africa. Also selling well is Rosalie Bertell's *No Immediate Danger*, a scientific study of the spread of radioactive pollution. This sold well, even before the Chernobyl disaster, but even better after it.[21] All its fiction titles sell well, that is, around 7,000 copies in the first year of publication. The reps, apparently, now love to sell the fiction. At first there was some resistance to the Zebra Stripes hallmark of the fiction titles, introduced in February 1982; but now the booksellers, recognizing the sales potential of the product, will take ten copies at once. When the Press first began trading in 1978, it was the radical booksellers who promoted the books, and in the early days they were vital: the reps simply did not believe that there was a market. The Feminist Book Fortnight and the International Feminist Book Fair held in London in 1984 proved to be a turning-point. *The Color Purple*, which had by then won the Pulitzer Prize for Fiction, was chosen as one of the key texts to be promoted, and for the first time W. H. Smith took large orders.

The Women's Press distribution is handled by Plymbridge in Plymouth. Since June 1986 its Scottish distribution has been handled by Bookspeed, which has increased sales in the north by 50 per cent. Since 1985 Books for Students has taken all Press titles and put them out on approval to school libraries and public libraries. In June 1986, after three years of diplomatic lobbying, Bookwise, the national wholesalers, agreed to take its titles. Pipeline also distributes its books. The Press does very little market research; but Katy thought that it did neither more nor less than any other publisher. Terms for their authors are $7\frac{1}{2}$ per cent royalties on home sales in paperback and 10 per cent in hardback; export royalties are 6 per cent in paperback and 8 per cent in hardback. The advance for a first novel – that is, the royalties on what the Press could expect to sell in 18–24 months – will usually be around £1,000. Well-known authors do not get large advances. These terms do not differ substantially from the usual terms offered to writers elsewhere in commercial publishing. It is a truth universally acknowledged, that publishers do it for money and writers do it for love. Staff salaries at The Women's Press vary between £8,000 and £12,000: it is a conscious policy not to have very large wage differentials. The age range of the women who work there is from twenty-two to mid-fifties.

The Press will accept around six titles from the pile of unsolicited manuscripts every year, and that includes the work which comes to them through literary agents. Katy said that they encouraged their writers to work both with history workshop groups and creative writing groups. On the whole, most of their non-fiction work is commissioned. Rosika Parker's *The Subversive Stitch* (1985), a radical history of women's embroidery, was commissioned in 1979. A feminist analysis of astrology, *The Knot of Time* (1987) was also commissioned some years ago. Titles in the 'Handbook' series, which includes the titles *Sexual Violence, The Anorexic Experience* and *Lesbian Mothers' Legal Handbook*, were all commissioned. Innovations since 1985 include the feminist science fiction list and the new 'Livewires' fiction series for young women.

I asked Katy what she thought were the disadvantages of working at The Women's Press. She replied that the ambiguity which persists with the residual desire to work as a collective could be a problem. She thought that the company probably had too little structure rather than too much. The enormous pressure of work and the desire to maintain a co-operative atmosphere were often in conflict: staff sometimes fall seriously ill and are forced to leave. Disagreements, she said, tend to boil up and then disappear, but there is so much pressure from external crises that the internal arguments which might emerge over a particular text can be contained. She felt that the Press published a wide variety of books, enough to contain and express contradictions. It did not want its politics, as a Press, to be too narrowly defined. I asked her what she liked about working there: this was easy to answer. 'Oh, the variety . . . And I feel that we are dealing with the issues that are important within feminism.'[22]

And their logo? The flying iron? Well, this is not altogether serious. The ironing has usually been women's work. John Osborne has the heroine of *Look Back in Anger* (1956) ironing for most of the play. Now the iron is given a progressive meaning, 'steaming ahead'.

Figure 3   *'Steaming ahead': The Women's Press logo*

Notes

1 Simon Shepherd, *The Women's Sharp Revenge: Five Women's Pamphlets from the Renaissance* (London, Fourth Estate, 1985), p. 23.
2 I must now declare an interest. As a result of the research and discussions I had with Onlywomen Press while I was working on this chapter I was asked to edit their next volume of Lesbian Short Fiction to follow *The Pied Piper* (London, Onlywomen, 1989), which included a piece of my own fiction work. The new volume, *In and Out of Time* (London, Onlywomen, 1990) contains work that reflects the concerns and interests of this book: the continuing battle to dismantle racist structures in publishing women's writing and in the representations we construct; the vexed questions of passion and desire; our relation to the world in which we work; our communities, our families – and the things which make us laugh.
3 dusty rhodes and Sandra McNeill (eds), *Women Against Violence Against Women* (London, Onlywomen, 1985).
4 Elsbeth Linder, *Women's Review*, no. 8 (June 1986), p. 11.
5 'Books For Fun', article on Silver Moon Books in The Women's Press Bookclub catalogue, Summer 1990.
6 Claire McNab, *Lessons in Murder* (1988; London, Silver Moon Books, 1990).
7 Irene Coffey, 'Lesbian Sleuths', *Spare Rib*, no. 217 (October 1990), pp. 34–5. The discussion continues in chapter 4 below, 'On Genre Fiction'.
8 'Can Black and White Women Work Together?', *Spare Rib*, no. 168 (July 1986), p. 19.
9 For an opinionated but intriguing read on the present state of the British literary publishing industry see Nicci Gerrard, *Into the Mainstream: How Feminism has Changed Women's Writing* (London, Pandora, 1989), esp. ch. 1.
10 Lilian Mohin (ed.), *One Foot on the Mountain* (London, Onlywomen, 1979).
11 'Notes from the Desk of the Many-headed Hydra', *Gossip: A Journal of Lesbian Feminist Ethics*, no. 6 (1988), p. 5.
12 *Lesbian Ethics* is available from LE Publications, PO Box 943, Venice, California CA 90294, USA.
13 Lilian Mohin and Sheila Shulman (eds), *The Reach: Lesbian Feminist Fiction* (London, Onlywomen, 1984).
14 Onlywomen Press Collective, *Breaching the Peace: A Collection of Radical Feminist Papers* (London, Onlywomen, 1983).
15 Sarah Lucia Hoagland and Julia Penelope (eds), *For Lesbians Only: A Separatist Anthology* (London, Onlywomen, 1988).
16 Sharan-Jeet Shan, *In My Own Name* (London, Women's Press, 1985). I discuss this text at length in chapter 3, 'On Autobiography'.
17 See chapter 7, 'Writing Against Racism', for an extended discussion of Riley's work.
18 This often results in the suppression and exclusion of certain titles from the reading market. See Noreen O'Donoghue's article, 'The Fate of *Out for Ourselves: The Lives of Irish Lesbians and Gay Men*', in Gail Chester and Julienne Dickey (eds), *Feminism and Censorship: The Current Debate* (London, Prism, 1988), pp. 224–8.
19 It has published Christian McEwen (ed.), *Naming the Waves: Contemporary Lesbian Poetry* (1988), Christian McEwen and Sue O'Sullivan (eds), *Out the Other Side: Contemporary Lesbian Writing* (1988) and Helen Hodgeman's novel *Broken Words* (1989), which is a Lesbian text.
20 Mary Daly, *Gyn/Ecology* (1978; London, Women's Press, 1979); Andrea Dworkin, *Pornography: Men Possessing Women* (London, Women's Press, 1981) and *Right-Wing Women: The Politics of Domesticated Females* (London, Women's Press, 1983).

21 Alice Walker, *The Color Purple* (1982; London, Women's Press, 1983); Marge Piercy, *Woman on the Edge of Time* (1976; London, Women's Press, 1979); Alice Walker, *In Search of Our Mothers' Gardens* (1983; London, Women's Press, 1984); Ellen Kuzwayo, *Call Me Woman* (London, Women's Press, 1984); Rosalie Bertell, *No Immediate Danger* (London, Women's Press, 1985).

22 News of the current upheavals at the Women's Press reached me while I was correcting this text. I gather that most of the staff to whom I had spoken have now resigned. If the problems are not resolved rapidly and peacefully the future for feminist publishing will be bleak indeed. For an account of what happened see Rukhsana Ahmad, 'What's Happening to the Women's Presses?' *Spare Rib*, no. 223 (May 1991), pp. 10–13.

3

On Autobiography

The highest, as the lowest form of criticism is a mode of autobiography.
Oscar Wilde, *The Portrait of Dorian Gray*

My solicitor is nearly ten years younger than I am. I am most interested in the way she reads. She consumes books in the way that some other women eat chocolates: with a voracious disregard for anything else except the matter in hand. She is also a resisting reader, in that she usually has very firm preconceived ideas concerning what it is she should be reading, and objects accordingly if the text fails to fulfil her desires or conform to her demands. A text which set out to seduce her would not get very far. While she was staying with me I let her loose on my books; and made the following note of one of our conversations.

Barbara is reading Rosemary Manning's *A Time and A Time: An Autobiography*.[1] It is clearly a ghastly experience; the unrelieved torrent of misery is beginning to get to her. Thus speaketh Barbara:
'In order for it to be an autobiography it has to be either all her life or all of her. And all I'm hearing about is Manning's suicide attempts and the reasons why her emotional life is in such a mess . . . '
So really, as a clinical investigation of suicide she would find the project more acceptable. But what if Manning considered her suicide attempt and her emotional mess to be the most important aspects of her life? I think that Barbara objects to the deliberate exclusion of Manning's professional life. Manning was a successful teacher, a headmistress. Well, perhaps, I suggest, she feared that revelations of her Lesbianism would result in scandal, resignations and unemployment. Or indeed, I speculate, libel suits from her colleagues. Barbara replies that a complete defence against the accusation of defamation of character is that it's true. And then she explains that her objection to Manning's narrative is simply that she doesn't tell all. Having promised to do so, she doesn't deliver the goods. She withholds too much which Barbara regards as important. What this reveals is that Barbara reads autobiography as if she were interviewing a witness. She has a fixed notion in her head of what is crucial in a life; this doesn't coincide with Manning's version.
So this is the expectation of autobiography. The reader wants honesty. And to be told everything.
'I want all of her. She's manipulating me . . . '
'But doesn't every writer manipulate the reader?' I ask gently.

'She shouldn't be caught doing it,' replies Barbara. A lawyer's response. I laugh at Barbara. But she is clearly gripped by the book, lies in front of the fire and goes on reading.

The autobiographical pact between writer and reader is that the fictional gap between writer and narrator shall not exist. The 'I' who speaks is the 'I' who writes, even if the project in hand is the construction of that 'I': the woman whose body passed through all the experience narrated, the woman who holds the pen. 'I want all her life, or all of her.' I didn't ask Barbara to enlarge on this distinction, which is an interesting one. Autobiography demands a certain nakedness from the writer. And it is always an egotistical gesture, or an assertion of pride. The woman writes: this is what happened to me, this is how I felt, what I did, and it's worth hearing.

Until this year I have never tried to write an autobiography, daunted by the sheer impossibility of ever saying it how it was – which made Maureen Duffy's defiant title *That's How It Was* seem all the more remarkable.[2] When Audre Lorde told one of her lovers 'I am writing an unfolding of my life and loves,' her lover replied, demanding the impossible, 'Just make sure you tell the truth about me.'[3] We all live our own lives in our own books; we can only tell our own truths. And the fears which surround writing an autobiography are numerous: the fear of ever finding the self who made that past, the fear of unearthing the dead, the conflicts unresolved, the griefs unmourned, the fear of betraying the living, of being seen naked.

Autobiography is often a search for coherence and explanation. And here we come to a central impasse in feminist theory; that is, the political over against the psychoanalytical in the construction of the self. Let me put this as simply as I can. The political, or socio-historical, approach to the construction of femininity is most often endorsed by radical feminists, that is, by women like myself whose priorities remain activism, campaigns around the issues that affect our lives as women, collective projects. Radical feminists have always been materialists in that yes, they do hold that women have been socially constructed by male ideologies as passive, masochistic and subservient – but they also hold that we need not remain so. It is possible for us – with a lot of hard work, hard thinking and hard decisions – to restructure both the political shapes of our lives and our sexual desires. The psychoanalytical approach to the making of femininity has been very influential in university departments. Here there is no autonomous subject, capable of decisive action or of changing her life. We are incoherent, fractured selves, at the mercy of seething unconscious desires which we cannot know or control precisely because they are unconscious. We are controlled by cultural and linguistic structures. Femininity can only be understood in relation to masculinity. It is as important to consider the social construction of men/masculinity as that of women/femininity. Women's oppression, even woman as a category, is unstable, shifting, unknown. We are strangers to ourselves.[4]

I am certainly not the only person to smell the rats here. It is actually much easier to regard your life as something of an inexplicable mystery, as does Elizabeth Wilson in *Mirror Writing: An Autobiography*, and to view your fractured self as an intriguing, changing, splintered fragment.[5] You can disown parts of yourself: these can be objects for discussion, which you too, from an Olympian position of unearthly detachment, can hold up to analyse. If there is no such thing as a unitary self, then, in some liberating sense, you really are no longer the same woman who was married, held those opinions, was racist, threw that bomb, took those drugs, or passed by on the other side.

The construction of sexuality and sexual desire becomes crucial here. It has always been a central issue in the international women's movement. It is a critical, difficult and emotional subject. It was the subject of many of the 1970s autobiographies. It is still a battlefield. But we have shifted our ground. On the whole, under the influence of the psychoanalytical approach to the construction of the self, the debates have become abstract and polarized; the arguments are no longer thrashed out within real lives, but set against each other as theoretical positions. The raw confusion of the 1970s autobiographies, their embarrassing muddles, passionate rage and articulate pain still read as naked, revolutionary documents of the period. That kind of courage, to acknowledge that feminism does mean that we must actually try to think and live in different ways and to reveal that struggle on paper, seems rare among us now. I do not regard this as a defeat; but it is a retreat. We are not giving these difficulties the same kind of attention any more. The struggle concerning sex and sexuality has moved out of the kitchen and the bedroom. It has become a highly abstract psychic debate, a Star Wars conflict between the Imaginary and the Symbolic, the Phallus and the Chora. When the argument is about masculinity and femininity as psychic constructs, and not about men and women, I think that we have in fact stopped arguing. We make our peace with men, for the sake of the children, or a home, a salary, a meal ticket: and that peace will be made on their terms, not ours. The debate about sex and sexuality is central to feminism. The issues are not resolved. And the flight into abstraction is always evasion if it does not bring us back to the raw edge of politics: the bedroom, the kitchen, the workplace and the streets. There are, of course, militant exceptions to this trend, usually to be found in the *Revolutionary and Radical Feminist Newsletter* which reports robust forms of direct action as well as developing a feminist theory which is rooted in women's resistance to men's oppression.[6] The sexual politics of the 1970s did not simply pass away with the decade.

But no amount of political activism can obliterate the power of the unconscious if it does indeed have a universal hold over all women. In a wonderfully convincing argument published in *Feminist Review*, Rosalind Minsky argues that not only is 'the human subject . . . fundamentally split into the conscious and unconscious', but that our unconscious is formed in early childhood, not a period of our lives over which we have much control, and is structured 'by what goes on emotionally within . . . [the] family, whether it be nuclear, single-parent or extended'.[7] We do not choose our biological or substitute families either. Minsky follows Melanie Klein in arguing that the unconscious is formed during the pre-Oedipal baby's developing relationship with its mother or mother-substitute, and not during the Oedipal crisis. But we all have an unconscious, and it is always traumatic, for everyone, in more or less the same way. Minsky then goes on to ask a very pertinent question. 'Why precisely is this such a problem for some people, except in terms of the intellectual difficulty of integrating a historical 'consciousness' central to social theory and an ahistorical 'unconscious' central to psychoanalytic theory?' (p. 9). Implied in Minsky's question is the assumption that consciousness and unconscious are difficult to integrate and that in some sense we all choose which method we want to use. My problem is not that of integrating the two but of separating them in the first place. Historical forces and political pressures are not always easily recognized, not always visible or even easily discussed. Nor is it necessarily true that unconscious drives can only ever be revealed by professional expertise, expensive individual psychoanalysis or lengthy therapy sessions. And even as we are inscribed in history, surely so too is the unconscious, unless it really does exist, like the Deist view of God, outside history, time and space.

Let me take a concrete example of what I mean by the impossibility of separating social consciousness and psychoanalytical unconscious. I once had a long and intimate discussion with a married woman who found her husband's sexual demands horrible and unpleasant. 'But if I don't give in,' she said, 'he takes it out on the children.' 'Why don't you leave him?' I suggested, when she had assured me that he was not persuadable, either by reason or by her mother's threats. 'Who would I be then?' she asked me desperately. She didn't ask me 'What should I do?' 'How would I live?' nor 'Who would pay the bills?' She asked me 'Who would I be?' Her sense of identity – economic, political, social, economic, affective, psychic – was entirely bound up with being that man's wife. Of course I told her that she was a person in her own right, who could make her own decisions. But in some sense she wasn't. And that is the point from which we had to begin. In the end, you'll be delighted to know, she left him.

The unconscious is rather like God. If it exists it will have an effect upon us, whether we like it or not; but it is perfectly possible to live, love, write, think, speak and take political action as if it did not exist. We can choose on what terms we want to understand ourselves. We can interrogate our rational and irrational desires. We may be strangers to ourselves, but we need not be our own victims. It is both an existential gesture and an affirmation of political responsibility to undertake the making of ourselves. For, of course, our self is constructed. It makes no sense at all to dream about discovering who we *really* are, as if there were a perfect doll hidden inside us underneath layers of seaweed. Our struggle is to achieve an identity – and most of us pass through a series of multiple identities, some chosen, others imposed upon us. Our bodies are the territory we occupy as well as the means we have of engaging with the world. I find my scars, the actual physical marks on my body, very reassuring. These are the marks of history on every woman's body. And to say that I am now quite different from the person I once was is not at all the same thing as saying that I am not the same person. Taking political responsibility for who you are does mean judging both the woman you were and the woman you have become. No part of the fractured self is let off the hook. If we acknowledge every part of the fractured self we will emerge as monsters; but at least we will be honest monsters.

For a woman to write her life as a perceiving subject, to be both the one who acts and the one who records, when we have existed for centuries simply as his mother, sister, mistress, daughter, servant, employee, wife, is to make a decisive political gesture. When men write their stories of lust, guilt, triumph and disaster the world admires them for their honesty, candour and courage. Think of St Paul, St Augustine, Rousseau. They become classics and we forgive them. Besides, their lives stand side by side with their achievements – or what are claimed to be their achievements: the founding of Christianity, the City of God, the transformation of European sensibility, the French Revolution. For women, the very fact that we lived, and more particularly that we loved, is sometimes our single achievement. Women's autobiographies are therefore often the stories of inner lives; not what we did, but who we loved and how we felt. And it is difficult to write about feelings which frequently render us ridiculous rather than achievements which lend us dignity.

The practice of autobiography is usually a web of special pleading, self-justification, myth-making, sentimentality and downright lies. The motives for writing an autobiography are often at the root of how a life is reconstructed and a past remembered. They will explain the priority of significance given to events, landscapes or people. Both Audre Lorde and Ann Oakley had cancer.[8] Lorde lost her right breast, Oakley lost part of her tongue. Both gave up parts of their bodies which were important in their erotic lives to an invasive, greedy, malignant disease. Both recognize their own mortality; and so they add up their lives, judge their peers, their world, themselves. Lorde turns to the women, Oakley turns to the men. Both women are fighters, survivors, determined to be heard. And their determination to impose their own meanings on their lives grows from the knowledge that those lives are fragile; that they already carry their deaths in their bodies.

The feminist autobiographies of the 1970s are tales of conversion. The deep darkness of muddled sexuality, the horrors of marriage, children and guilt, self-hatred and housework, precede the dawn of political consciousness, the first women's group, the discovery of other women. An autobiography is of course a self-portrait; the feminist women of the 1970s present portraits not only of themselves, but of their lives and times. They demonstrate the ways in which their lives were shaped by politics, and by a political movement of women. These books are chronicles of history.

I sometimes think that Kate Millett and Germaine Greer invented the women's liberation movement between them. Their books, *Sexual Politics* and *The Female Eunuch*, were both published in Britain in 1970. These were the maps of institutional misogyny, and the first moves in the game on paper. Millett became a superstar, she says, and then fell to bits. Her autobiography, *Flying*, spans the period of one year between two of her public performances as figurehead for the women's movement: the meeting at which she is forced to admit her Lesbianism and the non-violence panel where she pleads for her pacifist politics.[9] The subject of Millett's confessional autobiography is the conflict between heterosexuality and Lesbianism.

Behind every book lies another book. The books behind *Flying* are Violette Leduc's *La Bâtarde*, an unspecified book by Emma Goldman, possibly her autobiography, *Living My Life*, and Doris Lessing's *The Golden Notebook*.[10] Leduc's passionate history of her making as the literary Lesbian and Goldmann's uncompromising political convictions almost stifle Millett. 'These two women are art and politics. Reading them I am judged. Better not to try anything.'[11] This mental separation of art and politics is a dangerous one, as *Flying* proceeds to demonstrate. Millett actually meets Lessing in the course of writing her own book, and they discuss *The Golden Notebook*. Lessing keeps her life under the protective wraps of fiction and thus guards herself from personal criticism. Millett is braver; she takes the risk and the rap. Her own autobiography grows out of her documentary film, *Three Women*. The film, and the making of the film, are inscribed in the book. Millett turns the camera on herself; she is the fourth woman. Every moment of her life, present, memory, events, lovers, is recorded. She leaves out nothing but the verbs. This has a curious effect on the politics of the book. Everything is detailed in a desperate, luminous, eternal present. Verbs carry time, perspective, process, history. Leave them out and the experience stands raw, immediate and awful before us. But every experience is then of equal weight. There is nothing to tell us what is trivial, insignificant, and what actually changed the course of this woman's life. The writing of *Flying* is one of the pervasive themes of the book; we are being given the process of writing and the process of experience. This means that Millett never has to judge her own actions seriously. She is too busy actually doing it. She is not a fool; she anticipates the serious objections that can be made against her method and raises them herself. But she does not do this honestly. The objecting critic is Vita, one of Millett's more unpleasant lovers, who pounds about the book, demanding love and attention. Vita argues that *Flying* will end up as 'pulp Sappho' (p. 182) if it is solely erotic gossip with no analysis. Vita wants to put back the politics which fell out with the verbs. Millett uncharitably records Vita's criticism as reported speech. Vita is not allowed to speak for herself. ' . . . She unwraps her bright new ideology, it should all be political, it should wave a flag. I try to argue that propaganda is a bore, has no magic' (p. 181). Now politics cannot be dismissed as propaganda or flag-waving in favour of the magic of art. To reveal one's own raw contradictions is not weakness or stupidity, for we all live through them, but what Millett offers is a self-indulgent wallow in a sexual muddle of her own making. Millett has managed to suppress Vita's objections, for no reader in her right mind would want to think like Vita; and the fact that *Flying* was indeed a best-seller proves that there is a very healthy market for 'pulp Sappho'.

Millett proposes for herself a radical absolution: the process of telling all, leaving nothing unspoken, unadmitted, undescribed. ' . . . If I finish my book I will have no secrets to be afraid for, corrupted over, tied to, as I have been all my life, hiding . . . ' (p. 210). But there is nothing intrinsically radical about telling all. Events, erotic encounters, insoluble contradictions, fall on to the page, one after the other, unexpurgated, but also unanalysed. The politics of experience becomes meaningless monologue, simply because she offers us her experience, all of it, without the politics. Politics means self-criticism; and seeing oneself as a creature shaped by social forces. Feminist politics are about learning, and changing ourselves, by confronting other people; and, crucially, about realizing that what you do, and who you do it with, even or especially in bed, is not unrelated to the outside world. Significantly, *Flying* contains very few conversations or real dialogues. This is Millett's book, her story, her roaring. Occasionally she realizes that no one else has managed to get a word in: 'I am overcome with shame to see how little I have known her, almost a stranger to me . . . ' (p. 549). Millett has dozens of friends and lovers, but she wants to sleep with them, not listen to them.

Intriguingly, her husband, when he is allowed to speak for himself, talks remorseless sense. Men are not usually sensible about sex and sexuality. Fumio is. And Millet gives him his own voice, even his own original, unstable English. 'But you must be careful the sex. It is still dangerous. Everyone uses it for the weapon. I am off from that. I am getting myself. Living here alone. I am my work' (p. 489). Millett too is 'getting herself', but she can only do it by winning the coveted approval of others, preferably in bed. 'The joy of knowing I will get what I want, that it will not be withheld from me. As if acceptance in the flesh were all acceptance. And who can prove that it is not?' (p. 550). Indeed, I cannot prove that it is not; but it is frankly unwise to conduct our lives as if sexuality and power were not at all connected. As Fumio says: sex is a weapon.

Millett's returning agony is bound up with her own sexual confusion and her inability to detach herself from the pervasive bourgeois clichés about Lesbianism and marriage. She remembers her first affair with her teacher, JayCee, as 'depravity' (p. 116), imagining 'our bodies, clothes, walk . . . stamped with the certainty of our guilt, shouting our criminality' (p. 117). When she observes the brother and sister-in-law of one of her lovers she remarks: 'Reg and Julia, the real people, married with children, a status and authority we seem to lack . . . ' (p. 498). It is only because married people and the bourgeois family are given this authority within a sexist culture that Lesbians become nebulous unpersons. Heterosexuality assumes its normative centrality with quiet violence. But Millett never says that. Instead, she perpetually reminds us that she is a wife. 'A wife for Godsake, as a wife I'm a disgrace' (p. 513). Lesbian, but married nevertheless. Millett cannot afford to give a radical critique of marriage because she has a foot in both camps. And she is always careful to cover her back.

> Watching the two of them, one on each hand, man and woman in their world, knowing that in an hour I enter a cavern of Lesbians in a loft on an obscure downtown street. Watching them with loving eyes and feeling all the tension of two worlds, two cultures sealed away from each other, two entire societies separated so often it seems permanently, the crevasses between me tearing apart like a mulatto who passes. When do things come together? (p. 221)

What this passage presents is a false version of the crevasses. All is not well between 'man and woman in their world', otherwise none of us would be feminists. The cavern of Lesbians, which sounds savage and debauched, is presented according to heterosexist cliché, as a kind of underworld.

Millett knows that it is dangerous to live as a Lesbian. Early on in the book she describes a frightened gathering of Radicalesbians. One of them has been murdered by the male lover she has left. Sexual rejection is apparently sufficient provocation for murder. Millett takes this on board and then tries it out on her husband Fumio. She tells him – in bed – that she has slept with a woman, deliberately courting the danger. Fumio laughs at her and goes back to sleep. He takes neither Millett nor her trumpeted bisexuality seriously. And he is right not to do so. She is not serious. Millett and her masochism are simply screaming for attention. She says, 'I was very disappointed, and expected him to murder me or march out of the house forever' (p. 21). Millett was forced to admit, in public, that she was Lesbian: 'The line goes, inflexible as a fascist edict, that bisexuality is a cop-out' (p. 16).[12] Yet within ten pages Millett has made it quite clear that Radicalesbians, the source of the 'fascist edict', are justly afraid, even for their lives. The term 'fascist', which attributes the very worst of political methods to a small group of brave women, is therefore an irresponsible slander. Millett's treacherous politics, or lack of them, emerge in her language. She describes Zooey, one of her friends, who is brutally raped by one of Millett's lovers: ' . . . she wouldn't so he forced her, huge body of a football player pinning her to the bed, bruising, beating her . . . ' (p. 74). Three pages later she describes a row with one of her feminist friends. She recoils, 'raped by her hatred' (p. 77). Now, rape is not about hard words between friends, especially when they are both women. Rape is about violence which men commit against women. It is about penises, vaginas, vulnerability and force. And it is to abuse both women and language to pretend otherwise.

Books that are published by the commercial press cannot be for women's eyes only. The Lesbian sex scenes in *Flying*, erotic, potent and explicit as they are, appear within a context that renders them politically uneasy; insecure as affirmations of women's sexuality and women's power. On two occasions in the narrative Millett comes home to her husband bringing a woman lover. She then abandons the lover to sleep with her husband. Vita throws a fit of accusations. Claire, being a proud and dignified character, leaves the house, 'declares her independence, will sleep in her sleeping bag under the stars' (p. 458). On both occasions Millett gives us a thrust by thrust account of exquisitely tender matrimonial love. In her own bed it is Fumio who counts. For all her breast-beating flood of true confessions, Millett never asks herself an awkward set of questions. To describe oneself as bisexual may indeed be an accurate description of one's own sexual practice, but bisexuality is not a political sexual category. To claim it as such is to pretend that there is an easy equivalent between loving men and loving women; and it is to ignore the financial privilege and social approval which heterosexuals enjoy.

There is a myth, to which I do not subscribe, that underneath we are all really either Lesbian or straight. This is used against women who do not conform to the pathological Lesbian stereotypes of heterosexist cliché and yet still refuse to pass out of their 'Lesbian phase'. Mariana Valverde, in an acute chapter on bisexuality, points out: 'Would it not be better to work from the hypothesis that sexual orientation is not a given, . . . but is rather subject to profound changes – and is in fact constantly created and recreated – as our sexual and social experiences unfold?'[13] Those sexual and social experiences, moreover, will be governed by a society which punishes any lapse from the supposedly natural happy heterosexual norm. Valverde insists: 'Gay people do have a right to demand that bisexuals do not fall into the easy trap of being publicly straight and privately gay' (p. 117). No one could accuse Millett of doing that; if anything, she operates the other way around. But what she does do is use the power imbalance inherent in heterosexual and Lesbian experience against Lesbian women.

The accusing Lesbian ghost in Millett's machine is Jill Johnston, who makes two significant appearances. On page 48 she steps out of the shadows in her Levis and shades. She inhabits 'the other world'. This is in itself an insidious and dangerous notion: to construct a separation between Lesbians and all other women. Johnston is 'sinister, hazardous' (p. 47), even 'Mephistophelian' (p. 49) her 'butch disdain . . . more bullying than any male performance I can remember' (p. 50). Millett is transfixed by guilt at her own uncertainties and insecurities. She projects all her fear and resentment on to the uncompromising figure of Jill Johnston. 'I know as well as she does that if women are vulnerable to the dyke-baiting we are vulnerable to everything, a paper movement, helpless even before words' (p. 51). Quite so. But Millett has, only one page previously, irresponsibly transformed Johnston into a castrating dyke from the underworld. Later on in the book Johnston turns up in England. Just for the hell of it they go to a Soho strip show together. 'The stomach watches, weak with anger. Thought I heard Jill sob in her seat' (p. 391). Lesbians deny the right of men to consume the female body and define the erotic. And here Millett is honest, firm and clear. Her own sexual apotheosis with her scholar lover is explicit, lyrical and politically to the point. 'Complicity so close we are each others' cunts . . . our two bodies one I can no longer separate them . . . While I give I am given. The same storm, the same upheaval. One never has this with a man, his experience hidden as mine is. But two women have the same nerves' (p. 540).

Perhaps no one can be completely likeable and still be the subject of their own autobiography. First-person narrative is always raw and vulnerable. Millett is particularly open about her own mixed motives, her manipulative self-seeking and suppressed angers. But she renders the private public rather than the personal political. The difficulty resides in her egotism. She is writing *Flying* in order to salvage her Real Self, whoever she may be, from the wreckage of Kate Millett superstar, author of *Sexual Politics*. But in fact she loves the role of tortured superstar, she adores the limelight and wants to believe that she is essential to the movement in that capacity. This desire is confirmed when she is summoned uptown to save the abortion conference, which has collapsed in the fangs of a feminist disagreement. Millett arrives, like Superwoman out of a comic. 'Why didn't you get here sooner, where the hell have you been? A woman yells as I run in the door' (p. 448). Millett's conviction that the movement will be doomed if she fails or gives up is simply a bizarre, misplaced individualism.

Feminism, if we are to survive at all as a political movement, must be a collective political endeavour. Millett writes out of the conviction that she is in herself significant, and so are the people she knows. *Flying* is an exercise in name-dropping. John Lennon and Yoko Ono have walk-on parts: Yoko Ono is presented as an old friend from Japan. The other media stars of the US women's liberation movement are 'friends, peers, the best minds of my generation . . . Flo Kennedy, Anselma Dell'Olio, Gloria Steinem, Myrna Lamb, Robin Morgan, Martha Shelley . . . ' (p. 562).[14] Millett's ostensible reason for writing the book – to stop herself going crazy, to give herself back to herself – led me to expect a little self-searching analysis; but in fact she is writing within an already well-established American genre, the Confessions of a Superstar. And she succumbs to the conventions; the powerful, sexy, articulate image, but underneath it the real woman, masochistic, uncertain, confused, vulnerable, anxious to have her mother's good opinion. True Confessions are always an attempt to win back a fickle public, and they rely upon that contradiction. 'Good Heavens,' we are supposed to cry, 'is she really so helpless, muddled? We must forgive her, for she always seemed so powerful, sexy, articulate . . . ' The voice crying in the wilderness is underhand; her humility is a mask. Millett can only tell all and have it marketed in paperback as a best-seller because *Sexual Politics* made her own life a marketable product, instantly of interest to feminists, Lesbians, voyeurs and men who have fantasies about screwing dykes.

The autobiography of a feminist need not necessarily be written as a feminist autobiography. Millett's clouds of self-accusation should alert us to the fact that *Flying* is a saint's life, recording the sins. 'I hate confessionals. Bless me father for I have sinned. A whining form' (p. 24). But she's done it anyway, Dear Reader; six hundred pages stretch before you.[15]

Flying is the book behind Anja Meulenbelt's *The Shame is Over*; the inspirational heroines of Meulenbelt's political life story are Kate Millett and Jill Johnston: 'Jill Johnston who travelled to Spain, crying, to fetch her love back again. Hopeless, she could not compete with marriage to a man. And Kate Millett who mourns throughout a whole book for Celia.'[16] That book is, of course, *Flying*; there is a critique of *Flying* and other autobiographical feminist writing, including Verena Stefan's *Shedding*, early on in the book.[17] Meulenbelt claims: 'I have needed the other women who write without shame in order to become what I am' (p. 14). Their revelatory narratives set the terms for her own. White feminist writers, even across continents, are extraordinarily inter-dependent. I think that this is also true of Blackwomen writers. The history of the movement, and the making of contemporary feminism, is actually recorded on paper with peculiar intimacy. *The Shame is Over* is a torrid sprawl of sexual encounters. For Meulenbelt her life is her sex life. This is fair enough; Meulenbelt came of age during the sexual revolution. But we crawl from bed to bed, only gradually realizing that the 1960s model of sexual liberation was another cage for women, in which it was bad manners to refuse to be fucked. She describes it as ' . . . the sexual revolution that is indeed sexual, but not revolutionary' (p. 130).[18] Like Millett's epic, Meulenbelt's saga is written in a breathless present tense; and like Millett, she makes the writing of the book a critical part of its subject. But she is much more astute about her motives for writing, and much more ruthless about the politics of feminism. As she says, 'Sisterhood is powerful: it can kill you. And yet we can only go on, we can't go back anymore. Even the deserters who can't live up to their ideals, go on'

(p. 14). Initially, she staggers from one political movement to another; counter-culture theatre, the Black Panthers, the hard left, taking up everyone's cause except her own. There is a wailing litany for the lovers who treated her badly, but were at least a good screw.

O Shaun
Michael

These two selfish lizards stroll in and out of the book and are apocalyptically mourned. Meulenbelt is shatteringly frank about the Great Lie, otherwise known as romantic love. 'When he is gone, I stop living' (p. 14). Her affairs with men are like a drug; she is hooked, but the need is killing her. And the pattern which develops in her life is the triangle, with the man playing two women off against each other. Meulenbelt describes her experiences in harrowing detail; and then she does something which Millett never does: she struggles with the political analysis of that experience. And she does not do it alone: she turns to other women. Other women are, admittedly, the last port of call. 'It is no accident, I think later, that I was sensitive to the women's movement only when I had nothing more to lose' (p. 137). Indeed, the refrain from Janis Joplin's lyric echoes through the book: 'Freedom's just another word for nothin' left to lose.' But what is demonstrated in the book is political process.

Meulenbelt's own increasing political understanding gives her the power to take control over her own life. She begins to think and live differently. She is attacked in the street, she fights back; the man flings bricks at her. Immediately, she describes the experience with other women, and together they produce 'bits of theory that we are slowly developing . . . The only way to avoid it [sexual violence and assault] is to put yourself at the service of *one* man who protects you against all other men' (pp. 190–1). Her triangular affair with a married couple – she is sleeping with both of them – breaks down. The women, together, discuss her experience, develop the analysis. 'Surely it doesn't surprise you that Anna didn't choose you, say my women friends. Surely it wasn't a choice between Ton and you, it was a choice between two completely different ways of life' (p. 248). The autobiography thus becomes confessional testimony and political commentary. Meulenbelt never sees herself as psychically fragmented. She constructs herself as a woman in process, in movement, a growing political being; and so she takes responsibility for who she was and who she is. She never disowns or despises her past, knowing that to do so is to reject other women. 'I am still that woman, wounded, bitter, suspicious, at the same time as the strong, creative, independent woman I am' (p. 4).

Meulenbelt has plenty to say on tendentious issues. Her life was shaped by a turbulent period in left politics; her analysis is influenced by years of the male-dominated Marxist left and the equally male-dominated Black revolutionary movements, for both of which she filled a lot of envelopes and a lot of beds. Her conclusion is uncompromising. 'If a black man is beaten up in the street, that is politics. If a woman is battered in her home that is a private problem, a disturbed relationship' (p. 49). Meulenbelt becomes famous in the course of the book. By page 255 she can fill the hall with 'people who have come to see what the vampire really looks like' (p. 255). But her fame is irrelevant to the project of the book, whose themes are those of radical feminism – sexuality, Lesbianism, sex–class politics, separatism – and whose pattern follows the classical methods of radical feminism: theory and action growing out of a critical analysis of personal experience.

Autobiography as testimony is usually justified by the claim either that it is exceptional, or that it is typical. A unique woman, or everywoman, tells her story, writes her life. The idea that her life might be in some sense typical of a woman who discovers feminism and other women certainly never enters Kate Millett's head. She is unique, extraordinary, even (or perhaps particularly) to herself. But both Anja Meulenbelt and Verena Stefan in *Shedding* narrate their stories and awakening as exemplary lives; or at least, as the exemplary lives of white western women under capitalism. Here is Meulenbelt (her italics): 'Whoever thinks that this is all, *one* woman who wrestled with her shame, *one* unique herstory separate from all the others, has not understood' (p. 275). The 'we' in Stefan's *Shedding* appears in the poetry, like a Greek chorus. And it is 'we', the women.

> we hatch the world anew
> we stir up time
> we shed our shadow skin
> fire breaks out. (p. 85)

Millett and Meulenbelt both write unproblematic naturalistic narratives, and the Real Self who eventually emerges from the sheets is presented as a straightforward character, like someone in a novel whom they know well. But fiction is a game of masks. The gap between the writer and narrator, or the narrative perspective, is always shifting and insecure. Stefan disrupts the autobiographical pact, the promise that writer and narrator are speaking with one voice. Her text uses the tactics of fiction, the rhetoric of political polemic, the lyric of intimate confession. Her life and experience are not so much the substance of confession as the raw material to be analysed. On one occasion she writes two versions of an unpleasant experience with her male lover, after which she ended up with a bladder infection. One version is written in the language of loving cliché, in which the compliant woman consents and enjoys – 'On the way we decide we'd like to go to bed with each other . . . ' – the other version makes it clear that she is bullied into bed: 'On the way he keeps looking over at my bare knees, finally reaches over, touches them and asks, would I like to come home with him?' (p. 20). She puts the two accounts side by side. Then she draws her own political conclusion: 'Love can be a means of camouflaging brutality for a while' (p. 21).

Shedding is a catalogue of questions and doubts, another story of process; but one which leads into solitude rather than collective struggle. Bodiliness, and the repossession of bodily experience, is a central theme. 'Although occasionally I got the feeling that I could occupy my whole body, I was nonetheless evicted from it piece by piece' (p. 6). The final section, 'Gourd Woman', which is written in the third person, describes the woman who has at last gained possession of her body, and therefore of herself: 'I am my own woman' (p. 118). This, at last, is the woman who controls her own biological, and therefore psychological, reality. Freedom, according to Stefan, begins in the solitary body of the solitary woman. And, significantly, she is alone; and talking, triumphantly, only to herself. The theme of bodiliness should, I think, be considered more broadly than Stefan suggests. Certainly, as individual women, the right to control our own bodies is crucial; but we have, too, as women, a collective political body; and that body is exploited, sold, consumed, displayed everywhere in public – in art galleries, on billboards, in books and films. The freedom of the body is for women a public as well as a private affair, and a collective as well as an individual issue.

The book behind Stefan's book is Shulamith Firestone's *The Dialectic of Sex* (1970) which her current male lover refuses to read. ' "Why can't you just tell me what's in it that is so important? " he asked; "I don't understand how you can just plunk down a couple of books about all your problems and expect me to read them!" ' (p. 58). Stefan's text is about transforming what men see as women's problems into women's politics. The redefinition of sexuality begins with an analysis of the ways in which women cease to be human when they service men.

> One of them kissed passionately, madly, so that I felt teeth, nothing
>   but teeth –
> and I kissed passionately, madly.
> Another kissed gently and thought anything else adolescent and
> immature and I kissed gently, mature. (p. 35)

Stefan carefully examines the quality of passion between women. She does not raise the banner of Lesbian sex; instead she asks more questions. Eroticism becomes a map without markers. 'The expanse of unexplored territory . . . a new language of skin words' (pp. 74, 86). This is remarkably similar to the metaphor of the 'country that has no language/no laws' in Adrienne Rich's lyric sequence, 'Twenty-One Love Poems'. Rich too asks questions rather than haranguing the reader with certainties:

> whatever we do together is pure invention
> the maps they gave us were out of date
> by years . . . we're driving through the desert
> wondering if the water will hold out[19]

and she pursues the geographical metaphor in another poem in the same volume, 'Cartographies of Silence'. Both Rich and Stefan are aware that their subject is unwritten; that there are no rules.

Stefan's text, like that of Millett and Meulenbelt, locates the roots of the women's liberation movement in the sexual and political revolutions of the 1960s. She slouches through the same left-wing beds and has a Black male lover who gives her Cleaver and Malcolm X to read, then uses her body for, so he says, 'warmth and lubrication' (p. 29). Stefan's comments on the complex intersection of racism and sexism are savage, and occasionally offensive. Her Black male lover treats her as badly as the white men do. That Black men can be sexist comes as no surprise, especially not to Blackwomen, but her Black lover's behaviour does, I think, have a different political meaning, which Stefan does not examine. She says, 'A victim of oppression does not necessarily treat other victims of oppression more humanely' (p. 28). This is certainly true; but we cannot appropriate each other's pain as Stefan does when she writes, 'Women are every nation's niggers. This was my battle cry as I set out with Simone de Beauvoir's *Second Sex* and Valerie Solanas' *Manifesto* under my arm' (p. 32). She also argues that, for women, 'their sex is the colour of their skin' (p. 77). Both these comments deny the reality of racism for Blackwomen. Racism and sexism share a similar insane ideological structure of prejudice; but white women simply do not suffer racism because they are white. Stefan was writing in the mid-1970s before there was a visible and vocal autonomous movement of Blackwomen who put their challenge to the white feminist movement, pointing out that they shared neither white feminist priorities nor white feminist terms of reference. But Stefan's attitudes have been common currency among white women for many years. Audre Lorde records her unease at the denial of her Blackness by her white woman lover: 'Even Muriel seemed to believe that as lesbians, we were all outsiders and all equal in our outsiderhood. "We're all niggers," she used to say, and I hated to hear her say it. It was wishful thinking based on little fact; the ways in which it was true languished in the shadow of those many ways in which it would always be false.'[20] Lorde uses her experience of racism, heterosexism and homophobia each to inform the others; as a Black Lesbian she is marginal to her own Black community, and is doubly ostracized by a white society that is both racist and sexist. But Lorde uses that marginal cultural status to analyse with clarity and force the structures which have placed her there. In her acknowledgements to *Zami* Lorde thanks 'Barbara Smith for her courage in asking the right question and her faith that it could be answered'. What happened was this:

> *Zami*? Well, you know how I started to write that book . . . the first time I met Barbara [Smith] it was . . . in an NBA [National Book Association] meeting. I had gone to this, and this beautiful Black Woman stood up and said 'I'm a Black Lesbian Feminist Literary Critic, wondering whether I can live to tell the story' and I'm sitting in the audience thinking, isn't that sweet; what does she mean – 'Whether-she-can-live-to-tell-the-story – *I lived it*! . . . And I said to Barbara, 'Hey, I'm gonna tell those stories.'[21]

Lorde's reply is in answer to a quite specific demand from the community of Blackwomen. At the end of her essay *Towards a Black Feminist Criticism*, Barbara Smith calls for a book that would be both rooted in and reflect her experience. 'I finally want to express how much easier both my waking and my sleeping hours would be if there were one book in existence that would tell me something specific about my life. One book based in Black feminist and Black lesbian experience, fiction or non-fiction . . . when such a book exists then each of us will not only know better how to live, but how to dream.'[22] She demands The Book behind which there is no other book. So Audre Lorde is writing, quite explicitly, for Blackwomen and Blacklesbians. She understands that all oppressed people need both myth and history to give us continuity and authority; a pride in our present selves. And so she gives her community a new myth – 'Zami: A Carriacou name for women who work together as friends and lovers'[23] – and therefore, a new way to define themselves; a name that is rooted in the Black culture of West Indian Americans, not the culture of the whites.

Lorde confidently redefines the Freudian triangle of mother, father, child in her unfolding of the construction of her identity. It is the women who have shaped her – 'Every woman I have ever loved has left her print upon me' (p. 255) – and it is the women of her family who pass on her inheritance: 'I have felt the age-old triangle of mother father and child with the "I" at its eternal core, elongate and flatten out into the elegantly strong triad of grandmother, mother, daughter . . . (p. 7). This is the accepted pattern of raising children in many West Indian families; often the closest bonds that the children will forge will be with the grandmother or older women of the house. Oddly enough, I have watched this cultural pattern being reproduced within my own family. We are white West Indians, but the pattern prevails. My mother now lives very near her daughter-in-law and takes care of her two granddaughters. She assumed that it was important and natural that she should do this. In Jamaica very few women would ever expect to bring up their children on their own.

Lorde's mother dominates her childhood, and the process of definition, what it means to be a woman, what it means to be Black, begins with her mother's experiences. Being Black is not only a political category, a proudly chosen political definition; it is also how you are perceived by white racists. Linda Lorde was pale enough to pass for 'Spanish'; but the owner of the teashop where she works sees her husband. 'When the owner saw him, he realized my mother was Black and fired her on the spot' (p. 9). To be Black does not necessarily simply describe the colour of your skin; it is also bound up with the community you inhabit. Linda Lorde cannot protect her children from racism, and her inability to change that condition of being means that she must use the only weapon she has. She simply insists that it does not happen. 'It was so often her approach to the world to change reality. If you can't change reality, change your perception of it' (p. 18). For Audre Lorde, Black is a process of becoming: 'I grew Black . . . ' (p. 58), and a process of gradual awareness. Each experience of racism gave her a new meaning of what it is to become Black. In the Stamford ribbon factory 'It was standard procedure in most of the "software" factories to hire Black workers for three weeks, then fire them before they could join the union, and hire new workers' (p. 123). Racism affects every area of her life. And Lorde comes to realize that being clever and aspiring to a white education means that she has been denied her own Black history. She has never heard of Crispus Attucks. 'I had been taught by some of the most highly considered historians in the country. Yet I never once heard the name mentioned of the first man to fall in the american revolution, nor even been told that he was a Negro. What did that mean about the history I had learned?' (p. 138).

Lorde was a gay woman in the period before Stonewall; a Lesbian long before Lesbian feminism was a political movement.[24] This makes her analysis of her own sexuality a piece of history. Her description of her first sexual encounter with a woman is both erotic and comic; but it is, she insists, like a homecoming, 'as if I . . . was remembering her body rather than learning it deeply for the first time' (p. 139). Lesbianism, intriguingly, is not always regarded as a threat, because within the Black community she inhabits it is inconceivable that a woman could lead a whole life with other women. Her first lover's mother, Cora, is not alarmed; she simply refuses to take the relationship seriously, and the structure of power between women and men is such that Cora's attitude makes perfect sense. 'Friends are nice, but marriage is marriage' (p. 142). I have encountered this view many times. One very young friend of mine came out as a Lesbian. I went to her eighteenth birthday party, which was held at her parents' house, with her mother doing the cooking. As we watched dozens of Lesbians dancing on the lawn, her mother said to me, 'Well, we think it's a very good idea at her stage. Her girlfriends can't make her pregnant and won't beat her up, but of course we hope that . . . ' Both Cora and my friend's mother made an absolute separation between erotic sexuality and the serious business of marrying for money, status, power, security and children. And they both regarded Lesbianism as an adolescent phenomenon.

Lorde's adventure in Mexico as a young woman is crucial to both her political and her sexual education. Mexico is therefore a psychic space as well as another country. Here, to be Black is also to be beautiful: 'It was in Mexico that I stopped feeling invisible' (p. 173). And it is here that she becomes the lover of a much older woman who had had breast cancer and had survived a radical mastectomy and radiotherapy. It is Eudora, the Amazon, who is one of Lorde's teachers of love. Eudora plays a prophetic role in Lorde's life. Years later she records her own experience of cancer and mastectomy:

> Eudora Garrett was not the first woman with whom I had shared body warmth and wildness, but she was the first woman who totally engaged me in our loving. I remember the hesitation and tenderness I felt as I touched the deeply scarred hollow under her right shoulder and across her chest, the night she finally shared the last pain of her mastectomy with me in the clear heavy heat of our Mexican spring. I was 19 and she was 47. Now I am 44 and she is dead.
>
> Eudora came to me in my sleep that night before surgery in that tiny cold hospital room so different from her bright hot dishevelled bedroom in Cuernavaca, with her lanky snapdragon self and her gap-toothed lopsided smile, and we held hands for a while.[25]

Lorde mythologizes her women lovers; Eudora is the Amazon, Afrekete, the African Goddess. Her text attempts to create a new language of the body which re-defines the conventional conjunction of sexuality and food. She and her Black lover, Afrekete, become all the exotic, sensuous West Indian fruits and are part of Lorde's historical memories: cocoyams, cassava, plantains, ripe red finger bananas, coconut oil, avocado pear. But they also literally cover themselves in fruit, while love-making. As Lorde points out in her most matter-of-fact tones, 'Then we would have to get up to gather the pits and fruit skins and bag them to put out later for the garbage men, because if we left them near the bed for any length of time, they would call out the hordes of cockroaches . . . '[26] This is a great strength in Lorde's writing: the levels of the metaphoric and the actual are constantly fused. Afrekete, the erotic Black Goddess, is also Kitty from Atlanta, Georgia who has a seven-year-old daughter and smokes Lucky Strike. And this means that she always honours the particular woman, even when she re-creates her as a mythic figure of power and authority.

Lorde's need for other Blackwomen and her demonstration of the ways in which they have played an essential part in her survival are eloquently expressed. She is not at all sentimental about the Gay world in the McCarthy years, ' . . . the lesbians, virile as men, hating women *and* their own womanhood with a vengeance . . . ' (p. 225, Lorde's italics). But the fact that survival is such a struggle – 'It was hard enough to be Black, to be Black, female, and gay . . . ' (p. 224); and Lorde records many of the women who did not survive – gives her narrative an unusual wisdom and generosity of spirit. Lorde understands why so many women took to smack or committed suicide. Here she explains why. 'All of us who survived those common years had to be a little strange. We spent so much of our young-womanhood trying to define ourselves as women-identified women before we even knew the words existed' (p. 225). They had a community, but they did not have a conscious politics with which to articulate themselves, their pain and their hope. Now, possessing that politics, Lesbian feminism, Lorde looks back, clear-sighted; and she refuses to impose that politics in judgement upon her historical community of 'gay-girls' in the 1950s.

Lorde's mother, who dominates her childhood, takes no part in the later sections of her narrative, other than to disapprove. She says nothing, 'But my mother could make "no comment" more loudly and with more hostility than anyone else I knew' (p. 216). Yet her mother is given the last line in the book. 'There it is said that the desire to lie with other women is a drive from the mother's blood' (p. 256). Her love for her mother was, in a sense, her first unhappy love affair. While I know that this will confirm the worst fears of many mothers who have not yet come to terms with their own anti-Lesbianism and while I know too that there are many Lesbians who would savagely deny that their love for their mothers is the source of their Lesbianism, it appears to me not at all mysterious that many Lesbians either have or remember mothers of power, integrity and strength, who gave to their daughters an image of independence, creativity and force; and an example to follow. Lorde's mother, despite her poverty and vulnerability, and despite the racism which perpetually borders their lives, gives her children an absolute security through her dignity and pride. 'Nobody wrote stories about us, but still people always asked my mother for directions in a crowd. It was this that made me decide as a child we must be rich' (p. 18).

Maureen Duffy, a woman of Lorde's generation, describes herself as a fairly orthodox Freudian, and as homosexual rather than as Lesbian. Since 1970

Lesbian has become a political category: homosexual remains a technical, even a medical, description of sexual practice. Duffy's autobiographical novel *That's How It Was* is about her mother.

> She was absolutely incredible. One of the things I ask at the end of that book is how, if you had such a relationship for your first fourteen years, can you ever recover? Who will be able to take that place? How do you shift your emotions and your orientation? There are certain patterns which appear too often in the childhoods of homosexuals to be chance – statistically there are too many important mothers and unimportant fathers.[27]

The book at once establishes the uniquely Lesbian balance of I/She; the woman as perceiving subject and the woman as subject perceived. Paddy's memory of her mother is of a fighter, a survivor, who struggled against TB all her life. Duffy presents two white working-class childhoods, her own and that of her mother, through a shifting perspective. Sometimes the child interrogates her mother, demanding the stories, legends and mythologies of her mother's childhood. She is the solitary child in search of siblings, whom she finds in her mother's past. But the two childhoods interlock in sinister ways. Sentimental memories of ingenious mischief, energy and creative inventiveness overcoming the inertia of poverty, hunger and illness become seriously qualified when Paddy tries to re-create her mother's life with her step-brothers, the three Willerton boys. Casual violence, theft, begging and crime become her daily experience. Paddy perceives the boys as 'animals'; they eat like 'starving savages'.[28] With all the contempt of the freshly educated she sneers at these 'barbarians'. The effect of this is seriously to put in question the myth of British working-class childhoods like that of her mother where poverty, ignorance and pain are held at bay by a strong class consciousness, solidarity and joy.

Duffy is writing about the process through which Paddy achieves the coveted cultural literacy of the middle classes in order to write her story. And the middle classes are the audience for whom the book is written. This has serious implications for its politics. The scene in the X-ray department becomes a frightening metaphor for Duffy's portrayal of working-class lives.

> I stared fascinated. They were women of all ages, stripped to the waist, their clothing hanging dishevelled about them, hair awry. None of them had covered themselves as we had. They sat with sagging breasts, their faces distorted with caverns of shadow under high-lighted out-crops of nose, cheek-bone and jaw, like the pictures of waiting prostitutes in the big art books of French painters we had studied at school: the same listless postures, the lumpy bodies that gave me a shock of compassionate horror. We sat beside them at the end of the row.
>
> As their names were called they went forward, stepped into the machine and the plate lowered. Then, as the radiographer pressed a button, we saw into them, the dark rib cage, the linked spine, the shadowy organs filled the screen before us. (p. 149).

The narrator, her mother and the reader all become voyeurs. The women are brutally observed: dishevelled, sagging, distorted, listless. Only Paddy and her mother have covered themselves. Nakedness is always painfully vulnerable; and the narrator enforces this by the perpetual opposition of 'we'/'they' throughout the description. So, set apart, securely clothed, we too peer at those vulnerable bodies as connoisseurs. We become the customers, the consumers, the men watching the waiting prostitutes. We are the middle-class audience, secure in our understanding of the apt comparison with the works of French painters. We see into these women's bodies, but we do not see them whole, as discreet individuals with their own histories.

The class from which Paddy and her mother come is the rising aristocracy of poverty: East-Enders, sharp Cockneys, intent on making good. 'They were smart and undersized, stuck to their principles and their mates, hard working and drinking. Their children's children are teachers and nurses and television playwrights' (p. 22). The Willertons, on the other hand, are Wortbridge rural working-class: huge, illiterate and physically disgusting. Ted Willerton, her mother's husband, has 'fingers like little sausages' (p. 85) and 'carved great calluses from the palms of his hands, that seemed to grow again overnight, like Prometheus' liver' (p. 86). It is not only the burgeoning calluses which mark the man as deformed in Paddy's eyes; it is also the fact that he can barely sign his own name and would never have heard of Prometheus. Paddy's perceptions hammer him back on to the rock of his ignorance and illiteracy.

The tension and ambiguity of Duffy's theme lie in the fact that she is making her literary reputation out of the people she has despised and abandoned. And she knows it. 'The phrase "class traitor" has always been around in my background – the concept was discussed, employed in conversation. It was not applied to me, but I feel in a sense divorced. This is not just a personal thing, I think, but a layer of experience in our society.'[29] Duffy herself suggests that we should read *That's How It Was* with suspicion. The gaps, absences, shocks of the book are carefully placed. Louey's motives for marrying Ted Willerton are never completely clear. Of course, Paddy would want to think that she had done it entirely for her daughter's benefit; but we never see inside Louey's mind. Her frail physical presence and unyielding spirit dominate the book. But who she is, what she feels, how it was for Louey Millar, Louey Mahoney, Louey Willerton is never revealed. She is observed with possessive passion, but never understood.

In her preface to the 1983 Virago edition Duffy describes her own education, and her ambition to become a writer. Her hero was Keats. He too was working-class, struggled to educate himself, nursed enormous ambitions as a poet, and was haunted by the spectre of TB. The disease which her mother evades, confronts, eludes all through Paddy's childhood hangs over her daughter's life, and her desire to write. But unlike Keats, Duffy faced more than the shadow of disease. There were other threats to her ambition: 'The pressure to conform, to leave school and go into the mill or factory, to get a chap was unremitting except when I was at school or alone with my mother' (p. xi). Paddy's first love affair was with her mother. And her childish passions for her teachers take the same form of *amour courtois* that characterizes the expression of her love for her mother. 'She was the castle under siege and I was the desperate defender boiling the oil to send the attacker howling back to cover'

(p. 46). Her passion for Miss Tyson is described in comic clichés. 'Her eyes were like grey seas; I felt myself drowning' (p. 182). But Paddy actively courts other women. She is the woman who chooses, the woman who acts; not the woman who waits. To choose women was to choose ostracism from her class and from her community's cultural norm, but it was also to choose education, independence, liberty. And the longing for freedom comes directly from the mother who never disappoints the child. 'I'd like you to go to college. It's the one thing they can't take away from you, education. You're not going to be pushed about as I've been' (p. 86). Education becomes self-defence.

That's How It Was is both biography and autobiography. Paddy's mother shapes the book which begins with her childhood and ends with her death. The anonymous character of a white working-class woman's life, her story, is transformed into an epic battle about a heroine whose antagonists are bad housing, poverty, dirt, ignorance, disease. This is what Virginia Woolf describes as 'the dark country' of fiction. Dark here does, I think, mean both shadowy and obscure.

> In the early nineteenth century, women's novels were largely autobiographical. One of the motives that led them to write was the desire to expose their own suffering, to plead their own cause. Now that this desire is no longer so urgent, women are beginning to explore their own sex, to write of women as women have never been written of before . . . their lives are far less tested and examined by the ordinary processes of life . . . Her life has an anonymous character which is baffling and puzzling in the extreme. For the first time this dark country is beginning to be explored in fiction.[30]

Psychoanalysis is a theory about the construction of the self; a hypothesis, a possible map for this dark country. It is a suggested explanation of how we acquire an identity and take up our posts in the normative categories: mother, father, woman, man. Psychoanalysis has provided the only coherent theory of psychic identity; of how it is we come to interpret ourselves, of how we become who we are. Most women would probably agree with Freud's conclusion that 'femininity' is not easily acquired; and *mirabile dictu*, some of us manage never to acquire it at all. Now to say that a theory is coherent is not to say that it is either accurate or useful. The two objections which reappear most often in connection with the feminist fascination with psychoanalysis are, first, that the discourse itself creates a theoretical elite who talk an indecipherable tongue learned from men and therefore, under its evil influence, take no part in providing their womanpower stitching banners or running the Rape Crisis Line; second, that the theory collapses into a sort of psychic essentialism: we inexorably resolve our Oedipal difficulties and end up, whether we like it or not, women and men, feminine and masculine, with all our phobias and repressed horrors duly acquired in childhood and remorselessly intact. These two criticisms are in fact linked; women who are committed to reclaiming male discourses are not usually those who choose to be in the Women Only political front line. And it would therefore be in their interest to discover a bedrock of psychic determinism which makes masculinity and femininity irresistible. For if the oppression of women is actually caused simply by the fact of sexual difference then political, social and economic upheaval may prove quite unnecessary. All we have to do is splinter these psychic identities, deconstruct the ahistorical, almost metaphysical, polar oppositions of masculine and feminine by applying a lot of complex theory. But I notice that no one bothers to deconstruct the psychic difference between Blacks and whites, or between the proletariat and the bourgeoisie. These differences are matters of power, political, social and economic, and can only be altered by a messy struggle and the redistribution of wealth.

I realize that these objections do not do justice to the adventure of Freud's thinking, nor to the originality and speculative endeavour of much psychoanalytic writing; but the feminist love affair with psychoanalytic theory has not substantially challenged or transformed the terms upon which we, as women, live our lives. I find myself in broad agreement with Lynne Segal's intelligent critique of psychoanalytic theory, and with her conclusion: 'I also see no reason why a more complex notion of psychic conflict, fragmentation and instability in sexual identity need undermine or deny women's conscious and collective opposition to the many sites of men's power'.[31] I believe, too, that this can be demonstrated by the way in which feminists have transformed the genre of autobiography. Autobiography is central to feminist practice. As a genre, autobiography is also about the construction of the self; but it is not as closely related to psychoanalysis as it might at first appear to be. Feminist autobiography analyses personal experience, reassesses the trivial, the normal, the anonymous, and makes visible – *as a process* – the forces of oppression, rather than simply naming or defining them as static shapes. Thus, June Levine in *Sisters: The Personal Story of an Irish Feminist* can demonstrate the way in which her husband tried to destroy her, with a small but savage detail, which illuminates an expanse of sexual violence within marriage. Levine's sister, after visiting her in Canada, reported back to her family in Ireland, ' "They have this beautiful kitchen with formica counters and he was cutting bread and she asked him to use the board. He deliberately sawed into the formica. I'd have stuck the knife in him myself." '[32] The process of liberation and transformation, with all its painful contradictions, can also be enacted: and this affirms the possibility of radical change, a hope we can never abandon while we call ourselves feminists. The problem with psychoanalysis lies in its historical link with medical science and the claim that analysis itself can provide some kind of 'cure' for psychic disorders. Why should verbalizing the unconscious – if there is indeed such a thing, as I doubted earlier in this chapter, for its existence seems to me to be as hypothetical as that of the soul[33] – necessarily make anyone feel any better about anything? And why should the fact that it sometimes does work extraordinary changes be anything more than a happy coincidence? Might the confessional not have had the same effect in some cases? I am delighted to find that my scepticism is shared by psychoanalysts. Here are Stuart Schneidermann's doubts:

> It may be that there is no such thing as cure when we are talking about the psyche. The concept of cure in psychoanalysis may go back to a belief that psyche must

follow soma, that we can have the same degree of certainty in the one as we think we obtain with the other. Psychoanalysis ought to get out of the business of thinking about how people live their lives, about how they behave.[34]

I think that this is right, because then all the accusations against psychoanalysis as a normalizing therapy which has, as its aim, the taming of anti-social behaviour into the acceptable categories of masculine and feminine would become unnecessary. And to be unconventional, rebellious, Lesbian or Gay would not automatically be read as signs that the subject was sick, mad or bad. June Levine hated being a housewife. Her husband told her she was mad and handed her over to the medical professions to be analysed, drugged, shocked, destroyed. She didn't need analysis. She needed her freedom. One Black Lesbian friend of mine went into analysis, I believe of her own volition. The (male) analyst dismissed her love of women as a fixation on her mother's breasts. She walked out. She said to me, 'I knew he was wrong.' Both these women wer considered to be sick. Analysis, so said the experts, would cure them. They both survived; but some of us lie on the couch, writing cheques, for years.

However, the speculative insights of psychoanalysis, as a theory rather than as a medical discipline, have been used by some feminists as a tool with which to make sense of their own lives. Two relevant autobiographies here are Elizabeth Wilson's *Mirror Writing: An Autobiography* and Carolyn Steedman's *Landscape of a Good Woman: A Story of Two Lives*.[35] Both writers use the form of autobiography to disrupt our expectations of the genre and to question the assumptions built into the feminist chronicles of the 1970s. Both women chew over the contradictions of sexuality, identity, relationship and memory, that their lives have produced. And both women are academics: Steedman's text has vistas of footnotes and bibliography; Wilson has a modest page of notes but offers lengthy and learned reflections on various subjects, including Proust, psychoanalysis and feminist autobiography, within the text. Both books are much more insecure in their purpose and in their meaning then the feminist chronicles of the 1970s, which all had Jerusalem firmly defined and well in their sights. Wilson and Steedman unearth a quagmire of difficulties and contradictions which appear, to them, practically insoluble.

Wilson's theme is the mystery of her own identity. Her text has the logic of memory, or of dreams. She re-creates isolated moments, a period, an atmosphere, an attitude, intense and memorable. When she remembers her post-war home, she says of the street, 'We dwelt among peeling vistas of stucco . . . ' (p. 9) and of the 1960s, 'You sat on the floorboards, which were painted cream and strewn with mattresses and cushions. The rooms had dark brown walls and heavily fringed lampshades' (p. 216). Wilson's search for an identity is also a search for authenticity, continuity, confidence; not so much an unchanging essence as a certainty, an affirmation: yes, this is who I am. She perpetually describes herself in Sartre's terms, as amorphous, viscous, slimy. One of her male lovers has the magic gift. 'Once, long after, I caught sight of him in an Algerian café in Paris. He hadn't changed. Now there was someone with identity! . . . His identity remained implacably clear, deadpan . . . ' (p. 47).

Wilson questions the link between subjectivity and truth which was certainly assumed by the women who wrote their feminist testimonies in the 1970s. Is identity in fact continuous, a political process, as Anja Meulenbelt asserted that it was, or do we break up and reform as different beings? Wilson tries out different identities, like masks; as a Bright Young Thing at Oxford, as a Serious Psychiatric Social Worker, as a Writer and as a Lesbian. They all prove problematic. Being a Writer suddenly raises the question of gender. She is not taken seriously. Being a psychiatric social worker involves a dreadful abyss between a public world of respectable bourgeois norms and the '*femme damnée*' role of being a Lesbian. The Lesbian identity is particularly fraught with anxiety, because in the 1960s this was not a political identity, collectively asserted, but a sexual identity, often defined by others through disdain, fear, abuse or the sinister practices of the medical profession. And to be Lesbian was to be doomed, damned, preferably dead. 'Many lesbians rejected the idea of being paired off as masculine and feminine, but how else *could* we be defined?' (p. 145, Wilson's italics). She describes an intriguing muddle of feelings and points out that the problem of butch and femme roles was not nearly so interesting for male homosexuals. 'The expression of their sexuality was what interested them. Lesbians (in the sixties at any rate) had hardly known what their sexuality *was*' (p. 145, Wilson's italics). In a brief, incisive article Beatrix Campbell gives an idea of how this uncertain territory has been ploughed up by the debates on sexual practice in the 1970s.

> Anna Koedt's *Myth of the Vaginal Orgasm* asserted that men were doggedly resistant to the claims of the clitoris, and she identified penetration as a major fortification in patriarchal sexuality. One effect of this was to generate a sense of women's bodies which could ally heterosexual, homosexual and celibate women. As we have said earlier, lesbians' pleasure was in femaleness, rather than a refusal of the female – something which heterosexuality has still not registered.[36]

Behind the comic prose, in which the clitoris and heterosexuality become conscious agents in the epic struggle for sexual pleasure, lurks a subversive proposition: that women's sexuality and Lesbian sexuality might in fact be exactly the same thing. Elizabeth Wilson was uneasy as a woman because she was a Lesbian; for all people are assumed to be heterosexual unless they assert themselves as Gay, and in the mid-1960s there was still an absolute division between being 'normal' and being a 'pervert'.

Therefore, Wilson grasped a moment of authentic identity while she was a part of Gay Liberation Front, for it was here that she achieved a fusion of political and sexual identity, 'G.L.F. fused and united the impossible and made a statement simultaneously that homosexuality was "all right" and that it was "damned" ' (p. 123). Wilson's love affair with psychoanalysis was bound up with its religious mystique, the promise of secret knowledge. And this is, I think, also the basis for the passion for Freud in the women's liberation movement; the knowledge 'which might lead to the source and origins of women's subordination' (p. 135). In this respect Freud's secrets resemble the myth of the Matriarchal Golden Age of womyn's rites and women's rights, the age of Gentle Men who were kept in their place, a myth which has many converts and supporters. Wilson's final chapter is a reflection on the substance of identity and the books behind her book. Is identity opaque, as is Gertrude Stein's identity in *The Autobiography of Alice B. Toklas* (1933) – which is of course, Stein's version of Stein, the self seen from outside, the self observed? Or is identity simply a mask, a memory, a guilty secret? Feminist autobiography claims a new identity, a political and sexual authenticity within the community of women. The Book here, for Wilson, is Anja Meulenbelt's *The Shame is Over*. 'Thus have women tried to construct a collective identity out of a shared experience of collective oppression.' What is lost in this process, so Wilson argues, is 'our sense of individuality and of an unique past, an unique self' (p. 154). I don't think that this is true. Feminist autobiography certainly works as testimony; and, as in our consciousness-raising sessions we offered our unique lives, our story of that's how we thought it was, not simply to find the shared points of reference in an isolated and oppressive experience, that of being socially constructed as a woman, but to re-value our own particular, unique lives, to give ourselves to each other. For if we do not treasure each other's lives, as women's lives, no one else will do so. This is part of our work as feminists.[37]

I think, though, that there is a genuine difficulty in establishing a balance between subjective perceptions and a collective politics. For a while, some years ago, I lived in a monastery and was seduced by the idea of becoming a contemplative Benedictine nun. Sister Anne, exasperated by my preoccupation with my own individual identity, finally snapped, 'Look, Patricia, God doesn't save us as individuals, He saves us as a people.' This is a very catholic attitude. But Sister Anne's point was simply this: identity is constructed in relationship. It is the product of community. And I do think that Wilson is right when she argues that we must construct 'a plurality of positive images for women' (p. 155).[38] We can't all be Amazons, and why should we want to be?

Perhaps the obsession with identity, which Wilson describes as part of 'the sub-Freudian baggage of Western culture' (p. 136), only becomes problematic when we are no longer part of a strongly defined community? When I lived as part of an extended family I was firmly known as Mr Duncker's Daughter. This identity, in which I was utterly secure, was bestowed upon me by patriarchy. My subsequent insecurity has been healthy and politically invaluable. The freedom I claim as a feminist is to work with other women to create my own community. And nobody ever pretended that that would be easy.

The last metaphor of *Mirror Writing* interestingly shifts the terms of Wilson's questioning. Confronted with mirrors reflecting one another into eternity in an art exhibition, she hesitates. Her revolutionary friend Rosa, who has spent years in prison for practising a politics in which she presumably believed, has no fear. She leaps on to the glass floor, laughing. Wilson realizes her identity as a leap of faith, 'the triumph of the momentary, vulnerable "I"' (p. 160). But this is surely not the case. Rosa's identity is neither momentary nor vulnerable; she survived imprisonment. Her identity is bodily, political, enduring, earned, and triumphant.

Carolyn Steedman's analysis of her childhood in the 1950s, and the effect of her mother's life upon her own, is presented as a case study rather than as a personal narrative. 'This is not to say that this book involves a search for a past or for what really happened. It is about how people use the past to tell the stories of their life.'[39] Her book is a defiant subversion of the sentimental working-class autobiographies where working-class people have a simplified, unified psychology and identify themselves strongly with one another as an oppressed class. Freud and Marx loom in the texture of her prose; but the book behind her book is another feminist autobiography, Ann Oakley's *Taking It Like A Woman*, which cannot ever be her story. 'I . . . feel the painful and familiar sense of exclusion from these autobiographies of middle-class little-girlhood and womanhood, envy of these who belong, who can, like Ann Oakley, use the outlines of conventional romantic fiction to tell a life story' (p. 17). Steedman's book is about the way in which her story is marginal to all the interpretive discourses conventionally used to describe her life; 'Even the psychoanalytic drama was constructed to describe that of middle-class women' (p. 17). Steedman counterpoints her story with that of Mayhew's watercress girl and Freud's Dora; the working-class child who knows her value as a worker and brings home the money she earns in exchange for love and security, and the middle-class hysteric who knows that her sex is her exchange value. I think that Steedman intends we should see an absolute gulf between these two stories. But in fact both young women are imprisoned and exploited within their own situations. The difference between them is that Dora claims the power to walk out on her father's sexual deals and the bargain he struck with Freud. But after that, all she can do is strike her sexual bargain elsewhere; hardly a great freedom. If anything, Steedman's comparison demonstrates the fact that Dora and the watercress girl are sisters under the skin, insisting on their own realities, their own integrity, with great persistence and dignity.

Some odd arguments emerge from Steedman's book. The poverty of her mother's childhood and her own is bound up not so much with money as with expectations, confidence, the perpetual sense of exclusion and not belonging. Her mother operated with a politics of envy; she was 'a working-class Conservative from a traditional Labour background' (p. 8). And what she wanted was *things*. Steedman uses the prescriptive metaphors of the fairy-tales, which, she rightly argues, underlie modern psychoanalytic myths, the world of arriving princes and fathers who, like feudal kings, have absolute power, to make sense of her mother's unfulfilled desires and to explain her refusal of any solidarity with her origins, and the fact that she voted with the class which excluded her. But why is it strange that her mother wanted things? We are programmed by capitalism to desire material goods. And Steedman doesn't spend much time ruminating on the fact that it is a *woman* who does this, nor does she explicitly speculate that her mother's marginality to working-class culture, as the mother of two illegitimate children and as an exile from the north, might have reinforced her decision to embrace the attitudes of the class to which she could aspire but which she could never enter. Women's concerns do not define or even substantially influence working-class values.

Steedman's observation of her father's vulnerable powerlessness over against the authority outside his home, which represents the ruling class, leads her to argue that he did not *matter* within the household. The Oedipal incident occurred when she witnessed a confrontation with a park-keeper who ticked him off for picking a handful of bluebells. She cannot quite recall how he shouted back. 'His not mattering had an effect like this: I don't believe in male power; somehow the iron of patriarchy didn't enter into my soul. I accept the idea of male power intellectually, of course (and I will eat my words the day I am raped . . .) ' (p. 19). While I can imagine that it must be invigorating and useful not to have the iron of patriarchy in one's soul, I do question this analysis. Steedman sees male power in fairy-tale terms, the threat of sexual violence. I do not subscribe to the myth of the patriarchal monolith and the Giant Penis, but I do think that sexual violence is a central column in the edifice; and yet it is not the only means of wielding power. The rest of Steedman's narrative tells how her father wrecked their lives by denial. Her mother struggled to marry him, bullied him with babies, demanded things. He kept up his £7 a week payments, but refused the rest. Her mother built her whole life around the desire for a man who never delivered the goods or conferred the status of wife upon her. And yet the daughter denies the man's power, which he exercises relentlessly throughout her childhood. The daughter is coerced into being the mother's advocate with the father, but 'he never capitulated' (p. 60). The mother's longing is re-articulated in the daughter. 'When he died I spent days foolishly hoping there would be something for me' (p. 61). The father's power resides in what he withholds. Steedman's denial of the reality of male power in her own life is, I'm afraid, wishful thinking.

Steedman's mother's refusal to mother is examined at some length. She made her daughters feel that they were a crucial part of her burden; that they contributed to her 'sense of unfairness, her belief that she had been refused entry to her rightful place in the world' (p. 112). I think it is true that the politics of envy is always judged in moral terms as mean and small-minded, belittled as trivial and treacherous. I suspect that this dishonesty results from from the fact that is is those who have, rather than those who have not, who write the theory, the analyses, even the fiction, which deny her mother's desires any psychological validity. Steedman tries to make sense of the ways in which her mother's unsatisfied longing devastated her children's lives. The rage and bitterness in her narrative are detectable, but stifled behind the clenched teeth of her academic prose. The defence of scholarship and learning erected around her story is, I think, a strategy against the prejudice that would dismiss her mother's history as the cringing voice of envy and deny her own painful disquiet as insignificant. This is understandable, but I suspect that the rage unleashed would have been even more arresting.

Steedman keeps herself at a distance from her own story, which she presents as unromantic, painful, ordinary, anonymous. Ann Oakley, in the book which Steedman resents, *Taking It Like A Woman*, divides her narrative into two parts: one is the story of her life as a wife, mother and professional sociologist; the other is the progress of her Romantic Love Affair with an unnamed man, conducted in various continental hotel bedrooms. The first narrative is in the first person, which necessarily gives it authority and force; the second is in the third person, and written almost entirely in the language of breathless cliché. At first glance Sharan-Jeet Shan's *In My Own Name: An Autobiography* could not be a more different life.[40] Oakley is a committed feminist, white, married, middle-class, Oxford-educated, the privileged daughter of a public man. Sharan-Jeet Shan is a Sikh, born in the Punjab, an ambitious, clever woman, whose medical career was destroyed by her father when he discovered that she loved a fellow student who was a Moslem. He forced her to marry a Sikh who had already emigrated to England. Shan had to abandon her home, country, family, ambitions, to live in a country she had not chosen and had never seen with a man who was a complete stranger. The context is indeed radically different: but both women are caught in the tension and ambiguity between two opposing ideologies, dutiful marriage and romantic love.

Like the two poles, masculinity and femininity, marriage and romantic passion need each other to define their meanings, for the one has to be everything that the other is not. And for both women, consummated heterosexual passion is at the core of romantic love. Shan never describes sex directly; but she makes it clear that she knows what she is talking about, and leaves the rest to us. 'As a man, as a human being, he was simply beautiful. In our expression of love for each other, we were equally intense, passionate and sincere. Whatever the future held, our minds, bodies and souls had been enraptured by that glorious feeling called "love" ' (p. 32). But the atmosphere of apprehension never leaves her. In 1965 she was married to Aziz in an Indian court of law, but 'In India no court would have challenged such an explosive issue, that of a marital alliance between a Sikh and a Muslim . . . in the eyes of "tradition" my marriage did not yet exist' (p. 32). Shan is faced with the taboos of her culture and the wrath of her father. Oakley and her lover are faced with their sense of responsibility to their existing families. They are answerable only to their consciences; Shan is confronted with brute force.

Oakley's romantic affair is conducted in bed. These passages, written in a dense web of surging clichés, are the most disquieting in the book. To some extent the clichés must surely be deliberate; Oakley wants her readers to be aware of the contradictions involved when a strong independent feminist simply longs to drown in passion for a man whose lovemaking is pitched in terms of sexual domination. Here is a typical passage.

> Authoritatively, he demands that she discard her underwear so that his hands can have an interesting time under the starched white tablecloth . . . His fingers are sexual organs . . . She really feels she has lost her identity. She really feels as though she cannot, does not, exist apart from him . . . He could be the original Viking pillager for all she cares . . . This is the unpremeditated ecstasy . . . the peak that rises above the plain, the force that powers the waves, the wind, the lava flows and the cold bright stars. (pp. 50–1)

Here, heterosexual sex becomes the universal natural force. Romantic love cannot survive within dailiness; it must be both fleeting and overwhelming, and, within the codes of the Grand Passion, somebody else must be wronged.

Oakley argues out the conflict between love and the family, pleasure and ethics, responsibility and desire. She spends one night on her own, without her lover or her husband and children. And she comes to the conclusion that 'she is only sure that parenthood is worth it. Work, sexuality, feminism, poems, parties, these are fictions' (p. 103). I find this an alarming conclusion. For children have the most profoundly unequal relationship with their parents. We do have the absolute power, as parents, to nurture or destroy. We can pretend to be God. Parenthood, in Sharan-Jeet Shan's family, is 'but a pretext to tyrannise where it can be done with impunity, for only good and wise men are content with the respect that will bear discussion'.[41] And good, wise fathers, as both Shan and Mary Wollstonecraft (to whom I owe the above comment) know well, are very few.

White western feminists, whose dominant context is the nuclear family, have a tendency to romanticize the extended family, the tribe, which is the basis of the different kinship structures in many other parts of the world. Germaine Greer's lyrical celebration of a poor Italian community in Calabria concludes: 'The only perfect love to be found on earth is not sexual love, which is riddled with doubt and insecurity, but the wordless commitment of families, which takes as its model mother-love.'[42] The family, in whatever form, is of itself never a neutral or benevolent structure. Neither sentimentality nor tactless racist denunciation is an adequate response; both are dangerous. 'White feminists have fallen into the trap of measuring the Black female experience against their own, labelling it as in some way lacking, then looking for ways in which it might be possible to harness the Black women's experience to their own.'[43] And white feminists, including myself, cannot say that we have not been warned. Sharan-Jeet Shan herself denies that her autobiography is a case against arranged marriage. She argues that, if all parties are careful and sensitive, an arranged marriage has as good a chance, if not a better chance, of working well as a love match. Only one woman I have known well, a Greek Cypriot, actually went home to look over a man her mother had picked out for her. At that time, twelve years ago, I was scandalized. 'Why?' she answered. 'What are you going on about? My family know me. They wouldn't choose anyone unsuitable. It'll be someone I've heard of if I don't already know him. I'd look at anyone they suggested. And anyway they wouldn't force me if I didn't like him.' And therein lies the secret of my friend's trusting relationship with her parents; she knew she would never be forced to marry against her will.

Sharan-Jeet Shan was forced by her father to marry a man she neither knew nor loved and to betray her promise to a man she did love, in the name of the family's honour. If we accept marriage as a necessary institution, and I must confess that I do not, it is not arranged marriage that is the problem, but rather the abuse of power and trust within the family. And it is, I am afraid, generally true that cultures whose normal practice is to arrange marriages are less likely to accept a woman who refuses to marry at all. Another friend, herself a Sikh, told me that she was looking for a husband for their daughter. We discussed what sort of man would be best. Sur-Jeet, who is a very religious woman, was delighted that her daughter had explicitly said that she wanted to marry a man who wore his turban. 'But Sur-Jeet,' I suggested cautiously, 'what if she decides that she doesn't want to marry at all?' 'She's twenty-three!' said Sur-Jeet indignantly, 'so it's high time.' Remaining unmarried was simply unthinkable.

The relationship of a Black or Asian woman to her family and her community within a racist state is problematic; for her support, help, solidarity and financial security often come from the very same structures and institutions which she may want to challenge. The situation for white women is usually not so critical, as the world outside the family may well provide the opportunity to escape. We will be discriminated against because we are women, but not on grounds of race. A Blackwoman or an Asian woman who is Lesbian may find it much more difficult to come out to her family or community.

> The family! The family is very contradictory for us. There are emotional involvements, there are ties, the roots that it represents for us all as individuals in a fundamentally racist/sexist society. That's why Black people may decide not to come out as lesbians or gay for fear of being rejected by a group of people whom you not only love but who represent a real source of security, of foundation. That's a choice that has to be respected as a political choice, not just an individual one.[44]

The most moving, indeed devastating undercurrent in Shan's narrative is her continual longing; the appeal to her family, culture, religion, to accept her, to honour her perspectives, to understand her courage and her fears. She grasps the contradictions in her own religion that would have given her the freedom to love where she chose. 'If Muslims were so bad for Sikhs why were the teachings of the Muslim saints included in the holy book, the Granth?' (p. 35). But there are no discussions and no alternatives. She is imprisoned and beaten into submission by her father. The women do speak up for her, but they are insulted and dismissed. Women can be very influential and powerful within families; but their power always depends on circumstances and personalities. Within the structure of the institution itself, whether the extended or the nuclear version, they have no absolute power that cannot be brushed aside by men. Shan's mother can only recommend the consolations of religion.

Shan is a fighter; a courageous woman whose pride and self-respect save her life. Her disastrous arranged marriage ends in cruelty and violence. 'Only in motherhood was there an escape route for self-realisation and expression' (p. 87). Shan does not say so explicitly, but the fact is that only in motherhood does she have any power or influence over anybody else. In fact, Shan continues to support and uphold the ideal of extended family life which has shattered her own ambitions and desires. ' . . . I found it very difficult to get away from the thoughts of India, of grandparents for the children, of festive family occasions and of the very special position sons would have in an extended family' (p. 95). Perversely, she duplicates her brother's privilege and freedom, a freedom that was granted to her brother at her expense, in the way she rears her two sons. She perpetuates the contradictions which almost destroyed her life. But this passionate nostalgia is easy to understand; no one who has ever lived within a close community in which her place is assured and secure, and I speak now from personal experience, can ever completely reconcile herself to exile. And

yet, having lived both in an extended family and in a nuclear one, I now
ferociously defend my right to live outside both, and never to be afflicted with a
family of my own.

For both Shan and Oakley, men are the source of the agony and the ecstasy.
There are no other women whose significance is critical to their stories. Shan
dedicates her book to her Moslem lover and her two sons. Oakley writes, 'Much
of this book has been about men. Is this not in itself a most objectionable
contradiction? I think it is' (p. 197). In fact, she is disarmingly honest about her
objectionable contradictions. They are, in effect, the subject of her book.
Oakley knows that it is women's capacity for unselfish love that is their undoing.
'Male-dominated culture has designated as female all labours of emotional
connectedness . . . So, if it isn't in love that women are lost, it's in the family.
The tension between the interests of the family and the interests of women as
individuals has been rising for some two centuries. It is not possible for those
interests to be reconciled' (p. 201). Yet both Shan and Oakley give a crucial part
of their energy to other women; Oakley in her writing and research work on
peri-natal issues, Shan in teaching English to Asian women, for she is especially
able 'to help my Asian sisters to bridge the gap, not only between themselves
and the indigenous systems of education and employment, but also to get closer
to their children' (p. 100). Shan never was a masochistic advocate of
self-sacrifice and denial, but her last comments indicate a new self-awareness
of her right to happiness as a woman. 'I . . . am beginning to taste the joy of
freedom . . . I want to live a little for me now' (p. 174).

Ann Oakley had a rare but dangerous form of cancer. The sharpened
knowledge that she would not live for ever was the impulse behind her
autobiography. She wanted to come to terms with the woman who might cease
to exist, herself. Death is also the shadow on the edge of the page for Rigoberta
Menchú; but in her case it is the threat of murder by the army or the police in
Guatemala's repressive state. Menchú's narrative is a testimony for a people in
struggle: her people, the Quiché Indians. Just as Sharan-Jeet Shan understands
the need for an oppressed people to possess 'the powerful implement of
language', (p. 100) so too does Menchú. She learned Spanish, the language of
her oppressors, in order to organize against them. Her autobiography *I,
Rigoberta Menchú* . . . should be required reading in the Vatican.[45] It is a classic
story of rebellion and the absolute dignity of the wretched. Shan's religion was
used to crush her; Menchú and her people take up the radical message of
Christianity, which has been successfully smothered by the Church, to liberate
her people. The radical transforming power of Sikhism in Shan's life was never
allowed to flower.

Menchú told her story to Elisabeth Burgos-Debray, who has transcribed the
text, editing the original, terrifying simplicity of Menchú's voice as little as
possible. The book is a celebration of her people, her community and their
traditions, and their struggle to survive. The Quiché Indians base their religion
and culture on the earth's cycles; on the sacred power of the water, the land, the
maize from which they live, the sun. Again and again, Menchú stresses the
importance of the ancestors and of adherence to their ancestral traditions. It is a
culture based on respect for the past. Usually, a faith or society based on

carefully preserved traditions tends to be both reactionary and oppressive to women; but for the Quiché Indians their loyalty to their ancient customs has ensured their physical survival and shaped their political identity. And their reverence for nature leads to some surprisingly logical attitudes. 'Our people don't differentiate between people who are homosexual and people who aren't; that only happens when we go out of our community. We don't have the rejection of homosexuality the *ladinos* do; they really cannot stand it. What's good about our way of life is that everything is considered part of nature' (p. 60). The idea that homosexuality might be natural is an original one for any woman who has a Christian inheritance or who has read St Paul; on the other hand, the Quiché have natural sexism. Menchú says, 'It's not that *machismo* doesn't exist among our people, but it doesn't present a problem for the community because it's so much part of our way of life' (p. 14). Elsewhere Menchú describes *machismo* as a sickness. She does not always connect up her own observations. The racist mentality of the *ladinos*, which she finds so painful, has its counterpart in the veneration of male children within her community: 'The community is always happier when a male child is born and the men feel much prouder' (p. 14). I'm sure they do.

Menchú is not a typical Indian woman by any means. Her crucial role as a national leader in their revolutionary struggle gives her both freedom and authority; but even as a child, as her own narrative makes clear, she sidestepped the rigid sex roles of her people. She was very much her father's daughter. 'I hardly ever fought with any of the boys in my village, because I've got more or less the same attitudes as they have' (p. 194). For women engaged in a revolutionary liberation struggle, political consciousness is a process shaped by expediency and the daily emergency of living. Menchú declares herself firmly against separatist women's politics at this stage in the struggle, although she explicitly refuses to rule out the possibility of women's organizations in the future. She is utterly uncompromising in her stand against the *machismo* of the men who try to negate women's participation in the revolution.

> I came up against revolutionary compañeros who had many ideas about making a revolution, but who had trouble accepting that a woman could participate in the struggle not only in superficial things but in fundamental things. I've also had to punish many compañeros who try to prevent their women taking part in the struggle or carrying out any task . . . We must fight as equals. (pp. 221–2)

Radical change often dissolves impractical and irrational prejudice and throws up extraordinary contradictions. Catholicism, imposed upon the Indians by their oppressors, becomes another of the weapons of the revolution. Catholics, on the whole, read the Bible with caution. The Quiché Indians discovered there what many Black people have found, stories of slavery, rebellion and escape and the articulation of a God who is irrevocably on the side of the sufferers and the oppressed. They read the Bible through their perception of reality. God's Kingdom 'will exist only when we all have enough to eat, when our children, brothers, parents don't have to die from hunger and malnutrition. That will be the "Glory", a Kingdom for we who have never known it' (p. 134). The Bible has become their written authority, for women and men. 'We have the example of Judith . . . she fought very hard for her people and made many attacks against the king they had then, until she finally had his head. She held her victory in her hand, the head of the King. This gave us a vision, a stronger idea of how we Christians must defend ourselves' (pp. 131–2). The story of Judith's victory over Holofernes has been an inspiration to Black people, Christian and Jewish feminists alike. Biblical history achieves its realization and continuity in South American liberation theology and the revolutionary movements which that theology supports and inspires.

Menchú insists that her horrifying story of poverty, hunger and violence is not hers alone – 'it's the grief of a whole people' (p. 236) – and yet every life is unique, precious, different. Her insistence that her experience and suffering are shared has a political point. Her life and that of her community are bound together. Her story is not that of an inner life, the growth of a single soul, but that of the life, customs and traditions of a people. It is the story, not of how *I* saw the world, but of how *we* organized, how we fought, how we valued each other, how we died for each other, how we survived. And for feminist revolutionary politics and for feminist autobiography I think that this shift is crucial: the movement from the single perspective towards the basis for a collective politics, the shift from 'I' to 'We'. We start from where we are, we cannot do otherwise; but it is not enough to shape each single identity as an oppressed person and leave it at that. Nor is it enough for those of us who have enough to eat and a mattress at night to concern ourselves only with finding a better job, persuading our husbands to clean the loo or our sons to wash up. There are no single lives that can be lived without reference to others. There are no single issues. Other women in the world starve so that the wealthy of the west can eat well. The people are not free until the women, all the women, are free. That old slogan, which I first saw in the early 1970s, remains true. And the process of feminist consciousness is the realization that we are not alone, and that we need not fight on alone. But we must fight as equals.

Notes

1 Rosemary Manning, *A Time and a Time: An Autobiography* (1971, as Sarah Davys; 2nd edn, London, Marion Boyars, 1986).
2 Maureen Duffy, *That's How It Was* (1982; London, Virago, 1983).
3 Audre Lorde, *Zami: A New Spelling of My Name* (1982; London, Sheba, 1984), p. 190.
4 Paulina Palmer has written very clearly about this split. See her article 'The Representation of Lesbianism in Contemporary Women's Fiction: The Division between "Politics" and "Psychoanalysis" ', in Jane Aaron and Sylvia Walby (eds), *Out of the Margins: Women's Studies in the Nineties* (Lewes, Falmer, 1991).
5 Elizabeth Wilson, *Mirror Writing: An Autobiography* (London, Virago, 1982).
6 The *Revolutionary and Radical Feminist Newsletter*, available to women only, has been printed intermittently for around ten years now. Try: RRFM, 22 Finsbury Park Road, London N4 2JZ (send cheques, payable to RRFM). The last issue I managed to lay my hands on – and it was terrific – was issue 120, Spring 1990.

7 Rosalind Minsky, ' "The Trouble is it's Ahistorical": The Problem of the Unconscious in Modern Feminist Theory', *Feminist Review*, no. 36 (Autumn 1990), pp. 7, 6.

8 Lorde, *Zami*; Ann Oakley, *Taking It Like A Woman* (London, Cape, 1984).

9 Kate Millett, *Flying* (1974; London, Paladin, 1976).

10 Violette Leduc, *La Bâtarde* (1964; London, Virago, 1985); Emma Goldman, *Living My Life*, 2 vols (1932); Doris Lessing, *The Golden Notebook* (London, 1935).

11 Millett, *Flying*, pp. 14–16.

12 For the Radicalesbians' paper 'The Woman Identified Woman' and other documents from Lesbians in the USA in the early 1970s see Sarah Lucia Hoagland and Julia Penelope (eds), *For Lesbians Only: A Separatist Anthology* (London, Onlywomen, 1983).

13 Mariana Valverde, *Sex, Power and Pleasure* (Toronto, Women's Press, 1985), p. 112.

14 I am delighted to say I hadn't heard of most of them.

15 For a much more sympathetic analysis of Millett's autobiographical strategies and an intriguing psychoanalytical assessment of women's autobiography see Linda Anderson's essay, 'At the Threshold of the Self: Women and Autobiography', in Moira Monteith (ed.), *Women's Writing: A Challenge to Theory* (Brighton, Harvester, 1986), pp. 54–71.

16 Anja Meulenbelt, *The Shame is Over* (1976; London, Women's Press, 1980), p. 6.

17 Verena Stefan, *Shedding* (1975; London, Women's Press, 1979).

18 The best political analysis of the 'sexual revolution' of the 1960s that I have read is to be found in Andrea Dworkin's *Right-Wing Women: The Politics of Domesticated Females* (London, Women's Press, 1983), pp. 99–100.

19 Adrienne Rich, *The Fact of a Doorframe: Poems Selected and New 1950–1984* (New York, Norton, 1984), p. 242.

20 Lorde, *Zami*, p. 205.

21 "No, we never go out of fashion . . . for each other" ', Audre Lorde interviewed by Dorothea, Jackie Kay and Uma, *Spare Rib*, no. 149 (November 1984), pp. 26–9.

22 Barbara Smith, *Towards a Black Feminist Criticism* (1977; Trumansberg, NY, The Crossing Press, Out and Out Books, Pamphlet no. 5, 1980).

23 Lorde, *Zami*, p. 255.

24 'It is now common knowledge that the gay liberation movement started in New York in June 1969, when the queens in the Stonewall bar fought back police repression, and for the first time in history gay people began to stand up on a massive scale. The movement spread like a forest fire, first across the United States, then soon catching on in the rest of the Western world. In this intense struggle for the social recognition of homosexuality, a certain gay consciousness was formed.' *Come Together: The Years of Gay Liberation 1970–73*, edited and introduced by Aubrey Walter (London: Gay Men's Press, 1980), p. 7.

25 Audre Lorde, *The Cancer Journals* (San Francisco, Spinsters Ink, 1980), p. 35. My references are to the US edition, but there is also a British edition published by Sheba.

26 Lorde, *Zami*, p. 251.

27 'Maybe it's because I'm a Londoner . . . '; Maureen Duffy interviewed by Rachel Gould, *The Guardian*, 5 October 1983.

28 Maureen Duffy, *That's How It Was* (1962; London, Virago, 1983), p. 107.

29 Gould, 'Maybe it's because I'm a Londoner . . . '.

30 Virginia Woolf, 'Women and Fiction' (1929), in *Women and Writing*, selected and introduced by Michèle Barrett (London, Women's Press, 1979), pp. 49–50.

31 Lynne Segal, *Is the Future Female? Troubled Thoughts on Contemporary Feminism* (London, Virago, 1987), p. 128.

32 June Levine, *Sisters: The Personal Story of an Irish Feminist* (Swords, Co. Dublin, Ward River Press, 1982), p. 63.

33 'Psyche' is, of course, the Greek work for the soul. And psyche, as non-material mind, and the soul have always been linked. But many people who doubt the existence of the one defend the other, and attribute to it great and influential powers. This is very interesting.

34 Stuart Schneidermann, *Jacques Lacan: The Death of an Intellectual Hero* (Cambridge, Mass., Harvard University Press, 1983), p. 57. This book is an autobiography of Schneidermann's encounter with Lacan and his ideas. Lacan was his mentor, idol and analyst.

35 Elizabeth Wilson, *Mirror Writing: An Autobiography* (London, Virago, 1982); Carolyn Steedman, *Landscape for a Good Woman* (London, Virago, 1986).

36 Beatrix Campbell, 'Sex – A Family Affair', in Lynne Segal (ed.), *What is to be Done about the Family? Crisis in the Eighties* (London, Penguin, 1983), pp. 65–6.

37 And this work is being done. See, for example, *Shifra: A Jewish Feminist Magazine*, nos 3, 4 (Chanukkah 5747/December 1986), for a report on the work of the Jewish Women in London oral history project, which aims to recall and re-value the lives of Jewish women. This is only one of the numerous women's history projects in Britain.
   We have also begun to build a lesbian archive. The British Lesbian Archive, based in London, went through a particularly horrible period of internal trouble and strife after the Lesbian Summer School of July 1988. Accusations of every kind were made against both the two paid workers and the management collective. The situation was temporarily resolved after a public meeting held in London in January 1989. But the failure to keep this project running smoothly makes Caeia March's acknowledgement to the Archive in her novel *The Hide and Seek Files* (London, Women's Press, 1989) all the more saddening to read. If we don't defend and preserve our own history, no one else will.

38 Wilson is herself critical of some aspects of her own text. In an intriguing essay, 'Tell It Like It Is: Women and Confessional Writing', in Susannah Radstone (ed.), *Sweet Dreams: Sexuality, Gender and Popular Fiction* (London, Lawrence & Wishart, 1988), pp. 21–45, she has this to say about *Mirror Writing* and her novel, *Prisons of Glass*: 'Yet it may be that in their very rejection of a transparent authenticity they covertly claim the "higher" truth of the postmodernist flux of identity and disintegration of experience. And this too can become little more than a modish imperative' (p. 42).

39 Steedman, *Landscape for a Good Woman*, p. 8.

40 Sharan-Jeet Shan, *In My Own Name: An Autobiography* (London, Women's Press, 1985).

41 Mary Wollstonecraft, *A Vindication of the Rights of Woman*, ed. Miriam Brody Kramnic (1792; London, Pelican, 1975), p. 264.

42 Germaine Greer, *The Madwoman's Underclothes: Essays and Occasional Writings 1968–1985* (London, Picador, 1986), introduction, p. xxvi.

43 Valerie Amos and Pratibha Parmer, 'Challenging Imperial Feminism', in *Many Voices, One Chant: Black Feminist Perspectives*, special Black issue of *Feminist Review*, no. 17 (Autumn 1984), p. 11.

44 'Becoming Visible: Black Lesbian Discussions: Carmen, Gail, Shaila and Pratibha', in *Many Voices, One Chant*, p. 54.

45 Rigoberta Menchú, *I, Rigoberta Menchú . . .* (London, Verso, 1984).

4

On Genre Fiction

Not that I mistook fictional heroines for real women; the situations I was most affected by are those which seemed most like what would have happened in real life.

Anna Livia, *Gossip*, no. 5

When the book ends, exactly as you predicted and just as you wished, the satisfaction and the pleasure which you, the reader, have desired and enjoyed is as erotic as the first anticipated kiss and as comforting as an itch scratched. But for you, the writer who chooses a genre that is strongly marked by a traditional array of necessary motifs, characters, plots, locations and emotions, the conventions become a corset that is both supportive and confining. For the writer of genre fiction is bound to the reader's expectations – either to satisfy or subvert them. Of course, the best writing within any conventional form, be it the thriller, the science-fiction adventure, the horror story or the romance, does both. For genre raises the question of codes and patterns; patterns of plot, feeling, character. If the writing is to be successful the pattern must be suggested, even if it is to be shattered. What price then, can we put upon originality in this context? An original piece of writing will surely make the conventional gestures, begin the dance, convince us that we will not be disappointed, wherever we are taken on the journey as we read. Originality will consist in a clever use of form rather than the abandoning, the breaking open of the form itself.

But hard questions arise immediately. Does the patterning necessary within the form determine what the text must eventually mean? Is the thriller or detective story, doggedly committed to answering all the questions raised by the plot – who did it and why – inherently conservative? Can a romantic novel in which the woman eventually sinks into the tweed-jacketed, fur-lined or taut-leathered breast of the taller, older, richer man be anything other than a capitulation to the very structures feminist women set out to challenge and subvert – and which for Lesbian women constitute nothing less than a complete denial of identity? Yet here is the curious fact: women write genre fiction. Indeed, they are immensely successful at it. The early Gothic romances in the eighteenth century were written predominantly by women. The readership was also largely female. The most enduring science-fiction myth of all was a woman's myth, Mary Shelley's *Frankenstein* (1818). The romance is apparently a woman's form, written by women for women: Georgette Heyer, Catherine Cookson, Mary Stewart, Barbara Cartland and a flowering host of authoresses who write for Mills and Boon are all in the business of constructing men as the objects of woman's desire. Murder is also a woman's profession: Agatha Christie, Dorothy L. Sayers, Patricia Highsmith, P. D. James have all made it a very profitable one.

Science fiction, traditionally a form of writing dominated by men, is especially vulnerable to feminist infiltration and expropriation, for reasons inherent in the form. Sarah Lefanu points out that 'Unlike other forms of genre writing, such as detective stories and romances, which demand the reinstatement of order and thus can be described as "closed" texts, science fiction is by its nature interrogative, open. Feminism questions a given order in political terms, while science fiction questions its imaginative terms.'[1] I agree. The potential is certainly there.

The original thriller, indeed, perhaps the original psychological narrative itself is Sophocles' *Oedipus Rex*, the story of a man who murders his father and marries his mother.[2] Oedipus is both the murderer and the detective within an action that is beyond his control and has been determined by the gods. Thebes cannot be free from plague until the murderer of King Laius is brought to justice. The audience knows, of course, that it is Oedipus the King himself who is the curse and pollution upon the city; so the drama's suspense centres entirely upon the inevitable unravelling of his own crime by the criminal. And his deed remains a crime despite the fact that it was unknowingly committed. Oedipus is also his own judge. He chooses blinding and exile. Jocasta, his mother and his wife, hangs herself. Notice that it is the woman who ends up dead. Oedipus lives to become a repentant saint in a later play, *Oedipus at Colonnus*, able to offer interesting reflections on the justice of the gods. The weakness in detective stories is usually the motive. In *Oedipus Rex* there is no motive. The murder and the resulting incest were all a ghastly mistake and the retribution which follows puts radically in question the metaphysical order of a world where the gods kills us for their sport. There is therefore a theological dimension to the play – and to the story of Oedipus – which concerns fate, justice and the very possibility of free will. But these arguments and debates, which are disputed by the Chorus, are intrinsic to the dynamic of the plot. The oracle has determined the destiny of the main actors: we simply watch the impersonal will of the gods executed in destruction. The gods wrote the plot.

Now, detective stories are not realistic narratives about crimes. They are geometric puzzles which the reader is challenged to solve. They are texts with hidden signs, disguised meanings, at once duplicitous and self-subverting. No one in a good detective thriller should ever turn out to be quite what they seem. Authority, in the form of the police, is often deliberately set aside. The law rarely appears until justice has already been done. The finest detectives are usually amateurs. But they must be honest.[3] Raymond Chandler, in an essay on his own craft, describes the detective as a man of honour. 'But down these mean streets a man must go who is not himself mean ... I am quite sure he would not spoil a Virgin.'[4] Indeed? But what happens when the detective is a woman? The metaphysical debate on the destiny of human beings and the justice of the gods is the central theme in *Oedipus Rex*. An abstract idea governs the plot. But this is not usually the case with the detective story or the spy thriller. The mechanics of the plot are central. We read on to see how rather than why the narrative develops. A complex drama of ideas is not usually critical to the structure of the narrative.

Many detective writers make intellectual claims for themselves by using one character as a coat-hanger for their reflections concerning everything from philosophy to food. Dorothy L. Sayers made Lord Peter Wimsey a vehicle for her 'incidental dissertations'.[5] John le Carré's spymaster, George Smiley, has a passion for German Romantic poetry. P. D. James's Adam Dalgliesh actually is a famous poet, and all the people he investigates have heard of him.[6] But in all these cases it is a single character, rather than the form, which carries the burden of ideas. Feminist writers are trying to re-create and re-write the detective thriller as a form within which to argue politics and ideas, albeit not quite in the manner of Sophocles.

The codes of detective fiction are usually conservative and secure. We expect to be told who was in fact good or bad. The wicked and the guilty might get away with it; but we know who they are. Barbara Wilson's *Murder in the Collective* uses the traditional detective narrative as a vehicle for her discussion of two contemporary issues: American imperialism in the Philippines during the Marcos regime; and the split between the mixed left and the autonomous Lesbian movement.[7] The pacing of the tale, the twists of the plot, the necessary shifting finger of suspicion, are executed in the traditional fashion, with energy and verve. Objects are important: earrings, car keys, contact lenses. Mistaken identities are significant. But a peculiar set of difficulties emerges. Two kinds of murder are described in the book. First there is the usual corpse, found early on, a member of the mixed left printing collective, discovered neatly murdered in the darkroom. This is an individual murder committed in secret by person or persons unknown. Second, there are other murders, accompanied by torture, humiliation, castration, openly practised by the former totalitarian government of the Philippines.[8] This is murder sanctioned by the state. The first takes place within the codes of distinct literary genre; the second stands out, raw and unforgiven. 'He was tortured, his body was found . . . no, it's awful. Benny, he couldn't believe it. He went around like a crazy man, he wanted to go there and murder Marcos personally. Such a waste, Pam, to think of Amado killed like a dog and thrown out on a pile' (p. 92). Marcos was a real dictator who liquidated his opponents. Wilson's point is clear. Outside the fiction there is real murder – like that of Amado – in a real world. But few genres could be less realistic than the detective novel. So Wilson adds at the end of the novel a bibliography of information concerning the Philippines liberation struggle. She has been arguing a political case; she suggests that we put down her book, which should by the time we have finished it have ceased to be comfortable fiction, and read the truth about the politics of imperialism and torture. Her text is subordinate to other texts – and to political action.

I have no objection to this strategy; but it is surprising that it did not lead the author to cast a more critical eye at the politics of her fictional text: especially if the key issues are to be ones as sensitive as racism and Lesbian separatism. Two of the mixed collective are women of Colour. 'June was black, twenty-three, widowed with two children . . . ' (p. 8). That is, at first, all the information we

are given about June. Then she is arrested on suspicion of murder and we are
told something else, which was withheld previously by both the writer and the
narrator. 'She grew up in Seattle, went to Garfield High and got married right
after. To a nice guy, I guess, a really nice guy. But he was shot, in one of those
weird freak accidents. June says a bunch of them were fooling around, they
were still teenagers, someone had an "unloaded" gun and somehow it went off.
I think June was holding it, though she's never been able to say it' (p. 48). White
racism constructs Blackwomen as passionate; if necessary, murderous. We all
know this, and June points it out. 'They gave me a Black cop, see. Get the truth
out of me. Someone from my own "culture", knows about us Black girls'
murderous instincts' (p. 65). But the problem is that, in Wilson's text, the two
white women are central, they are the detectives, and the Blackwomen are the
murderers. The stereotypes are held up for inspection, then endorsed. There
are two interlocking fictional crimes, the murder of a man and the wrecking of a
printshop. The women accused are the women who did it; the Blackwomen and
the Lesbians.

When the Lesbians muscle their way into the book they are huge, husky and
hairy. 'Fran . . . looked every inch the traditional dyke, with her flannel sleeves
rolled up, her big, unbound breasts propped up on her full stomach . . . she had
a droplet of beer in the faint dark moustache over her full well-formed lips'
(p. 32). Fran is an alcoholic. Statistically this is likely. The figures for
alcoholism among Lesbians are staggering: 'The statistics are: 38% alcoholic,
30% problem drinkers. For a lesbian these statistics mean you either are one,
or you love one.'[9] But there are good and sad reasons why a woman who tries to
live as a Lesbian in a heterosexist society, which at best treats her as an
unnatural pervert and at worst advocates her liquidation, should take to the
bottle. And Wilson never analyses why Fran drinks.

Our heroine, Pam, falls for the long-limbed Texas dyke who is strong, silent,
tall as a man and adept at softball. She also has an androgynous name, Hadley.
'She was all legs, almost hipless, with wide strong shoulders and elegant
collarbones . . . ' (p. 27). And the seduction on the disco dance floor is acted out
within the codes of heterosexual romance. 'She bent her head so that her breath
touched my ear, but she didn't say anything. My knees were going a bit
weak . . . ' (p. 101). Hadley is the acceptable face of Lesbianism, the nearest
equivalent to Prince Charming without the penis: older, more experienced,
bony and with enormous feet.

There is a fusillade of anti-Lesbianism towards the end of the book. Wilson
uses one of the Lesbians as her mouthpiece.

> But I'll tell you, Pam, I've seen more fucked-up women who are lesbians and even
> more who are lesbian-feminists. They're jealous, they gossip and lie, they're
> promiscuous, they drink, they fight, they hurt people, they don't live out any
> feminist ideals in their own lives, they think they can judge everyone but
> themselves. They're nothing but goddamn hypocritical bitches . . . (p. 162).

. . . and so on. Across several pages Lesbians are denounced with prophetic
zeal. Lesbian feminists, so it seems, would clearly be wise to forget all about it,

find a good man to take them in hand and settle down. But this is one of the classic sexist tactics of male writing – to show women glorying in their own self-hatred; to write our minds, voices, bodies, into a discourse which confirms every venomous cliché ever used against us. Wilson is writing Lesbians into a heterosexual discourse which has a long tradition of sick and sorry perverts moaning jealous violence and self-recrimination. And because that is the dominant discourse the passage above cannot be read as ironic, however it was intended.

Intriguingly, alcoholic Fran surprises us all by transforming herself into an image of middle-class respectability. The description of Fran's flat clears her of suspected murder. 'An old Persian carpet on the polished wooden floor; an enormous stereo set-up, framed photographs and several original paintings; fresh flowers on the table. I'd expected clutter; there was none; had been sure I'd find a revealing lack of taste – plastic, velour, lesbian kitsch. Nothing like that' (p. 169). But what has been revealed by all this excellent taste? No woman who has a Persian carpet and polishes the floorboards could possibly be a murderer? Elena, on the other hand, who lives in a 'ramshackle' house – 'the tar-like shingles were peeling off the outer walls at a great rate, the porch was rotting underneath and the door had ominous black scorches along one side' (p. 75) – clearly could be violent. After all, she sags in her 'plastic kitchen chair' (p. 76), and plastic seems to be a conclusively significant material.[10] The message coded in the décor is clear: once we whites, Lesbian or otherwise, slither away from middle-class standards nearly everything is possible. Not murder, however; we leave that to the Blackwomen.

The two Blackwomen in the narrative are both involved with the man who ends up as the corpse. On a midnight raid into his flat our heroine detectives, Pam and Hadley, discover piles of pornography under the bed. No woman would weep for his loss. The other man in the collective does: the weeping is to his credit, even if the object of sorrow is undeserving. But the true facts of Jeremy's iniquity do leave the Blackwomen oddly exposed. Were they not sharp enough to see through him? As Hadley comments pityingly, 'Poor June'. All this amounts to a sort of textual tactlessness. It is neither good sense nor good politics to present Blackwomen as killers and Lesbians as alcoholic monsters in a world which assumes we are like that anyway. But at least in most feminist thrillers, unlike *Oedipus Rex*, it is the men who end up dead.

Is it a crime for a woman to kill a man in self-defence when the world we inhabit has transformed violence against women into an unremarkable institution? Valerie Miner's *Murder in the English Department* takes up that question within the conventions of the university novel.[11] The university or campus novel is an interesting phenomenon. It is set within a small, self-enclosed, self-preoccupied community, and is usually spattered with literary or philosophical references, coterie academic characters, faculty politics and jolly in-jokes. The genre is largely addressed to the audience it describes. The best-known British practitioners are men – David Lodge (*Changing Places*, 1975) and Malcolm Bradbury (*The History Man*, also 1975) – and the seduction and exploitation of female students by male academics is a critical element in the plots. Miner's central character is a woman professor involved in a campaign against sexual harassment. Nan is in opposition within every space she inhabits: in the academy, with her family, even alone in her car. 'Sometimes Nan worried about this habit of talking to her car. . . . And if a cop pulled her over? Well, she could always say she was taping a lecture on the cassette recorder. Nan had it all figured out . . . ' (p. 2). This is not the thinking of a paranoid obsessive; Nan is critically at risk. She is up for tenure, and her sexual politics are regarded with suspicion by her colleagues. She is casually and constantly bullied by the wicked Angus Murchie, the most overt misogynist in her department. She turns up early for meetings: 'Another survival tactic: you get there first and watch the adversary walk in' (p. 67). And that is what it's all about: survival.

The two communities within the book are the university and the family. Both are patriarchal institutions. Nan's petit-bourgeois lower-middle-class home, Hayward, to which she constantly returns, is a nightmare world of jellybean yellow ranch houses, pumpkin pie, synthetic fibres and eggnog.[12] Her women relatives are obsessed 'with their interior decorating and their plans for children' (p. 15). Both Nan and the reader are constructed as middle-class. We are expected to understand and share Nan's discomfort when confronted with all this bad taste. We are expected to recognize and appreciate all the literary references. Class politics take an unnerving turn at the moment when sexual harassment on campus and the sexist struggle within the family come together, because the encounter exposes Nan's sister Shirley and her appalling husband Joe as bigoted, inconsiderate and stupid. Their daughter Lisa is embattled, fighting to get out of the conventional roles and expectations forced upon her. Her only hope is to follow Nan's example and educate herself. She develops a mystery disease, her body registering the protest. Her father orders her to stay home. ' "But what'll I do, Dad, sitting home all day?" "You'll be with your family," he said, "where we can keep an eye on you. Don't you remember that a man was murdered on the same floor where your poor aunt has to work? That place is dangerous, Lisa, especially for a delicate girl" ' (p. 95). But another apparently delicate girl stabbed a professor to death when he was trying to rape her. For the women, the family and the university are equally dangerous places. Joe harasses his sister-in-law with impunity. 'Joe had managed a grope along Nan's back to determine if she were wearing a bra. An old trick of his' (p. 17). His daughter, caged, frustrated, becomes seriously ill. The three women central to the text are critically unalike. Nan is the lower-class *arriviste*, who has successfully risen to teach women's writing as a university professor. Shirley remains a Hayward housewife. Marjorie, the murderer, is a rich princess, an upper-class intellectual, a performer who plays with disguise. She is equally at home in each fantastic set of clothes. But all three women are forced to play parts, as women who conform to the rules of patriarchy in any way are always forced to do. Marjorie's costumes simply make the game of role-playing utterly explicit.

In contrast to most thrillers, here we know both the murderer and the motive. The point at issue is a question of silence: Nan's silence. She knows why Marjorie killed Angus Murchie; her violence was a response to attempted rape. Understanding this, Nan becomes her accomplice, and refuses to speak. The political structure of Miner's novel is startlingly similar to that of Marlene

Gorres' film *A Question of Silence,* although Gorres makes the problem of motive central. The witnesses to the murder of a man, the other women in the shop, refuse to come forward. Nan protects Marjorie simply because she is another woman, and all women live with rape and the threat of rape. Her silence is heroic. Marjorie's silence is not judged. This is a learning silence. She was not a feminist. She refused to support the campaign against sexual harassment on the grounds that 'a girl [sic] learns to avoid certain situations . . . Besides, the "victim" in some cases might be the male professor unjustly accused' (p. 20).[13] This calm assertion masks an abyss of self-hatred. Who manipulates and creates the situations we should learn to avoid? Are not those 'situations' bound up with the deliberate *intimidation* of women by men? By men who stand to lose power, position, authority and status if women move freely in the public world, define their own sexuality and earn their own (equal) wages? Sexual harassment is one end of a sliding scale of violence against women which begins with sexy jokes, comments about clothes and leering looks and ends with rape. Campaigning against sexual harassment is about redefining male sexuality and heterosexual exchange. In the case of male professors and women students sexual threat is a violent abuse of power and breach of trust, however flattered and willing the women student may have appeared to be. The sexual politics of *Murder in the English Department* are quite explicit. Marjorie Adams learns the hard way.

Angus Murchie does not live to learn and makes a quite disgusting corpse. 'For the first time, she noticed that his pants were down around his thighs. His penis looked like a purple magic marker . . . Momentarily she contemplated whether murder would be the perfect climax to every rape' (p. 45). Nan's wonderful reflection illuminates the moment; in violent pornography the rape and murder of the woman jointly form the climax. Here the man, killed by the woman, lies dead at her feet.

But can the genre of murder mystery contain this dangerous material? Well, not altogether. Nan protects Marjorie and goes to prison; the resolution comes during the trial scene when Marjorie reappears and speaks her confession, not to the patriarchal court, but directly to Nan. ' "I killed Angus Murchie," Marjorie was speaking directly to Nan, "while he was trying to rape me" ' (p. 145). Trial scenes are necessarily confrontational and intrinsically dramatic. They usually work in one of two ways. Either we do not understand all the evidence which is being developed in the text, so that we are ranged alongside detective, jury, lawyer and judge, knowing that when we have resolved the plot of the novel we will also have resolved the mystery. In this case the writer/narrator and the reader are on different sides. The writer has information which she withholds. Or, as in *Murder in the English Department*, we are the murderer's accomplice, alongside the narrator. This utterly transforms the nature of our relation, as the reader, to social justice, to the police, authority, prison. We too are outside the law.

Both *Murder in the English Department* and *Murder in the Collective* treat the social structures of authority with cynicism and suspicion. The prison in Miner's novel is full of Blacks and Chicanas. Against this realistic assessment of racist white justice the conclusion of the book is alarmingly utopian. 'Judge

Marie Wong ruled that rape is an act of such physical violence that it warrants substantial use of force in self defence' (p. 166). The judge is a woman, a woman of Colour at that, and she sides with other women: Marjorie goes free; Nan stops worrying about her tenure and drives off into the dawn. But whoever argued that detective fiction was anything other than fantastical? What is truly radical about this novel is the way in which the women stick together, across all their divisions. Judy Milligan the whore and Nan Weaver the professor share a cell and become friends. Nan's family, led by her sister, believe in her unconditionally. And Nan's reason for shielding her student is subversive simplicity itself. 'She was another woman . . . she needed help. You should understand that' (p. 148). Well yes, I do, because she speaks from the core of radical feminism.

Both books refer to the genre within which they are written with cautious self-consciousness. Hadley, at the end of *Murder in the Collective*, comments: 'Somehow I always thought that the solution of the case would hinge on you and Penny being twins . . . It never even came up' (p. 179). Nan's niece Lisa realizes that Marjorie must be the missing piece of the story by listening both to Nan's silences and the silences in the text.

> 'Nan, you used to talk about her all the time.'
> 'Did I?'
> 'Sure, you were always going on about her clothes and how smart she was. I guess I was even a little jealous.'
> 'Oh, Lisa.'
> 'And then all of a sudden you stopped talking about her. Right after the murder.'
> 'Sherlock Holmes,' said Nan.
> 'Nope. Agatha Christie,' said Lisa. 'I read ten of her novels when I was home . . . ' (p. 155).

And the other unspoken thread in the text, the Lesbian silence, is of course Nan's attachment to Marjorie, of which even Nan herself is largely unaware.

Detective fiction is, on the whole, written within a naturalistic mode, however fantastical the plots. This has implications for a writer who describes violence against women, and may explain Miner's implausibly optimistic conclusion. Miner does not want to reinforce women's status as victims, both of individual violence by men and of the institutional violence of the patriarchal state, by writing yet another book within which the aspirations and energy of women are crushed by force. But it is extremely unlikely, however much sense it makes to kill a man in a self-defence,[14] that Marjorie Adams would ever have been exonerated and set free.

Violence of some kind there must be in this fiction. The corpse is crucial. The plots may be unlikely, the social and physical setting need not be. Two thrillers sporting women detectives which use the verismo settings of the 1980s, the glooms of recession, cuts, racism, political unrest and decayed urban misery, as a presence in the fiction are Mary Wings' *She Came too Late*, set in Reagan's Boston, and Gillian Slovo's *Death by Analysis*, set in the London of 1981, the year of the Royal Wedding and the inner-city riots.[15] Wings' novel addresses the politics of the women's community directly. Our present situation is bleak, and rapidly getting worse. 'Our city was a sinking ship, women and children going down first' (p. 4). Women will now do more or less anything, even kill other women, for continuing funds. Wings gets round the problem of power differentials and violence against women by turning everyone into Lesbians: two of the corpses, the murderer and the investigating detective. The book is in the mean-streets-and-tough-talkin'-guys mould: first-person narrative, short sentences and plenty of strong verbs. Some of the one-liners are arresting: 'Rumour had it that she was celibate, but her convent training made me suspicious of that' (p. 5). 'Dyke reality promises heaven between the sheets and struggle on the streets' (p. 39). Wings is sharp on the institutional racism of fiction. She describes one woman as white, not often done, because we are all assumed to be white unless described otherwise, and she withholds the fact that the detective heroine's best friend is Black until the last time we meet her: 'Jonell is the darkest black person I know. I am always shocked by how white and lifeless my skin looks next to hers' (p. 168). The central political issues, critical to the plot, are the new reproductive technologies; the fictional triumph is parthenogenesis or, as the heroine's lover puts it, in drunken joy, 'Lesbian frogs' (p. 186). But Wings does not try to use the form of detective fiction in innovative ways. And, as always, the weakness is the motive. Personal ambition never seems to me enough of a reason to commit murder. But I am probably being very naïve.

There is a lost opportunity lurking in the text of Slovo's *Death by Analysis*. The theme of psychoanalysis is important in feminist theory; Oedipus provides the link, for solving a mystery in the manner of detective fiction is precisely what psychoanalysis is about. Freud's case studies read like detective novels. Finding out who did it and to whom involves asking awkward and unavoidable questions, establishing a motive or motives, digging up a lot of raw emotion which the protagonists would rather keep buried, and coming upon a revelation which is also a resolution. Black politics are central to the book. And the Black West Indian community is all too firmly gripped by the class struggle to bother with therapists at all. Only the whites sit around contemplating their childhoods and their phobias; the Blacks are too busy confronting the police and fighting to survive in racist Britain. We are given some gripping sessions with the therapist which make the power relations inherent in these encounters appallingly explicit. I emerged from these passages convinced that political action was the answer to therapy.[16] But Slovo does not exploit the potential metaphor of psychoanalysis and detective fiction. Instead, the real argument of the novel, which surfaces intermittently like a ghostly thread, is the contrast between the 1960s and the 1980s. The women's liberation movement is oddly absent and implictly dismissed. Whatever happened to the revolutionaries of 1968? Well, most of them played safe and signed up for middle-class security. But one of them works in a women's refuge. This is a handsome, clean, freshly painted 'monster house', and, amazingly, it is presented as a soft option.

' . . . I enjoy it, living with women and kids, sharing each other's experience.'
'Is it really enough,' I asked, 'restricted to your small niche?'

'It's what I've got,' she said. 'Sometimes the world gets too large. Even to be contented is an achievement.' (p. 120)

Now, the women's movement did change the world, but not along the lines prescribed by a definition of politics which only includes class struggle and violent revolution. Slovo's women's refuge sounds like a well-heeled holiday home with added sunshine, cheerful children and healthy salads. Perhaps I move in the wrong circles, but the only kind of women's refuges I have ever encountered were overcrowded, underfunded and hunted out by murderous men. No one ever thought that this was the soft side of politics. It felt like the bloodiest raw edge. Feminism has had an effect, however. The men are less confident. 'The changes feminism had wrought had only further twisted their insecurities. Ten years ago they would have felt safe at least in their own homes. Now even their personal conduct was up for examination' (p. 95). There is one other encouraging detail. The heroine is so absorbed by her detective work that her love affair falls to pieces. It is her male lover Sam who is concerned with their relationship and with building nests. There is at least hope for her feminist future.

The current flowering of crime writing by women has produced some good stories, but they are not necessarily feminist in either intention or execution. Hannah Wakefield's *The Price You Pay* is a fluent, gripping political escapade, but a few references to sexism, women's issues, a sturdy woman sleuth and one comment on the women's movement do not add up to a feminist novel.

> '...And they let me cover the woman's issues.' She smiled. 'In their system – which I'm ashamed to say was mine as well when I started – the women's movement isn't "political". It's classed as "human interest" and isn't considered in the slightest threatening to the established order. Isn't that pompous? Do you believe it?'[17]

Well, on reading Hannah Wakefield I'm afraid I do. *The Price You Pay* is an excellent conventional thriller reproducing all the innate conservatism of the form. As a residual left-winger I enjoyed being told that the USA was more or less run by the CIA; that Castro and Allende were good guys and that, had they been left to get on with it, they would have turned Cuba and Chile respectively into a socialist paradise. The simplicities of crime writing always work against the complexities of feminism. Woman, within patriarchal sign systems, stands for duplicity, treachery, betrayal and emotional instability. And so she does in *The Price You Pay*. The woman, who ends up as one of the corpses, is duped by the CIA into being one of their agents, but is constantly torn by her gut reactions whenever she is confronted with fine, honest, upright socialists. She changes sides, chooses goodness, justice and dissidence and is therefore saved just before she ends up dead. The wages of sin is always death in conventional crime fiction. In *The Price You Pay* the detective-solicitor runs a women-only law firm; but that really is an incidental detail we can forget all about. We are back on the high road of patriarchal forms and discourses; the feminist clues lead nowhere.

All the women's presses, in the last days of the 1980s and on into the 1990s, have been engaged in promoting women's genre fiction because the combination of feminist textual noises and a brisk escapist read sells extremely well. It is clear from what I have written here that I am not a convert to this kind of writing, although I respect the enterprise of women who wish to subvert and explode genre fiction.[18] Lesbian crime fiction is, necessarily, more subversive, because the insertion of Lesbian meanings into any kind of genre fiction disrupts the heterosexist codes of desire. In her second Pam Nilson thriller, *Sisters of the Road*, Barbara Wilson challenges the authority and power of the detective in relation to the victims of crime, who are usually duped, ignorant or dead.[19] The final scene, where the detective is brutally raped by the murderer, has been criticized for re-inscribing women's vulnerability to male violence into fictional forms, and thereby disrupting the utopian pleasure of reading about superwoman detectives. The scene is shocking. It is intended to be. And afterwards it is the young prostitute, supposedly the victim, who comforts the detective. The power balance shifts. The form of the genre breaks down. And we are reading a new kind of political fiction: feminist fiction – where everything still remains to be said.[20]

Wilson has been one of the women saying it. Her most recent work, *The Dog Collar Murders* and *Cows and Horses*, continues this development. *The Dog Collar Murders* has a skeleton murder mystery which dissolves into detailed feminist discussion. Some readers do not like this: I do. *Cows and Horses* is a less polemical fiction, a return to the small-scale realist mode dealing with work, love, sex and friendship in an elegantly written winter setting. Understated and thoughtful in the prose and the characters, the book was accused of being a text in which nothing happens by the reviewer in *Gay Scotland*. Must Lesbian fiction have action? Perhaps we have lost interest in fiction where women feel, rather than do.

Imagine a world where a woman could take 'a walk at night under the stars. She imagined herself ambling down a country road and feeling only mild curiosity when she saw three men coming toward her. She imagined hitching a ride with anyone willing to give her a ride. She imagined answering the door without fear, to see if anyone needed help . . . '[21] Marge Piercy's dreamer, Connie Ramos, the *Woman on the Edge of Time*, imagines utopia, a world where women would live free from the violence of men. Utopia – Thomas More's imaginary world which has given its name to a whole genre of writing – began life as a Greek joke. The name means both the good place, $\epsilon\bar{\upsilon}/\tau o\pi o\varsigma$, the ideal world, and $\bar{\upsilon}/\tau o\pi o\varsigma$, nowhere; it doesn't exist. Twentieth-century versions of imaginary futures or other worlds, written by men, have usually been the substance of nightmare: Golding's *Lord of the Flies*, Orwell's *1984* and Huxley's *Brave New World*.[22] In each case the nature of man (*sic*) proves to be too greedy, power-crazed and violent to reconstruct paradise. A utopian vision is a necessary element in all feminist thought. The wild wish of feminism, voiced by Mary Wollstonecraft, to see the distinction of sex confounded in society, is necessarily utopian. And there is a strongly utopian impulse behind the arguments and suggested possibilities for change in feminist theory. To imagine a radically different world for women is to imagine a radically different world.

Shulamith Firestone's *The Dialectic of Sex* offers some 'dangerously utopian' concrete proposals for a society no longer based on the reproduction of the labour force through the nuclear family. But, she complains, 'We haven't even a literary image of this future society.'[23] Firestone goes on to postulate alternatives to love and marriage, alternative households and ground rules for personal politics which would inevitably advance the prospect of radical social change. Mothering surfaces as a critical issue in both the imaginative and the discursive prose which argues for a new way of living and a new world, simply because the fact of our reproductive capacity as women has always been the basis of our exclusion and oppression in a world which sees the fathering of a child as the act of a moment and the imperative to mother a child as a lifetime of commitment and dedication, a profession of caring.[24] Motherhood is at the core of Charlotte Perkins Gilman's early utopian text *Herland*, in which every woman is mother to every child; for Piercy the process of birth is handed over to technology, and mothering, even breast-feeding, is shared between women and men; in Sally Miller Gearhart's *The Wanderground: Stories of the Hill Women* every child has seven mothers.[25]

Utopias always reflect the society which has produced them, and against which they are written, in interesting and significant ways. The secret of happiness in an ideal society is the key to the political meaning of the fiction. For William Morris in *News from Nowhere* (1890) the secret is socialism. For Perkins Gilman, writing during the Great War, the answer is motherhood itself. 'The power of mother-love, that maternal instinct we so highly laud, was theirs of course, raised to its highest power; and a sister-love which . . . we found it hard to credit' (pp. 57–8). Perkins Gilman's notion of mothers is for women only; they reproduce by parthenogenesis which is represented as a spontaneous overwhelming desire to have a child. 'Herland' is perceived through the alien consciousness of three men who visit it. They are alien in every sense, both as men in a women's society and as Old World outsiders in utopia. The novelist plays games with their – and the reader's – expectations. But she also polarizes her readership along the sexual divide. A woman reader sees past the men's shoulders. She has an immediate appreciation of the utopian perspective; for the writer is on her side. The text is a joke which excludes the men. They imagine an Amazon utopia of ravishing young women. And indeed the first three they see are young and beautiful; the Amazons of patriarchal cliché. But the women who deal with the intruders are old.

> In all our discussions and speculations we had always unconsciously assumed that the women, whatever else they might be, would be young. Most men do think that way, I fancy.
> 'Women' in the abstract is young, and we assume, charming. As they get older they pass off the stage, somehow, into private ownership mostly, or out of it altogether. But these good ladies were very much on the stage, and yet any one of them might have been a grandmother. (p. 20)

In all feminist utopian writing women grow old, but always with immense strength and dignity. Nobody becomes objectionable, smelly and incontinent. Nobody dribbles.

Marge Piercy's *Woman on the Edge of Time* offers a future world of mixed-sex, small-scale communes, where the power to give birth has been relinquished by the women in exchange for equality with men. The babies are produced by a technological womb, a battery brooder. In Mattapoissett even the men are mothers. But Piercy speaks of the power which women must give up; she does not tell us what privileges the men have ceded. It seems that motherhood becomes an honourable profession as soon as it is open to men.

The structure of Piercy's book is interesting. She moves between the lunatic asylum where her heroine, Connie, is incarcerated and Mattapoisett; she holds the balance between naturalism and science-fiction fantasy, and makes that split the breach between the present world and utopia. Thus all the characters in the lunatic asylum, the appropriate setting for our world, and in utopian Mattapoissett, are counterparts to each other. There are radical implications here, for Connie's imagination is her most potent source of freedom and revenge. She, like every other imprisoned woman, can imagine a better world. And it is precisely this power, the power to think herself free, which the white medicine men seek to control and destroy. But she escapes them and imagines utopia. The problem with Piercy's fiction is the disjunction between the politics of the framing section, Connie's nightmare as a medical guinea-pig in an asylum, and the politics of the ideal utopia. Let me explain. Piercy's message is terrifyingly simple: the future depends on us, all of us, now. She takes as her central focus of consciousness a woman who is at the bottom of the heap, a poor Chicana in a rich white world. Connie is systematically reduced; she loses home, freedom, family, self-respect, and it is as the most powerless and vulnerable of people that she finds her strength. Piercy's text does not reject violence as a means to achieve radical change. Indeed, she argues that violence is the context within which all women are forced to live. Domestic violence opens the book, and from there we watch Connie pitched into the institutional prison violence of the hospital. Connie's first and last acts in the book are violent, and they are both blows struck against men; the men who are firmly and unhesitatingly identified as the sources of coercion and oppression. Piercy's heroine is neither a saint nor a feminist. She survives, rather than lives. But she has a woman's anger, which becomes productive and liberating when it is turned outwards, against the men, and not inwards, upon the self. 'Living in enforced contemplation, she found that clean anger glowing in her still. She hated Geraldo and it was right for her to hate him . . . She had struck out not at herself, not at herself in another, but at Geraldo, the enemy' (pp. 19–20). Connie's final murderous act is justified and endorsed by everyone involved in her conspiracy: the writer, the reader, the text.

The alternative to Connie's resistance is embodied by her niece, Dolly, who perceives her reproductive power as her only manipulative strength. She gets pregnant in order to blackmail her pimp and force him to marry her. The plot fails and he forces her to have an abortion. Dolly is a male-identified woman caught in an economic trap. Geraldo forces her to work as a prostitute; she needs him to protect her from the tricks. And so she accepts the sexual status quo. Women are there to be used by men. 'He is my man . . . What can I do?' (p. 24). The reality of her life, of all woman's lives, is imprisonment; within economic and sexual prisons. Thus the asylum becomes a metaphor for a condition of being. Given the terms of these conditions, the women betray one another. Dolly betrays Connie because she is afraid to speak the truth with her man present, justly fearing the consequences. Language also imprisons Connie. She is not able to define herself against the rest of the world; thus her blind lover, Claude, becomes 'a black handicapped pickpocket', and her daughter becomes 'the abused and neglected child' (p. 26). But, without any theory or analysis, and with precious little support, Connie draws her own conclusions from her own bodily experience, and resists. The framing narrative plays out the realities of our lives with all the savage clarity of a radical feminist tract.

Piercy's utopian future, on the other hand, is a small-scale, socialist co-operative venture, in which we have all learned how to work together. Mattapoissett re-defines the family as tribe. It is a society based on rituals, in which emotions are natural and encouraged, madness is an acceptable way to discover yourself, automation means liberation and work is determined by the natural cycles of the land. The exhausting consultative process of complete democracy is described with optimistic realism. No one owns anybody else; adolescence has been neatly abolished. Everyone has a magnificent ecological awareness, racism does not exist, and a complete unity of purpose has rendered cultural diversity obsolete. Different cultures are, however, artificially main-tained as a picturesque national heritage.

So far, so good. The cracks show – and indeed, it is here that they usually do show – when Piercy argues her utopian sexual politics. The men, who in the framing narrative are, on the whole, murderous egotistical monsters, are now thoughtful, acceptable comrades. Or are they? Jackrabbit appears to be in a perpetual state of erection. And his behaviour towards Connie reads like the crudest form of sexual harassment. Connie's utopian double and guide, Luciente, assures both Connie and the reader that sexuality has been reduced to its proper place; but the civilized form of free love which is the usual practice in this utopia looms large within the narrative. For Piercy, writing in 1976, revolution still really means sexual revolution, and while many other economic and social problems have been solved, sex still fouls up the system. Jackrabbit and Bolivar's 'holi' – a sort of holographic light show of visual images (which, incidentally, sounds horrible to watch) – is justly criticized by Luciente. She sees the struggling male and female figures which resolve into androgynes as an inadequate analysis of the destructive struggle of history. 'I can't see male and female as equally to blame, for one had power and the other was property. Nothing in what you made speaks of that' (p. 211). And, curiously enough, this is the only moment in the Mattapoissett sections of the book where a radical feminist analysis, so cogently argued elsewhere, is allowed to challenge the sexual system.

In utopia the men no longer deny and abuse the women openly. But they still practise the tactics of liberal sexism: ignore, omit, suppress. The power imbalance between the sexes has still not been destroyed. This is particularly evident when Bee gives Connie a night of bliss. The language of heterosexual lovemaking, and indeed the act itself, is, Piercy assures us blandly, 'constant in any time' (p. 187). This is patently untrue. The significance and practice of sexuality differs across cultures and through history. And every heterosexual feminist will surely be disturbed to find that even in utopia the male remains remorselessly in control. Connie is certainly willing, but sex is still something a man does to her. The language of eroticism gives the game away. The male leads, the female collapses: ' . . . was leading her . . . he drew her down . . . Her head fell in (*sic*) . . . he moved up on her and entered her . . . he rode into her.' Bee even re-creates Connie's body: 'He slowly began to build her body out of the dark' (p. 188). Penetrative heterosexual sex has a potentially unpleasant meaning in the history of contemporary sexual relations, for it is not an act performed between equals. The radical feminist analysis which links penetration and rape is obviously not one that Piercy would accept; Bee and Connie's encounter is offered as Paradise Regained. This it may well be; but it is described in a language of cliché which has rightly been criticized as endorsing the sexual subjection of women.

The clichés which surround the delights of heterosexuality are matched by unthinking anti-Lesbianism. Lesbians are defined, in Piercy's text, as primarily sexual beings, nothing else. 'The hospital regarded Sybil as a lesbian. Actually she had no sex life' (p. 85). And Sybil's counterpart in Mattapoissett, the mystical Diana, turns out to be a risky sexual partner. Luciente remembers, ' . . . it was a binding, you know, we obsessed. Not good for growing' (p. 64). Utopian Lesbianism apparently has the effect of reducing women to a state of arrested adolesence. Not that male homosexuality gets a good press either; Bolivar and Jackrabbit also cause trouble by their intensity. Piercy is not concerned with the process of imaginatively re-defining sexual difference. Does she lose her nerve? This may well be the case, for Luciente is first introduced into the text as a man. Connie fears him as a mugger and a lunatic, a fear which vanishes when Luciente indignantly asserts the triumph of biology. 'Of course I'm female' (p. 67). This revelation causes a genuine shift of perception in the reader's understanding of how we read the inscription of gender in the text; but it never happens again. The androgynous persons of Mattapoissett are really women and men underneath. The sexual absolutes remain unchallenged.

Piercy does give us a brief glimpse into an nightmare dystopia where women are physically constructed as grotesque sexual objects, 'a cartoon of femininity' (p. 288). The alternative hell is urban, centrally owned and pornographic. But it is not our inevitable future. We can choose, even the most apparently powerless woman can choose; and that is the most subversively radical truth in *Woman on the Edge of Time*. 'The powerful don't make revolutions' (p. 198).

It is the Earth herself who revolts in Sally Miller Gearhart's *The Wanderground*; and hers is a revolt against male violence and force. The society against which the 'hill women' revolt is uncannily like Piercy's dystopia, an urban hell where women either teeter provocatively on high heels as whores, or become 'breeders': ' . . . a woman had a few options if she'd cooperate. She could keep her senses and be a whore or a wife or she could have a little tinkering done with her brain and be a whore or a wife anyway. If her body was too ugly or too old they could use her for maintenance work' (p. 165). If this sounds unpleasantly close to the present state of affairs, I believe that is Miller Gearhart's intention. For in her fiction the dream of a common language is over, men are irrevocably the enemy and the only survival hope for women is to head for the hills. Here the women discover a new 'connectedness' with Nature and The Earth, who are, conveniently, both female. They develop new concepts to describe this process of connection, both with the earth and with one another: hardself, softself, fallaway, root touch, windriding, first-tellings. Miller Gearhart does not give us a glossary; she simply allows the meanings to evolve from the text. The hill women's society is perceived in its dailiness; it is a women's community, based on consent, not force, and all living or natural things are part of that community. Alaka on a journey receives encouragement from a flotilla of fish and her feet are warmed by a helpful tree. Manaje can only have a kitten if the animal consents. 'I'm told to tell you that Terpsichore brought forth seven kittens. One solid black which will be for your special care if you choose each other' (p. 146). The myth at the core of the hill women's ethic is the story at the centre of the ancient Eleusinian mysteries, the myth of the season's cycle, the myth of Persephone and Demeter. This is, of course, a story of rape in which male force is equated with death, and the union of two women, mother and daughter, is the key to resurrection and the healing of the earth. In Miller Gearhart's version the critical refrain emphasizes the woman's essential liberty to choose. 'Oft will I ask her, but never can I take her if she does not choose to go' (p. 80).

The Wanderground is not a continuous narrative but a spiral of interlocking stories, each of which focuses on one woman's experience, but which relates her to the community of women. The effect is therefore cumulative, presenting the customs, ethics and practices of a women's society in a way which insists on a collective perception and presence rather than isolating single women as heroines of the narrative. Even the women's memories are collective: they live through one another's experiences in the remember rooms. The novel, as a linear narration of events building up to a climax and resolution, might well be regarded as a predominantly phallic form, with one set of characters and events privileged over another. Miller Gearhart's interlocking stories break down this parabola, offering instead a whirlpool of mirroring perspectives.

Motherhood in the Wanderground is a collective enterprise as it is in Piercy's narrative and in Perkins Gilman's *Herland*; but pregnancy still happens in individual wombs. Sisterhood rather than motherhood is the key between women. We are not inhumanly idealized; indeed, the text opens with anger – 'two older sisters who had over visited with each other' are busy quarrelling – but in the Wanderground Lesbian sex appears to present no difficulties whatsoever. Nobody's passion or lust proves uncontrollable, nobody gets jealous. In fact, the erotic becomes interestingly diffuse. Clana's encounter with the snake is an orgasmic communion. Blase, Huntsblood, the big cat and the pine tree finish singing in the language of completed sensual love. 'The singing faded softly into rhythms. The rhythms seemed to resonate for a long parting time . . . there were two figures, one far larger than the other, but both locked in the sweeping embrace of a gently swaying pine.' (pp. 81–2).

The Wanderground is a women's society that is not at peace, but still in the process of becoming. The women live under threat from the men who still possess the cities, just as Piercy's Mattapoissett is threatened by a potential future which could rob them of their imagined existence. Both narratives describe, as warnings, the societies against which their ideal worlds are written into being. Both utopias are small-scale, agrarian communities, based on tribal rituals and natural cycles. Miller Gearhart's hill women live close to the earth, without elaborate technology, by choice. 'We can do anything that the old machines could do. And with a good deal less effort' (p. 156). They have, potentially, an enormous power: 'All of them were preparing for the time when it would be possible to gather their power, to direct it, and to confront whatever murderous violence threatened the earth' (p. 133). The inevitable source of that violence would be men; Miller Gearhart presents them to us as callous rapists, brutal murderers, subhuman – not by crude caricature, but simply by presenting the games of sexual politics and the fictional dystopia entirely from a woman's perspective. In one of the escape narratives a woman plays for time, knowing that she cannot hold the men at bay for long, ' . . . walking that thin line between go-to-hell and come-to-bed . . . Just the right proportion of righteous indignation, haughty self-control, pleasant rebuff, and implicit familiarity' (p. 95). Deceit is the necessary weapon of those without power. No woman who walks that thin line can ever win in the long term. Men have no access to women's minds, just as the master has no access to that of the slave. But the outcome of every encounter ultimately depends upon who holds the whip.

In an article on feminism and science fiction, Gwyneth Jones argues against futuristic prophetic writing which envisions the logical consequences of male oppression, ' . . . too many pages dwelling lovingly on the nasty powerful men and the poor helpless women. This is cathartic but dangerous. It is bad magic; reinforcing the models of defeat.'[26] This is, substantially, her objection to *The Wanderground*. Certainly, recitations of our oppressions like a masochistic rosary do not advance The Cause. On the other hand, by no means all women accept that the situation is as bad as it is, let alone as Miller Gearhart imagines it could become. We shut our eyes; to open them is too horrifying. Feminist fiction reaches a broader audience than feminist theory. Women who might not broach Mary Daly's *Gyn/Ecology* might well read *The Wanderground*. In fact, I think that Miller Gearhart's vision of atrocity is cleverly pitched. Every woman will recognize Evona's discomfort in the city bar: 'Men were boasting, women were listening, barmaids were hustling . . . ' (p. 123). Or the restrictions on dress. At one job interview my prospective employer informed me: 'And Miss Duncker, we do not wear trousers.' We didn't. I got the job. In some parts of the world women's dress is prescribed by state law. How much would it take for a police warning to women to stay home at night, or only to go out with a male escort, as in the North of England during the last decade while the Yorkshire Ripper was free and the police were proving themselves significantly unable to catch him, to become a legal curfew against women being outside at night? Rape, and the threat of rape, is already a form of social control. Peter Sutcliffe became a media star not only because he conformed to the sex-beast-loose-in-the-dark stereotype, but because he articulated a hatred towards women which our society does not in fact condemn.[27] We are not usually battered and attacked by strangers in the night, but by the men we love. Most women attacked and raped are assaulted by men known to them. Here is Miller

Gearhart: '. . . state laws were being revised to require every woman to be married . . . curfews on women went into effect early. Any woman caught wearing pants went to a behaviour modification unit; she emerged wearing a dress and a very scary vacant smile' (p. 165). She has simply taken present reality one more step along the way. Her strategy is simple. By imagining what could happen she forces us to recognize what is happening. This is not a self-indulgent litany of horror but political analysis and feminist polemic, a simple unfettering of the radical imagination.

The politics of Miller Gearhart's text are those of ecological radical Lesbian feminism; the women's strength lies in 'their common knowing' (p. 133). Men, even the ones without the whips (called the Gentles), are outside this knowing and irrevocably alien. It is not explicitly stated that the Gentles represent Gay men; but they are men who have refused to exploit and oppress women and who struggle to become close to one another. This is not easy. 'Somehow men – even Gentles – found it difficult or impossible really to share power' (p. 124). Yet without the Gentles it would be impossible for the women to maintain their watch in the cities. In the section called 'Meeting the Gentles' it is the politics of separatism or co-operation that are at issue. This story in the book makes painful and interesting reading. The confrontation takes place in a courtroom. The two sides, the women and the Gentles, argue their case; the reader is the judge. We choose. The Gentles manage to communicate telepathically with one another only when they arrange themselves in a phallic line. They cannot encircle and embrace other beings, only force themselves invasively outwards. Their language of hopeful conquest and speculative capitalism gives them away: 'If only we can develop it . . . ' (p. 193). Despite the women's anxiety and fear the men still talk the language of chivalry and force. 'You have to trust us now lady. You may sicken at that thought, but you've got no choice' (p. 195). The precarious security of the hill women is demonstrated to be fragile, under constant threat. Indeed, women and men are frighteningly polarized by this text.

The suggestion that the hill women have natural powers of connection with each other and with the earth is problematic. Women, in Miller Gearhart's fiction, represent spontaneous feeling, sympathy; men represent order, discipline, control. 'Evona sensed behind his small dark eyes an openness that was practised and disciplined – not a gift of nature, but the product of some painful growth' (p. 184). I am not at ease with the notions of women's natural superiority or men's innate brutality. I would agree with her that men are every bit as brutal as she says they are; but they are monsters because they benefit from being so and because they choose to be so. They could choose to be otherwise. If we subscribe to the potential reality of Miller Gearhart's *Wanderground* thesis, '. . . women and men cannot yet, may not ever, love one another without violence; they are no longer of the same species' (p. 125), then we are all doomed. For women are not naturally in touch with one another, as her own text demonstrates; the city whore runs screaming to her death when she recognizes the hill woman, yelling, 'A dyke! A dyke!' (p. 70). The struggle to build a common political consciousness is, in my experience, precisely that, a struggle. We cannot hope for a natural common mindstretch. We need instead an uncompromising feminism which puts women first. And that too is always 'the product of some painful growth'.[28]

That the Earth herself should intervene on our behalf and fight for women is, however, a most engaging idea. But we should not assume that Gaia is a Lesbian spirit. In Jane Palmer's science-fiction comedy *The Planet Dweller*, a sensual erotic planet called Moosevan, covered in a lavishly seductive vegetation, falls for a dotty Russian scientist. Moosevan embodies a barrage of undulating heterosexist clichés; she is an 'obstructive, temperamental creature' given to moods.[29] She tempts the bewitched Yuri into escaping from his scientist wife, an autocratic, bad-tempered shrew, and into all kinds of pornographic speculations. 'Perhaps Moosevan was like the sea, fluid and reshaping. Perhaps she was like the sand he lay on, soft, warm and yielding.' Moosevan panders to male fantasy. ' "I like your touch . . . " whispered Moosevan, "You are not like anything I have touched before" ' (p. 92). And she does not much like other women. When Diana, who is also trying to save the brooding planet from extinction, arrives on the surface Moosevan ladders her tights in three different places. 'No perfumed blanket of ardour for her, just an efficient snatch into emptiness and a sudden jolt as she landed' (p. 95). Palmer's text is, of course, a joke. The real woman are independent, unsentimental and middle-aged. If men have erotic fantasies of infinitely yielding women they will have to take to space travel.

Science fiction, broadly interpreted as an inclusive genre which covers aliens landing in the back garden, fantasies of technological futures, stories of worlds after nuclear holocaust and 'what if . . . ' tales, is enjoying something of a renaissance in feminist writing in all these variations. Some of the problems which emerge in this kind of writing are evident in Palmer's *The Planet Dweller*. The women writing do not seem able to contemplate non-individual subjective perception or non-human emotions. This results in a peculiarly conservative imaginative construction of other worlds. All Palmer's colourful aliens are in fact bourgeois individuals, with the seven deadly sins, especially greed and lust, all healthy and intact. The toes, tusks, splay feet and tails worn by the aliens are carnival costumes, easily changed at the writer's will.[30] In *The Planet Dweller* many of the old oppositions go unquestioned – for example, the split between Nature and Technology. 'Most of them at some time or another had resorted to genetic engineering to preserve themselves from extinction, and their efforts had produced far less pleasing results than Nature's' (p. 27). Nature (female) is spontaneous, beautiful and pleasing; Technology (male) has never quite caught up. In fact, Palmer's naturalistic style is really the source of the laughs. The creatures from beyond are described in exactly the same tones as the comic English village. The hierarchies in both dimensions reflect each other: the wicked upper-class landlord, keen on hunting and killing, is Mrs Daphne Trotter; her outerspace equivalent is the Mott, 'the multi-footed creature with the dental problem' (p. 50). But this joke wears thin when it appears again and the Olumke are described as 'three individuals with the complexion trouble' (p. 102). I began to wonder whether imagining aliens from outer space might not always be racist, for within most science fiction, even feminist science fiction, The Other From Beyond is always either good or bad, malicious or benevolent – never simply different. Science fiction, like utopian writing, is always addressing a contemporary world, in an oblique rather than a direct fictional mode. Outer-space narratives and encounters with other cultures, planets and races do veer dangerously towards the metaphors of imperialism; for the language of voyages, adventures, struggles and conquest does slide easily into a fictional language which endorses the crudest forms of colonial racism. On the whole, futuristic speculative fiction in which the present is brutally on trial has proved a more fruitful source of radical feminist writing.

There is a traditional utopia/dystopia split which divides the country from the city. It is there in George Orwell's *1984* (1948). London is hell; the country is Paradise Remembered. Miller Gearhart sets utopia in the country; a non-industrial low-tech culture in the woods. Piercy's decentralized rural communes dramatize much the same division: hell is New York. That easy split between the city and the green wilderness[31] becomes more complicated in Anna Livia's first science-fiction novel, *Bulldozer Rising*. Livia's brave band of oldwomen and a few chosen youngwomen are left hurtling into the hinterland as the city explodes behind them. They have mixed feelings. 'Karlin loved the city of glass and water, the beauty of skateboards and traffic; she would not easily have left it for the salad splendour of the countryside.'[32] The salad splendour is second choice and second best. *Bulldozer Rising* articulates an old romance structure: that of the Grail Quest. Three youngwomen, each representing a crucial aspect of the city's high-speed culture, set off into the wilderness on a mission. They are: Ithaca, our heroine, and the city's Ideo Logician, who makes up the reasons for oppressive social structures; Zay, her ex-lover, a high-speed artist on skates; and Scimitel, a tiny little nelly, that is, a woman being trained for sexual service to men, whom Mary Daly would no doubt recognize as a fembot. The journey is of course a psychological reckoning; a dark night of the soul. It contains some of Livia's most sharply visual writing. The landscape around the women is animate, waiting to be perceived. Here, oldwomen have become rockwomen, ancient, eternal, perpetually in process, rock becoming. 'The three youngwomen were surrounded by rock. The hooked noses, cavernous eyes and wrinkled skin were more prominent since Scimitel had grown used to looking at them' (p. 121). In this novel, age becomes a touchstone of value; the most marginal categories, the old, fat, blindwomen, become the most important – eternal, radical, the real revolutionaries. Livia's fiction directly addresses issues which have been under discussion during the period in which she wrote the novel: age, ageing, ageism and the politics of disability. She uses these questions – What happens to old women? Who cares for us when we are old? Is a blind person powerless, dependent? Is fat beautiful? Is an old body desirable? – to interrogate received opinion on these issues.[33] The women who set out on the Quest are young, lithe and lovely; but it is the old women who have all the political answers. The awareness that she is writing against current clichés about old age marks Livia's text as a white western book. In many other, non-western, societies age is greatly respected, honoured, cherished. And this has its dangers; oldwomen in Livia's text are the keepers of the revolution, but in other societies the old have a stranglehold on change, and the power to reinforce the subordination and oppression of women.

Livia's construction of her fiction works best when the new words do not simply correspond to some aspect of our world – as do travelators, Quantums and the northern conduits of the motorways – but actually transform and illuminate our present reality. The divisions in Livia's city, the ideologies of division, re-named and re-defined, did actually have the effect of shifting my consciousness of structures. The Tramontanes, outsiders from the scrub, are treated as an underclass of workers in the city. Some wish to become assimilated into the city, others guard their difference. Through the shift in seeing which Livia offers, the initial impulse to divide and distinguish then appears as exactly what it is: arbitrary tyranny. Zappers and nellies; youngmen, youngwomen; these are new words which became filled with meanings given to them by the encircling fictional structures of Livia's city. And I must say I hope they catch on.

The great advantage of science-fiction writing is, of course, that some things – in Livia's case, the passionate and erotic connection between women – can simply be taken for granted. That Lesbianism should be primary is neither argued for nor constrained by realism. Thus the focus can be entirely upon the conflicts and successes between women. Livia is gloomily pessimistic concerning the possibility of co-operation between groups of women with conflicting interests. The section 'Twenty-fourth Sighting: Songs of Civic Pride' made very painful reading. Here are the mechanics of feminist politics in the process of disintegration. ' "You can't reduce politics to a small group of friends," Desde objected. "I have more faith in the durability of friendship than in an amorphous crowd held together by slogans," said Soren' (p. 159). In the end the politics of survival demand precisely that – a small group of friends, a tiny cell in a hostile world. This does, I think, accurately reflect what has happened to many women who were radicals in the 1960s and 1970s and who have refused to sell out, back down or otherwise make their peace with patriarchy. On the other hand, there are many women coming to radical feminism for the first time now, and their first contact with these ideas might well be through reading a book. I therefore welcome the quite devastating and terrifying description of the Rest Room in Livia's text. This is a sci-fi version of a women's geriatric ward in a hospital, and not far off contemporary realism. I hope that a significant number of nellies and zappers will read it.

Women science-fiction writers, even those who do not specifically identify themselves as feminists, have addressed the issues of sexual politics. Ursula Le Guin's *The Left Hand of Darkness* imagines an arctic world in which members of the indigenous humanoid species, the Gethenians, are 'five-sixths of the time hermaphrodite neuters'.[34] Once a month, echoing the woman's menstrual cycle, they pass into a state called 'kemmer' and become quite uncontrollably sexy. They then transform themselves each into one half of a heterosexual couple. Everyone has the chance to be either a man or a woman, to sire or to conceive a child. But all this is not as revolutionary as it sounds; and the prison of gender, inscribed in our psychic perceptions of each other, was never more dreadfully visible. Conventional sexual roles and characteristics do not disappear, nor do the values attached to them change. The visiting Alien, Genly Ai, our perceiving consciousness, is a man, and a sexist man at that. He views his 'landlady' as a creature with 'fat buttocks that wagged as he walked, and a soft fat face, and a prying, spying, ignoble, kindly nature . . . He was so feminine in looks and manner that I once asked him how many children he had' (pp. 46–7). Whether a human being is constructed as 'he' or 'she' is crucial to our understanding of who they are and how we should treat them. This is no less true of a human sign, a character, constructed in a text. We read them according to the sexual codes. Le Guin gives her game away completely when she argues, through the voice of her visiting alien, that 'Lacking the Karhidish "human pronoun" used for persons in somer, I must say "he", for the same reasons as we used the masculine pronoun in referring to a transcendent god: it is less defined, less specific, than the neuter or the feminine' (p. 85). Unfortunately 'he' proves to be quite specific and defined, both sexually and textually. 'He' means a man. And the Gethenians are all men. Conventional human sexual behaviour is naturalized; there are 'kemmer-houses' – brothels, for orgies – and 'vowing kemmering', which is to all intents and purposes monogamous marriage. Homosexuality is not unknown, but 'If there are exceptions, resulting in kemmer-partners of the same sex, they are so rare as to be ignored' (p. 82). The only other reference to homosexuality is in connection with the Pervert; a human permanently fixed in the masculine role. 'They are not excluded from society, but they are tolerated with some disdain, as homosexuals are in many bisexual societies. The Karhidish slang for them is *half deads*. They are sterile' (pp. 59–60). That homosexuals should be connected with unfortunates who are 'half-dead' and 'sterile' is not a coincidence, but is symptomatic of the sexual politics of the text.

Women's experience is imaginatively appropriated by men; at one point the King of Kerhide gets pregnant, but then he is marginalized. We never see anyone caring for children. Instead a traditional, male notion of politics is made central. The polarities within the text are not the two sexes but the two states, Karhide and Orgoreyn; one is an unstable feudal monarchy and the other is 'a genuine fullblown bureaucracy' (p. 125) ruled by committee and controlled by SARF, the secret police. But exclamations such as 'By Meshe's tits' don't sound all that alien to me, and they reinforce the notion that we are dealing with a race of men. Indeed, the set-piece of the book, an adventure escape across the northern landscape of volcanoes, glaciers and ice flows, recalls the iconography of the Norse sagas where two men fall in love with each other's courage and endurance. It is an existential voyage, and a fine sustained piece of descriptive writing; but the two men, journeying towards one another, form a brotherhood on ice. We, the women, have been written out of the text.

The Left Hand of Darkness demonstrates the necessity for a feminist politics in science-fiction writing. We are there now, the women engaged in writing the women back on to the page. Women's communities and the politics of Lesbian separatism inform the futuristic fiction of many Lesbian writers. In Anna Wilson's 'The Reach', title story in *The Reach and other Stories: Lesbian Feminist Fiction*, the alien world is rural England, and the Lesbian is the Other, the space invader, as peculiar as a being from beyond the stars, 'in one of those out-of-the-way country places where you can't relax over your drink for fear some crazed yokel will be in through the door waving a hand-carved axe'.[35] The narrative takes an interesting risk; the voice is that of easy comedy, the Lesbian stereotype of black leather jacket, cords and untipped Players, the Byke Dyke whom heterosexuals regard as a-man-in-everything-but, walks on to the page before us. But this is her disguise to 'reach' other women. And it is an elaborate joke. This is a narrative written for other Lesbians; for once, heterosexuals read over the Lesbian shoulder. The Lesbian community is a physical space, the subject of the fictional text, but it is also created by the textual perspective itself and the physical presentation of the book as 'lesbian feminist fiction'. 'The Reach' both posits and creates the very community it describes. Wilson nods elegantly towards the theorists of Lesbian politics who underlie this imaginative 'reach'. 'I knew very little about the riding school branch of lesbian existence [Adrienne Rich, *Compulsory Heterosexuality and Lesbian Existence*] . . . It had never seemed to me that mucking out with the upper classes was likely to produce the kind of lesbian nation that I wanted anything to do with . . . [Jill Johnston, *Lesbian Nation: The Feminist Solution*]' (p. 14). The radical insecurity of every 'women only' space emerges in the voice of the old woman: 'Reaching is always a dangerous business . . . But we are built on risk . . . We must take the risk to survive' (p. 18). Reaching out risks betrayal. Interestingly, as in Livia's *Bulldozer Rising*, old women, crones, are made central by the Lesbian community – in its more speculative fictional form at least – which makes old women the source of authority, power and respect. 'When d'you go to the crone house?' the narrator asks cautiously. And the answer makes it clear that the crone house is not the Old Dykes' Dustbin: 'When the others think you're worth talking to' (p. 21).

Caroline Forbes's novella 'London Fields', one of the central stories in her collection *The Needle on Full: Lesbian Feminist Science Fiction*, opens with an old woman remembering, and she too has an honoured, central place in the New Women's World.[36] As in Perkins Gilman's *Herland*, the men have been obliterated, not by selective nuclear holocaust or a rockfall, but by The Death. Boy children simply 'wasted and died . . . Some subtle blend of poisons had caused the Y chromosome to mutate and the change was irreversible. The XX combination was still a winner, but for mankind it was the end' (p. 82). Mankind is at last used to mean precisely what it does mean: men.

Forbes's plain-grained prose can be comically ungrammatical: 'She was in the middle of doing the dishes when they landed in the back garden' (p. 64). We might indeed be dealing with flying saucers. But her naturalistic method and the precision of her urban geography create a powerful and disturbing landscape in ruined London. The abandoned city, slowly being re-possessed by the women, is a known space that is already made strange by the absence of the dead masters. The central metaphor of the novella is the dismantling of one of the tower blocks which at present blight the skyline of East London. The women are taking down the products of patriarchy, brick by brick. Men are, or were, in Forbes's fiction, unequivocally the Enemy. 'Then she'd fled to the countryside to escape the vengeance of the last few men, who would watch pregnant women and kill those that bore healthy daughters, such was their dying hatred' (p. 91). This is of course, already happening. Madhu Kishwar's essay on 'The Continuing Deficit of Women in India and the Impact of Amniocentesis' makes it clear that Forbes's futuristic fiction has already long been a reality. 'The acute preference for sons and viewing the birth of daughters as a curse has a long history in India . . . More careful investigation in certain areas which showed especially dramatic population differences between the sexes showed that in some instances, the low sex ratio of women was, among other things, related to female infanticide.'[37] The birth of a daughter has been regarded as a curse in western Europe too. And often, as I am writing, many women are terrorized into murdering both their daughters and themselves.

One of Forbes's surviving women is Julie, writer and historian of The Death. 'She had written about the mass rapes and the beginnings of organised women's resistance' (p. 92). Thus the writer herself is privileged and justified as the recording angel, chronicler of the destruction of the old world. The atrocities committed by men against women are not described in any detail – Julie, and Forbes, only gesture towards them – but men emerge as an 'insane race', a race apart from women. Forbes does not argue that women are in any sense superior: the issue is one of power, not of genes. The critical issue, both for contemporary feminism and for the futuristic new world of women, is the right to control our own bodies and our own fertility. The Seven Demands of the British women's liberation movement centre upon those issues: our right to live without the fear of rape, to define our sexuality for ourselves and to control our own reproductive power. The polemic of 'London Fields' is not addressed to Lesbian feminists, but to anti-feminist women. It is a fictional threat.

> Those who could remember men, healthy men, men that they thought they loved, that they shared their lives with and whose children they bore willingly. All these and more felt a terrible guilt. A guilt that it was their inaction for so long that had caused the catastrophe of The Death. They saw themselves as having supported the rule of men which had led to such destruction, even of the race itself. The women felt that they had betrayed their children and themselves by their weakness . . . Among all of us are women who were married to men of power, who might have done something but did not, an inheritance of inaction over so many years. So much fear for so long (p. 128).

British feminism has produced an apocalyptic form of anti-nuclear science fiction rising from the mud of Greenham Common. And it is a fiction which poses precisely the choice of 'London Fields': which side are you on?

> Are you on the side that beats your wife?
> Are you on the side of death or life?
> Which side are you on?

Greenham songs always insists that we do in fact make that choice, whether or not we perceive ourselves as political creatures. We are all implicated. The songs also reaffirm the vision of women's solidarity within the context of a political struggle.

> Stand up women; women make a choice
> Create a world without nuclear death
> Now together we are strong
> To break the nuclear chain.

The challenge of the choice is always there.

It is not surprising that Greenham became a symbolic place from which to contemplate the future, because many women felt that the present might end there. The political meaning of Greenham has been a focus for debate within the British women's movement. In a discussion on 'Feminism and Class Politics' Beatrix Campbell argued for a generous reading of the phenomenon of Greenham.

> At a point when it was difficult to imagine forms of politics outside the institutions, it regenerated the radical traditions of direct action which had disappeared off the agenda of left politics during the 70s. Greenham was something completely different – to inhabit a piece of space permanently, to contest the opposition's right to hold it, to say we are going to stay and we are going to watch every move you make. And it drew on a culture of femininity and radicalized it. Initially, a lot of people had a problem with all the talk of embroidery, sticking things on the fence, grannies coming along; thinking about the future they wanted for their children. Yet it created an atmosphere in which it was possible to speak of your care for the planet and for those who live on it, ideas that are not always part of the vocabulary of the left.[38]

Greenham is not simply a place, or even just a USAF base in Berkshire. It is a network of values; a political attitude which mythologizes women's culture as a basis for an alternative world. The central symbol of Greenham is the web. The weekend action on 13–14 December 1985 was called 'Widening the Web'. The web spreads itself over a broad spectrum of ecological issues and liberation movements. The recurring emphasis, however, is on the special connection – assumed, not argued – between women and the earth.

> All women are spinners
> We spin webs on the fences.
> We spin stories of our love for the earth
> We weave our memories into the fences.[39]

This proposition is either challenged or endorsed by the science fiction of Greenham.

Margaret Elphinstone's 'Spinning the Green' is an alternative fairy-tale in the collection *Despatches from the Frontiers of the Female Mind*.[40] The narrative follows a familiar pattern, both that of the fairy-tale, Beauty and the Beast (a merchant with three daughters goes on a business voyage and gets lost in the forest) and that of feminist science fiction (alien man stumbles upon a women's community). In fact, 'Spinning the Green' draws on a number of British

Figure 4   *'Widening the Web': an illustration from Greenham*

national institutions. Elphinstone's women are descendants of Robin Hood, concerned with the redistribution of wealth, armed with bows and arrows, clad in Lincoln green. The two elder sisters who decide on marriage and bourgeois life as opposed to the women's community stumble into Shakespeare's *A*

Midsummer Night's Dream, where the forest is the unconscious world of sexual confusion and blurred identities. Rather than come face to face with the unknown and the unthinkable, that is, the community of women, they marry identical men, Lysander and Demetrius. The fairy-tale pattern is reversed; usually it is the youngest sister who wins the prize and marries the prince, but here marriage is the fate of the Ugly Sisters, the trap. The green world reverses the conventional opposition; the choice is marriage or the open woods, duty or freedom. And 'Sister, the choice is yours' (p. 26).

It is the women who spin the green of the world, the web of life. 'Across the firelight he saw that they were spinning, spinning green threads, green threads twining together, spindles growing heavy with green. He watched neat fingers twisting the thread, and then weaving it, a green web woven, the circle of spinners became a circle of weavers' (p. 18). The Beast of the fairy-tale is the mentality which endorses the destruction of the green world: the mind which creates 'a place her father owned where the wind blew across scarred soil until red rock showed, where once a forest stood' (p. 24). The Beast is in the heads of men – and, incidentally, lay housed in Berkshire, surrounded by nine miles of razor wire and searchlights. But the fact is that the choice is offered only to women; only women can spin the green. As in *The Wanderground*, the polarities have become so fixed that there is no obligation upon men to change. The gulf becomes absolute.

Zoë Fairbairns' 'Relics', a narrative in the same collection as 'Spinning the Green', is about Greenham and feminism in the 1980s; the attempt to silence the women's movement by turning feminism into a marketable commodity rather than an independent passion for revolutionary change. The narrator is the voice of consoling compromise, the feminist who still talks to and even cheerfully seduces the men who provide her with the opportunity to sell out her sisters. The narrative begins and ends with the men making offers, ' . . . and the fact that we're having this conversation should prove to you that you can stop fighting because you've won' (pp. 177, 188). Greenham is the place where the choice has to be made, the choice between women and men, patriarchy or freedom. The narrator visits the base for the Fire Dragon Festival, 25 June 1983, which involved sewing an enormous patchwork dragon to encircle the base. I too was there on that day, and had the same bizarre experience she describes: of being the woman who refused to learn to sew at school and then finding myself 'surrounded by women with beautiful homemade tapestries, quilts, shawls and tablecloths' (p. 178). That women should know how to sew is a patriarchal imperative; for some of us it was never part of our culture, it was one of the things we refused to do. And 'Relics' is about refusal, the refusal to conform, to compromise, to dance to the men's tunes.

Greenham is based on ritual. Fairbairns' Catholic metaphors inform the narrative: the peace women become relics in a post-nuclear world, frozen like Catholic saints in our nuclear shelters; but unlike the saints we refuse to support our ecclesiastical masters. The voice of Sister St Laur, the nun who failed to teach the narrator to sew, is the woman's voice who refuses. 'Piss off . . . We have all the choices in the world' (p. 185). The holy relics retain all their passion for autonomous rebellion.

Aileen La Tourette's *Cry Wolf* is a post-nuclear-holocaust narrative. The entire fiction is set in the future, either the near future or the world without seasons beyond the bomb. That there ever will be any kind of world after the bomb is in itself a piece of pure science fiction. *Cry Wolf* is a parable which lurches uneasily into a discourse on writing fiction and telling stories, a meditation on imagination and memory. The narrative voice is that of Curie, the last survivor of the Old World, the keeper of wisdom, telling the stories to the innocent. The danger of describing a new world, or even the Old World, from the perspective of a post-nuclear future is the temptation to write the sententious wisdom of hindsight. Here are some examples.

> All learning is learning to pay attention.
> To live close to the earth was to live close to death.
> All history is gossip.
> Imagination is a child crying wolf . . . The cause of death is lack of imagination.
> We must meditate, we must discover, the relationship between mind and world.[41]

Most of this is, of course, unarguably true; but it is delivered with pompous unease, as if the narrative were uncertain of its own didactic purposes. Like other feminists writing the future, La Tourette makes motherhood central. But in this case, 'They were all M-others, three syllables in one breath, male and female, young and old. They were born maternally responsible for themselves and their planet. It was the only title that existed in the Gods of the Body, the only form of address they knew. It covered everything' (p. 12). M-other is the nurturing core and the other self; self and other bound into one M-other, so that the separation is both acknowledged and contained. And the book is really about mothers and M-others. The most haunting thread in the novel is the narrator's grief and anger against her dead mother, Bee Fairchild, who was shot dead climbing the fence at Greenham Common. Curie, the daughter, perceives herself to have been sacrificed to the mother's political desire to save the world, when that world sees the mother as martyr, the woman who sacrifices her life for her child. Curie takes on her mother's mission and fails, as her mother had done. The men destroy the world.

But it is supposedly women's values, the collective enterprise of a women's commune, and the women themselves, significantly all Lesbian women, who re-think, re-make, re-build and re-imagine the world. All agree that religion and ritual are to be the crucial binding strands in the new world. This is the common longing which draws the founding M-others together in the Old World, 'We had all reached some kind of impasse or spiritual ennui . . . ' (p. 73), and it is their central invention in the New World. 'Religion, they decided, the bonding of religion, its stricture against murder, must be the cornerstone . . . One without gods . . . People had always needed icons, idols' (p. 24). The primary function of religion, now and in La Tourette's post-nuclear future, is social control. The founding M-others invent a religion based on the body, in which death and the demystification of death have a central place. It sounds horrible; a sort of dissecting house of cults in which the body is worshipped and celebrated in pieces. The annual fertility festival culminates with a mass orgasm in the river. The problem here is that religion, any religion, is seldom a cohesive force in any body politic. Religion generates schism, hostility, enmity, murder. And apart from the M-others there are also the Potters, a separate race, mutants left over from the Old World, and now bearing a suspicious resemblance to a middle-class view of the working classes. Their bodies are different from those of the M-others; they are not all part of the same spiritual body. That women have been the keepers of religion is not surprising. Religions, patriarchal religions, are usually at the root of the politics which control us, as women. La Tourette is quite right to perceive that the metaphysical structures we choose as our means to apprehend and make sense of the world will govern our treatment of each other. But I am uneasy with any politics which naturally connect women with religion, the body, the earth. And the 'Gods of the Body' uncannily reproduce the same patterns of human self-representation and response which we have developed over hundreds of years. 'They had plotted a society without history, then. But perhaps some memories, like some words, like some ideas, were carried in the body itself, the body whose word was law' (p. 28). I would resist the determinism buried in this notion of the body as law; neither religion nor the body, our interpretation of the meaning of the body, is natural or constant; they are both the products of history.

And history proves inescapable. The women's plot to save the world by telling stories to the men with their fingers on the button fails. The stories are witty squibs, often biblical. Sodom and Gomorrah become 'the Promised Land of the gay community' (p. 128); but they fail to stave off the nuclear holocaust. Neither novels, nor stories, nor even books of political criticism, have ever been substitutes for direct action. Words cannot hold the bombs at bay. Nor did the protest at Greenham Common forestall Cruise: but I know of no woman who ever lived in the mud at Greenham without coming away, enraged and empowered, with a passion to transform our world.

The separatism of Greenham politics was easily the most controversial aspect of the camp; and the women-only anarchist structure of the protest has been sadly and irrefutably justified by events at Molesworth, which is a mixed peace camp. Between autumn 1985 and July 1986 three women were raped by men who lived at the camp. When the women spoke out, they were blamed. 'The peace movement never got to grips with the idea of Greenham or women's protest. By magic, Molesworth was supposed to be a mixed equivalent to Greenham – there isn't any such thing.'[42] Feminist separatism acknowledges men as the problem, if not the enemy. In Suzette Haden Elgin's *Native Tongue* the separatist argument is devastatingly simple.[43] Women can shape their freedom, indeed, simply think themselves free of men, by inventing another language. This proposition is enthusiastically advocated in some quarters of the women's movement. Nelly Fuman's essay, 'The Politics of Language: Beyond the Gender Principle?', puts the case succinctly: 'We are moulded into speaking subjects by language and that language shapes our perceptual world.'[44] The language we possess thus determines what we think; and, according to Furman, what we are able to experience. 'Not only are we born into a language which moulds us, but any knowledge of the world which we experience is also articulated in language.' Haden Elgin is herself a linguist, and an expert on Native American (Indian) languages. The privileged class in her future world are the linguists, a sort of elite civil service, mastering Alien languages, servicing the world's contacts with the rest of the universe. In this dystopia women are utterly subject to the laws of men, and the wives of the linguists are no exception. But the most intriguing thing about Haden Elgin's text is the way in which she refutes Furman's propositions. Michaela is, arguably, the heroine of the text. She is not a linguist, but the wife of an ordinary man. The chapter describing their marriage, chapter 3, is one of the most devastating in the book, simply because it depicts an utterly ordinary marriage, described from the man's point of view. Ned Landry is a monster of smug, banal sadism, the male ego rounded out. Michaela is a blank. And the quality for which he prizes her is the one required by every tyrant of his flattering slave; she listens. Virginia Woolf has this to say on women and male narcissism:

> Women have served all these centuries as looking glasses possessing the magic and delicious power of reflecting the figure of man at twice its natural size . . . That serves to explain in part the necessity that women so often are to men. And it serves to explain how restless they are under her criticism; . . . for if she begins to tell the truth, the figure on the looking-glass shrinks.[45]

Michaela has never learned a language other than her native tongue and she never does. She constructs another kind of perceptual world, other than the one she was taught in the 'wife factory', out of her own experience. When her child is taken from her and brutally destroyed she becomes pure rage; she becomes the woman who sees herself as an autonomous subject, not the fembot, the woman who exists only in relation to men. She sees the men clearly, as selfish and murderous. And she develops her own consciousness; cunning, accurate, deadly, she sets about killing them. Nazareth, her counterpart within the Linguist household, is cured both of romantic love and even any human fellow feeling for men by the systematic humiliation she receives at the hands of the men who own her; her husband and her father. 'Nazareth was never again to feel even the smallest stirring of affection or even of liking for any male past toddling age. Not even her own sons' (p. 202). Feeling, not language, is at the core of these women's experiences. And both of them trust what they feel. Their oppression and pain are experienced not in language, but in the flesh. To articulate an experience in language is to analyse, theorize, to give conceptual meaning to that experience. Michaela simply murders her husband; and that act, a deed of self-affirmation, self-liberation, is hardly linguistic. It is not said, but done.

The women's language is developed in the Barren Houses, the separatist households, where the redundant, the belittled, the despised, plan their freedom. When Nazareth returns to the Barren House and lives among women for the first time, 'she realized that she was like someone who goes home at last after a lifetime of exile' (p. 243). The women already have a shared experience of pain; their language is simply a tool, a root, to build a power base from which to create their own lives. It is not the language itself which causes a revolution in perception; it is the use to which it can be put. Michaela's silent ears become those of the spy in the camp of the men. She listens while they pour out their secrets. Her revolutionary gesture is not to learn her own woman's language, but to understand theirs.

The change-the-language-and-you-change-reality argument is certainly floated in *Native Tongue*, but the radical alternative, the flight into the wilderness to escape the power of men, is also given a necessary hearing. 'What would really solve the problem once and for all, is a colony of our own. A colony just for women. Somewhere far away, and so lacking in anything worth money, that men would never be interested in taking it away from us' (p. 268). And some of the women do try this solution in the sequel to *Native Tongue*, entitled *The Judas Rose*.[46] This sequel demonstrates the fact that there are very few fictional ideas strong enough for a re-run and that sequels are, on the whole, not advisable. The same plot is turned inside out. Instead of Michaela as the lay-woman spy in the Linguist male camp, we have a Linguist-born spy, masquerading as a nun, in the lay-men's camp. She is propagating the women's language, Láadan, by translating the Bible, literally spreading the Word. But whereas we saw into Michaela's mind, watched her develop and change, we never see the inner cogitations of Sister Miriam Rose. She is a demure blank, both to the men and to the reader, waiting for permission to speak at endless men's meetings. In fact, the entire novel is largely taken up with men's meetings: men getting it wrong, summoning each other for arguments, power games, tantrums, a series of talking heads. The Linguist women know that their men, and indeed, all men, are selfish, dangerous children, carrying loaded guns, and for 360-odd pages the reader watches this fact being proved.

Fundamentalist Christianity, which must loom large in the experience of American women writers, is the basis of much idiocy and sadism in the minds of Haden Elgin's men of power, especially one Hykus Clete. This medieval understanding of the faith alongside the technology of science fiction was interesting, disconcerting and instructive. The imperialism built into gospel-spreading, evangelistic Christianity – a problem inherent in all science fiction which deals with aliens and voyages – is made quite explicit. Terran (Earth, of course) trouble-makers, presumably communists, Jews, gypsies, hippies, homo-sexuals and the mentally handicapped, are shipped off to the colonies. But the sexual politics of the book, so sharply imagined in *Native Tongue*, become less prominent. It is as if Haden Elgin were not interested in what might go on in the Womanhouses and the Convents, inside women-only space. The moments of conflict and confrontation are left to the men. On three occasions the problematic dynamic between male power and women's resistance surfaces sharply, disturbing the banality of much of the writing. Chapter 6 describes the usual male meeting with reports, but the content of the report challenges the gradualist approach to changing the world adopted by the women of the Linguist household. Here is the Amazonian separatist alternative. A small group of women murder their husbands and attempt to build the Wan-derground on another asteroid. What do women want? The eternal male question here receives its answer. Freedom. 'Free to starve. Free to die of exposure. Free to choke on foul air. Free to die of diseases no doctor has seen in a century. Free to suffer unspeakably. They want to be *free*, to do all those things?' (p. 90). Here is the echo of the Savage in Huxley's *Brave New World* (1932), demanding the right to experience his own life, whatever the cost. But the meaning of freedom is interestingly different for women who have never been defined in terms of anything other than the flesh. Needless to say, the men of *The Judas Rose* cannot understand what has gone wrong.

Lesbian desire has presumably also been transported to the asteroids, as it never surfaces in Haden Elgin's texts at all. We have one devastatingly horrible scene of male heterosexuality, all of chapter 23, in which Belle-Sharon slaughters her own sexual desire in the sure and certain knowledge that her husband will never bother to satisfy her, for the most pessimistic of reasons. ' "But what it *really* is, sweet Belle-Sharon, is that the men are perfectly contented with what they're doing. Why should they change it, when it suits them so well? " ' (p. 299). Quite so. Which makes the desperate escape attempt of the women who fled to the stars seem more rational. I clung to chapter 20, which was the only truly optimistic moment in the novel. Here we have an inter-galactic heterosexual dinner party. It is just like twentieth-century ones, only with floating tables and talking doors. Haden Elgin formalizes the bitchiness and competition between the wives, whose heads are full of dresses, food, interior decoration and doing the other woman down. In comes one of the Lingoe women, dressed simply, hair brushed, natural, straightforward, affection-ate, apparently in harmony with her husband – and she invites the other women to stand beside her, 'My dears, won't you come and play too?' (p. 270). This is a woman in control, and her first gesture is one of solidarity towards other women. Haden Elgin argues that we should, most assuredly, be our sisters' keepers.

The sympathy between women is the source of Michaela's sacrifice of her life and freedom for the Linguist women and their language at the end of *Native Tongue*. She never understands any of the political, philosophical or metaphys-ical implications. She does it for Nazareth, for the love of another woman: 'if Nazareth had known of this, she would have been grateful . . . It was a fitting gift to leave for her' (p. 282). The solidarity of the women becomes inevitable simply because Haden Elgin insists on the reality of Michaela's inarticulate perception, a perception based not on language or theory but on her sense of herself as a woman, on her woman's dignity and her woman's love. 'Loving someone who considered you only one small notch above a cleverly trained domestic animal, and made no secret of it – that is, loving any adult male – was not possible for her. It would be a perversion, loving your masters while their boots were on your neck, and she was a woman healthy of mind' (p. 258).

Romantic novels are about learning to do precisely that, learning to love the boot on your neck. Tania Modleski, in her study *Loving With a Vengeance: Mass Produced Fantasies for Women*, argues that 'the formula rarely varies: a young, inexperienced, poor to moderately well-to-do woman encounters and becomes involved with a handsome, strong, experienced, wealthy man, older than herself by ten to fifteen years'.[47] Modleski's reading of the politics of romance gives more weight to the anger and longing for revenge that the women feel for the men who mock, ignore, bully, persecute and eventually marry them, than seems plausible to me. The blunt truth is, as she admits: 'The novels perpetuate ideological confusion about male sexuality and male violence, while insisting there is no problem' (pp. 42–3). And who reads romance? Well, we do. According to the sociologists of Sheffield University, 30 per cent of women reading a book at any one time are reading a romance. This is a terrifying thought. The formula Modleski outlines is, I believe, quite unsubvertable, because the erotic in romance is intrinsically bound up with an unalterable imbalance of power. The man is older, wealthier, dominant. The woman submits; she never wins. Even the romance parable of *Jane Eyre* concludes with 'the sad – not triumphant – admission that a woman only achieves equality with – not dominance over – men who are crippled in some way' (p. 46). Rochester's symbolic castration, his blinding, is also mutilation. He can no longer dominate Jane because he needs her as his eyes. In many ways *Jane Eyre* reflects both the object of desire in conventional romance and the despair of its achievement. So, if heterosexual romance presents an impossible dilemma from a feminist perspective, does Lesbian romance solve the problem or present a new set of difficulties?

That two Lesbians, or indeed two Gay men, could live happily ever after in this world does sound like a romantic fantasy. That they could have done so in history, without any Lesbian political consciousness or Lesbian community, requires a real flight of the imagination. Two romantic historical Lesbian novels from the women's movement are Isabel Miller's *Patience and Sarah*, set in early nineteenth-century America, and Ellen Galford's *Moll Cutpurse: Her True History*, which purports to be the real story of Middleton and Dekker's Roaring Girl and comes packaged, somewhat unpromisingly, as 'The adventures of a swashbuckling lesbian heroine in the colourful, teeming world of Shakespeare's London'.[48] (It doesn't say with what Shakespeare's London is supposed to 'teem'.)

One of the problems Isabel Miller sets herself is to imagine a Lesbian love affair long before the category of Lesbian – which is, after all, a medical, clinical category of recent date – was ever invented. Miller puts the sex back into Romantic Friendship.[49] Something of a 'did they do it or didn't they?' debate rages around the historical phenomenon of Romantic Friendship. On the one hand we have Lillian Faderman, whose *Surpassing the Love of Men* and *Scotch Verdict* are essays in Lesbian history, both of them refusing to impose a modern Lesbian consciousness on women whose sexuality was certainly perceived in very different terms, both by the women themselves and by the people around them.[50] On the other hand, Sheila Jeffreys' considered reply 'Does It Matter If They Did It?' in *Trouble and Strife* makes the sensible point that, if we exclude women whose passionate connection was to other women, simply on the grounds that they did not define themselves as Lesbians, we are in danger of losing all the Lesbian history that we have.[51] Furthermore, in whose interest is it that we should insist that Lesbianism is simply a sexual practice? 'Lesbianism then becomes part of a list in sexological textbooks with bestiality and paedophilia.' But Lesbianism as 'a passionate commitment to women, a culture, a political alternative' (p. 27) is and always was a threat to the institutions of heterosexuality and male supremacy. A simpler solution to this stirring debate might be 'How do we know they didn't do it?' I have yet to see it argued.

Miller and Galford both imagine Lesbian women who desired and loved one another in the way that we do now. But these women are isolated, solitary lovers, freaks in a heterosexual world, the only ones of their kind. One lover of each couple dresses and behaves like a man. Here is Miller's heroine: ' "Is it a woman or a boy?" I asked. . . . but it was Sarah Dowling, dressed just as her reputation claimed, in boots, breeches, jerkin, fur mittens, fur hat with a scarf tied over her ears" ' (pp. 12, 15). And here is Galford's: ' "Turn me into a man," was all she said. She was of middle height, stout and thickset, with short-cropped yellow hair that looked as if it had been struck off in desperation with a blunted knife. She was dressed in a rough jerkin and breeches, and carried a tobacco pipe. If I hadn't heard her speak I might have taken her for a boy' (pp. 14–15). Galford's Moll Cutpurse markets herself as a freak. Her breeches and her exploits are pure exhibitionism. Women who dressed as men, or 'passing women', that is, women who lived disguised as men, have always existed. Their refusal of the female gender need not necessarily be ascribed to Lesbianism, although, given that many passing women of whom we have records actually married other women, I think we may safely assume that these women were Lesbians. 'Women who dressed as men had, above all, access to the jobs that were limited to males. They enjoyed more freedom of mobility, less fear of sexual attacks, better employment prospects, with better pay. They were also free to have sexual relationships with other women or to avoid sex with men.'[52] But the penalty for transgressing the boundaries of gender was often imprisonment, torture, death. Even in the Romance genre this threat is always there, like an uninvited ghost. Miller's boyish heroine is beaten up by her father when he hears that she loves another woman. And whenever the disguise is discovered or breached the prison of gender inexorably closes around the heroine. The men are no longer her comrades, her equals. Thus Miller: 'You wouldn't think just a word could change a whole friendship like that. I didn't get weak and gal-ish. Nothing happened but a word. But we couldn't fix it . . . ' (p. 83). And Galford: 'I was furious that night, when they made me sleep alone in a separate chamber, as if the weeks I'd served them and been their comrade had never happened. I knew that in the morning all of them, except Tom, would treat me in a different way than they had before, and I wouldn't stand for it' (p. 33).

Interestingly, both women are propositioned by men who insist that 'men have loved and embraced each other since the beginning of time' (*Patience and Sarah*, p. 81). Homosexuality is very far from unthinkable; the men move easily in the company of other men and can live independently of women if they wish to do so. For the women it is not so simple. As in our own times and outside the pages of fiction, economic and sexual freedom are inextricable. Miller's lovers are able to escape with the aid of a past legacy from an enlightened father; Galford's Moll makes a living as a thief, her lover Bridget inherits her father's apothecary's shop and learns his craft. Both of them are, knowingly, confidence tricksters. This is witty and apt, for all Lesbians, at some time or other, use

disguise. Lesbianism becomes the best-kept open secret of Galford's panto-
mime Elizabethan England. 'It's a well-known fact that women's touch is
sweeter . . . It takes little wit to realise that women's joys are safest when kept
secret' (p. 59). And because this is a Romance Galford does not spend much
time explaining why women's joys are best kept secret, as even (or perhaps
especially) in Elizabethan England this would result in some unpleasant
discussions about sexual politics.

In both novels one of the women, and in both cases the more conventionally
womanly lover, knows about Lesbian sensuality. Miller's Patience, wearing the
skirts, argues that 'it's better to be a real woman than an imitation man, and that
when someone chooses a woman to go away with it's because a woman is what's
preferred' (p. 23). The question of what a 'real woman' actually is does not pose
the problem in Romantic fiction that it does in Lesbian theory. Galford's
apothecary talks like a radical Lesbian feminist. 'You've been mixing too much
with men. The world is full of brave, strong women. If you're too stupid to see
them, it's your loss, not mine . . . if you looked farther than the end of your
nose, you'd find a lot of us about. I promise you Moll, you can be as bold and
strong and free as you are now, and still be a woman, and the wisest of your
sisters will love you for it' (p. 23). Both Miller and Galford divide the narratives
between their heroines. This simple device means that each lover tells us her
own story as a first-person confessional narrative. All lovers are egoists; and in
egalitarian Lesbian romance the agony and the ecstasy are evenly balanced
between the two women. In heterosexual romance the narrative is governed by
the woman's – and by implication the reader's – perspective. The man, his
intentions and desires, remain a blank. It is only when he capitulates to the
formulaic resolution, love and marriage, that his behaviour is ever explained.
And even then, it never is. Quite.

The women who write romances are rarely historians, which means that we
are given a very conventional pasteboard version of history. In Galford's comic
picaresque, all the clichés have walk-on parts, severe kill-joy Puritans and
glamorous hard-drinking playwrights alike. The real points of reference are the
fantasies of other women. Shakespeare's sister Judith, copyright Virginia Woolf
in *A Room of One's Own*, makes an appearance and tells us her own tale: the
story of oppression, misery and male sexual duplicity.[53] Woolf's creation kills
herself; but Galford ends her tale with a kind of triumph as Judith writes and
sells her own ballads and broadsheets. 'My humble wares are a long cry from
Sidney's noble *Arcadia* or the richly-wrought verses of the *Faerie Queene*, but let
those jeer who will, for I do what I set out to do – I earn my bread through
poesy' (p. 163). Galford and Miller are committed, as are all romance writers,
to Hallelujah happy endings, even for the minor characters. Miller's lovers,
reunited after the obligatory tribulation, become sexual and territorial pioneers.
'We were free to remember and invent with no one to say that our way would
never do. Sometimes indeed, our ways did fail. But often they did not' (*Patience
and Sarah*, p. 188). Lesbians have to be creative, simply because there are no
rules as to how we should live. Memory and invention are the necessary
qualifications for survival, and the basis of Monique Wittig's triumphant and
inspirational command, 'Make an effort to remember, and failing that, invent.'[54]

Inventing history has always been a writer's prerogative. Schiller made up most of the history in *Don Carlos* and had Joan of Arc in *Die Jungfrau von Orleans* die on the battlefield because her actual fate did not suit his dramatic purposes. Re-writing history so that we too are actually *dramatis personae* has been one of the projects of contemporary feminism. Virago Press grew out of this enterprise, re-publishing women's writing that had been discarded, ignored and suppressed. It is therefore entirely suitable that it should have been the publisher of a book that combined both fiction and feminist history. Zoë Fairbairns and the editors at Virago cooked up the project together. It was to be 'a big, fat, family saga full of feminist history'.[55] The product, *Stand We At Last*, combines two recognizable, highly marketable popular types of genre fiction: the domestic family saga and the romantic novel.[56] *Stand We At Last* begins in 1855, the heyday of women novelists and time of increasing public debate on the 'Woman Question', and ends in the early 1970s with the advent of the contemporary women's movement. Fairbairns uses the device of two sisters, making different choices, to generate two radically different contrasting narratives. One woman marries a conventional, suitable husband; the other emigrates to Australia. Precisely the same device is used to much the same effect by Arnold Bennett in his *Old Wives' Tale* (1908), a historical novel covering the first half of the same period. Fairbairns' problems are to do with psychology and dialogue. Is the book a 1980s feminist reconstruction of history and of the Victorian period, or is she writing a version of the 1850s that is constructed and interpreted by writers living at the time? Each section deals with a 'women's issue' identified as an important milestone by our own feminist historians: the medical and sexual abuse of women, the prostitution laws, the fate of illegitimate children, the struggle for the vote, the fate of women in the professions, women and war, the End of Empire, and the emergence of the present women's liberation movement out of radical student political movements in the 1960s. The focus of the narrative is not, however, on the condition of woman, but on the condition of individual women. The plot therefore tends to coerce each woman into representing an attitude or an issue. History is generally perceived from the viewpoint of the individual; the suffragette movement lurches into the novel, apparently from nowhere, in the form of an omnibus packed with women, to collect Aunt Sarah, the only really radical woman in the book (and, significantly, the woman who leaves no children and no heirs behind her). There is no sense of any wider suffrage movement. Politics, social change, crises simply hit the characters with all the random force of a passing bus. Character is never shaped by history. Discrete individuals are overwhelmed by events. The *Titanic* sinks – as indeed it did – with Aunt Sarah on board.

The sexual politics of the book are peculiar. Fairbairns makes women's experience of oppression central, but reinforces convention in odd ways. All the women, including Jackie, the last daughter of the family whose fate is described, are sexual victims. They experience heterosexual sex as inevitable, unpleasant and grotesque, with horrible consequences: unwanted pregnancy and venereal disease. Even the redoubtable Aunt Sarah has a bloody miscarriage in the Australian dairy.

Here are Helena's reflections on matrimony: 'Had he gone mad? had some rapid illness struck him while he was away? Or had he always wanted to be like this . . . waiting for the first month of marriage to pass before revealing himself, bringing her a beautiful nightgown to console her for what he would make her endure while she wore it?' (p. 34). All Victorian middle-class women 'endured' sex, apparently. 'Would it surprise you to know that Pearl has a deep fear and disgust of anything to do with men or marriage?' (p. 181). Well no, it wouldn't; given Aunt Sarah's discovery that ' . . . undetected gonorrhoea is one of the main causes of sterility and ill-health among virtuous married women' (p. 161). Ruby 'knows passion' once on the drawing-room floor with a lover, but ' . . . her husband was a bitter disappointment to her in ways that she could only wish she did not know. He had little passion and less delicacy . . . Now he gave a pompous and trembling performance once a week' (p. 348). And by the time we get to the 1960s all the chicks are on the pill, or ought to be, for the men to fuck. This is Jackie's experience. 'He said casually, once in the aftermath, I suppose you're on the pill, chick? And I said, yeah, dreamily . . . And when I told Calvin what had happened, he said, can't be mine, chick, you were taking those pills when you were with me' (p. 448). Lesbianism remains absolutely invisible in Fairbairns' text; as it does in the work of most heterosexual feminist historians. There is not even the occasional chaste Romantic Friendship.

Fairbairns herself admits that the book is not a success; 'there is an overreliance on cliché'.[57] And the clichés are sinster when it comes to sexuality, because Fairbairns simply reproduces the sexual values of romantic fiction, which are anything but feminist. 'Ruby felt a little shock at passion's violence, but the peace of its aftermath quite made up for that, the peace spreading from his body to hers' (p. 315). Sex is still something men do to women, and the yoking of passion and violence, which certainly do seem to go together in the male mind, is, I would have thought, something we should all want to challenge.

The reasons behind the political and textual uncertainties in *Stand We At Last* are interesting. Virago commissioned the book, but wanted to influence the writing to a much greater extent than Fairbairns expected. They wanted a text that would fit in with their marketing strategy. All genre fiction is written with a market in mind; all genre fiction must operate within textual expectations which are indeed clichés. To write well within a particular genre without disrupting or subverting the form is, I believe, impossible. Most of the consumers of genre fiction eat the novels like a favourite meal. They want to know what they are buying, even if it is junk food. Feminism, on the other hand, should always be disruptive, unsettling. And it is this dis-ease, symptomatic of the transforming breath of change, that a feminist reader will want. It is dissatisfaction with murder mysteries which rely on dead blondes with big breasts, horribly hacked to death, which makes a reader desire the pleasure of fiction where the woman is not always, automatically, the victim. And a historical family saga which spans the period of two women's revolutions, a period within which the condition of women has been profoundly changed, needs to envisage that change with a radical reading of history, not a heaped accumulation of isolated issues.

Fairbairns' title comes from Cicily Hamilton's song, set to Ethyl Smyth's music, 'The March of the Women': 'Strong, strong, stand we at last'. Stirring words; Smyth and Hamilton were both radical spinsters of the suffragette movement; but their spirit does not inhabit the text of *Stand We At Last*. We are not standing at the end of the book. We are still holding the baby and we are still on our backs. However, I take the last women-only grouping of the novel as a positive, if somewhat desperate gesture. 'I've had to leave home. I've got an old woman and a toddler and no money. And I don't know what to do' (p. 510). But at least – and at last – our heroine is asking another woman for help; knowing that the woman at the other end of the telephone has a political commitment to feminism, and to other women.

Notes

1 Sarah Lefanu, *In the Chinks of the World Machine: Feminism and Science Fiction* (London, Women's Press, 1988), p. 100. Lefanu argues a good case for seeing science fiction as 'feminist-friendly'. I might disagree with some of her readings, but not with her general conclusions. See also, for a more detailed discussion of the issues raised by feminist writers' use of genre, Anne Cranny-Francis, *Feminist Fiction: Feminist Uses of Generic Fiction* (Cambridge, Polity, 1990). Cranny-Francis is more optimistic about the subversive potential of feminist ideas and discourses within genre fiction than I am; but we share similar misgivings.

2 The story of Oedipus enjoys an enormous and pernicious influence in our culture. 'Recently, critics, following Roland Barthes, have plausibly argued that most popular of "classic" narratives reenact the male oedipal crisis. We need not list here the dreary catalogue of devices used in the male text to disable the female and thus assert masculine superiority . . . At the end of a majority of popular narratives the woman is disfigured, dead, or at the very least, domesticated.' See Tania Modleski, *Loving with a Vengeance: Mass-Produced Fantasies for Women* (1982; London, Methuen, 1984), p. 12.

3 For a brief, perceptive analysis of the central characteristics of British detective fiction see Robert Graves and Alan Hodge, *The Long Week-End: A Social History of Great Britain 1918–1939* (1940; London, Faber, 1950), pp. 300–3.

4 Raymond Chandler. 'The Simple Art of Murder', in *The Chandler Collection*, vol. 3 (London, Pan, 1984), p. 191.

5 Graves and Hodge, *The Long Week-End*, p. 303.

6 There is an interesting interview/profile of P. D. James and her work by Polly Toynbee: 'More Deadly than the Male', *The Guardian*, 2 June 1986.

7 Barbara Wilson, *Murder in the Collective* (London, Women's Press, 1984).

8 Since Wilson wrote her book the Marcos regime has collapsed. This a cause for celebration; but dictatorship is a creeping evil, and too often founded on the liquidation of all opposition. The central thesis of Wilson's book remains, sadly, very relevant.

9 Jean Swallow (ed.), *Out From Under: Sober Dykes and Our Friends* (San Francisco, Spinsters, Ink, 1983), p. ix. This is a heartening book; very American in style. It is, as the title says, about becoming and staying sober, with a lot of help from our friends.

10 My thanks for this observation on the fixtures and fittings to Nicola Bourdillon.

11 Valerie Miner, *Murder in the English Department* (London, Women's Press, 1982).

12 The US class system does not easily map on to the British. The nuances of class are hard to read in other cultures, but this does not mean, as some Americans have claimed to me, that there is no class system in the United States. In Britain, class is

where you come from; in America class is where you end up. Thus, an Oxford don of my acquaintance, well established in the college hierarchy and his profession, could claim to be working-class. I suspect that had he not been so securely embedded in the upper middle classes, he would not have mentioned it. On the other hand, I know Americans who proudly boast of their humble origins while writing enormous cheques to indicate their own prowess in rising from the rubble.

13 Useful discussions concerning the issue of sexual harassment on university territory are: Deborah Cameron, 'Sex with your Tutor? It's his Fringe Benefit', first published in *Spare Rib*, no. 99 (November 1980) and reprinted (slightly edited) in Marsha Rowe (ed.), *Spare Rib Reader* (London, Penguin, 1982); '*The Ones who Just Patronise seem Genial by Comparison . . .': An Enquiry into Sexual Harassment of Women in Oxford University*, a survey published by the Oxford University Student Union Women's Committee, April 1984; and an especially good article by Melissa Benn, 'Isn't Sexual Harassment Really about Masculinity?' *Spare Rib*, no. 156 (July 1985), pp. 6–8. There is also an interesting case study by Riva Krut and Elaine Otto, 'Danger! Male Bonding at Work', *Trouble and Strife*, no. 4 (Winter 1984), pp. 41–7.

14 See – or, indeed, hear – Ova's song on this theme, 'Some day I'm gonna kill a man in self-defence/it makes sense.'

15 Mary Wings, *She Came Too Late* (London, Women's Press, 1986); Gillian Slovo, *Death by Analysis* (London, Women's Press, 1986).

16 I am not alone in this opinion. See Sara Scott and Tracey Payne, 'Underneath We're All Lovable', *Trouble and Strife*, no 3 (Summer 1984), pp. 21–4; also Lorraine Davies' thoughtful response to that article on the letters page of the next issue: *Trouble and Strife*, no. 4 (Winter 1984), pp. 9–10.

17 Hannah Wakefield, *The Price You Pay* (London, Women's Press, 1987), p. 232.

18 I have been influenced by and disagreed with two excellent essays on Lesbian crime fiction: Sally Munt, 'The Investigators: Lesbian Crime Fiction', in Susannah Radstone (ed.), *Sweet Dreams: Sexuality, Gender and Popular Fiction* (London: Lawrence & Wishart, 1988), pp. 91–119, and Paulina Palmer, 'The Lesbian Feminist Thriller and Detective Novel', in Elaine Hobby and Chris White (eds), *What Lesbians Do in Books* (London, Women's Press, 1991). Both these writers are interested in psychoanalytical interpretations of fiction; Palmer has an especially interesting section on the tension between the individualism of the detective as opposed to the collectivist ideals of Lesbian feminist politics. Munt talks about the shifting sexual subjectivity of Wings' heroine Emma Victor in *She Came Too Late*, and the explicit sexual themes; she occasionally slithers into unreadable academic prose, as in: 'Lesbian crime fiction provides a site of struggle over definitions, positing the lesbian at the centre of meaning dissemination' (p. 109). I often felt that the critical acadamic ingenuity of both Munt and Palmer was much more sophisticated than the fiction they discuss. Perhaps they will now both write thrillers themselves. I hope so.

19 Barbara Wilson, *Sisters of the Road* (London, Women's Press, 1987).

20 See Wilson's third novel in her Pam Nilsen series, *The Dog Collar Murders* (London, Virago, 1989); also *Cows and Horses* (London, Virago, 1989). For a commentary on women and crime fiction see Linda Semple, *An Unsuitable Job for a Woman: A History of Women Crime Writers* (London, Pandora, 1988) and for the real thing Barney Bardsley, *Flowers in Hell: An Investigation into Women and Crime* (London, Pandora, 1987).

21 Marge Piercy, *Woman on the Edge of Time* (London, Women's Press, 1979), p. 207.

22 See Francis Mulhern, 'Writing for the Future: The Politics of Literature', *New Statesman*, 22 March 1985, pp. 24–6.

23 Shulamith Firestone, *The Dialectic of Sex* (1970; London, Women's Press, 1979), p. 211.

24 For an extended, illuminating feminist argument on the subject, see Adrienne Rich, *Of Woman Born: Motherhood as Experience and Institution* (1976; London, Virago, 1981).

25 Charlotte Perkins Gilman, *Herland* (1915; London, Women's Press, 1979); Sally Miller Gearhart, *The Wanderground: Stories of the Hill Women* (1979; London, Women's Press, 1985).

26 See Gwyneth Jones, 'Imagining Things Differently', *Women's Review*, no. 3 (January 1986), pp. 10–11. She provides a useful bibliography of feminist science fiction.

27 For an original if somewhat self-indulgently speculative analysis of the trial of Peter Sutcliffe see Nicole Ward Jouve, *The Streetcleaner: The Yorkshire Ripper Case on Trial* (London, Marion Boyars, 1986). For a serious and realistic assessments of the issues see The London Rape Crisis Centre, *Sexual Violence: The Reality for Women* (London, Women's Press, 1984); dusty rhodes and Sandra McNeill (eds), *Women Against Violence Against Women* (London, Onlywomen, 1985); Jalna Hanmer and Sheila Saunders, *Well-founded Fear: A Community Study of Violence to Women* (London, Hutchinson, 1984); and for an American perspective, Andrea Dworkin, 'The Rape Atrocity and the Boy Next Door', in *Our Blood: Prophecies and Discourses on Sexual Politics* (1976; London, Women's Press, 1982), pp. 22–49. See also Deborah Cameron and Elizabeth Frazer, *The Lust to Kill: A Feminist Investigation of Sexual Murder* (Cambridge, Polity, 1987).

28 I think that there are substantial political differences between British and American versions of radical feminism. The attitudes developed in Miller Gearhart's fiction are much closer to those of the Greenham women who endorsed the natural connection of women and the earth. British radical feminism has always been urban-based, materialistic rather than mystical in its analysis of the oppression of women, and impudently, wonderfully confrontational against male power. We are more likely to burn down a porn shop than connect with the earth for a gatherstretch.

American science-fiction writer Joanna Russ advocates a version of radical feminism that is closer to British political women. See Ruth Wallsgrove's review, 'The Four Lives of Joanna', *Trouble and Strife*, no. 5 (Spring 1985), pp. 30–3, where she claims *The Female Man* (1975; London, Women's Press, 1988) as 'an utterly radical feminist novel'. I have not dealt here with Russ's work, for two reasons. First, her writing has been carefully discussed by Sarah Lefanu in *In the Chinks of the World Machine* – see her last chapter, 'The Reader as Subject: Joanna Russ', in which she argues an excellent case for Russ's exploitation of feminism and modernism. But the second reason is the real one: I don't much like her work. I get bored. This is why. The forms of science fiction can be a game. Joanna Russ is one of the American feminist writers who plays games with the forms. Her *Extra(Ordinary) People* (1984; London, Women's Press, 1985) is a sequence of stories that form a meditation on the possibilities of the genre, the games of the imagination. Yet her work, ironic, self-reflecting, also exposes the limits of the genre. Women venture forth into space, conquer technology; her heroine Irene in *The Two of Them* (1978; London, Women's Press, 1986) has an epic, intellectual battle with the spaceship's computer. Russ writes futuristic fantasy, parables of inner and outer space; but her perpetual and most interesting subjects are the expectations placed upon gender and the forms of sexuality. 'The Mystery of the Young Gentleman' in *Extra(Ordinary) People* is a gender-bender. We are left in textual uncertainty for much of the narrative as to whether the hero is a heterosexual man, a Gay man, a straight woman, or a Lesbian woman dressed up as a man. The insecurity generated in the reader is genuinely, disturbingly erotic. Our interest and desire are thoroughly confused. As the 'young gentleman' proceeds through the cliché scenes of a bad western the surface of the action is ruffled by the ironic, ambiguous narrator. ' . . . Why is it that acts of manliness always involve damage to the furniture? – which is, you must understand, *something a woman cannot do*. That's faith. I repeat: What a woman cannot do' (p. 88; Russ's italics). 'Souls', the central narrative in *Extra(Ordinary) People*, is set in a medieval abbey. It is a meditation on power: women's power, imaginative power, and the power of the weaponless. The resolution of the tale exemplifies the difficulty endemic in the form. The cunning peasant abbess, Radegunde, almost outwits the Norsemen who come – as they do in all Viking stories – to do a little raping and pillaging all down the coast. But finally Radegunde becomes a chosen magic saint, a Creature from Beyond, not quite human after all; but an extra-terrestrial who vanishes among the trees with her shining collective. The power we initially read as human is no longer so, and the mortals she abandons – and, incidently, the all-too-human reader – become less than human, belittled, diminished. The most haunting and infinite subject for science-fiction remains, interestingly, human passions, human actions, the remorseless longing of the human heart.

29 Jane Palmer, *The Planet Dweller* (London, Women's Press, 1985), p. 108.
30 Monique Wittig's Amazon utopia *Les Guérillères* (1969) does try to present 'The Women' as a collective subject – as, to some extent, do Charlotte Perkins Gilman and Sally Miller Gearhart. See also Sarah Lefanu's reading of *The Wanderground* as 'a portrait of a culture rather than of individuals' (*In the Chinks of the World Machine*, pp. 64–70).
31 For the most intelligent analysis of this split in our culture that I have read, see Raymond Williams, *The Country and the City* (1973; London, Paladin, 1975).
32 Anna Livia, *Bulldozer Rising* (London, Onlywomen, 1988), p. 181.
33 See Susan Hemmings, *A Wealth of Experience: The Lives of Older Women* (London, Pandora, 1985) and Barbara Macdonald with Cynthia Rich, *Look Me in the Eye* (London, Women's Press, 1984). See also carol anne douglas's report on a conference held in Washington, DC, in January 1988: 'Passages: Lesbians Aging', in *Off Our Backs*, vol. 18, no. 4 (April 1988).
34 Ursula Le Guin, *The Left Hand of Darkness* (1969; London, Futura, 1981, repr. 1983), p. 47. But see Le Guin's own political shift on this point in her essay 'Is Gender Necessary?' (1976) and the comments in her 'Redux' (1988), both in *The Language of the Night: Essays on Fantasy and Science Fiction* (1979; rev. edn London, Women's Press, 1989), pp. 135–47. Le Guin now agrees with what I have said here. She has changed her mind. Bravo.
35 Anna Wilson, 'The Reach', in Lilian Mohin and Sheila Shulman (eds), *The Reach and Other Stories: Lesbian Feminist Fiction* (London, Onlywomen, 1984), p. 9.
36 Caroline Forbes, *The Needle on Full: Lesbian Feminist Science Fiction* (London, Onlywomen, 1985).
37 Madhu Kishwar, 'The Continuing Deficit of Women in India and the Impact of Amniocentesis', in G. Corea et al., *Man-Made Women: How New Reproductive Technologies Affect Women* (London, Century Hutchinson, 1985), p. 31.
38 Beatrix Campbell, 'Feminism and Class Politics', *Feminist Review*, no. 23 (Summer 1986), p. 16.
39 Juliet Lamont, 'Many of Those Burned as Witches were Weavers', *Women for Life on Earth*, no. 14 (Summer 1986), p. 17.
40 Jen Green and Sarah Lefanu (eds), *Despatches from the Frontiers of the Female Mind* (London, Women's Press, 1985).
41 Aileen La Tourette, *Cry Wolf* (London, Virago, 1986). Sententious wisdom in order

of appearance: pp. 10, 27, 73, 174, 191.
42 See Barbara Norden's article and interview with 'Julia', one of the women who was raped: 'Utopia is Dead', *Spare Rib*, no. 174 (January 1987), pp. 40–3. Also important are the articles in *Peace News*, no. 2276 (5 September 1986), pp. 14–15. This issue carried a bold cover statement 'RAPE IS AN ACT OF WAR' and firmly linked militarism and male violence against women. Subsequent correspondence in nos 2277 (19 September 1986) and 2278 (3 October 1986) gives a terrifying insight into the sexism, bigotry and sheer hypocrisy of some sections of the mixed peace movement.

You will have to search the library archives for these issues of *Peace News*: the magazine ceased publication shortly after the publication of the Molesworth rapes. Undoubtedly, the crisis at *Peace News* forms part of the general lull in activist support for the peace movement. Mr Gorbachev's initiatives seemed to dampen protest; but I am certain that the magazine's decline was also due to its outspoken stand on the issues of sexual politics, which was not supported by the 'traditional' – that is, sexist and anti-Lesbian/anti-Gay – readers. Friday 26 May 1989 saw the first issue of the resurrected *Peace News*. Good luck to the team.
43 Suzette Haden Elgin, *Native Tongue* (1984; London, Women's Press, 1985).
44 Nelly Furman in Gayle Greene and Coppélia Kahn (eds), *Making a Difference: Feminist Literary Criticism* (London, Methuen, 1985), p. 69.
45 Virginia Woolf, *A Room of One's Own* (1928; London, Penguin, 1972), p. 37. See also Sally Cline and Dale Spender, *Reflecting Men at Twice Their Natural Size* (1987; London, Fontana, 1988).
46 Suzette Haden Elgin, *The Judas Rose* (1987; London, Women's Press, 1988).
47 Modleski, *Loving with a Vengeance*, p. 36. Horrifying but helpful was Polly Toynbee's review of Mary Wibberley's book *To Writers with Love: On Writing Romantic Novels* (Buchan & Enright, 1985) in *The Guardian*, 22 July 1985.
48 Isabel Miller, *Patience and Sarah* (London, Women's Press, 1979); Ellen Galford, *Moll Cutpurse: Her True History* (Edinburgh, Stramullion, 1984).
49 Relevant here are the Ladies of Llangollen, Eleanor Butler and Sarah Ponsonby, who achieved notoriety and some admiration for their lifestyle. See Elizabeth Mavor's biography, *The Ladies of Llangollen: A Study in Romantic Friendship* (1971; London, Penguin, 1973). Mavor goes to some lengths in her introduction to eschew the world 'Lesbian' and refuse any kind of Freudian interpretation. I can see that 'The Lesbians of Llangollen' is a somewhat more tendentious title, but Mavor's anxieties on the subject can produce a statement like this: 'Indeed, much that we would now associate solely with a sexual attachment was contained in romantic friendship: tenderness, loyalty, sensibility, shared beds, shared tastes, coquetry, even passion' (p. xvii). Well, frankly, I can't spot the difference between this interpretation of Romantic Friendship and contemporary Lesbianism, and I would be inclined to attribute Mavor's delicacy to creeping homophobia.
50 Lillian Faderman, *Surpassing the Love of Men: Romantic Friendship and Love Between Women from the Renaissance to the Present* (1981; London, Women's Press, 1985), and *Scotch Verdict* (New York, Quill, 1983).
51 Sheila Jeffreys, 'Does It Matter If They Did It?', *Trouble and Strife*, no. 3 (Summer 1984), pp. 25–9.
52 Lynne Friedli, 'Women Who Dressed as Men', *Trouble and Strife*, no. 6 (Summer 1985), p. 27. This brief article is based on Friedli's doctoral thesis (University of Essex) and gives some useful source references. On the theory of cross-dressing see also Annette Kuhn, 'Sexual Disguise and Cinema', in her collection *The Power of the Image: Essays on Representation and Sexuality* (London, Routledge & Kegan Paul,

1985). See also: Julia Wheelwright *Amazons and Military Maids: Women Who Dressed as Men in Pursuit of Life, Liberty and Happiness* (London: Pandora, 1989) and Rudolf M. Dekker and Lotte C. van de Pol, *The Tradition of Female Transvestism in Early Modern Europe* (Basingstoke, Macmillan, 1989).

53 ' . . . so it seemed to me, viewing the story of Shakespeare's sister, as I had made it, [is] that any woman born with a great gift in the sixteenth century would certainly have gone crazed, shot herself, or ended her days in some lonely cottage outside the village . . . ' (Virginia Woolf, *A Room of One's Own*, p. 51.) Woolf might have been describing what happened to her, born with a great gift in the late nineteenth century and living on into the twentieth, in that she went fairly crazed and eventually committed suicide. At least she lived to write the books.

54 Jo Jones uses Wittig's epigram as the introduction to the last section in her novel *Come Come* (London, Sheba, 1983). There is a special issue on Wittig's writing of *Vlasta: Fictions, utopies, amazoniennes*, no 4, available from Collectif Memoires/ Utopies B.P. 130, 75663 Paris, Cedex 14.

55 From Fairbairns' own assessment of her career, 'I Was a Teenage Novelist', *Women's Review*, no. 8 (June 1986), pp. 8–11.

56 Zoë Fairbairns, *Stand We At Last* (London, Virago, 1983; Pan, 1984).

57 Fairbairns, 'I Was a Teenage Novelist', p. 10.

5

Fables, Myths, Mythologies

A police spokesman for the Neru district, Nkubu, said that, after a quarrel with his wife, Mr Ndola Kianyaga fed the supper she had cooked for him to his dog, whereupon Mrs Kianyaga fetched an axe from the kitchen and beheaded him.

The Nation, Nairobi, 18 August 1988

Draupadi is one of the heroines of the Indian epic, the *Mahabharata*. She is married to the five sons of Pandu. Her eldest husband is about to lose her in a game of dice. This is what happens.

'The Scriptures prescribed one husband for a woman; Draupadi is dependent on many husbands; therefore she can be designated a prostitute. There is nothing improper in bringing her, clothed or unclothed into the assembly.' (*Mahabharata* 65:35–36.) The enemy chief begins to pull at Draupadi's *sari*. Draupadi silently prays to the incarnate Krishna. The Idea of Sustaining Law (Dharma) materializes itself as clothing, and as the king pulls and pulls at her *sari* there seems to be more and more of it. Draupadi is infinitely clothed and cannot be publicly stripped. It is one of Krishna's miracles.[1]

The assembly is the company of men. Draupadi's body is private property, the property of men. Like all property, she can be bought, sold, exchanged. She is the goods to be viewed. I notice that Krishna's gesture does not alter her status; but it does call into question the motives of the men: the buyers, the audience, the pornographers. Mahasweta Devi's story 'Draupadi' places myth against history. Her narrative reverses the events of the myth in particular circumstances at a particular moment in the history of India.[2] But does the narrative endorse or transform the original meanings of Krishna's miracle and the story of Draupadi? What, in any case, was that original meaning? How could it ever be recuperated, given that the making of meaning is always a contract, however informal, between the reader and the text?

Mahasweta Devi's story is set during 1971, in the midst of the Indian army actions against the Santal tribal revolutionaries in West Bengal. The text was written in Bengali, with a revealing smattering of English words. All the technical vocabulary of the army is written in English. Gayatri Spivak, the translator, indicates which words these are by leaving them in italics in her translation so that they stand out of the text. Draupadi, or Dopdi, as she is also known, is a revolutionary. She lives and works alongside her husband and comrades as an equal. Her responsibility, freedom and political resolution are insisted upon by the narrator. The other aspect of Dopdi which Mahasweta Devi emphasizes is her identity as a tribal; her strange language, shared with her people, and her black, black skin. The revolutionaries exploit the racism of the special forces to protect themselves. Dopdi can vanish among her people by simply taking another name: ' . . . not merely the Santals but all tribals of the Austro-Asiatic Munda tribes appear the same to the Special Forces.'[3] This is a classic characteristic of racism – to racist eyes, they all look the same. Individuals do not exist. People are objects.

In the *Mahabharata* the woman is property, to be exchanged between men. She is held and captured by the male gaze; her nakedness would be her shame, a fact witnessed by Krishna's miracle, which clothes her in her defence. Shame is man's threat against women: a woman without shame is a woman without worth, a shameless woman. Not surprisingly, this was one of the first threats we exposed for what it was in the early days of the contemporary women's liberation movement. Shame could no longer contain us if we refused men's definitions of what was shameful. Anja Meulenbelt deliberately entitled her magnificently brazen autobiography *The Shame is Over*.[4] For what becomes of a man's power to intimidate, to overpower and to destroy, if a woman refuses to be ashamed? Mahasweta Devi's heroine is recognized, betrayed and brutally raped by the Special Forces upon the orders of their commander Senanayak. Senanayak fancies himself as an expert on revolutionary thinking. He has read all the books. Intriguingly, this works. His philosophy, *'In order to destroy the enemy, become one'*[5] enables him to capture Dopdi. But the one thing about which he cannot inform himself is the meaning a woman constructs and places upon herself and her body when she refuses men's meanings. It was not something he could study beforehand because we are now writing the books. When Dopdi is released from the posts where she has been tied, spread-eagled and repeatedly raped by many soldiers, she refuses to cover her bleeding, mutilated body and – refusing to be shamed – she marches straight up to Senanayak. 'There isn't a man here that I should be ashamed. I will not let you put my cloth on me. What more can you do?' (p. 196). Dopdi refuses Krishna's miracle, because she refuses to acknowledge the authority of men.

All myths are culturally specific. They legitimate power structures, endorse and justify existing social arrangements. They explain politics through symbols and metaphors. They offer truth, spiced with eternity. The least likely stories will be most warmly accepted and believed as revelation. The *Mahabharata* was not one of the mythic texts I knew in childhood. I had never heard of Draupadi until I read Mahasweta Devi's story; and so, her re-writing of the myth, upon which the impact of her narrative depends, carries no mythical emotional resonance for me. There was no sudden shift of consciousness or perception in my mind. Draupadi's sari was already simply a sign, something to apprehend intellectually. But what I did see, an image which had enormous force, was a woman, a specific woman, Dopdi Mejhen, unashamed of her raped, torn, bleeding body, confronting her enemy. I saw her 'walking towards him in the bright sunlight with her head high'. And I noticed that when the woman refuses to be shamed her captor is made to feel not morally guilty, but 'terribly afraid' (p. 196). She has refused to endorse men's systems of value. She has refused the meanings he placed upon her body. She has refused to bend, give way, give herself up. He can kill her – she demands that he does so, threatening him with her naked body. He can kill her; but her power, her spirit can never be broken.

The original myth of the *Mahabharata* had no authority over me as a woman reader, but the idea in the story of 'Draupadi', that a woman's naked body is an object of which to be ashamed, obviously did. My religion, Catholic Christianity, and the master-text which does have power over my life and my perceptions, the Bible, are both saturated in exactly the same nexus of ideas: women as sexual objects, sexuality as sin, and the wages of sin as shame and death. The influence and authority of the Bible in my culture and language, and especially within British literature, is both terrifying and immense.[6] For myths, once they are translated into theology, cease to be speculative and become prescriptive. They transform the political and changeable into the metaphysical, and therefore into supposedly immutable structures. As women, we are inscribed in biblical myth. Our nature, as women, is imagined and defined by men; and then, subsequently, forced upon us. The fact that Christianity was the imperial religion of Britain, and indeed, one of the tools used to justify that imperial endeavour, means that a good part of the world's population has been afflicted with Christian assumptions and institutions. One of the peculiar strengths of the Scriptures is the frequent absence of an author. The master-texts, the Books of Patriarchy, therefore exist as God-given, Godspeak, the Sacred Word.

But of course, like all the works of men, the Bible is fractured by contradictions, gaps and silences. The feminist challenge to the Bible has been consistent over the centuries; we have pointed out the same contradictions, even the same texts are cited, trotted out like seaside donkeys. Sometimes women cite text after text against text in our own defence, as Rachel Speght did in her reply to Joseph Swetnam's attack on women. Her pamphlet, *A Mouzell for Melastomus* (1617), is a defence mounted solely on the authority of biblical citation.[7] Elizabeth Cady Stanton's *The Women's Bible* (1895–8) argued, passionately and rationally, that the time had come to read the Bible as a book, rather than worship it as a 'fetich', and moreover to read it as a book which is 'not above the application of reason and common sense'.[8] In the most recent resurgence of the women's liberation movement, both Jewish and Christian women have tried to construct a women's theology. We have re-read the Bible from a feminist perspective and, even more radically, we have begun to re-tell the stories and to re-write the texts. Often, the same women have undertaken both the scholarly and the imaginative work of re-thinking Christianity. Sara Maitland wrote one of the first British accounts of the women's liberation movement in the white western Anglican and Catholic churches: *A Map of the New Country: Women and Christianity*. She co-edited, with Jo Garcia, an anthology of women's writing about spirituality, *Walking on the Water*, and in the same year published a volume of short stories, *Telling Tales*, many of which are re-writings of Judaeo-Christian and Classical Greek myths.[9]

The temptation to challenge the myths through their re-telling, to change their shapes and emphases, is obvious. Jan Montefiore explains. 'For the appeal of such traditional material as myth and fairy-story, especially for feminists, lies not only in its archaic prestige, but in its strong connections with human subjectivity, so that using this material seems to be a way of escaping the constrictive hierarchies of tradition and gaining access to the power of definition.'[10] Feminist writers have taken advantage of this imaginative freedom. Nothing, not even the Word of God, goes untouched. Feminist re-writing and re-telling of the Bible has revealed two things to me: first, that the Word of God is, indubitably and irrefutably, the word of men; and second, that women's words do not come from some sacred, separate, female space. Re-making meanings is both an individual and a collective project. It cannot be done by one woman alone. It cannot be done once and for all. Not only must the old stories be continually challenged and re-told; sometimes they must simply be mocked and abandoned. We need to make up new stories of our own. Let me explain.

The 1970s feminist writers' group which first published *Tales I Tell My Mother* in 1978 was a Gang of Five: Michelene Wandor, Sara Maitland, Zoë Fairbairns, Valerie Miner and Michèle Roberts.[11] They have now all found a published home with Methuen, although they published their anniversary issue *More Tales I Tell My Mother* with Journeyman Press in 1987. Three of these women, Maitland, Wandor and Roberts, have published work explicitly dealing with religious myth and its structuring power in women's lives and western culture. Wandor's poem sequence, *Gardens of Eden*, uses Jewish myth, the voices of Lilith and Eve as Jewish women making sense of sex, God, cookery and family life, and above all, re-interrogating the old stories. At one point Eve takes a tour of ancient Greek myth, asking some difficult questions. Michèle Roberts, brought up as a Catholic, has worked on Catholic themes, Christian myth and Christian theology in all her fiction, even taking *The Visitation* as the title of her second novel. Her third novel, *The Wild Girl*, is a fifth gospel, the women's gospel according to Mary Magdalene; and she has made both the Bible and Greek myth central to her fiction *The Book of Mrs Noah*.[12] Sara Maitland is the wife of an Anglican priest; she is involved with the church in every way, personally and politically. This is the subject of her fiction. I want to write about this work because it is crucial to make the links between feminism and Christianity and because it is impossible ever to resolve the quarrel between free women and the Church.

The first of Maitland's *Telling Tales* is 'Of Deborah and Jael', a re-telling of the story narrated in Judges 4 and 5. This narrative is crucial to any feminist reconstruction of the Bible. Deborah's song for Jael is one of the oldest texts we have. Deborah judged Israel. She is a prophetess, a woman of power and decision: a woman who speaks for God and who dwells with God. She tells the children of Israel that the Lord will deliver their enemy Sisera into the hands of a woman. Barak, the leader of Israel's army, will not go into battle without her. Sisera, his army duly defeated, flies to the tent of Heber the Kenite, assuming that because peace reigns between the two tribes he will be safe there. Jael, the wife of Heber, lures him into her tent, gives him milk to drink, and urges him to rest. While he sleeps she hammers a tent peg into his temples.

> Blessed above women shall Jael the wife of Heber the Kenite be, blessed shall she be above women in the tent.
> He asked water, and she gave him milk; she brought forth butter in a lordly dish.

> She put her hand to the nail, and her right hand to the workman's hammer and with the hammer she smote Sisera. She smote off his head when she had pierced and stricken through the temples.[13]

Male commentators, Jewish and Christian alike, have taken a predictably negative attitude towards murderous women in the Bible. They are happy praising Moses, but become uneasy when faced with Judith decapitating Holofernes, so much so that she is not part of the official version. And so with the story of Jael: they point out that the codes of hospitality in the desert necessarily involve both friends and foes. They argue that the fact of being a guest is sacred. Jael murders a guest while he sleeps. Her sexual manipulativeness is seen as cowardly and dishonourable. Feminists read the story rather differently.

The irony of Jael's situation is made explicit in Deborah's song, celebrating her victory for Israel. The reality of war – all wars – for women, is that we are the spoils. Men are killed, women are raped.

> Have they not sped? Have they not divided the prey? To every man a damsel or two.[14]

This passage in the Hebrew text is literal and shocking. The Authorized Version's polite rendition – 'To every man a damsel or two' – might be better translated as 'a cunt or two for every prick'. Woman is written here as 'rachamata'im', which means womb; 'rosh' is the head of a man, but can also mean prick. Jael knows, as does every woman, that we can never win against men in open combat. They are physically stronger than we are. Women's weapons are, and have always been, guile, cunning and trickery.

In Maitland's story of Deborah and Jael, one women fulfils the prophecy of another; one woman honours another in song. Deborah sings Jael's victory with 'her public authority';[15] she celebrates a solidarity in slaughter between the two women. Barak cannot look at the bloody mess in Jael's tent, nor at 'that crazy little woman' (p. 3). However, the women 'look at each other, they smile at each other – they are friends . . . They reach out hands, unspeaking, almost shy with excitement, and touch each other very gently. They know their husbands will never want to touch them again. They know who the enemy is' (p. 4). Maitland does not explicitly say who the enemy is; but what her narrative does is transform the biblical victory of Israel over the Canaanites into a violent sexual victory of women over men. She describes Jael's murder of Sisera not as a careful, cold-blooded political murder, but as an expression of orgasmic, sadistic sexuality. Her murder of Sisera is the violent reversal of a man raping a woman, a sexual murder. The tent peg becomes her penis, 'the pointed stick no longer alien but a part of her person', her weapon of penetration. She enters Sisera's brains in a frenzy, 'becomes berserk, and long after it is necessary, bang, bang, bang, rhythmical and powerful'. When she has finished Jael collapses exhausted, 'worn out by her own excitement' (p. 2).

There is in fact some evidence in the original text for this interpretation of Jael's act as sexual murder. Rabbi Sheila Shulman reads Judges 5:27 as an inversion of birth and rape. Here is the verse.

At her feet he bowed, he fell: where he bowed there he fell down dead.

The structure of the verse, as in the repetitions of a ballad, flings the weight on the last word, 'dead'. Literally translated, the word means 'destroyed'. In her essay on Deborah and Jael, 'Versions of a Story', Shulman had this to say about that verse.

> There is, here, a sense of extreme violence and then, if we can call it that, release, carefully built up through the structure. These same elements are present in two other human experiences; the overwhelming visual images become, here, on the one hand a parody of birth, as Sisera falls between Jael's feet, and a triumphant *reversal* of rape. Again, the image is hieratic, larger than life.[16]

What this murder does in Maitland's story is release both women from male meanings. Deborah, whom Maitland imagines as 'an ugly woman; she had wept about it through her youth', is set free from male expectations of beauty. 'Her words are strong and beautiful instead: she has delivered the mighty Sisera into the hands of a woman' (p. 3). Sexual murder is a genre of crime that is – at present – peculiar to the male of the human species.[17] Yet both women delight in the bloody slaughter of men, 'breathing in the exhilarating stink of fear that comes to their nostrils' (p. 4).

Maitland is interested in writing about experiences and perceptions that are, or have been, sexually unacceptable. Sometimes her writing is too clearly saturated in the clichés peculiar to sado-masochistic eroticism, which simply reproduce what men have always said about women. But here, I think, her method works. 'Of Deborah and Jael' is obscurely shocking; four brief pages that need to be re-thought, re-read. I do not think that her re-telling of the biblical story tells us in any definitive way either what women are or what they could be like. But it does tell us what men fear. They fear that we are as capable of killing them as boldly, bloodily and cruelly as they kill us. They know, and we know, that we have ample reason for doing so. But what is odd, and slightly sinister in Maitland's story, is that she should suggest that women might find sexual murder erotically gratifying. The idea is certainly present in Judges 5. But then, who wrote that version of the story?

The myths we have not made and do not own always operate in reference to male-constructed meanings. It is therefore most fruitful for us to deconstruct and re-write the patriarchal myths that already contain cracks, fissures and contradictions; or those where women have a dominant and subversive role. Women painters, working in the genre of epic historical or biblical painting, have often chosen to work with these subjects – as, for example, in Artemesia Gentileschi's dramatic depiction of Judith decapitating Holofernes.[18] Feminist writers have been drawn to the stories where we were present, but silent; they have given women voices, motives, feelings, but above all, meanings.

The holy texts of any culture, as I have already indicated, present the greatest challenge to women. In white western culture we have a political, metaphysical and social structure which draws on Christian biblical concepts both to prescribe and to justify the subordination of women. We, the women, were of course present in the making of history. But in the writing we appear only in brief passages, fragments. We are always interpreted. We rarely interpret ourselves.

Maitland's second book of short stories, *A Book of Spells* continues and develops her early themes: biblical narratives, fairy-tales, modern fables, magic, metamorphoses and ambiguous, unpleasant sexual feelings.[19] The boldest piece of writing is her 'Triptych', an interpretation of Genesis 12–21, the story of Hagar, Sarah and Abraham. No simple moral lessons here. None of the preachers I have ever heard using this story has ever gone into the morality of surrogate motherhood terribly carefully. Abraham's wife Sarah is barren. Hagar the handmaid bears Abraham's child so that he will have an heir. Nobody ever denounced Abraham. Instead, I have listened to lengthy exhortations to wait patiently until God sees fit to hand out sons in our old age, and to make male visitors welcome just in case they turn out to be angels.

A triptych is usually an altarpiece with three paintings of unequal size and significance. The most important event, usually the Nativity or the Crucifixion, will be in the middle and will be the largest; two minor characters will be on either side. Sometimes the Nativity has the Virgin on one side, the Angel Gabriel on the other. Sometimes the donor who paid for the painting is there in attendance with his patron saint. Maitland takes her three characters and makes the woman who has the least power, the woman abused and betrayed, the foreigner, the handmaiden, the slave, the central figure in the triptych. It is Hagar's perceptions and Hagar's story which become central. We interpret Sarah and Abraham, all their actions and motives, through her intelligence and judgement. But Maitland does one single thing which transforms and electrifies the story, and overdetermines the inherent political meanings. She describes Hagar as a Blackwoman. In Genesis, Hagar is described as Hagar the Egyptian, as the bondwoman, a handmaid, Sarah's maid; never as Black.

In the Bible it is Sarah who persuades Abraham to remedy her sterility by sleeping with Hagar.

And Sarah said unto Abraham, Behold now, the Lord hath restrained me from bearing: I pray three, go in unto my maid; it may be that I may obtain children by her.[20]

In the Bible it is Sarah who persuades Abraham to banish Hagar and her son Ishmael into the desert.

Wherefore she said unto Abraham, Cast out this bondwoman and her son: for the son of this bondwoman shall not be heir with my son, even with Isaac.[21]

In Maitland's 'Triptych' it is Abraham who lusts after Hagar, Sarah who says, 'Oh do it, Hagar, for God's sake. Get the old goat off both our backs' (p. 106). The relationship between Sarah and Hagar is a Lesbian one, despite a vast difference in age. To Hagar, Sarah is everything: mother, sister, lover, friend. It is when their actual relationship in history, that of mistress and bought slave, is made visible between them, that the bond breaks for ever. In Maitland's 'Triptych' it is Abraham who forces Hagar out into the desert and to certain death. Abraham is a madman, a lecher, a bully, a coward, a fanatic: a man who batters his wife into submission and insists that the Blackwoman slave and her son, his son, are cast out. Blackness is Hagar's sign of difference. Certainly, it is her Blackness which rouses Abraham's lust. 'Abraham in that week they had been together had venerated the purple blackness of her breasts . . .' (pp. 108–9). And it is her Blackness which Sarah finds beautiful. 'That Sarah, who had taken her from the land of the Pharaoh and told her she was loveable, who had touched her black skin and found it lovely, found in it the source and power of resistance and had given back to Hagar that strength which she had drawn from her . . . ' (p. 110). Black pride and Black power are the strengths which Blackwomen give to themselves and each other. No non-Black woman could ever give that to her Blackwoman lover. Sarah, Maitland's narrative implies, is not-black. She is Hagar's white lover. And so Hagar is a victim – a proud victim, but a victim nevertheless. If God had not intervened on her side – and He did, so the story goes – she and her son would have been doomed.

Maitland's narrative retains the broad outlines of Genesis. She ascribes every evil action to Abraham. But was there no muttering among Abraham's people at his violence and injustice? Or were they glad to see the back of Hagar, Sarah's favourite? Were there any other Blackpeople in the camp? I can ask these questions because Maitland offers alternative solutions, other endings, and because she is re-imagining a master-text, dismantling its authority. My point here is that the conjunction of Black/woman/slave/outcast/powerlessness is an unwise conjunction. Maitland is writing racism into a story where no racism is implied. Abraham and Sarah were probably not whites, and it is not only Blackpeople who have been slaves: the Israelites were themselves enslaved in Egypt.

But there are good things here too. Hagar sees God and lives. And the vision of God is of a Blackwoman; God as Black, female power. And it is extraordinary and wonderful to imagine 'the great black smile of God' (p. 111). The vision of Hagar dancing, and the holy darkness of God, are beautifully written; but, but, but . . . Why was it so impossible to imagine Hagar brewing up a slave rebellion? The only retribution Hagar can have is that permitted by the Bible story. Hagar and Ishmael are saved and blessed by God. 'The great nation' that Ishmael founded is thought by some to be the people of the Islamic faith. In the Qu'ran, Sura II: 127, it is written:

> And remember Abraham
> And Isma'il raised
> The foundations of the House.

Ishmael/Isma'il is here placed before Isaac. Moslems celebrate Abraham as one of their spiritual ancestors, as do the Jews and the Christians. Therefore the narrative in Genesis has implications for the women of all three faiths – although Allah inspired Mohammed, wisely I suspect, to leave out the incendiary elements in the story, the story of Hagar and Sarah. Hagar is powerless without God. She goes out into the desert to die. God rewards her meek submission to her fate. 'Blessed are the meek, for they shall inherit the earth' (Matthew 5:5). This is a most mischievous text. I am opposed to meekness in women. We have never inherited the earth. And meekness is not a quality that would enable us to do so. The third figure in Maitland's 'Triptych' is Abraham himself. With resolute bad temper and obstinacy Maitland refuses to imagine his side of the story. She displaces Abraham with her own voice, as the writer. The woman speaks and silences the man. If you want to know his version, she says, read Genesis. Maitland refuses to produce what she describes, very critically, as her 'hyped-up prose'. Instead she gives us an angry biblical commentary on the text which is, as she describes it, 'edgy, cranky, cynical' (p. 119) – and, to my mind, delicious. She breaks the illusion, refuses to write beautifully. She stands before us as an angry feminist woman: a woman writer, who stands in relation to the church and the Holy Scriptures as Hagar does to Abraham's encampment. They are both driven out, despised; the outcasts, the strangers, full of just rage. Maitland finally sets her text against Genesis, and says, as Hagar must have done, 'I cannot forgive' (p. 119). Bravo.

Touching the sacred texts results in the most appalling violence from those whose vested interests are thereby put in question. I preached a sermon at Cuddesdon Theological College near Oxford on 1 March 1985. My theme was the contentious subject of Love. The woman friend who read the passage from the New Testament was a revolutionary feminist and a Catholic. The first Epistle of St John, chapter 3, beginning at the thirteenth verse: 'Marvel not, my brethren, if the world hate you.' Standing at the lectern she transformed the text, so that it would speak to women. 'Marvel not, my sisters and brothers, if the world hate you. We know that we have passed from death unto life, because we love the sisters and brothers. He or she that loveth not their sister or brother abideth in death.' Afterwards she was publicly insulted and abused by a priest sitting opposite her at supper, because she had dared to touch the text. Their voices rose in anger; the table took sides. She refused to eat with him. The Principal of the College pressed the fire alarm and we all downed our cutlery and fled. We were never asked back to Cuddesdon again.

In 1984, Michèle Roberts published her re-writing of the sacred text: her fifth Gospel, the Gospel According to Mary Magdalene, entitled *The Wild Girl*. She decided to re-imagine the events of the Gospel narratives from the marginal perspective of a woman who was both the lover of Jesus of Nazareth and a whore. Refusing the intricacies of biblical scholarship, or indeed of history, Roberts decided to re-possess the myth. She accepts the traditional teaching of the Church which combines the three women, Mary of Magdala, Mary of Bethany and the unknown woman of St Mark who anoints Jesus. 'I wanted to dissect a myth; I found myself at the same time recreating one.'[22] Re-imagining the Gospels is a project that has already been undertaken by men, either in the interests of agnosticism (as in Strauss's *Das Leben Jesu*, which George Eliot translated) or to promote their own quasi-religious doctrines. Two twentieth-century examples of this are Robert Graves, in his numerous studies and fictions, and D. H. Lawrence. In 'The Man Who Died' (1928) Lawrence described a preposterous sexual resurrection involving pagan priestesses and erotic rites which made for thrillingly titillating reading when I was about sixteen. The process of re-making Christian myth continues in the most popular twentieth-century medium, cinema. Violent denunciations greeted the showing of Martin Scorsese's film *The Last Temptation of Christ* in 1988. Fundamentalist Christians kept up a prayer vigil by the box office in Paris and a right-wing Catholic group attacked and burnt out the cinema where the film was being shown. Reverential reconstructions such as Cecil B. de Mille's fabulous *The Ten Commandments* got away with presenting pure Hollywood behind a great masquerade of rabbinical and exegetical consultants in the credits; but versions that suggest Jesus of Nazareth was human and might have fancied 'girls' meet with a different response.

Other religions and cultures have responded in similar ways when their prophets and gurus are presented as ordinary men. One of my teachers, an Indian and a Hindu, who had actually known Gandhi as a child, told me that someone had demanded that Richard Attenborough's film *Gandhi* should not represent her spiritual leader in the flesh, but by a sort of moving light with a voice. More recently, Moslems in Britain publicly burned Salman Rushdie's book *The Satanic Verses* because it contained what they argued was an insulting portrait of Mohammed.[23] 'Because the Rugby-educated son of an Indian Muslim family writes a thick and richly literary novel suggesting that the Prophet was human and the distinction between good and evil is not always crystal clear, his book is not only banned in India, Egypt and Saudi Arabia, but burned in the streets of Bradford, and withdrawn from the shelves of W. H. Smith's bookshops there.'[24] The emotions aroused by the Rushdie affair suggest to me that we need more and different versions of the Prophet: and more open discussion between Christian, Jewish and Moslem women. We, after all, have very little to lose.

All the re-visions of the life of Christ have one thing in common; they all identify (hetero)sexuality as the missing element in the Gospels.[25] Christianity does not have a good track record on sex. The received view has been that it is better to marry than to burn – but only just – and that all forms of homosexuality are an abomination. Anything other than holy wedlock opened the gateway to mortal sin, and we, the women, were the gateway. Roberts radically re-writes the Gospel story by placing the debate about sexual politics firmly at the centre of the Jesus movement. The project of her myth-making is not just to salvage Jesus for feminism – not an easy task – but to re-write the debate, which did actually take place, between the Gnostics and the orthodox faction, led by St Peter, which eventually became the Christian Church. This is a crucial work to undertake because it has been Christian men who have invented women either as sexless virgins or as an embodied rapacious sexual urge, as either virgin or whore; Mary, mother of God, or Mary, the sinner forgiven. Roberts takes her stand on the contradictions in the texts and within the stories of the tradition. She does what feminist writers have always done and continue to do: she articulates silences, absences, gaps, imagines women as speaking subjects. To make a woman's perception central is not, however, a simple thing. We have been written, imagined and re-written for too many centuries, by the men. And the figure of Mary Magdalene has always been a painted cardboard cut-out, endlessly re-drawn, as nun, as whore.

Christianity works through the construction of opposites and a subsequent marriage between the two, in which the darkness is redeemed by the light. Behold.

The Church	Christ
Earth	Heaven
Darkness	Light
Flesh	Spirit
Woman	Man
Whore	Virgin
Nature	God

Exponents of Christian theology worry away at the problem of re-uniting the irreconcilably opposed. Thus, so the story goes, God enters Nature as Jesus of Nazareth, the master becomes the slave, heaven descends to earth, the first becomes the last, the light shines in the darkness, and Christ saves the Church. For Death to become Life we have to enact the drama of the Crucifixion and the Resurrection. For atheists in post-Christian times this scenario – the spectacle of brutal suffering willingly undertaken by the victim, who presents it as some kind of necessary sacrifice on behalf of the torturer – will seem bewilderingly familiar. It has been endlessly reproduced in the philosophy and fantasy of the Marquis de Sade. It is no coincidence that de Sade's most sophisticated theoreticians in his elaborate sexual scenarios are powerful clerics. Christianity is da Sade's source, his framework, his working metaphysic. The scenario in which the victim willingly chooses suffering, indeed, becomes erotically involved in the orgasm of death, is simply the libertine version of the first scenario, in which the victim is forced. The theology of Crucifixion, therefore, transforms the version in which the victim capitulates under duress into the joyous embracing of utter destruction.[26] It is all very unpleasant.

Roberts' theological thinking proceeds along the tram-line dualities. At one point in her text Jesus gives a long sermon on the need to unite the male and the female, the marriage in the soul. 'You must remember that you can know God only when you know both parts of yourself and let them come together, the light of the Father married to the darkness of the Mother . . . '[27] and so on. The Jesus movement is represented in Roberts' text – very realistically – as a lot of dusty travellers, 'united in our yearning dissatisfaction with this world' (p. 56). Even homosexuality is cheerfully accepted as long as the women and the men concerned are busy uniting the male and the female on a metaphysical plane. 'There are men and women in our company who love only the members of their own sex. They must still let the marriage happen in their souls.' (p. 63). Only when this happens can we know the 'fullness' of God and become 'whole'. Now all this is what Rabbi Sheila Shulman describes as The Zip Fastener Theory of Sexual Politics: the polarities are all set out, then zipped up. But these polarities are, in every sense, man-made. They exist only through cultural representation and political force. Men invented both the Virgin and the Whore; men made themselves cultural subjects and women the object–other. So there is no point whatever in accepting man-made terms of reference, endorsing them as natural, or even as existing in some absolute sense, and then arguing for their destruction in a marriage of opposites. I am of the opinion, which Roberts too makes explicit in her text, that Mary Magdalene and St Peter are more alike than different, that the schism between male and female is more ideological than biological, and that the splintered, fragmented nature of our consciousness, whatever sex we happen to be, is an aspect of human being. This is why we make art, fear death and reflect upon our own condition in order to transform ourselves.

The myth of wholeness, indeed, the search for wholeness, is an idea which comes from the acceptance of polarity and division, and from the Christian doctrine of the Fall, where our oneness with Nature and with God, whatever or whoever they are, was originally lost. Roberts is absolutely right to engage with these contradictions and dualities: if we are the products of centuries of western Catholic Christendom, then we have no choice but to do so. We can, though, at least re-think the terms of the debate. Roberts follows the Gnostic theology of inspiration. Her Magdalene hears voices. 'How do I know? I whispered to the Saviour's mother: whether the voices that speak in me and make me sing come from God? Did I blaspheme when I invoked the power of the Mother? She shifted, and looked at me. – Trust the voice, daughter, she said: as we trust you' (p. 65). Here Roberts and I part company again. She clearly endorses Magdalene's voices. Mary's visions form the philosophical substance of *The Wild Girl*. But all my life I have mistrusted voices and the people who claim to hear them. Joan of Arc followed her voices, and so did Peter Sutcliffe. One slaughtered men honourably as a soldier, the other butchered women as a sexual murderer. They both left a trail of blood. On the whole, the Bible suggests that voices from God will ask you to do irrational things: kill your son, go and order entire cities to repent, marry disgraced pregnant women, spend time starving in deserts. The wonderful thing about voices and visions, as the Gnostics discovered, is that no one can gainsay your revelations. You possess access to divine authority; you are your own authority, your own witness. Roberts' Magdalene envisages the polarities becoming fused in a mystic marriage. This is the central theology of *The Wild Girl*. And no mythic structure in western culture which might lend weight to this argument is left out. After Jesus' death Mary goes into a lengthy death-like trance in which she re-enacts the myth of Cupid and Psyche. Nearly all these myths of mystic lovers reinforce existing heterosexist structures. The men descend as gods; we, the women, the mortals, wait passively to receive them. Heterosexual union is the longing for death. 'I have followed your mysteries, I whispered: I am an initiate. I have shared in the sacred drama of sexuality and death' (p. 125). Salome the midwife turns into the Triple Goddess, Maiden/Mother/Crone, a useful structure taken over by the Church and re-named the Trinity. 'Receive the blessing, she said: of the virgin and the mother and the crone' (p. 144). The problem with the Triple Goddess is that she endorses an interpretation of a woman's life that is based upon her relation with men: the virgin, woman as prepubescent girl, awaiting the mystic lover; the mother, woman as reproductive vessel; crone, woman as past menstruation, past childbearing. There is no need even to consider a woman's virginity as a phase in her life unless there is a value placed on her unbroken hymen.

On the whole, Mary Magdalene's symbolic visions are far less convincing than the Revised Standard Version of Christianity elaborated by Jesus around camp fires or jugs of wine. Mary's visions are too laden with obvious meanings – for example, Ignorance = Phallic Men who refuse the Mystic Marriage. But in her re-writing of Genesis, in which the children of Ignorance, bent on male power, fling Adam and Eve out of Paradise, Roberts is imaginative in interesting ways. Genesis has always been interpreted as a whites-only myth, given the apartheid of conventional theology. But Roberts makes it clear that Adam and Eve were Black. 'Both were of great beauty, with black skins that shone like the most precious jet or ebony and signified the marriage of the lightness and the dark in them' (p. 80). I must confess that, given my political reasons for arguing against cultural polarities and the metaphor of marriage, mystic or otherwise, it is unlikely that I would ever be converted to Roberts' views. Still, she is attempting to write a version of Christianity that is not aggressively alienating to women, and that is worth doing. Jesus himself, however, remains a guru and an immortal, not just a wandering prophet or a man of ideas. Mary asks him what he thinks her visions mean and meekly accepts his explanations. After the Crucifixion, the tomb remains inexplicably empty. So Jesus never is just a man. Not quite.

Christianity is not often presented as comic and the New Testament narrative is not a funny story. But for Christians or ex-Christians like myself, who know the Bible well, there are some irresistibly funny lines. Roberts and her predecessor, D. H. Lawrence, found that putting the sex back into the text was not all that easy; because sex is often comic, and Roberts and Lawrence are remorselessly serious. Lawrence's Man Who Died looks down upon his erect phallus with holy awe. 'He crouched to her, and he felt the blaze of his manhood and his power rise up in his loins, magnificent. "I am risen!" '.[28] Roberts is more lyrical, but the thesis is the same. Here is Mary Magdalene's orgasm. 'I rose, I pierced through the barrier of shadow, and was no longer an I but part of a great whirl of light that throbbed and rang with music – for a moment, till I was pulled back by the sound of my own voice whispering words I did not understand: this is the resurrection, and the life' (p. 67). I'm afraid I laughed out loud at these passages. To lay so overwhelming an emphasis on (hetero)sexual sex as a mystical experience places Roberts historically. In the late twentieth century we have given sex an extraordinarily exalted position as both the problem and the solution in our lives. Sex has not always loomed so large.

But there are some good political points too. On being told to forget about the housework, Martha answers Jesus back: 'It's well for you, she astonished us all by spitting, it's I who'll do it later when you're asleep' (p. 35). And so Roberts' Jesus and his disciples do the washing up. Amen, sister, Amen. Most marvellous of all is Roberts' version of the feeding of the five thousand. This becomes Martha's miracle. 'People called it a miracle afterwards. I called it good housewifery. I daresay we meant the same thing. Within minutes Martha had the disciples organised . . . ' (p. 76). This miracle is rather more waspishly presented by Christina Roche in *i'm not a feminist but . . .* (see figure 5).[29]

Nevertheless, the most valuable theological idea arising from Roberts' fiction is not a new one but the old Jewish concept of *tikkun olam*, mending the world. The relevance of this idea for feminist spirituality is elaborated by Rabbi Sheila Shulman:

> . . . *tikkun olam* usually refers to two notions, both of which are relevant here. One is that there is a kind of crack in the world, a sense that the world lacks integrity (which I should remind you is the root meaning of *shalom*) because the people persistently do not walk in God's ways . . . The other notion has a more cosmic dimension . . . It is that *tikkun olam* is the human work in a creation that is not yet complete. We, humans, are partners in the work of creation.[30]

This is not so much the partnership of woman and man, but of human beings and God. Roberts writes the same thought. 'Your dreams tell us how creation did not happen all at once, but over time, how creation must continue, and must be renewed' (p. 82). Roberts insists that we are in and of this world. Our visions inform the world. We must live fully, in and through the flesh. The apocalypse ending of *The Wild Girl* affirms this-worldiness; the love between mother and daughter, and of women together. Finally, Roberts adopts another Catholic myth, that of the Four Marys washed ashore near Massilia, Marseilles in southern France, at Saintes-Maries-de-la-Mer, where they build their vision of a community run by women, living in harmony with the land and one another, and at peace. The fifth Gospel, Roberts' text, has a crusading purpose: 'to warn against Ignorance and to preach an Idea' (p. 130). That Idea hinges on the value of women. And because she has an unhesitating sense of the preciousness of each woman, Roberts refuses the endemic sado-masochism of Christianity. The crucifixion is simply horrible. There is no ecstasy in pain, and no salvation. There is no virtue in denial, nor in suffering. Here are the sayings of Roberts' risen Jesus. 'We are part of nature, and, in that fierce embrace, we must celebrate the action of spirit and matter in ourselves, through dance and song, through meals shared, through conversation. These acts of everyday become holy, and become our sacraments, the way we meet God in ourselves and in each other' (p. 109). Roberts denies the other-worldiness of Christianity, but remains ambiguous about the life to come: we are never told what happened to Jesus. Even in his role as the returning traveller he keeps marvellously quiet about the other side. But with the authority of the risen dead, albeit seen with visionary eyes, he sits down in the grass and tells Mary Magdalene that we must get on with the 'mystic marriage '*in this life*' (Roberts' italics). 'Those who are reunited in the marriage chamber will never be separated again. *This* is the restoration. *This* is the resurrection. There are those who will say of me that I died first and then rose up, but they are in error, for first I was resurrected and then I died. If you do not first attain the resurrection then your souls will shrivel and die' (p. 111). This ominous threat to the soul does not confront the fact that no matter how hard we strive to unite matter and spirit, inner woman and inner man, darkness and light, God and nature, when we die we separate and

146

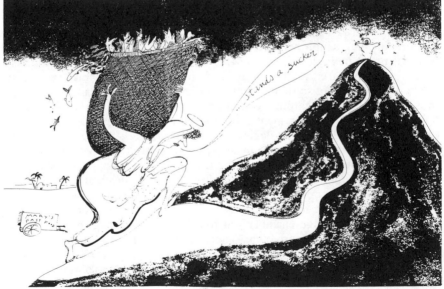

Figure 5   *Mary's fast food*

dissolve. We cease to be as we once were; and however we try to imagine otherwise, in some absolute sense we cease to be. It is a strength in Christianity, as in all mystery religions, that the faith confronts this absolute loss head-on, and concludes by reversing the dénouement of the human plot. 'Death, thou shalt die.' The denial of the world, the flesh, the devil and all their works is the traditional Christian solution. But we, the women, are inextricably bound up with all three in the Christian structure of metaphysics. We give birth to the world, we are the flesh and the devil's gateway. Christianity has never been a women's religion. And only by denying the centrality of death in Christian mystery and arguing for sexual resurrection can Roberts argue what a friend we have in Jesus.

Women's actions are central to the myths of Christianity: Mary of Nazareth singing the Magnificat, the woman at the well in Samaria telling truth, the Magdalene's extravagant love, the fact that we were last at the cross and first at the tomb. Despite men's attempts to control the interpretation and meaning given to those actions, the Gospel stories make women central and crucial.[31] Even as odious a book as C. S. Lewis's *The Lion, The Witch and the Wardrobe*[32] has to give us credit for loyalty and persistence. Roberts' controversial theology, though I have deep reservations about it, is more than worthwhile; it is necessary. These are the principal myths of white western culture; they must be re-written, re-imagined, re-constructed, or thrown out, again and again and again. Unlike many of my sisters and colleagues in the women's liberation movement I do not believe that religion – any religion, Christianity, Islam, Judsism, Sikhism, Hinduism, Buddhism or whatever – will go away if ignored, or proved to be irrational, mad and unjust. Religious myths are at the roots of our politics and social structures, the core of white western male philosophy, the source of many persistent ambiguities in our own thinking.[33] Unless they are actively argued over, dismantled and re-shaped they can never be resisted and withstood.

Roberts herself may have sensed the limitations of directly re-telling Christian myth. For it can only be done by recalling again and again the patriarchal myths upon which the narrative is based. In her next novel, *The Book of Mrs Noah*, she takes the re-writing of myth, both the story and the process, as her subject. Here, the Bible becomes the master-text, the book behind the Book; but the author, the voice of God, is forced to put in a comic appearance and to justify His version to a women writers' group of disagreeing sibyls, all of whom represent fairly recognizable white feminist stereotypes. This is fantasy fiction and the Ark of Mrs Noah is the Ark of Stories. So this is the book about writing The Book; first base, making myths, and telling the stories that were left out of the main text.

And so the structure of the book proceeds, unfolding, absorbing, with each of the five sibyls telling a story; the unwritten mythic history of women. For the Ark is also the Arkive, the library, the womb, the psychic space for the re-telling of lost women's stories. There is a rhythm to *The Book of Mrs Noah*; the stories alternate with the sibyls' discussions of feminist writing and Mrs Noah's adventures on surreal and menacing Italian islands. These adventures give the text a coherence and urgency, which is just as well: I was perpetually disappointed and frustrated that none of the sibyls' stories was resolved or developed. This text is also middle-class fiction with a vengeance. Mrs Noah's husband has the kind of job which means that you can afford *pensiones* in Venice, and most of the sibyls have houses, husbands, children, cars, private bathrooms. The Babble-On Sibyl has a family of in-laws that go to church: 'Departing up the path to the car in a flurry of silk headscarves, leather handbags, walking sticks, white socks, they exclaim how good she is to stay home and make the lunch . . . ' (p. 27). Only the Forsaken Sibyl has discovered Lesbianism. No one is declared to be Black and it is not an issue.

What this means is that despite the fragmentation of the form, the density of the prose, the candour of Roberts' continuous analysis of the process of writing, despite her indignation on behalf of all women, which is not a feature of any man's fiction, it still all feels like familiar well-written ground. The six stories, mostly first-person narratives, are all disturbing and often about sex. The first two deal directly with issues of theology and spirituality. The first story, by an unnamed Mrs Noah, tells the story of the Flood and takes up the theology of *The Wild Girl* and the old argument of God-Immanent or God-Transcendent.

> I flow out of myself and become pot, hide, fish, earth, leaf. I worship the creation of the world day by day by letting myself become part of it, by working. God is in my hands as they scrub, wring, knead, scour, caress, sew, carve. I act, I create, and God pours through me . . . For Jack God is different. He is a mighty father in the sky, who punishes us when we do wrong. (p. 72)

The transcendent God is malevolent, 'ready with his thunderbolts'. God-Immanent is the feminist version. Yet both Gods emerge as an aspect of the soul, the self, a faith in Be-ing, the God within. Roberts' Mrs Noah of the biblical myth ceases to be the good wife and mother. She goes off to live on her own as a result of her reflections on the couples of animals entering the Ark. 'What a strange way to live, I suddenly think to myself: couples couples couples. I want to live on my own' (p. 78). She settles down on Ararat for ever, invents writing and re-names the world. Naming the world and creating the world become one. The inadequacy of our shared public language, our shared concepts, the impossibility of expressing women's ideas, women's myths – this is one of Roberts' obsessions. The public language is owned by men. But Roberts worries away at the contradictions. The State Dictionary is interrogated every time Mrs Noah consults the book of riddles. Nearly all the words are linked to childbirth.

p. 63.   When is a *confinement* . . . not a *confinement*?
p. 97.   Does *want* also mean *want*?
p. 132.   *Life. Sentence. Life-sentence?*
p. 183.   Does *to bear* mean also *to bear*?
p. 211.   So why . . . does *to conceive* also mean *to conceive*?

The Ark is also the Arkive, a reference library with Mrs Noah as the librarian. Books and wombs are linked in sinister fashion in Roberts' texts. But even Mrs

Noah's longing for a child becomes ambiguous as public meanings slither across the words. Roberts adheres to a line of thinking more often found in American radical feminism; especially in the linguistic work by Mary Daly. Inventing new words and re-naming the world is supposedly a source of power. 'Naming is power: the hidden world yields up its secrets when you link the right names in nature together, when you trace the correspondence, taut as a fishing line, between star, herb, season, humour and beast' (p. 109). I disagree. Naming is in itself not power: it is identifying the world made not-in-our-image. But naming it in our own words can only be a prelude to changing it – which is something we still need to work out how to do.

The second story in *The Book of Mrs Noah* directly confronts the sado-masochism of Christianity; this peculiar ecstasy of the flesh associated with Christian sensibility. Here Roberts' narrator is a medieval nun whose repressed sexual desires find orgasmic expression in flagellation.

> I have already been taught to meditate on the passion, wounds and sacred blood of our Saviour Lord Jesus Christ. I have spent hours in church kneeling under the enormous crucifix, gazing at the thick nails driven through his hands and feet, the gashes torn in soft flesh. I have learned to enter his suffering, to share it. So it does not seem strange to me that my new brothers show me the way further in.
> At first their whips only tickle me . . . (p. 111)

Meditating on the Passion clearly has its dangers when it is combined with the traditional Christian hatred of the body, matter, nature, women. In Roberts' narrative, the torture and ecstasy of the flesh are firmly linked with the medieval painting of the Last Judgement on the walls of the parish church. 'One of these ladies is held down by two scarlet devils, while a third tears off her breasts with red-hot pincers. The other lady, tied to a gridiron, is having her eyes put out, and a glowing poker thrust between her legs' (p. 105). Women are the damned. And our damnation is bound up with the definition of our flesh as sin and the orthodox Christian meanings imposed upon our bodies. Roberts' fictional theology makes this visible and explicit. Thus public ideology and private experience endorse and affirm one another. Men hate women. Women hate themselves. Men paint Last Judgements of women being butchered. Women butcher themselves, with their own hands.

But how can these public meanings be unwritten, undone? The real energy of *The Book of Mrs Noah* does not go into the stories told by the sibyls. These are, in any case, simply a pastiche historical canter from the biblical Mrs Noah down through the Middle Ages, via the Renaissance and the eighteenth century, to a modern fairy-tale about middle-class heterosexuals into S&M scenarios and an inner-space science-fiction future about two street boys, who, miraculously, and against all the statistics, go in for mothering rather than abusing girl children. The main electricity of the *Book* is generated by the discussion of writing and of all the criticisms and dismissive accusations which silence women – and which women use to silence each other. In chapter 25 the Correct Sibyl answers the critics, all engagingly dressed up as the Seven Deadly Sins for women writers: Laziness, Intensity, Lack of Political Bite, Arrogance,

Unsisterly Behaviour, Lack of Avant-Garde Originality, Lack of True Artistry. They appear as different characters in the mirror; but they are invented by the sibyl herself. They accuse us of failing to satisfy their prejudices; they all demand different writing, different words. Of course, no ideal reader exists. There is no one who will agree with all that we have to say. But that does not mean they will refuse to hear us out. 'One of the pleasures of being a writer is that you can take power, please yourself and nobody else, choose your own words' (p. 181).

And yet all this still seemed like coterie writing. The one working-class woman in *The Book of Mrs Noah* is Meg, heroine of the eighteenth-century story. She is seduced and abused by the men who are the narrators of her story; she has her history appropriated, interpreted, re-told by a man, because she can neither read nor write. But of course, the meanings are slippery here. For it is Roberts, a woman's hand, creating the male narrators who write Meg into existence. So what is the meaning of Meg? Follow Richardson's *Pamela*, my girl. Or better still, Brontë's *Jane Eyre*. Learn to read and write so that you can marry the boss, not murder him. The sibyls from the world outside western Europe, who take part in Roberts' finale, the Writers' Dinner Party – a wonderful piece of comic jumble – were not part of the original writers' collective. I like to think that the Guatemalan Sibyl might have been Rigoberta Menchú. Would she have bothered about any of those Seven Deadly Sins? Laziness, Intensity, Arrogance, Unsisterly Behaviour, Lack of Avant-Garde Originality, Lack of True Artistry? No one could ever accuse her of Lack of Political Bite. My point here is that even Roberts' critical concerns touch a very narrow band of writing, creating women. But her re-writing of Christian myth touches every woman who has ever been slapped in the face by Christianity. There are Seven Other Deadly Sins, waiting to be re-written.

Roberts' argument about reading women's writing is firmly non-separatist. We must read and be read alongside the men. The comic Judy Chicago-style dinner party has each writer arguing her side of the case, and arguing for the right to be insiders, not outsiders.

It takes two to make a baby, murmurs Ahkmatova, bending forwards: why do people say literature has no sex? Meaning just one? Keep me in isolation from the male poets of my generation and you'll never understand my contribution to Russian poetry.
– Deny my friendship with Dickens, remarks Mrs Gaskell: and you'll never know what he learned from me. (p. 272)

I agree with Mrs Gaskell. Of course she is right. But male literary historians are far more likely to notice her friendship with Dickens than with Charlotte Brontë – or with her daughters. And it need no longer take two to make a baby.

In the very linking of making babies and making books Roberts moves on to ideological ground where I cannot follow her. 'Writer. Mother. Two words I have linked through this voyage on the Ark, this arc of stories, a distance of so many nights, such longing' (p. 275). The Ark turns out to be the unconscious mind as well as the womb: the storehouse of language. And so Mrs Noah marches back into Venice and daytime consciousness, pregnant and ready to begin The Book. To write. To give birth. Men have always used women's reproductive capacity to deny their creative ability in any other sphere. Men have always scorned and abused barren women. Men are never barren. Women are mothers. Women create babies. Men create Art. Roberts sets about unknotting these myths. But only by saying that we can do it all, have it all, be everything. We can give birth to daughters (she does not usually risk sons) and to books.

I think that my problem with the woman/writer/mother metaphor is bound up with the fact that birth is a natural process; which means that the womb as the storehouse of language is a sort of organic darkness out of which we make words. This is all much too close to the notion of writing as a sort of savage inspiration; or to the religion of psychoanalysis where images surge up from the unconscious mind. We have gone right over the edge into a sort of mystic lunacy if the words choose us. At least Roberts still chooses her words. But only just. Writing is not, and cannot ever be, a natural process. When we think from the heart and the blood, as D. H. Lawrence would have us do, we are usually giving voice to our grandparents' prejudices. Writing is about thinking, making, judging: often choosing against nature, against instinct – even against the received idea of what is beautiful or constitutes good writing. It is neither easy nor the prerogative of white, Oxbridge-educated, middle-class British women like Michèle Roberts, Sara Maitland or myself. Not every woman can give birth – or wants to – metaphysically, metaphorically or literally. Not every woman can write.

Roberts is one of the women who can. Not only does she re-write biblical and classical myth; she also looks hard at the fairy-tales. In the sibyl's story about 'food and punishment' a middle-class journalist and her S&M-inclined husband are lost in the Alps. Roberts takes the fairy-tale model of Hansel and Gretel finding the house of the witch. Feminist re-telling of the fairy-tales has tended to concentrate on the relationship between the bad woman and the good girl; that is, the witch and the princess. Roberts' bad woman turns out to be an old man dressed up, who is murdered as part of a New Year's ritual. Food and sex litter the pages; but the narrative remains simply sinister, without consequences or conclusions. More telling on the issue of sado-masochism is the story of Cinderella and her step-mother in Sara Maitland's *A Book of Spells*. In 'The Wicked Stepmother's Lament' Maitland gives a psychological account of calculating sadism; the relationship between victim and torturer as a kind of complicity, an appalling embrace. Unlike the writers who invest this embrace with an erotic thrill, Maitland pinpoints the boredom of persecution, which, as the pain inflicted on the other woman intensifies, actually ceases to be interesting. I would have thought that daily sadism and malice requiring considerable imaginative effort to sustain really would cease to be enjoyable for the torturer. However, neither the fairy-tales nor my (by now considerable) experience of humanity bear out Maitland's thesis. Most people who persecute others love doing it, and if anything, their pleasure increases as the years go by. And the people women persecute are usually their children.

One of the aspects of relationships between women which the fairy-tales allow us to examine and re-create is cruelty, brutality and hatred of woman against woman. Fairy-tales really are the stuff of Freudian nightmare. They are about archetypal family relationships, mothers, fathers, sisters, brothers, husbands, and how we all hate and love one another.[34] The fairy-tales are often the first stories we hear; traditional wisdom, told by experience to innocence. These are the tales of initiation, addressing the transition of puberty, from childhood to adulthood; and they teach the lessons of sexuality. Beauty translates into female power in the fairy-tales, for it is this which gains male devotion and approval. Snow White's step-mother asks the mirror 'Who is the fairest of them all?' not out of sheer vanity, but because it is a question of survival. When she is supplanted by her daughter she is forced to dance in red shoes till she dies. The punishment for not being the fairest is death. The curse of the fairy-tales is ugliness, because beauty is the condition of male desire. And it is not enough simply to be beautiful. We have to be the most beautiful woman, outshining all the others. As the mirror says:

> Queen thou art of beauty rare,
> But Snow White living in the glen
> With the seven little men,
> Is a thousand times more fair.

Relationships between women in the tales are always based on rivalry and competition. And so the Ugly Sisters abuse Cinderella, Snow White is poisoned, and it is the Mother in Hansel and Gretel who suggests that the children should be abandoned in the forest in order to solve the food shortages at home. The solitary woman in the gingerbread house is not just a witch, but an ogress who eats children. The maiden Rapunzel, seized by an old enchantress – old women are always wicked crones in the fairy-tale patterns – and imprisoned in the tower, transgresses all the fairy-tale laws by making love to the Prince. Her punishment, handed out by the enchantress, is banishment to the wilderness; as for the Prince, he is blinded, the symbolic gesture of castration.

Whenever a mother betrays her child in the fairy-tales, that child's life is in jeopardy. The only possible feeling between sisters is envy. Thus the uncompromising message in tale after tale is women beware women, as one woman after another plots her rival's destruction. The heroines – the good girls, the princesses – cannot initiate the action; they cannot lay claim to any autonomous sexuality. Princes act, princesses react. In fact, all we can do while we are dressed up as the princess is sit still and wait. The penalty for following desire, not orders, is death. Red Riding Hood's wolf is clearly the embodiment of predatory male sexuality; but the girl cannot be saved either by her own initiative or by an alliance with her grandmother. She can only be saved by the handsome Huntsman, the representative of respectable matrimonial sexuality. In some versions of this tale she is not saved at all. She is eaten up; sexually possessed. And, so the fairy-tale clearly implies, it serves her right for talking to strange wolves in forests.

Bluebeard's fourth wife, overcome by curiosity, desires to know what manner of man she has married. In his secret chamber she discovers the three tortured bodies of his three former wives. Rescue comes, not through the helpless wife, or her sister Anne, but her galloping brothers, who appear on the hill like the cavalry, just before she descends to the courtyard to be beheaded. Bluebeard is the man who consumes women's bodies. Marrying him spells certain death. Bluebeard is a husband. The disarming of male sexuality – by implication, always violent and bestial, except in the case of very refined princes – is a task for womanly virtue and submissivness. 'The Frog Prince' and 'Beauty and the Beast' tell the same story. It is the woman's assent to the unacceptable hideousness of male desire which turns monsters into men. But women's desire is seen only as response and as passive acquiescence to male sexual demand. That woman should possess her own sexuality is quite unmentionable, indeed, unthinkable. Snow White lies dead in her glass coffin when the passing Prince decides that he fancies her. Sleeping Beauty is stretched out, almost as dead as her enchanted castle. The women of the fairy-tales are both powerless and stupid. Each of Bluebeard's wives – all unnamed, for they were nothing but corpse-fodder for his Bloody Chamber – was handed out in marriage by her parents. Rapunzel was tricked into letting down her plaits for the Prince: but she believed his story. Red Riding Hood, despite the warnings, presumably thought she was just chatting to a friendly wolf.

The fairy-tales are dangerous. Identity is defined by role. We are offered patterns of behaviour to follow, menaces if we transgress. The divisions between mothers and daughters, between sisters, between all women, are the cornerstones of patriarchy, and the fairy-tales endorse these divisions with sinister predictability. Of course, there are fairy-tales specifically addressed to boys. 'Tom Thumb', 'Puss in Boots', 'Jack and the Beanstalk' are examples. The father, as ogre, must be slain. Cunning, daring and deception are highly recommended to the boys, because these are the tales of legitimate courage and endeavour. The son takes possession of the ogre/giant's wealth and power and thus comes into his own inheritance. The Father is never killed by name in the fairy-tales; he always appears as a wicked oppressor in another form. The woman, or the mother, can be named. And then murdered.

So the messages are clear. The boys must go out into the world, fight giants, gain wealth and power, possess women and become kings. For girls the critical metamorphosis into adulthood is sexual. Sleeping Beauty's bleeding finger is the sign of menstruation and sexual maturity. From menstruation she proceeds into marriage: all her life between is one long sleep. As I say, all we have to do is lie still and wait.

One of the modern collections of feminist fairy-tales is promisingly entitled *Don't Bet on the Prince*. Indeed, the new titles say it all: *The Clever Princess*, *Rapunzel's Revenge*, *Ms [sic] Muffet and Others*, *Mad and Bad Faeries*, *Sweeping Beauties*; these last four collections from a group of Irish feminists.[35] But no ideology, however confining, sexist and unjust, is ever monolithic. And the contradictions are there in the fairy-tales. Who is the Fairy Godmother? Or the witch who fights on the side of the Oppressed Princess? Bluebeard's unnamed wife has a sister, Anne, who is the warning voice from the top of the tower.

What is she doing there? The miller's daughter outwits Rumpelstiltskin and keeps her child. It is Gretel, not Hansel, who saves both their lives by her courage and her cunning.

Women's courage, women's cunning, are both survival qualities, and it is these virtues that are celebrated in feminist fairy-tales. There are many reversal stories, like Diana Coles's *The Clever Princess*, in which all the traditional elements appear: a tyrannical, greedy father who sells his daughter to a wizard, three tasks for the princess to perform, talking animals, a supportive witch and a fairy godmother who cooks. What is interesting about Coles's narrative is that the princess achieves her tasks by using her common sense, cleverness and patience; she does not use magic powers. Nor does she end up with a suitably anti-sexist prince. Instead, she decides to take time off from being a princess and travel. Fairy-tales are always didactic; so is feminism. The medium is ideal.

Not so the material. And of course the problem with reversal stories, which are usually about aggressive Cinderellas, pushy Snow Whites, and predatory Red Riding Hoods who do for the wolf, is that they persistently recall the patriarchal first versions, and depend for their effect upon the shock value of the reversal. This is especially true of stories like Jeanne Desy's 'The Princess Who Stood on Her Own Two Feet' (1982).[36] Desy's princess is too tall, too clever, too argumentative and too fond of riding astride to suit the prince. She gets a better prince; but the message from Mirabelle, her talking cat, is worth hearing – ' . . . sometimes one must *refuse* to sacrifice' (p. 47). The effect of this story depends upon the reader's assumption that most princesses are silent, helpless and persecuted. Anne Claffey's 'The Plastic Princess' is more radical.[37] Her princess starts life in 'an environment that was happy, frugal and female' (p. 23), but she is unfortunately cursed at birth with conventional happiness by an antique and conservative fairy godmother. All the modern fairies are handing out feminist gifts like assertiveness, a good head for business and a talent for mathematics. The formula for patriarchal happiness in conventional fairy-tales becomes the curse. 'My gift to the princess is that at the age of fifteen, she will fall in love with a handsome prince and live happily ever after' (p. 22). This fairy-tale addresses the predicament of contemporary feminism after twenty years of re-thinking the world. For now there is a generation of young women for whom feminism is a lot of unfashionable dated nonsense that is anti-sex and not stylish. They would like to wear nail varnish, short skirts and go out with princes. Claffey's princess fills the role for a time, until 'further rumours suggested that the Princess' serene appearance might owe more to tranquilizers than tranquility' (p. 26). Eventually she runs off with one of her ladies-in-waiting to 'join a women's commune in a neighbouring country'. The ideal of collective political action is reasserted, and the princess returns to the position from which she started before she was cursed with conventional happiness. What Claffey does is radicalize the women's space; the space that is always present, and always dismissed and despised, in traditional fairy-tales. It is this which separates her writing from the more liberal re-writings of the fairy tales where the princess has everything going for her: intelligence, rank, beauty, wealth and – usually – a prince who can be made to shut up and listen.

Sylvia Townsend Warner often used fairy-tale structures to discuss modern political conditions. Commenting on her use of the fairy tale, or the fable, Wendy Mulford has this to say: 'Fable distances and depersonalises; it allows the artist to work from the impersonality of traditional forms, detached from character, setting and superfluous incident. All the elements of story-telling are pared down in the fable to its essence.'[38] Fairy-tales reduce character and identity to role. Therein lie both their strengths and their dangers. For women's identities are usually confined to role. I learned this suddenly from a mature student in one of my undergraduate classes. She always looked up with a beaming smile whenever I called her by name, Marcia, and asked her opinion. At the end of the year I found out why. It was hearing her name. She had been Mummy, Mother, Mum, dear, my wife, my mother, my daughter-in-law, for years. And it is no coincidence that many feminist fairy-tales have particular heroines, in particular circumstances, with strong characters. Even when their names are traditional the fusion between identity and role is broken. Rapunzel Murphy of *Rapunzel's Revenge* has a particular friend, Pauline, who rescues her from Rory Prince, marketing manager of a lethal hair-growing shampoo called New Improved Sunsoft. This is a particular Rapunzel, whose name carries an echo, but not a fixed meaning. Mary Maher's Snow White was called that because she was born in a snowstorm: her real name is Margaret. In Maher's tale, 'Hi Ho It's Off to Strike We Go', Snow White organizes the seven dwarves into a union to get better wages out of the Prince Precious Jewel Mining Company. This is in fact an ingenious little fable about capitalism and the trade union movement. 'She set about negotiating with the bosses, ogres and princes, on a wide range of benefits.'[39] I think most of us work for ogres. In Maher's tale it is Mr Prince who chokes on the apple; and the wicked stepmother becomes Snow White's real mum, a sensible sharp-tongued woman who sees right through her husband's con-trick on other women – manufacturing Magic Mirrors, which give us a false view of the world and of ourselves.

One of the interesting contradictions in the traditional fairy-tales was the genuine instability of the society reflected within them. Frogs could be princes, miller's sons could get to be rich kings. The one thing that could not and did not change was women's subordination to men. If women became rich it was by marriage, not by wits. By transforming women's definitions of themselves, feminist fairy-tales at a stroke complete a pattern of subversion implicit in the old stories. Maeve Binchy's Cinderella in 'Cinderella Reexamined' chats up the old king rather than the prince, the latter being an alcoholic foot-fetishist, and so eventually becomes Chief Executive of Palace Enterprises, minting money.[40] All done with brains rather than with wedding bells.

The Irish writers who produced *Rapunzel's Revenge, Ms Muffet and Others, Mad and Bad Faeries* and *Sweeping Beauties* (and other collections to come, I hope) also translate fairy-tale characters into contemporary settings to comment on contemporary issues – including corruption in the use of EEC funds, which gets sorted out by the versatile Rapunzel Murphy. The Tired Trainer of Hamelin removes all the men from the town, which leads to interesting speculations as to who the real rats are. These fables fuse fairy-tales and political comment. They are 'what if . . .' and 'just imagine . . .' stories – as are all political utopias – for the fairy-tale licenses the imagination to change and translate social arrangements. The apparently powerless prove not to be so. The ogres and giants get their come-uppance.

And yet, not surprisingly, the most telling tales of all are those that use the form of the fairy-tale to re-imagine, in radical literary ways, characters and themes which are already central concerns in the traditional stories. Women are once more made speaking subjects in the territory we had already occupied. But now the mirror has been shifted again; we see our own faces at a different angle, and we are speaking, thinking, remembering ourselves in different ways. Tanith Lee re-thinks Red Riding Hood in 'Wolfland'; Margaret Atwood re-writes Bluebeard and his unnamed wife in 'Bluebeard's Egg'.[41] Neither of these narratives is a reversal story. Tanith Lee takes up the Gothic and the triangular relationship of the man, the maiden and the crone: that is, Red Riding Hood, the grandmother and the wolf. Atwood's tale is a self-conscious modern fable, setting the characters from Bluebeard in white North American middle-class suburbia. Both tales are about masculine sexuality and women's powerlessness – as were the original stories.

Male sexuality is socially constructed as insatiable, unstoppable, unknowable, predatory, sinister and dangerous. Bluebeard is one of the fairy-tales that contribute to the myth. Male lust is portrayed as ultimately the lust to kill. Men consume women; and the most complete possession of a woman's identity, body and soul, is achieved by sexual murder. Bluebeard's greatest pleasure is in not just slaughter, but in disembowelling women's bodies. And it is woman's curiosity, the desire to know the inner secrets of the man she has married, which leads directly to the bloody chamber. This is the desire for knowledge, the sin of Eve, and the penalty is death. Atwood gives Bluebeard and his wife a social context and a name. Sally is what readers of Mary Daly's *Gyn/Ecology* would immediately recognize as a fembot: a woman made in the image of men, one who anxiously tries to please, and whose identity is determined by the impression of niceness she makes on other people. Ed, the husband, the heart-surgeon, Bluebeard, is a blank. And what is so intriguing about this narrative is the unstated, unresolved sexual menace of Ed, beneath his studied quotidian normality. Bluebeard always has a secret. Bluebeard is always masked. 'Ed is a surface. One she has trouble getting beneath' (p. 173). Atwood then begins to hand clues to the reader so that she, along with Sally, can begin to guess the identity of Ed. He is the third son, the amiable, bumbling, lucky son. He is handsome, and apparently never notices the crushes other women have on him. He is sinisterly normal, average, unexceptional. He has been married twice before, and has no idea (men never do have any idea) what went wrong. The most disquieting clue is given by the other woman in the story; the woman who is divorced, independent and earns her own living. Marylynn is the witch. And she says of Ed, 'If he were mine, I'd get him bronzed and keep him on the mantelpiece' (p. 164). In other words, trapped, captured, controlled. Ed's new heart scanner is situated in his bloody chamber, the hospital where he anatomizes women's hearts. Sally insists on trying it out; and it is in that moment that she senses Ed's sexual power as terrifying. 'This transaction, this whole room, was sexual in a way she didn't quite understand; it was clearly a dangerous place. It was like a massage parlour, only for women' (p. 170).

But it is the fairy-tale story itself, in an older version, which gives Sally her meanings. Like all bored wives, Sally takes evening classes. She has worked her way through Cookery and Comparative Folklore and is now doing Forms of Narrative Fiction. There are advantages to random education. Sally discovers that the key to Bluebeard, to Ed, is the egg. In the older version of the folk-tale it is not the key which becomes stained with blood, but Bluebeard's egg. Who is the egg? Sally is asked to re-write the story from another point of view, as a class assignment. 'But how can there be a story from the egg's point of view, if the egg is so closed and unaware?' (p. 178). At a dinner party Sally suddenly realizes that her version of Ed is completely invented. Her husband is unknown, terrifying. 'Sally has been wrong about Ed, for years, forever. Her vision of Ed is not something she's perceived but something that's been perpetrated on her, by Ed himself, for reasons of his own' (p. 181). Sally herself is the bloodstained egg, the woman at last alive to the reality of her husband; the woman at last facing the possibility of another life and other feelings. 'This is something the story left out, Sally thinks: the egg is alive and one day it will hatch. But what will come out of it?' (p. 182). Atwood's narrative describes comfortable lives, but suggests the unspeakable – and remains open-ended.

Tanith Lee's 'Wolfland' moves deliberately into the sealed world of the Gothic.[42] It's all there: lonely château in the forest; young ingénue, lured out of her secure environment, travelling alone; the sinister coach, horses waiting in the dim light, the château's appalling secret. Lee uses Gothic to discuss the traditional theme of the genre: ritual imprisonment and persecution of women by men. But she refuses to inscribe women as victims in her text. The story of brutal sadism is told by Anna the Matriarch (the grandmother) to Lisel, her granddaughter (Red Riding Hood). The original text is about sexual danger, the danger male sexuality presents to women. Men are the wolves with large jaws, all the better to eat us with. And this is the conventional wisdom offered to Lisel by the magnificent Anna.

> I tell you, Lisel, because very soon your father will suggest to you that it is time you were wed, And however handsome or gracious the young man may seem to you that you choose, or that is chosen for you, however noble or marvellous or even docile he may seem, you have no way of being certain he will not turn out to be like your beloved grandpère . . . You see what it is to be a woman, Lisel. Is that what you want? The irrevocable marriage vow that binds you forever to a monster? And even if he is a good man, which is a rare beast indeed, you may die an agonising death in child-bed, just as your mother did. (p. 131)

There must have been, and must be still, many married women who wish that some other woman had spoken as frankly to them. The Gothic and the fairy-tale are worlds ruled by absolutes and extremes: so the marriage vow is irrevocable, men are always monsters, addicted to 'outbursts of perverse lust and savagery' (p. 124). The châteaux are unknowably immense, the cold unendurable. Anna's husband was a brute in the Sadean mould whose pleasure is to persecute, torment, destroy. Driven to desperation because she is not given to masochism, Anna seeks out the secrets of Wolfland. There she finds the power of 'the spirit, the wolfwomen, or maybe she's a goddess, an old goddess left over from the beginning of things, before Christ came to save us all' (p. 142). The irony of this is written into the text, for whoever Christ came to save, it wasn't Anna. She invokes the Wolfland goddess to save herself. Catching her husband alone as he returns through the forest to torture her at his leisure, Anna becomes the wolf and tears out his throat.

The narrative centres on women in a way that Gothic never does; Lee emphasizes women's magic, women's cunning, women's power. This power is the inherited wolfpower, passing from the grandmother to Red Riding Hood. Now women possess the wolf. The use of Gothic and fairy-tale to present revolutionary feminist material is startlingly at odds with conventional writing. Here is the matter-of-fact justification for her actions which Anna gives. 'If I had left him, he would have traced me, as he did the child. No law supports a wife. I could only kill him' (p. 145). Outside the Gothic this is still the last resort left to many women confronting violent men. Lee has not altered the theme or the action of the traditional fairy-tale; instead she has shifted the balance of power within it and re-written the finale. She is very forthright on the subject of male violence. But Anna's husband does not have to become a werewolf in order to torture and kill, whereas women's violence must be magical, the avenging power of the returning goddess. It is up to us to find a practical way of turning into wolves, and tearing their throats out.

I looked for other versions of male sexuality and the myth of the wolf in cultures other than my own. The most interesting that I found was a traditional Chinese folk-tale called 'The Seven Sisters'. This begins: 'One starry, moonless night seven wolves transformed themselves into seven young men and went down the mountain-side in search of food. On the side of the mountain there lived seven maidens who spent most of their time at home spinning. The seven wolves saw the seven girls through a chink and banged on the door of their house . . . '[43] The wolves are gradually revealed to be wolves as the maidens notice their hairy feet and lethal claws. The first three sisters decamp in terror, abandoning the four younger sisters to their fate. The remaining sisters are terrified, but under the cover of their whirling spinning wheels they plot to lure the wolves, one by one, to their fate at the top of the house, where the sisters split their heads open with gnarled oak cudgels. The last three wolves escape into the yard and are locked out. 'The spinning wheel was humming once again, but this time it sounded like a soft chuckle of satisfaction' (p. 37). The last three wolves discover the three eldest sisters cowering in the yard and take a bite out of all three respectively. 'Thus the three elder sisters, because they were timid and selfish, paid a heavy price for their folly. The fourth, fifth, sixth and seventh sisters, because they worked together, were able to think of a way to kill the wolves. And what is more, each of them was able to add a fine fur to her dowry' (p. 38). Collective women's action is firmly endorsed; but further feminist interpretation is stopped in its tracks by the last line. For this is one of the central mystifications of patriarchy: that there are bad men who rape and kill and good men whom you marry. Most women have to conduct their lives on the strength of this hypothesis. Radical feminists argue otherwise. There are no good men and bad men. There are simply men; men who have power over women, a power that is structural and endemic in the well-tried institutions of marriage, heterosexuality and patriarchy. There is no way to tell a man from a wolf.

This is Suniti Namjoshi's starting point in her *Feminist Fables*. Here is her satirical version of Red Riding Hood.

Case History

After the event Little R. traumatized. Wolf not slain. Forester is wolf. How else was he there exactly on time? Explain this to mother. Mother not happy. Thinks that forester is extremely nice. Grandmother dead. Wolf not dead. Wolf marries mother. R. not happy. R. is a kid. Mother thinks wolf is extremely nice. Please to see shrink. Shrink will make it clear that wolves on the whole are extremely nice. R. gets it straight. Okay to be wolf. Mama is a wolf. She is a wolf. Shrink is a wolf. Mama and shrink and forester also, extremely uptight.[44]

Namjoshi picks up the ambiguous identity of the wolf. The forester is both a nice man and a wolf. Women are facing a world of wolves. Namjoshi is Indian, now living and working in the west. Her early poetry was published in India; her fiction, *Feminist Fables*, *The Conversations of Cow*, *The Blue Donkey Fables* and *The Mothers of Maya Diip* has all been published in Britain. Namjoshi's central writing work is poetry, and her fables read like prose poems: sharp-toothed, condensed, story-telling pared down to its essence.[45] Paradoxical, prickly, ironic, the stories read like a sequence of stilettoes. Namjoshi ransacks western and eastern culture for narratives, themes, characters and, above all, metamorphoses. She has wise and foolish talking animals, recalcitrant princesses; modern parables addressing the contradictions of Lesbian and feminist theory. Namjoshi's tales reflect on their own sources and makers. Hans Christian Andersen's drakes send a delegation to their author demanding his agreement to their preference for their own gender.

Happy Ending

. . . As for the ducks, they also sent a delegation, and from then on they were permitted to like one another.[46]

In Namjoshi's democratic fables, the animals – and the witches – have a chance to answer back. The sexual debates within feminism are distanced by the metamorphosis into animals, so that an allegorical fable like 'The Female Swan', in which the Ugly Duckling never turns into a swan but is rewarded by a paper 'which clearly stated that thereafter she would be an Honorary Swan' (p. 18), wins its point by becoming irrefutable. Women can act like men, can wield power like men, study to think like men, but they cannot be men: just as ducks can never be swans. They are not the same species. Thus the history and literature of swans, the growth of swanhood, are forever alien to ducks. The argument in favour of recognizing an absolute difference is made by sleight-of-hand. What we do with the 'nature of ducks and the value of swans' is then up to us. The fables argue a coherent politics, even directly addressing particular issues, while changing the terms of the argument. Whether Namjoshi herself thinks that women and men are different species, or that Black and white people are irrevocably separate – for the fable would be equally applicable to an analysis of racism – is immaterial. The fable is about difference; told through the traditional medium of fables and fairy-tales, where the beasts can teach us how to be human.

Taking radical feminist liberties with traditional themes, Namjoshi explodes the clichés of gender. In 'A Moral Tale' – 'Beauty and the Beast' – she simply changes the sex of the beast.

> The Beast wasn't a nobleman. The Beast was a woman. That's why it's love for Beauty was so monstrous. As a child the Beast had had parents who were both kindly and liberal. 'It's not that we disapprove of homosexuals as such, but people disapprove and that's why it grieves us when you think you are one. We want you to be happy, and homosexuals are not happy, and that is the truth.' (p. 21)

This circular thinking need not be read as so brutally cruel as it looks. Most parents are victims of their own belief in the public/private myth, and never realize that they *are* society. Society begins in the kitchen and the bedroom of your own home. Confronted with the sexual structures of most western fairy-tales, young Lesbians and feminists might well think of themselves as either witches or Beasts. And here Namjoshi's critique of humanism is invaluable – as is her Indian perspective. In the prose essays linking her selection of poems *Because of India*, written over twenty-five years and across three continents, Namjoshi has this to say about women and the Beast.

> To me a beast wasn't 'bestial' in the Western sense. To me a bird or a beast was a creature like anyone else. Hinduism is, after all, pantheistic; and the popular notion of reincarnation attributes a soul to everyone. This may sound odd to Western ears, but for me, it was as familiar as it was unconscious. . . . in a humanistic universe, which has been male-centred historically, women are 'the other', together with the birds and the beasts and the rest of creation . . . I don't want to be separated from the birds and the beasts, nor do I want to 'humanise' them particularly.[47]

The Beast and the Women are therefore natural allies – and should have a lot to say to one another.

Namjoshi's beast characters continue from book to book, becoming part of her particular literary mythology. There is even a character called Suniti, the writer's mask. The one-eyed monkey, who appears in *Feminist Fables*, reappears in her children's fiction and in *The Blue Donkey Fables*. The monkey loses her eye in the fable 'The Monkey and the Crocodiles', a tale which can be read in many different ways. The monkey's friends are two crocodiles who protect her. When she sets out on her journey they warn her against other unspecified beasts who are 'long and narrow with scaly hides and powerful jaws'. When the monkey returns she has 'lost her tail, six of her teeth and one eye'. ' "Did you encounter the beasts?" "Yes," said the monkey. "What did they look like?" "They looked like you," she answered slowly. "When you warned me long ago, did you know that?" "Yes," said her friends and avoided her eye.'[48] The focus of the fable is not upon the monkey's adventures, but on her relationships with the crocodiles. We all have friends among The Others; we are Blackwomen, with white women friends, Lesbians who are friendly with heterosexual women; we are women who trust men, even when their kind is not on our side. The narrative – this is characteristic of Namjoshi – remains open-ended. The crocodiles knew that the monkey had everything to fear from them. Their power and privilege, which indeed amount to the power of life and death, are masked by their friendliness. They can cease to be friendly at any time of their own choosing. Which is why they avoid her eye. But they are, however, still talking in the next book.

Namjoshi's first novella, *The Conversations of Cow*, is about the encounter between cultures; about being Indian in white North America. It is also a book about cultural metamorphosis, and achieves its disruptiveness through the disjunction between Indian Lesbian perceptions and the ordinary daily clichés of the white West. Bhadravati is a Brahmini goddess and a Lesbian cow. She is also another part of the writer Suniti, and assumes a pedagogic role in her life. The narrative is hilarious, ridiculous, because it is entirely straight-faced. The insecurity of constant metamorphosis, the flux behind the masks, is the theme and part of the game. *The Conversations of Cow* follows the traditional rules which indicate the presence of the supernatural. Everything is normal and everyone behaves normally. Only one element in the fictional veneer of reality is different. Bhadravati is a cow. This becomes comic and startling in the dinner-party scene where Suniti introduces Cow to her friends.

> It's a small party. I've invited three of my colleagues. They are mostly white – I am not colour conscious – and entirely liberal, of this last I am sure.
> . . . They talk solemnly about the joys of the country, the pleasures of pastoral. B. occupies the entire sofa. She has thrown a turquoise and gold Benarasi stole across her shoulders. She looks magnificent . . .
> . . . Don't they realise that Cow is an animal? My palms are clammy. I feel a little sick.
> . . . At last they leave, I wave feebly. Cow has been a great success. My nerves are in shreds. (pp. 38–40)

The theme here is the collision of cultures and opposing groups. The sign 'Lesbian' – or 'Black' – is shifted to the sign 'Cow'. Namjoshi simply juggles the counters of fiction. The tension of the scene consists in this: can the liberal surface of harmony and common assumptions be preserved from the abyss of difference that lies beneath? For it is the everyday lives of the Others that are anathema to Us. One of the guests narrates the accident of her freezer overflowing cutlets to Cow. Cow, who might herself have been related to one of the cutlets, decides, to Suniti's relief, to be gracious rather than livid. The surfaces are saved; but only just.

Bhadravati's voyage is of course the journey into different aspects of the self, where identity is fluid, dependent on social context and individual desire.

Bhadravati becomes a man, a cow, an Asian Lesbian at will, teaching the meaning of difference and how to manage your difference in a white, alien world. The subject of racism and all its emotional convolutions is tackled directly in *The Blue Donkey Fables*. There, torrents of grey donkey guilt are given short shrift in the tale 'The Sinner'.

> One afternoon, as the Blue Donkey was reciting some verse before an audience, an ordinary grey donkey marched up to her, fell at her feet and cried out in a loud voice, 'Sister, I have sinned! I seek absolution.' The Blue Donkey was most embarrassed. . . . The donkey at her feet refused to budge. 'I have been snotty and snobbish and often thought to myself that I despise blue donkeys and would never go near one or have one for a friend.' (p. 36)

The response from the Blue Donkey is savage and appropriate. 'Fall at the feet of the other donkeys here and explain to them – as you did to me – that you excuse their greyness' (p. 36). Again the colour signs are shifted. The grey donkey, like many white women bent on breast-beating, puts herself centre stage. But there are no blue donkeys in the audience. There is only one Blue Donkey who performs and it is her blueness which makes her special. She does rather well out of being Blue and because no other blue donkeys are ever in sight, never needs to fight to put an end to discrimination against blue donkeys in general.

Namjoshi's fiction is filled with gurus and their disciples, a very Indian way of teaching. And she uses English as an Indian language, creates India in the rhythm of her prose. Even the emphatic 'like anything' – an idiom that is found in different Indian languages – transforms the shape of her descriptive writing. 'It was winter. The sun was shining like anything. It was pleasant, it was cool. The temperature was about seventy degrees.'[49] Understated, hilarious, the text undercuts western expectations. And, suitably enough, the central theme of *The Blue Donkey Fables* is the making of writing and the landscape of poetry; both the private joy and the brutally commercial aspects thereof. The publishers lose manuscripts and are jeered at cheerfully. The critics are effectively vanquished: by creative instincts. The readers are reasoned with.

> *Dear Reader*
> I have the power? I define? And I
> control? But it takes two live bodies, one
> writing and one reading, to generate a sky,
> a habitable planet and a working sun. (p. 51)

Indeed. Readers are not powerless. They can always disagree: or put the book down. But in Namjoshi's fiction we are invited, addressed, given room to object, wooed. The love affair with writing, and above all with poetry, is in Namjoshi's work precisely that – a Lesbian love affair, an erotic relationship. It is the subject of the finest sequence in *The Blue Donkey Fables*, the 'Three Angel Poems'.

Here, in her control over her voices, Namjoshi unites her themes: poet and muse, human and animal, Suniti and her Angel. The first poem, 'Familiar Angel', is the dialogue in poetry between the recalcitrant muse and her less willing poet. Angel has all the power, all the last words and all the best ones. Angel jeers at her poet, but never lets go. In 'Visiting Angel' Namjoshi returns to the fable form. Angel and poet go visiting in the world; a world where there are no words to welcome angels, or Lesbian lovers, or Blackwomen. 'But we shall have to explain when we meet other people that I am me and we are us. "How nice" they will say. "Do come along and bring your bird" ' (p. 14). Finally, in 'Unfallen Angel', Namjoshi uses the Shakespearian sonnet, three linked quatrains and the aggressive, clinching couplet, to celebrate her Angel. This time, despite Angel's impossible appearance and behaviour, Suniti and Angel are on the same side, defending each other against propriety, respectability and expected values. Shakespeare defended his Dark Lady and her unlikely beauty against all comers.

> And yet by heaven I think my love as rare
> As any she belied with false compare.

And Namjoshi defends her overweening, unfallen, Angel.

> And yet, by heav'n, though Angel struts and Angel grins,
> she's Angel still. Then who shall say that Angel sins? (p. 14)

This is a poetry that is irreverent, sometimes deliberately unpleasing. 'Angel, crow, sparrow, sitting on my shoulder and shitting when you please, who are you Bird?' (p. 14). In the dance of woman, bird and beast, neither Angel nor Suniti Namjoshi ever comes clean, giving easy answers. But within Namjoshi's medium, paradox, contradiction, irresolution, is never the opposite of clarity. Difficulty is contained and examined within form.

> Angel sings. Angel grins. Angel fluffs out her feathers
> and preens.
>   And a voice declares,
> 'Game and set and match to Angel.'
>   Angel wins. (p. 13)

Just so. Angel dictates the verse. Three logical steps: dialogue, fable, sonnet; three faultless moves in a game won by Suniti Namjoshi – and her Angel.

Notes

1 I read Mahasweta Devi's story in the translation from the original Bengali by Gayatri Chakravorty Spivak – with Spivak's meticulous foreword, interpretation and explanation. Despite all her learned exegesis, I read the story rather differently. See Spivak, *In Other Worlds: Essays in Cultural Politics* (London, Methuen, 1987), pp. 179–96. This quotation is from page 183.

2 See Spivak's foreword in *In Other Worlds*.
3 Spivak, *In Other Worlds*, p. 187.
4 See chapter 3 above. For a modern male view see Salman Rushdie, *Shame* (London, Cape, 1983).
5 Spivak, *In Other Worlds*, p. 189.
6 In a *New York Times* symposium on 4 December 1988, various authors were asked which of the classics they could do without. Angela Carter, herself a maker of women's myths, said 'the Bible troubles me; it is great literature but has caused lots of grief in its time'. Amen, amen.
7 The entire controversy has been usefully re-published: Simon Shepherd (ed.), *The Women's Sharp Revenge: Five Women's Pamphlets from the Renaissance* (London, Fourth Estate, 1985).
8 Also re-published: Elizabeth Cady Stanton, *The Women's Bible*, introduced by Dale Spender (Edinburgh, Polygon, 1985), p. 112.
9 Sara Maitland, *A Map of the New Country: Women and Christianity* (London, Routledge & Kegan Paul, 1983); with Jo Garcia (eds), *Walking on the Water* (London, Virago, 1983); *Telling Tales* (London, Journeyman, 1983).
10 Jan Montefiore, *Feminism and Poetry* (London, Pandora, 1987), p. 56.
11 See chapter 1 above for a critical look at collective creativity.
12 Michelene Wandor, *Gardens of Eden* (London, Journeyman, 1984); Michèle Roberts, *The Visitation* (London, Women's Press, 1983), *The Wild Girl* (London, Methuen, 1984), *The Book of Mrs Noah* (London, Methuen, 1987).
13 Judges 5:24–30, Authorized Version. I cite the AV not only on account of its linguistic authority as a text in our culture, but because, after hours working on Isaiah 1–7 with Christian and Jewish scholars at the Bendorf Bible Week (1987) I am greatly impressed by the accuracy of the translation.
14 Judges 5:30.
15 Maitland, 'Of Deborah and Jael', *Telling Tales*, p. 1.
16 For my discussion of the story of Deborah and Jael I am infinitely indebted to Rabbi Sheila Shulman, without whom the Hebrew text remains – to me at least – an impenetrable mystery of signs. She has given me permission to quote here from her as yet unpublished essay 'Versions of a Story', submitted to Leo Baeck College, 1988, as part of her rabbinical studies.
17 For explanations, definitions and horrifying examples please see Deborah Cameron and Elizabeth Frazer, *The Lust to Kill: A Feminist Investigation of Sexual Murder* (Cambridge, Polity, 1987) and Jane Caputi, *The Age of Sex Crime* (London, Women's Press, 1988).
18 See Germaine Greer, *The Obstacle Race: The Fortunes of Women Painters and Their Work* (London, Secker & Warburg, 1979), ch. 10, esp. p. 191.
19 Sara Maitland, *A Book of Spells* (1987; London, Methuen, 1988).
20 Genesis 16:2.
21 Genesis 21:10.
22 Roberts, *The Wild Girl*, author's note, p. 9.
23 Salman Rushdie, *The Satanic Verses* (London, Viking Penguin, 1988).
24 W. L. Webb, 'Judgement on Salman', *The Guardian*, 18 January 1989. See also Rana Kabbani, *Letter to Christendom* (London, Virago, 1989) for a sustained and interesting portrait of what it is like to be a Moslem woman living in the West. I assume that Kabbani is a Sunni Moslem, although she does not say so. She gives no indication that Islam is as varied as Christianity when it comes to sects and political perspectives. Other Moslem women will certainly have quite different responses to Rushdie's novel. I recommend *Letter to Christendom* – but cautiously.

25 I have never managed to read James Kirkup's poem of homosexual desire, addressed to the crucified figure of Jesus of Nazareth. *Gay News* was prosecuted, on a charge of blasphemy, for publishing the poem in 1977.

26 In the following discussion I am deeply indebted to Suzanne Kappeler's extraordinary book *The Pornography of Representation* (Cambridge, Polity, 1986).

27 Roberts, *The Wild Girl*, p. 63. These are all genuine Gnostic ideas. For more information about the Gnostics in history see Elaine Pagels, *The Gnostic Gospels* (1979; New York, Vintage, 1981), where the whole story is rivetingly re-told.

28 D. H. Lawrence, 'The Man Who Died', *The Short Novels*, vol. 2 (London, Heinemann, 1972), p. 43.

29 Christina Roche, *i'm not a feminist, but . . .* (London, Virago, 1985). Ms Roche's aggressive cartoons deal briskly with a good deal of academic waffle.

30 Sheila Shulman, 'Some Thoughts on Biblical Prophecy and Feminist Vision', *Gossip: A Journal of Lesbian Feminist Ethics*, no. 6 (1988), pp. 68–79: p. 75.

31 This curiosity in the religion has been seized upon and developed by Christian feminists and theologians. See especially Elizabeth Schüssler Fiorenza, *In Memory Of Her* (London, SCM, 1983).

32 First published in 1950 and still, I am sorry to report, a children's best-seller.

33 A good deal of the language of sado-masochism is derived from Christianity – especially the notion of the willing victim's consent to being tortured. For a particularly illuminating discussion see Sara Maitland's essay 'Passionate Prayer: Masochistic Images in Women's Experience', in *Sex and God: Some Varieties of Women's Religious Experience* (London: Routledge & Kegan Paul, 1987), pp. 125–40.

34 I have written elsewhere about the sexual patterns in fairy-tales, with specific reference to Angela Carter's *The Bloody Chamber and Other Stories* (1979). See Patricia Duncker, 'Re-imagining the Fairy Tales: Angela Carter's Bloody Chambers', in Peter Humm, Paul Stigant and Peter Widdowson (eds), *Popular Fictions: Essays in Literature and History* (London, Methuen, 1986). Some of the material here first appeared in an article 'The Sexual Politics of Fairy Tales', *Lilith: Oxford Women's Paper*, no. 14 (January 1984), pp. 4–5 – and, I am delighted to add, in the WIMMIN column of *Private Eye*, where a few of my sentences appeared under the rubric of 'Loony Feminist Nonsense'. As I say, I am delighted.

35 Jack Zipes (ed.), *Don't Bet on the Prince* (Aldershot, Gower, 1986); Diana Coles, *The Clever Princess* (London, Sheba, 1983); 'Fairy Tales for Feminists': *Rapunzel's Revenge* (Dublin, Attic, 1985), *Ms [sic] Muffet and Others* (Dublin, Attic, 1986), *Mad and Bad Faeries* (Dublin, Attic, 1987), *Sweeping Beauties* (Dublin, Attic, 1989).

36 Included in Zipes, *Don't Bet on the Prince*, pp. 39–47.

37 Included in *Rapunzel's Revenge*, pp. 21–6.

38 Wendy Mulford, *This Narrow Place: Sylvia Townsend Warner and Valentine Ackland – Life, Letters and Politics 1930–1951* (London, Pandora, 1988), p. 124.

39 Mary Maher, 'Hi Ho It's Off to Strike We Go', *Rapunzel's Revenge*, pp. 33–4.

40 *Rapunzel's Revenge*, pp. 57–64.

41 Both included in Zipes, *Don't Bet on the Prince*, pp. 122–47 and 160–82. For an excellent essay on Tanith Lee's work see Sarah Lefanu, 'Robots and Romance: The Science Fiction and Fantasy of Tanith Lee', in Susannah Radstone (ed.), *Sweet Dreams: Sexuality, Gender and Popular Fiction* (London, Lawrence & Wishart, 1988), pp. 121–36.

42 I am using 'Gothic' here to refer to a particular genre of fiction, extremely fashionable in the late eighteenth century and never completely out of fashion since. The iconography of Gothic never changes: castles, maidens, brigands, ghosts, illicit and incestuous sex, male violence against women, madness, damp, first-person

confessional narratives. It is a literature which emphasizes sadism and paranoia. Its most respectable practitioner is Ann Radcliffe (e.g. *The Mysteries of Udolpho*); better known for carrying the implications of the form to their logical conclusions is the Marquis de Sade. For a good introduction to Ann Radcliffe see Janet Todd, *The Sign of Angelica: Women, Writing and Fiction 1660–1800* (London, Virago, 1989). For a pugilistic commentary on the Marquis de Sade I recommend Andrea Dworkin, *Pornography: Men Possessing Women* (London, Women's Press, 1981), ch. 3.

43 *The Seven Sisters: Selected Chinese Folk Stories* (Beijing, Foreign Languages Press, 1965), p. 32.

44 Suniti Namjoshi, *Feminist Fables* (London, Sheba, 1981), p. 3.

45 *The Conversations of Cow* (1985), *The Blue Donkey Fables* (1989) and *The Mothers of Maya Diip* (1989), all published by The Women's Press. Namjoshi's published poetry includes seven single collections and one joint collection with Gillian Hanscombe, *Flesh and Paper* (Seaton, Devon, Jezebel, 1986). Her selected poems and fables *Because of India* were published by Onlywomen Press in 1989. Here, I am primarily concerned with her fables and the way that she uses her fable forms in relation to her poetry.

46 Namjoshi, *Feminist Fables*, p. 13.

47 Namjoshi, *Because of India*, p. 28.

48 Namjoshi, *Feminist Fables*, p. 26.

49 Namjoshi,*The Blue Donkey Fables*, p. 9.

6

Writing Lesbian

*And yet, I remain other than Woman; there remains a distinction between what
the world expects of a woman's view – and what I see . . . If it seems important to
retain my sense of difference, to guard the oblique angle from which I see the
world, what does it mean that I write as a lesbian?*

Anna Wilson, 'On Being a Lesbian Writer'

Subah means morning. It is the title of a feminist – and radical – Indian film
starring Smita Patel, an extraordinary south Asian actress who died young. The
film is set in a women's prison – a metaphor for the position of women in India.
In *Subah*, Smita Patel plays a young, middle-class university graduate who, after
a spell of being a bored, married mother, takes up the post of superintendent at
the prison. The narrative includes the stories of the women who are incarcerated there. It is a horrifying film. I saw it while I was taking an informal crash
course in south Asian culture from a friend, herself an east African Asian and a
Lesbian. I was gazing at the video when she said, 'Watch out. Here comes the
only Lesbian scene in the entire Indian film industry. You'd better concentrate
and don't blink or you might miss it.' Two women, fully dressed in their saris,
are pinioned in aggressive flashlight, hastily disentangling themselves from their
mutual embrace. The venom of the other women in the prison is vicious and
disturbing. The Chairman of the Board wants them separated and sent to
different prisons. The young superintendent defends them; but her support is
neither enlightened nor radical. They must be helped, she declares, sent to
psychiatrists, cured of their illness. Her arguments, within the terms of the
politics of the film, are presented as a courageous stand. Both sides agree that
the two young women should be either suppressed or destroyed. It is the
method which differs.

My friend's mother tongue is Katchi. I asked, 'What is the word for Lesbian
in your language?' She replied, 'There is no word. There are only bad words.
The same words you use for prostitute, whore.' So the experience of
Lesbianism exists only in disguise; it cannot be publicly articulated, without the
word.

Personal narratives, *Bildungsromane*, life stories, are both important and
frequent in Lesbian writing. They represent the search for definition, and the
search for a way to articulate and inhabit the word 'Lesbian'. Within British
culture, at the beginning of this century, Lesbian was a forbidden word, and a
word defined by men.[1] And the woman who tried to re-make and re-claim that
word, Radclyffe Hall, was prosecuted for obscenity by the British government.
The Well of Loneliness (1928) remains the definitive Lesbian novel, as brief field

research in several London women's bookshops revealed. One shop sold at least two copies a week. I asked at another. The woman at the desk, who was also a Lesbian, threw up her hands. 'Oh, God. We must sell at least twenty copies a week.' This actually meant between four and six. She explained, 'Very often it's the first thing that the young women read. I hate to give it to them.' One other Lesbian woman I know, busily censoring her bookshelves before her mother arrived, found that this was the only novel she needed to remove. It is a marked text, acknowledged, known, a public symbol. Esther Newton, in her intelligent analysis of Hall's fiction, points out that 'the mannish lesbian, of whom Stephen Gordon (Hall's heroine) is the most famous prototype, has symbolized the stigma of lesbianism and so continues to move a broad range of lesbians'.[2] But the reaction of the woman in the bookshop was also typical: 'I hate to give it to them.' As Newton argues, 'Hall's vision of lesbianism as sexual difference and as masculinity is inimical to lesbian feminist ideology' (pp. 23–4). Lesbian feminists object to Hall's insistence on the absolute difference between Lesbians and other, 'normal', women; and to her assumption that the only possible expression of Lesbianism was that of the swaggering, childless, masculine woman. Hall also assumed that her heroine's lover, the womanly woman, was really heterosexual. Lesbianism is therefore innate, biologically determined in some obscure way, which manifests itself in muscular shoulders, slender flanks and small, compact breasts. While this is clearly nonsense if taken literally – many Lesbians are either magnificently large or superbly unmuscular – we must remember that Hall's attempt to define her heroine's identity and her own as Lesbian involved appropriating the only available discourse of Lesbianism and presenting herself in those terms. And that discourse was determined by the medical sexologists: Havelock Ellis, Krafft-Ebing and Freud.[3] Lesbian feminists are in the business of defining our own terms; Lesbianism is no longer a matter of biology, but of politics.

Raclyffe Hall's novel is, bravely and unshakably – however deplorable we might find her capitulation to the sexologists' discourse on inversion – about sexual love between women. In the *Gay Studies Newsletter* Judith Fetterley writes; 'The wonderful thing about *The Well of Loneliness* is that it is an out text. You may well hate Hall's politics or her prose, but at least she gave us a book that people will agree is about lesbians. Truly it is a butch/bulldagger text. And this is the kind of text I want more of.'[4] But if *The Well of Loneliness* is an out text, does that imply that there are closet texts? And is there a clear distinction between Lesbian writing and Lesbian feminist writing? And what marks a text as Lesbian? Content? Form? Style? Grammar? Fetterley argues that Alice Walker's *The Color Purple*, despite its Lesbian theme, is not marked as Lesbian, but 'as black in a number of ways, perhaps primarily by her decision to write the most important part in black English'.[5] But there are many American Black people who do not talk or think as Celie does in *The Color Purple* and never have done. Do they recognize the text as Black in general or as a Southern Black novel? Lesbianism takes on a very different meaning in Black communities, has a different history. I certainly do not read *The Color Purple* as a Lesbian novel; but perhaps a Black Lesbian would read it differently. And then we are left with the vexed set of questions. What exactly is a Lesbian novel? A piece of fiction by a woman who is avowedly Lesbian, as is *The Well of Loneliness*? Does that make all Hall's other novels, even those texts where there is not a dyke in sight, Lesbian novels? Or are texts which deal with Lesbian experience the real thing? If so, could a heterosexual woman write a Lesbian novel? Could a man?

In the midst of the muddle Catharine R. Stimpson offers clarity, severity and absolutism.

> My definition of the lesbian – as writer, as character, and a reader – will be conservative and severely literal. She is a woman who finds other women erotically attractive and gratifying. Of course a lesbian is more than her body, more than her flesh, but lesbianism partakes of the body, partakes of the flesh. That carnality distinguishes it from gestures of political sympathy with homosexuals and from affectionate friendships in which women enjoy each other, support each other and commingle a sense of identity and well-being. Lesbianism represents a commitment of skin, blood, breast and bone.[6]

What this literalism assumes is that the physical and social experience of Lesbianism will be, in some way, necessarily expressed in the writing. Stimpson goes further: 'Because the violent yoking of homosexuality and deviancy has been so pervasive in the modern period, little or no writing about it can ignore that conjunction' (p. 244). The Lesbian narrative, therefore, becomes either 'a narrative of damnation' or one of 'the enabling escape'. And I think that these broad categories, when we are discussing texts by avowed Lesbians, are helpful and do hold good. But what of the closet texts? Are they simply not Lesbian novels, because they were written before 1970, in a social climate which equated Lesbianism with obscenity?

Some women took refuge in obscure codes. Gertrude Stein lived openly as a Lesbian in Paris at a time when it was certainly not hard to do so if you had the money; but it was still impossible to write as a Lesbian. Lillian Faderman points out: 'If she is difficult and often impossible to read it is because she felt that one could not write clearly about homosexuality and expect to be published.'[7] Stein did write about Lesbian love and Lesbian sex; she changed the genders of her characters as closet writers often do, but she could be bawdy, explicit and – even in the most deadpan style – full of tenderness.

> I am being led I am being led I am being gently led
> To bed.[8]

The problem with closet texts is not so much obscurity as ambiguity. In a Modern Fiction Group I once attended we were reading Marguérite Yourcenar's *Memoirs of Hadrian*.[9] One of us had read the text in French. It is an extraordinary *tour de force*, embracing love, death, power and the Meaning of Life. As we began to discuss the book we had to raise the question of homosexuality, for the emotional core of the story is the passion of the Emperor Hadrian for his boy lover Antinous. One of the men in the group suddenly said: 'This isn't about male lovers. It's about a Lesbian relationship.' We were all slightly shocked without knowing why, and looked at once for biographical rather than textual evidence. The author's notes in our edition referred to 'her great friend, Grace Frick', and declared that her letters and journals, including the correspondence between them, were to be sealed up until fifty years after their deaths. This, surely, was the closet code. But we abandoned our wild surmise as critically irrelevant and demanded that the man who had claimed that this was in fact a closet Lesbian novel explain himself, and, preferably, indicate the pages upon which this was made plain. This he was unable to do. We were left with the vexed problem of authorial intention. Finally, he was able to say that it was a question of *attention*: that men do not observe or remark other men, even their lovers, with that kind of attention. We were not convinced.

And yet Lesbian writers often do write of love between two men, an attachment which has historically always been easier to express and more openly celebrated. It is a conventional Lesbian disguise. One example is the historical novelist, Mary Renault. But the question of *attention* is more complex. American Lesbian feminist philosopher, Marilyn Frye, has this to say:

> Attention is a kind of passion. When one's attention is on something, one is present in a particular way with respect to that thing. This presence is, among other things, an element of erotic presence. The orientation of one's attention is also what fixes and directs the application of one's physical and emotional work.[10]

So, even if Lesbian sexuality was not the immediate topic a Lesbian writer had chosen, the orientation of her attention would be perceptible in her treatment of whatever subject she chose. Many years after completing *Memoirs of Hadrian*, Yourcenar discussed her work in a literary interview.

> 'Everything that has lived a human life is me,' she wrote at the end of 'Hadrian'. It is a remark she likes to quote. 'Of course all people have a mass of memory which makes of them an important receptacle of all life . . . Everything goes through us all the time, a series of vibrations . . . in general I would consider myself rather a subversive writer. Hadrian is essentially a subversive.'[11]

Yourcenar gives nothing away. She identifies herself with Hadrian only in so far as every writer's chameleon camouflage, the imagination, enables her to enter the skins and spirits of other beings. But subversive is a strong, charged, sinister word. Subversives usually court the veneer of respectability but are never entirely what they seem. Lesbian perceptions are too often hidden, deliberately encoded, whispered, disguised, for wild critical speculation to be dismissed as irrelevant.

I have said that personal narratives, confessions and testimonies are particularly important for Lesbian writers. Generally, these narratives will assume a mixed homosexual and heterosexual audience. They are often a case of special pleading, an explanation of how the writer's sexuality was formed, articulated and expressed. They are, often, a search for a first cause. Nobody ever needs to explain how they came to be heterosexual, although to do so might be a good exercise for anyone seriously disturbed by their own homophobia. So far as writing is concerned, I believe that it must remain irrelevant to the reader whether the author herself lives as a Lesbian, committed in 'blood, breast and bone' to other women. It is the writing itself which reveals or conceal, is successful or not, on its own terms. For writing has its own rules, and can be remote from a writer's life, a life lived on different terms and in different ways. I have often had the experience of meeting women whose writing is wise, generous and acute and finding myself bitterly disappointed by an author who is small-minded, egotistical and selfish. This is a naïveté on my part, for while it may seem obvious to say so, it is perhaps worth pointing out that the imagination can be both powerful and unfettered; and that writing is based upon craft, not experience. In the 1911 preface to his novel of 1908, *The Old Wives' Tale*, Arnold Bennett outlines the response to his description of a French public execution.

> Mr Frank Harris, discussing my book in *Vanity Fair*, said it was clear that I had not seen an execution (or words to that effect), and he proceeded to give his own description of an execution. It was a brief but terribly convincing bit of writing ... I wrote to Mr Frank Harris, regretting that his description had not been printed before I wrote mine, as I should assuredly have utilized it, and, of course, I admitted that I had never witnessed an execution. He simply replied: 'Neither have I'. This detail is worth preserving, for it is a reproof to that large body of readers, who, when a novelist has really carried conviction to them, assert off hand: 'O, that must be autobiography!'[12]

And yet, and yet ... we must remember that, as Catharine Stimpson points out, 'Like masturbation and the orgy, homosexuality has become a counter in the game of erotic writing.'[13] In the years before the women's liberation movement was visible, articulate and publishing, very often the only Lesbian material available was produced and sold as pornography for men. And there are many writers within the women's movement who use Lesbian material to spice their narratives, while being careful to refer to their husbands and children in the dustjacket notes. Sara Maitland's *Virgin Territory* uses precisely these textual tactics. The ambiguous mood of the narrative, tortuous, overwritten, sodden with symbols and portentousness, hinges on the sexual awakening – or smothering – of an American nun, Anna, who encounters a British 'gay feminist', Karen, in the British Library. Will they, or won't they go to bed? The gratuitous tension of the entire book hinges on Lesbian desire; repressed, unacknowledged or perverted. The two women come together over a translation of a deposition on the Rose of Lima: ' ... it was a report on the ecclesiastical investigations into whether Rose's self-inflicted penances and mortifications could really have been of God, so extreme and bizarre were they. Beatings and bindings and fastings and flagellations ... '[14] Tortures, penances, sexual ecstasy; the sado-masochism inherent in patriarchal Christianity forms the substance of Maitland's text, which yokes 'the sweetness of orgasm and the violence of self-disgust' (p. 169). This is difficult and complicated material, but it has been courageously confronted both by women who describe themselves as Christian feminists and women who discard the structures of Christianity for different forms of spirituality – Wicca, paganism and the Craft.[15] Maitland's fiction renews and affirms some elderly, recognizable, but dangerous clichés: that many nuns are thwarted, suppressed Lesbians, and that 'out' dykes spend a good deal of their time manipulating other women into bed. In this context, some of Maitland's reflections on Lesbian desire begin to sound alarming. 'She was prowling, predatory for Anna . . . ' (p. 99); 'I'm a bright lesbian feminist and I can sleep with anyone I want to . . . ' (p. 153); 'I've never known you do without for so long. For God's sake, girl, get down the bars and get laid' (p. 161); 'And she knew that she was physically stronger than Anna and that delighted some part of her' (p. 166). Desire, mutual or otherwise, is presented as predatory, irrational, potentially violent, 'the dark side of the moon' (p. 106). Desire is about power and force.

Now, it is certainly true that sexual desire of every kind does sometimes take precisely this form; and we can and do argue about whether that is a good thing. But given that our sexual responses, like every other so-called natural response – mother-love, women's passivity, man as killer, and so on – are constructed by the society we create and inhabit, it is politically contentious to write as if this were something mythical and inevitable, which we can neither challenge nor change. Maitland's presentation of Lesbian desire is framed by a mythic context of male violence. The novel opens with the rape of a virgin nun, described thus: 'The rape, like all rapes, was not a sexual, but a political assault' (p. 6). The rape echoes through the book. The separation of the sexual and the political is odd, for rape does, I think, tell us something appalling about male sexuality. All the nuns respond with prurience and horror. 'It worked its way into their flesh, the hard fact of the rape . . . each morning they looked at each other over the breakfast table – unwilling to tell their dreams, to expose their unholy images . . . discovering in themselves new and nasty things' (p. 4). The rape supposedly unleashes uncontrollable fantasies of desire; rape and desire grow easily out of one another in Maitland's sentences. 'There was Anna's place of passivity, of denial, the place where Persephone was *raped* by the God of Hell and then *desired* to stay with him in the darkness for a very long time' (p. 106; my italics). Eroticism and killing have the same root. One of the nuns, the radical Sister Kate, leaves her order, joins a revolutionary group and is shot. Anna, her friend and *alter ego*, imagines Kate's murder: 'The horn of the unicorn had gorged into her belly, seeking out her uterus, her womb' (p. 152). It is penile violence which encircles and awakens Lesbian desire.

The rape of women is linked, within the Christian symbolism of the book, with the supposedly penetrated Body of Christ. The raped nun is trying to forgive her rapists; 'She has something in common with all women everywhere, and something in common with her friend and brother on the cross' (p. 209). This is a peculiar, offensive idea. Jesus of Nazareth was brutally murdered, but he was not raped. And, so the story goes, he chose to die. The symbolic weight of *Virgin Territory* is carried by the mythological discourses of virginity and penetrative sado-masochistic heterosexuality; the Lesbians are necessary ingredients in this scheme of things as the potential Amazons, the warrior virgins. But they are also there simply as erotic titillation.

I am not arguing that Lesbian experience should be a forbidden zone for writers who are not themselves Lesbian. If we carried that argument to its lunatic conclusion women could never write about men, or whites about Blacks; and in any case, most people have usually had some kind of homosexual experience. But not everybody speaks with equal authority in this culture. Men have determined the meanings available to women, as have heterosexuals for Gay people, and white writers have written across Black experience. The argument is, as always, about politics and style. The issue is not what we describe or imagine, but how we construct our representations. Politics and style can never be severed. A writer's attitude to homosexuality will always be revealed in the text. And this does mean that writing which exploits Lesbianism in a voyeuristic way, even if the writer herself is a Lesbian, committed in blood, breast and bone to other women, will still read as pornographic and pernicious.

On the question of pornography, context is all. There are Lesbians interested in writing pornography, that is, explicit sexual material which is intended to arouse, for other Lesbians. Mary Wings, the author of the Emma Victor thrillers, has said that she is interested in precisely that; and her first novel *She Came Too Late* has been described by one heterosexual woman friend as a 'pubic hair curler', so she must be counted successful.[16] The language of Lesbian eroticism remains problematic partly because images of Lesbian sex have been so abused within male pornography, and partly because, simply, there are no words. In *Shedding*, Verena Stefan points out that the naming of our bodies is alien to our experience of them. 'Clitoris has nothing in common with this part of my body which is called clitoris. In order to find new words I will have to live differently for as many years as I have lived believing in the meaning of those terms.'[17] Lesbian time also transforms the nature of Stefan's sexuality. 'In the time it took for us to exchange a single kiss, I would in the past have already had intercourse and found myself standing there fully clothed and ready to depart' (p. 93). The expression of Lesbian sexuality always becomes problematic within a feminist analysis. It is much harder for women than it is for men to refuse the structures and institutions of heterosexuality, simply because there are chilling economic imperatives which force us either into marriage or into alliances with men. Most Lesbians, therefore, either are or have been married. The decision to live as a Lesbian is entirely different from the decision to enjoy an erotic relationship with another woman. Lesbian feminism articulates above all a political analysis which makes sense of those decisions, and spells out all their implications.

Novels about Lesbian experience which reproduce the clichés of anti-Lesbianism, like Maitland's *Virgin Territory*, usually deal in heavily overwritten psychological interiors, laden with the rhetoric of psychoanalysis and sado-masochism. The reason for this is that were the writers to deal with Lesbianism within a social, public context they would be forced to confront the sexual politics of patriarchy; and Lesbian love could then no longer be reduced to one form of exotic sex. Their books would have to address a less mystically Oedipal and more violently nasty set of questions about the freedom of women to define their own sexuality and to live as they please.

An elegant example of mystical Oedipal discourse is Dacia Maraini's *Letters to Marina*. Maraini neatly avoids any political difficulties about describing 'deviant' sexuality by keeping her narrator's desire for the prick (her phrase, not mine) firmly before us on every page.[18] The beloved Marina of the letters never appears in person. She is remembered, reported, narrated, described. Bianca's passion for Marina is therefore surrounded by descriptions of her affairs with men. Indeed, the book is saturated with every peculiar sort of sexuality, an endless unfolding of random and uncontrolled desire. One potential love relationship which is never described, however, is the equal and mutual love of one woman for another. Marina's love only ever arouses the comparison of love for mother or daughter. There is never any sister-love. 'Am I jealous? Yes I am: of how you snuggle close against her how you make her feel she is your mother and your daughter how you eat her up with the fire of your brazen love . . . ' (p. 155). Bianca's neighbour, Basilia, comes to massage her back and tell her bizarre horror stories. The fairy-tales which surface in the texture of the narrative are offered as repositories of sexual wisdom. But the only crime horror story which is re-told in any detail is a torrent of anti-Lesbian ideology which manages to dramatize all the clichés in almost one breath. Here is the story. Sabina and Aminta are supposedly aunt and niece. They are also the local witches. The older woman, Aminta, is found brutally hacked to pieces. Gradually it is revealed that Sabina was being preyed upon by the older woman, a Lesbian, and sexually abused by her – mutual desire between women being unthinkable. Sabina, of course, really desires men. She becomes pregnant. The wicked Lesbian aunt finds out and drives the man away. She slaughters the baby in the womb. The child is male, to make the point clear that Lesbianism is about man-hating, even unto murder. And for all these deeds Aminta receives the grim but just retribution at the hands of her abused companion. This nasty story confirms all the usual clichés to be found in the public imagination and the popular press: that Lesbians are predatory witches, ensnaring and molesting younger women, murdering babies and putting spells on men. Anti-Lesbian tales always end with death and retribution; the Lesbians either murder each other or commit suicide. Justice is done. The key sentence which gives the game away runs as follows: 'So Sabina told the whole story to the sergeant – how her aunt had wanted her *just like a man* . . . ' (p. 16; my italics). This is the essence of Lesbian transgression: to desire a woman is to usurp the prerogative of a man. Lesbian love has, of course, nothing whatsoever to do with men.

Maraini serves up this little story with no comment – except ecstatically to describe the beloved Marina, three pages later, thus ' . . . and of course your graceful body set so firmly on those sturdy legs of yours that tonight are surely riding a broomstick above the roofs of Rome'; and to deliver another story of a witch tortured and murdered by the Church. In this version the woman is a heroic victim of male atrocities; but a victim, nevertheless. The message is clear: to be either a Lesbian or a witch is to be already doomed. Identity is destiny.

And yes, the men are monsters; Maraini describes a rogue's gallery of quite appalling duplicitous exploiters and sadists, child-molesters and maniacs, all of whom think they are God's gift to women. Maraini makes it clear that, despite their better judgement, Bianca, the narrator, and all her women's group think so too. 'We all felt guilty over our dependence on the umbilical cords that bind us navel to navel to our lovers our fathers our husbands our sons.' (p. 148). The treachery begins in the womb. For Bianca it is her unchecked, unquestioned, unironic desire to bear a son. And so biology, that old warhorse, plods on, intact and triumphant. So too continues the Long March of the Phallus. For the *coup de grâce* comes in the final pages. 'This morning I was woken up by a phone call from Giorgia who gave me your latest news. She told me you had begun a love affair with a "student from Padua called Gerado". I jumped up in bed. What Gerado? And what of Guiomar? And all your theories about the phallus – the natural enemy?' (p. 200). Even for the magnificent Marina the phallus proves to be an old friend. And what of the continual beatings, betrayals and desertions the women endure? Well, it's all part of the cost of being a woman, and sons are our reward.

This kind of book is not harmless. This is a version of Lesbianism domesticated and packaged; made safe for men. There is indeed a great deal of implicit criticism of men's sexual practice and the institution of heterosexuality; but there is also a knowing resignation. Criticism never becomes critique, irritation never becomes rage. Men are forgiven; because they are our husbands, our lovers, our sons. 'He was the other: different from myself. He contained all the mystery of the universe [*sic*]. He was not like the reflection of myself in the mirror. He was the start of a journey through the thorny paths of the world in search of the golden apple' (p. 134). Here we find the usual cluster of received opinions: sexual difference as necessarily erotic and mysterious, the lie of the androgyne – that is, that only woman and man make a perfect whole, all else is perverted and incomplete – and the mythic structure of desire with the sexual Other as the goal of the quest. Maraini writes beautifully; but she is quite incapable of thinking outside the hegemony which rules both her pen and the rest of the world.

There is a footnote to all this. When Maraini's book was published in English she gave a reading at Sisterwrite Women's Bookshop in London, on 3 June 1987. I was not able to go, so I asked Florence Hamilton, one of the women who worked at the bookshop, to tell me what had happened. Michèle Roberts chaired the evening, at which around forty women were present. The occasion had been billed as a reading with discussion of the Lesbian erotic novel. Roberts said that as neither she nor the author was Lesbian they would drop that aspect of the discussion. Maraini was asked point-blank why she did not come out as a Lesbian. Her reply: 'If I identify as a woman writer, that's enough.' She spoke fluent English, so she cannot have misunderstood the question. Florence told me that many of the women there did feel a bit cheated and were of the opinion that if Maraini felt that her book was about Lesbianism, and addressed to Lesbians, then the very least she could do was show a bit of solidarity. In fact, I think Maraini was sensibly avoiding a nasty can of worms: the question of what constitutes Lesbian identity. There is no single meaning of the word Lesbian; it does not mean any woman who has had an affair with another woman. Maraini wanted us to buy and read her book. That's all. She had nothing further to say. The writing speaks. I have indicated here what her writing said to me. And Florence sold over £60 worth of books after the reading.

Thinking differently about sexuality need not involve a party line formulated elsewhere. Violette Leduc's *La Bâtarde* was published well before the advent of the contemporary women's liberation movement.[19] Leduc had probably read de Beauvoir's *The Second Sex*; but in the late 1940s Simone de Beauvoir was something of a voice crying in the wilderness, and I suspect that Leduc would not have been interested in a coherent political analysis of either Lesbianism or patriarchy, even if it had been possible for her to become part of a mass movement of women. *La Bâtarde* is a huge book of sensual memory; and it is about seeing oneself as special, extraordinary. Leduc indicates that her Lesbianism is rooted in her passion for her mother, her fear of rejection and her unending need for a woman's love. She is never troubled by Oedipal guilt, only by endless desire. What is also clear from her story is that sexual orientation and its expression are not necessarily a constant within one individual life; nor an unchanging biological fact, as Radclyffe Hall suggests in her analysis of congenital inversion. Our sexuality is something we invent, or re-invent, day after day, according to our circumstances and the political and sexual pressures upon us. In short, Lesbians are made, not born. For Leduc it is her illegitimacy rather than her Lesbianism which is the mark of Cain, the sign of her exclusion, marginality and difference. 'A bastard must lie, a bastard is the fruit of evasion and lies, a bastard is an infringement of all the rules' (p. 56). Her earliest homes were households of women. She adored her mother and grandmother, and her attachment is always expressed in the explicit language of lovers. 'I weep with the passion of a woman torn from her lover's arms. Fidéline, my grandmother, you will always be my betrothed in your mahogany bed with your failing lungs' (p. 35). Her mother had been the maid, seduced by the son of the house. Understandably, she gives men a bad press.

> Each morning, she made me a terrible gift: the gift of suspicion and mistrust, all men were swine, men had no hearts. She stared at me with such intensity as she made this statement that I would wonder whether perhaps I wasn't a man. There wasn't a single one among them to redeem the race as a whole. To take advantage of you, that was their aim. I must get that into my head and never forget it. Swine. All swine. (pp. 39–40)

Leduc never presents herself as a Lesbian in the sense of a sexual identity that is also a marked category. Her first lover is one of her schoolfriends, and their mutual desire is untaught, unproblematic, celebrated. Leduc's description of Lesbian lovemaking is an extraordinary piece of erotic writing, which is effective because she blends the lyricism of pure metaphor with the matter-of-fact whispered words the girls share. Leduc's language is therefore never clinical or analytic; it is purely sensual, descriptive. She conveys the endlessness which is possible in women's eroticism, the flood of accumulated sensations. And yet she makes it perfectly clear, even through the torrent of metaphors, what is actully happening. 'Isabelle's fingers opened, closed again like the bud of a daisy and brought my breasts through pink mists out of their limbo. I was awakening to spring with a babble of lilacs under my skin. "Do it more," I said' (p. 86). Leduc presents herself as a gargoyle, a grotesque with an enormous nose, a muddle, a failure. She very seldom gives any reason for who she is and what she does. She insists on her own intellectual vacuousness, her inability to read philosophy, to understand the 'adequate cause' What she gives instead are sensations, perceptions and textures. 'Quickly, reader, quickly, so that I can give you more of the old, familiar things: the soft ocean of the open country, the mown hay, the waves at rest with the far distance between them' (p. 466). The memory, image, sensation recalled and re-created is the thing itself, without cause. That which is perceived and felt is that which is.

This method of writing is inimical to self-critical analysis. Leduc is a woman obsessed. Each person, woman or man, with whom she involves herself receives the same desperate passions and persecutions. When her woman lover of nine years, Hermine, finally gives up and decamps, her mother says grimly, 'I saw it coming a long while ago. She'd had enough' (p. 244). When Leduc does give reasons for her behaviour they are extraordinary, bizarre. She marries Gabriel for all the conventional reasons; the fear of being an old maid, an ugly Lesbian. Yet she still calls herself by her maiden name, still pretends to be a single woman. Her sexuality, about which she is unflinchingly explicit, never apparently disturbs her. She is obsessed with homosexuality. Her attachment to Maurice Sachs represents a desire that is not so much prurient as thwarted. She longs to be a boy so that he will desire her. This is translated into her desire for her husband to sodomize her. 'So I asked Gabriel to make love to me as a man makes love to another man . . . But the truth, now I think back on it thirty years later, lay deeper. The deeper truth was my desire to have two male homosexuals in my bed' (p. 289).

Leduc's mother perfectly understands her daughter's self-dramatizing obsessions and never rejects her; which is perhaps why Leduc sees her love of women as a shelter. 'I had gone toward women as the lonely peasant, cut off one snowy night, makes his way toward a sheepfold' (p. 276). Leduc is perpetually uneasy with the fact of being a woman; but it is impossible to judge whether her Lesbianism is the cause or the effect of this unease. Of Gabriel she writes: 'I was his man, he was my woman in our friendship, in our wrestling match. He reappeared. But he came to see us less and less. Hermine was turning me into a woman, and that infuriated him' (p. 188) Hermine and her mother are trying to persuade her to wear more feminine clothes, to disguise herself behind the conventional mask of gender. In one extraordinary episode Leduc steals women's underwear, make-up and jewellery from a large store in Paris. 'I was reaping a harvest of knickers . . . I was stealing too in order to rob the other women of the things which made them feminine' (p. 179). Leduc's apparently perverse behaviour is – and she knows it – a complicated refusal of gender. She aborts her husband's child at five months, forces Hermine to make love in a brothel before a man for money, and feeds her obsession with Sachs to the point where it becomes a 'luxurious insanity'. Sensation, and the liberty to indulge her own obsessions, are all that matter.

Eventually, Leduc's sense of her own power and success comes not from her career as a writer – she takes us only as far as the end of the war in *La Bâtarde*, before the publication of *L'Asphyxie* – but from her success as a war profiteer. 'I looked at myself in the mirror, I saw the face of a woman beginning to succeed' (p. 428). She ran a black market in food from the villages in Normandy. This part of her narrative is, oddly enough, as sensual as the explicitly erotic passages. Even the food is animate. 'My eyes goggled as he offered me long strings of sausages, slabs of pork pâté, coils of black pudding, slabs of lard. The pâtés lay dozing beneath their veils of fat' (p. 430). But beneath the dangerous, glamorous life, the (male) lovers, the infatuations, the smuggling which makes her rich, there is an evil undertow: the transportations of the Jews. A Jewish family in her Paris apartment block vanish one by one; she finds Sachs's commentary on the Bible. 'I leafed through the Old Testament and discovered that Maurice had underlined all the passages that could be construed as having some connection with the deportation of the Jews and their extermination' (p. 412). But Leduc makes no further comment; she observes, she accepts. In fact, Leduc's contrived muddles and deliberate refusal ever to be satisfied ('I came into this world and I vowed to entertain a passion for the impossible . . . ' (p. 468)) are the source and subject of her writing. She desires to possess everything; and writing gives her complete power over everything she imagines. 'I could have anything I wanted, all I had to do was imagine it' (p. 316). The fact that her lovers are both men and women, and that her understanding of sexuality is individualistic rather than political, means that each encounter takes place in a moral void. As Simone de Beauvoir pointed out in her preface to *La Bâtarde*, 'Wherever she may chance to meet them, she is always interested in those who have reinvented sexuality for their own purpose.'[20] Leduc's pen serves no cause except her own. Her writing, her sensuality, her desire, is an end in itself. She is a radical, liberated from conventions and taboos; but she is also the amoral angel of good prose. She records, but never judges.

Leduc may be a sexual radical, but she is certainly not a feminist. Yet her work has influenced feminists and Lesbian feminists writing now. *La Bâtarde* has been successfully republished in the 1980s and is widely read; Jo Jones dedicated her first novel *Come Come* to Violette Leduc.[21] And Lesbian feminism certainly does not set the terms for every kind of Lesbian writing, even within the contemporary women's liberation movement. One personal narrative novel, which actually won patriarchal prizes despite its subject matter, is Jeanette Winterson's parable *Oranges Are Not the Only Fruit*.[22] This novel, presented as autobiography, tells the story of the Mighty Struggle between Unnatural Passions and The Fear of The Lord in a flurry of Comic Capitals. On the one hand this method is entirely suitable, in that pentecostal evangelicals do tend to live in a world that is emphatically punctuated; but on the other hand it is an easy irony against an easy target. The literal-minded always appear ridiculous to those who have a firm critical grasp of metaphor. Winterson's 'Jeanette' did always feel Chosen and Different. Being Lesbian simply becomes another form of being Chosen. She is picked out by satanic demons, bearing oranges. This is a literal, speaking device in the fiction for the inner voice of self-preservation. Thus, the struggle against the Family of God is presented in their terms, rather than in those of a Lesbian feminist consciousness. The story represents a shift from the black and white of evangelical faith to the grey world of relativity and uncertainty.

There is nothing at all problematic in 'Jeanette's' head about being a Lesbian or Lesbian sexuality. One day you just see a woman, fall in love with her and there you are. It is important to the structure of her parable that the pathological view of Lesbianism which involves distress, grief, shame and fear is very clearly shown to be in the minds of Other People. The only problem with this assertion is that most of the time this is not the case; it is in our minds too. But this is a narrative which works in terms of oppositions, the terms set by its heroine and real subject, 'Jeanette's' mother. 'She had never heard of mixed feelings. There were friends and there were enemies' (p. 3). Winterson comments on her own narrative by including a sequence of fairy-tale metaphors, adaptations of myths. She re-writes the narratives of the Grail knights and the popular stories of sorcerers and princesses. I did not find these excursions particularly convincing or helpful, simply because they are not necessary. It is clear that the central narrative effectively operates as a fairy-tale, the story of how the enchanted princess escapes from the wicked witch. The witch is of course 'Jeanette's' mother: the woman who is not only pernicious, but also remorselessly comic, hated and loved.

What is excellent well done in the book is the analysis of what constitutes betrayal; and this saves the novel from being either smug or complacent. 'There are different kinds of infidelity, but betrayal is betrayal wherever you find it. By betrayal, I mean promising to be on your side, then being on somebody else's' (p. 171). 'Jeanette's' mother betrays her trust in unforgivable ways, hands her over to the Pastor and the righteous of her church, burns every written scrap of her love life. This is all emotionally well written; and the world is full of women whose lives have been destroyed by someone else who said it was all for their own good.

The other aspect of *Oranges Are Not the Only Fruit* which is truly fascinating is the way in which 'Jeanette's' absolutist faith so clearly contributed to the shaping of herself as a Lesbian. Radical protestant churches where there is a great emphasis on the Spirit are often women-dominated. For the Spirit of God, if addressed correctly, is no respecter of sexual difference and may light upon whomsoever she wisheth. This is made perfectly clear when 'Jeanette's' mother takes off to Wigan. 'My father was at work at the time, so she left him the address and a note which said: "I am busy with the Lord in Wigan." She didn't come back for three weeks' (p. 56). The women operate on the instructions of the Ultimate Authority. The Lord calls them to preach, travel, speak their minds, behave in extraordinary ways. 'The women in our church were strong and organised. If you want to talk in terms of power I had enough to keep Mussolini happy' (p. 124). 'Jeanette's' Unnatural Passion for women is used to reassert male power in the church.

The real problem, it seemed, was going against the teachings of St Paul, and allowing women power in the church. Our branch of the church had never thought about it, we'd always had strong women, and the women organised everything . . . She ended up by saying that having taken on a man's world in other ways I had flouted God's law and tried to do it sexually . . . (p. 133)

And this is how Lesbianism is often judged, especially among the godly who have St Paul to back them up. Lesbianism is unnatural because women are not only created to be submissive to men, they are sexually reserved for men. It says so in the Bible.

Winterson's fictional argument does equate Lesbianism with intellectual as well as sexual liberty. The combination of heterosexuality and motherhood is envisaged as a sort of brain death. This is the fate of 'Jeanette's' first lover. 'If she had been serene to the point of bovine before, she was now almost vegetable' (p. 171). So much for that. But what 'Jeanette' does miss, and He seems to go with the heterosexual package, is God. He was the Beloved Friend whose love is stronger than death and who never betrays His own. She also misses the immense security of certainty, which spared her the pain of thinking. Nor can she ever be free of the dynamic, lunatic mother whose CB call sign is 'Kindly Light'. The text of this hymn is not irrelevant.

> Lead Kindly Light, amid the encircling gloom,
> Lead Thou me on.
> The night is dark and I am far from home,
> Lead Thou me on.

'Jeanette's' escape is also a Fall from a paradise of solidarity which would have remained supportive, if she could have accepted the terms. But no sane person ever could have done.

One of the early Lesbian feminist texts, and another personal narrative novel to come out of the women's liberation movement in the United States, was *Rubyfruit Jungle*, Rita Mae Brown's fictional autobiography of Molly Bolt which has been a best-seller on both sides of the Atlantic.[23] It is a Southern picaresque adventure story which, like *La Bâtarde*, tells the story of a bastard and a Lesbian. But the comparison ends there. Leduc chanted her failures; Molly Bolt manages to transform being gay into something of an all-American achievement. Rita Mae Brown bills her heroine as 'different'; the child who seeks approval and success, but who fiercely guards her sense of self. 'I don't care whether they like me or not. Everybody's stupid, that's what I think. I care if I like me, that's what I truly care about' (p. 36). This is the modern version of Jane Eyre's emphatic credo, 'I care for myself.' And like *Jane Eyre*, *Rubyfruit Jungle* is a rags-on-the-way-to-riches parable of the self-made girl. The option of marrying the boss is, however, not open to Molly; so the narrative remains open-ended. She hasn't made it in a man's world yet; but she is determined to do so: 'Then watch out world because I'm going to be the hottest fifty year old this side of the Mississippi' (p. 246). But the moral of her story is: I did it my way – with a little help from my friends. 'I wanted to go my own way. That's all I think I ever wanted, to go my own way and maybe find some love here and there' (p. 88). This is Gay sensibility on the offensive, taking on all the clichés of the American good life – the family, the prom queens, the college sororities, psychotherapy, the flash world of film – and looking at them from a perspective that is not so much excluded as aggressively, radically different.

Rita Mae Brown offers a comic and uncompromising analysis of heterosexuality from a Lesbian perspective. It is not only Lesbians who transgress the bourgeois boundaries. Mr Beers and Mrs Silver, 'our esteemed principal and our respected dean of women', are caught *in flagrante delicto* at a traffic light. Here, the power of censure works in favour of the High School girls. 'It's not us that has to worry about facing them, it's them that has to worry about facing us' (p. 83). Rita Mae Brown's narrative demonstrates the ways in which heterosexuality maintains its normative surfaces, disguising the hypocrisy beneath. The mechanics of heterosexual sex are also thoroughly discussed and divested of both the mystery and the lies of romance.

> Over eggs that looked as though the chicken rejected them, she began, 'Is it always such a mess? You know, when I stood up all this stuff ran down my leg. Larry said it was sperm. It was so disgusting I nearly barfed . . . Yech. And another thing – what am I supposed to do during all this, lie there? I mean, what do you really do? There they are on top of you sweating and grunting and it's not at all like I thought. (p. 100)

Violette Leduc tried to make love to her husband Gabriel as her woman lovers had made love to her. He remained completely uninterested. Rita Mae Brown's Molly Bolt simply maintains that as erotic partners, women can never be beaten. This is the trenchant Lesbian pride of Gay liberation after Stonewall. 'I bet I've slept with more men than you have, and they all work the same show. Some are better at it than others but it's boring once you know what women are like' (p. 198). One of Molly Bolt's lovers, Polina Bellantoni, author of the satirically entitled academic treatise *The Creative Spirit of the Middle Ages*, proves at first to be the 'classic heterosexual bigot', who along with all the prejudices ' . . . you look like anyone else . . . don't be silly; you can't be a lesbian' (p. 194) also has all the voyeurism and curiosity of the hypocrite. Even Leduc's school headmistress wanted to read the love letters first, then expel her. But Polina turns out to entertain the same fantasies as Leduc. She wants to imagine two male homosexuals in her bed and can only come if her partner is talking about touching her big, juicy cock. Molly's experiments with Polina's male lover, undertaken in the spirit of research, reveals that he can only reach orgasm by pretending to be a woman. Both the woman and the man have to imagine they are the same sex as their lovers to experience real desire. It is the heterosexuals who are peculiar, and desire is therefore Gay. Rita Mae Brown's jeering hostility towards heterosexuals is matched by an equal irreverence towards the convention of the butch/femme Lesbian bars and the role-playing of straight dykes, a phrase which has always struck me as an interesting contradiction in terms. Her perspective is that of Lesbian feminism. 'What's the point of being a lesbian if a woman is going to look like an imitation man?' (p. 147). Nothing remains sacred.

The anti-racist perspective of *Rubyfruit Jungle* is important and explicit. The first two people who help Molly to find her feet are both Black and Gay. They are also articulate, streetwise and politically aware. Their root solidarity is with other homosexuals. Calvin, the Black street hustler, listens to Molly's tales of horror and reflects, 'Looks like nobody wants their queers, not the whites, not the blacks. I bet even the Chinese don't want their queers' (p. 151). And I bet he's right. The 'goddam fucking closet fair[ies]' (p. 128) don't get a good press either. It is characteristic of Molly Bolt that she never pretends to be other than what she is. Sensible precautions usually give way to plain speaking in each of her confrontations. And it is this blazing honesty which exposes the coercive institutions of heterosexuality for what they really are. Most revealing is the psychiatric experience. Molly is handed over to the doctors to be cured of her Lesbianism and her aggression. She escapes by playing their game. 'It's also very important to make up dreams. They love dreams. I used to lie awake nights thinking up dreams. It was exhausting' (p. 129).

Molly Bolt survives by a mixture of guts and guile. The narrative takes us up to the moment when women's liberation and Gay liberation began to transform the radical political consciousness of the late 1960s and early 1970s. The twist in the tale is her reconciliation with the woman who adopted her: Carrie, a convinced racist and homophobe. Molly makes a film tribute to her adopted mother. Despite the implausible sentimentality of the leavetaking and the unlikely gush of love which Molly feels for the woman who treated her with nothing but cruel brutality, the political message is absolutely explicit. Carrie's story of unhappiness and betrayal has its counterpart in Molly's history. Women have more in common with each other than they do with any man. And every woman could be a Lesbian. Molly Bolt is the trickster, the fool; and in this she is also, recognizably, the picaro, the troublemaker who survives all her adventures. She is the woman who cannot be bought. In a world where everyone else has their price and sells out Molly stays ferociously 'proud but poor'. And it is this savage insistence on doing things her way which she has inherited from Carrie.

Rita Mae Brown's confrontational attitude – 'I don't give a flying fuck what you do . . . ' (p. 67) – indicates her assumption that she is writing for a mixed readership, Gay and straight. But it is a characteristic of Lesbian feminist fiction written in the late 1970s and 1980s that the writers assume a Lesbian reader. *Rubyfruit Jungle* is addressed to all the world, a defiant claim to be an all-American queer; now the straight world reads over the Lesbian shoulder. Leduc wrote extravagantly for herself and her beloved, solitary, unknown reader. The new Lesbian feminist writers, knowingly or otherwise, serve a cause. Whereas Leduc and her women lovers are utterly isolated, Lesbian feminist writers today propose the community of women, both as the subject described and as the subject addressed. But the old questions, the old insecurities, the old fears still haunt Lesbian writing, even the writing produced from within the feminist movement. And the central fear is this: what will happen to us all if the movement disappears, is suppressed, belittled, denied? What will happen when the bars, clubs, bookshops, publishers vanish or cease to be? What will happen to us when we grow old?

Barbara Deming's testament *A Humming Under My Feet: A Book of Travail* is dedicated to 'all my lesbian sisters who are struggling as I struggle in this book – with the difference that we struggle now in less isolation – to believe in our right to offer this kind of love. An odd "right" to have to struggle to claim – the right to be who we are.'[24] The desert which both influences and haunts recent Lesbian writing is the immediate post-war years, the 1950s; the period of the Family as Octopus, child care manuals, perfect cooking, perfect homes and polished bourgeois prosperity. These numbing years, filled with propaganda for consumerism, sexism and heterosexuality, are the background to Deming's autobiographical narrative. In the first years of the 1950s, Deming, who was an American, travelled to Europe for the first time and fell in love with a painter, another American woman, who was living in Italy. Deming realized the importance of the entire experience and began to write her book in 1952. She was dissuaded from continuing by friends who 'were embarrassed for me' (p. vii). It was over twenty years before she touched the material again; the book was finally finished in 1984, shortly before Deming's death. Her companion, Jane Gapen, says of *A Humming Under My Feet*, 'Since the writing was postponed twenty years, we get the benefit of Deming's later perspective on this material – showing us a young woman in the process of her radicalizing, before she was aware of theory . . . a woman's epic for our age of awareness.'[25]

The lurking crisis behind Barbara Deming's narrative is the loss of her lover Nell, who married her brother. This was a profoundly dishonest and somewhat nineteenth-century solution. The woman Emily Dickinson had loved also married her brother, Austen Dickinson. But this dishonesty was also a product of the period. Deming is disturbingly frank about the way her consciousness was influenced by the ideologies of the 1950s. 'Back then, the idea of marriage still inspired in me a kind of awe. He could offer her marriage; I could not – I could offer it only *through* him, my twin. In another part of my soul of course I felt that everything had gone wrong' (p. 16; Deming's italics). In the sexual wastes of the 1950s and in the Lesbian narratives describing those years, heterosexuality is the context within and against which Lesbian women attempt to make sense of themselves. The woman whom Deming loves, Carlotta, produces the most peculiar reasons for refusing to live with her and be her lover. 'It is too easy. I think there has to be more struggle between two people who live together' (p. 142). Then she insists that Deming take her to bed, but it is she who proceeds to do the seducing. 'I think it was you who kissed me. I lay in awe of you . . . at the evening's end you came into my bed again. To say goodbye. I didn't know how to say it. But you knew. Your hands spoke to me. To my confusion they seemed not to say goodbye but to discover and greet me' (pp. 143, 153). Carlotta speaks lies, and her body tells the truth. Eroticism, in this particular narrative, proves to be the easiest expression of Lesbian connection; the difficulty resides in negotiating the world. Carlotta, like every other woman living under patriarchy, knows this; and marries the nearest man at once. Her dishonesty is forced upon her. It is Deming who has the courage to think – and live – differently. Yet the climax, and the resolution to her book of travail, is not political but religious, or, in the deepest sense, spiritual. Crossing a field in Greece, Deming comes upon the marble fragment of a woman's body.

> Had I the courage to be the sexual self that I was? To act out truthfully this part for which it seemed no play was written? . . . It was a fragment of a fallen statue – a woman's torso . . . The stone breasts shone among the tossing grasses.

'Yes I am, I am this sexual self,' I said. And stood up, trembling, and went over and knelt and put my hands against the shining ancient breasts. And said: 'I am this self that I am . . . And I will not be shamed.' The stone breasts were cool under my hands, with the coolness of water found at a spring, life-giving. I felt the spirit of the stone enter my hands with this coolness and enter my soul. (p. 221)

This existential moment marks her decision to be the author of herself. I AM THAT I AM is, of course, God's declaration from the fiery bush. Deming refuses the definitions imposed upon her by patriarchal religions, in which shame is the common lot for women. The shining ancient breasts of the goddess root her, so she believes, in a more ancient past. 'A time had once been in which I would have been more free to be the self that I am . . . the joyful sense came to me that here within the present time it might be possible to invent such a world unlike the given world' (p. 207). I confess that I remain sceptical concerning the ancient matriarchal past in which Lesbian women were the revered priestesses of Eleusis; but the Age of Women's Power, however mythical, has been a haunting source of inspiration for many Lesbian feminist women. And the need to invent our own world, the unwritten play, is clearly critical and necessary. Sheila Shulman, as part of her contribution to the collective's statement at the end of *Love Your Enemy? The Debate between Heterosexual Feminism and Political Lesbianism*, makes exactly that point. She also indicates the difficulty of trying to live without context or history.

It seemed to me that I was trying to live in a world that didn't exist yet, that I had to make it, out of nothing and out of buried and silenced bits of the past. I could not make it alone but only with other women who had stepped off the same cliff with nothing but their naked and largely unknown selves. To this effort, except as an obstruction, men were and are irrelevant.[26]

A good part of Deming's European Odyssey is spent fighting off disbelieving men, who simply cannot understand that she would rather be on her own. But the hardest, most solitary voyage is the journey into herself. That she can eventually affirm that self with pride is her victory. Her book of travail has a happy ending. But, on the whole, Lesbian happy endings were not possible in the 1950s. An American exception, reprinted to warm acclaim in the 1980s, was Claire Morgan's *The Price of Salt*. Morgan, in her afterword to the new edition, tells us that after the paperback first appeared in 1953, she had thousands of grateful letters from Lesbians and Gay men who were delighted that someone had dared to tell a story 'about two people of the same sex in love, who actually came out alive at the end with a fair amount of hope for a happy future'.[27] But *The Price of Salt* is, in some ways a harrowing story. One of the lovers, Carol, has been married. Her attempt to escape with her younger lover, Therese, for a holiday in the west of America, becomes a nightmare journey as they realize they are being pursued by her husband's hired detectives, anxious to prove that Carol is perverted and depraved; a woman who should clearly lose the custody of her daughter. Their nights of love in bugged rooms, the blackmail scenes, the ghastly separations and court cases all reveal the tortured reality of Lesbian existence against what now appears to be a bizarre background of cocktail lounges, scarves and matching handbags. Therese had a boyfriend, and he is given all the clichés or anti-Lesbian bigotry to regurgitate. ' "This relationship which I am sure has become sordid and pathological by now . . . disgusts me. I know that it will not last, as I said from the first . . . It is rootless and infantile, like living on lotus blossoms or some sickening candy instead of the bread and meat of life" ' (p. 239). This represents the conventional – and presumably, in the 1950s, the largely universal – view that to love a woman is to be out of touch with reality and actually unwholesome for the stomach. Heterosexuality is bread and meat, the real thing, adult food; Lesbianism is a form of childish gratification, with sweets. The boyfriend assumes that the departing woman could have been 'saved' and that her passion is a medical condition, a sickness. There is even the psychoanalytical suggestion of arrested development in the term 'infantile'. Therese is still, he supposes, polymorphously perverse. But Morgan's lovers choose each other, rather than husbands, homes, money, children and heterosexual imprisonment. Whether they remain rootless or not will be up to them.

Anna Wilson's first novel, *Cactus*, spans the period from the 1950s to the 1980s. The plot, such as it is, revolves around two Lesbian couples and two stories: Lesbian love, ancient and modern. The women who come together in the 1950s are forced apart when one of them abandons her lover for husband, home, money, children and heterosexual imprisonment. The lack of any context or community simply makes a life together unimaginable. 'You can't begin to explain to anyone else; and then you realise that there really is no way of explaining it – that it's so totally inexplicable to the rest of the world that it doesn't exist. You can't live it. Everything we do out there denies it. Everything.'[28] Lesbianism in the 1950s was locked in the closet of private existence. With no public or social context the women are simply obliterated. The battle for Stonewall in June 1969 defended the right, which *Cactus* argues is necessary for survival, to gather as Gay people, the right to a public context. Wilson opts not for drama, but for detail, the detail of understatement. Her text is built with the bricks of naturalism: conversations, observations, the gestures of dailiness. Eleanor, the older woman who never marries, but chooses instead to live alone and run her own grocery business, makes the following reflection on the supposedly natural order.

> The cries of the children seemed to her louder and more piercing, the women carrying babies a little weary in the sun. What could she care that she and Bea had stood apart, unnatural? This was the natural world, she thought, in which she would have had to have her place, these tired people spending their brief summer Sundays in the park, among the staked roses. (p. 35).

Wilson's textual method, and indeed all Lesbian perception, is always oblique, because our discourse lies outside the central argument of the world. The effect of those two past participles used as adjectives, 'tired' and 'staked', illuminates her perception of harrowing limitation; a muted, but telling judgement. And most of Wilson's commentary is developed in this way, through internal reflection and monologue. *Cactus* is in many ways a nineteenth-century novel of manners, which looks both 'out there' at the heterosexual world which occupies the public space and inwards to the Lesbian community; to the women who are isolated, shut off, as is Eleanor in her shop, or to the new generation of Lesbian feminists, Ann and Dee, who have retreated to the country to find out what kind of commitment they can make to each other. The central encounter of the novel is between two couples and two attitudes. Eleanor is marginal to everyone else's life, to her village, to society. She thinks of Lesbians as 'they' – and certainly as no part of herself: 'She thought they lived in London, in the cities, out in the open, went about declaring themselves' (p. 59). Dee and Ann have withdrawn from their community, 'refugees from the ghetto' (p. 69). And they too have grown weary from the realization that they have little significance in the world. They come from 'a group of women alienated from their culture, so alienated that we are always trying to identify new assumptions we have from it, root them out. But that is something you can only experience . . . ' (p. 70). What the women have in common are the cactus skills of the novel's title, qualities which the text demonstrates: 'Grow a thick skin to withstand the heat of a hostile environment, go sit in the desert for a year drinking your juices meanly' (p. 26). In that this is how Eleanor lives, she is very recognizably Lesbian. 'It was as if Eleanor had no public space around her where strangers could approach without danger. It was none of it neutral but all angry, spiked with barriers and defences' (p. 40). If you have no power, no visibility in the public world, then all the spaces outside yourself have to be encountered with aggression, muted hostility or self-assertion. The effect of being marginal to a culture in which you encounter a daily and perpetual repudiation of your existence is to leave your skin raw. Almost all the conversations in the novel are antagonistic, even when they are daily, apparently uncontroversial. For this is a novel of tiny gestures, understated symbols. One of the most eloquent moments, characteristic of Wilson's method, is her description of Bea, the woman who abandoned her lover for marriage, looking at the waste of her life after her daughters have left home. 'Bea stood at Nell's bedroom window watching a rotting elm swaying in the wind . . . There had once been a line of elms, large and alive and green, where that rotting hulk stood. The view from Nell's window had changed with their felling: now you could see further, across more flat fenced and hedgeless fields' (p. 97). Wilson uses the claustrophobic landscape of southern rural England with extraordinary economy; it becomes a psychological landscape, a marriage gone stale, children grown up and departed, a row of rotting elms.

The novel wears its politics on its sleeve. All the clichés of Lesbian feminist life trot cheerfully off the tongues of Ann and Dee; phrases about 'taking energy' (p. 26), 'a necessary support system', 'In the lesbian feminist ghetto . . . the curent idea is that multiple relationships are a necessary part of the life style' (p. 71). But the clichés, so irrelevant to Eleanor's life, are also questioned. Nothing is taken for granted, except the necessary connection between women, whatever sexual decisions they may choose to make and however they betray each other or themselves.

The 1950s is the period within which the American lesbian writer Jane Rule set her first two novels, *Desert of the Heart* and *This Is Not For You*.[29] Her first book has since become notorious through Donna Deitch's film version *Desert Hearts* (1985). In the 'Personal introduction' to her study of twelve twentieth-century Lesbian writers, Rule describes the hostile critical reception of *Desert of the Heart* in 1964.[30] The objections were, quite simply, that Lesbians should not exist and that it was in bad taste to write about them. The film version is in quite unbelievable good taste. This is Lesbianism marketed as an acceptable, heterosexual package. When I showed some stills from the film to two French *Lesbiennes radicales*, they gazed sadly at the slender white stereotypes of Acceptable Hollywood Female Beauty and said, 'Ahhh . . . Hetero-de-Luxe . . . ' Sibyl Grundberg's comparative article on the book and the film in *Gossip* argues a similar dissident case. Rule's novel is about two independent-minded women who fall in love and a jilted man who tries to stop them; Deitch's film is about two women who go to bed together and a mean, twisted alcoholic woman roaring abuse from the sidelines. Positive film images of Lesbians are a relatively recent phenomenon and many Lesbians, like the women who wrote gratefully to Claire Morgan, are simply relieved to see a narrative in which the lovers are not doomed, damned and dead. But Grundberg has this point to make: 'Heterosexuals can see themselves, and their relationships portrayed critically on film without feeling personally threatened; I don't think Lesbians can.'[31] And to some extent, especially in the early 1970s, this was also true of Lesbian fiction.

When Rule began writing, she and her fictional Lesbian characters had no visible political context or community. She really was representing loving hearts in a social desert. But Rule consistently portrays Lesbians as part of a heterosexual world – as a literary strategy. 'In all of my novels my gay characters move in an essentially heterosexual world as most gay people do.' Rule takes a stand on 'telling it how it is': 'I decided to be a writer . . . because I wanted to speak the truth as I saw it.'[32] And part of her version of the truth is the heterosexual context for homosexuality. The heterosexuals can either help or hinder; in Rule's fiction they do both. And because the people she represents never inhabit Lesbian ghettos, the Lesbians are always significantly outnumbered. But in the 1950s, there was no politically visible ghetto to inhabit.

Rule is sensitive to Lesbian feminist criticism of her work. In her introduction to *Lesbian Images* she also notes that with 'the advent of women's liberation . . . the independence of lesbians became a symbol of a new political identity for women' (p. 9). This has proved to be a problem for Rule and her writing. She had been courageously and quietly insisting, in understated prose, that Lesbians were human beings and that theirs was simply a different form of love, which should be accepted and respected by all decent liberals. In the meantime, the early feminist challenge to heterosexuality gave way to an altogether more trenchant critique. 'Those uncertain young women have now been replaced by militant lesbians who find me a political sell-out of the worst sort, living behind money and class protection, writing books which don't suggest that the lesbian way of life is the best way of life for everyone in all circumstances always' (p. 10). Behind this wounded tone lies a refusal to see that that the sexual is indeed the political; that there can be no easy assumption that some people choose to be heterosexual, and to claim the same easy choice for Lesbians. I have always found the notion of choice, with its built-in consumerist assumptions, particularly offensive. It is as if we were all faced with a sexual cake, all the slices of which were the same shape and size, and the price for each slice was exactly the same. This is not the case. And the realization that it is not is the basis for feminist debates on the issues of sexuality and sexual expression.

Rule makes the usual plea for ART. 'Neither my life nor my work can be simple propaganda' (p. 11). Well, propaganda is very rarely simple, and all writers and critics argue a case. Rule's case has been challenged and she is on the defensive. That is all. But any Lesbian feminist who decides to dismiss Rule's work as irrelevant to The Struggle would be wise to think again. *This Is Not For You* stakes out a piece of our history. The entire text is about waste; about a love not given and a life not lived. The reader is surely intended to view the narrator's representation of herself as an advocate of manly martyrdom with sceptical irony, but on the whole the expression of Lesbianism in that period, the 1950s, is described from a point of view which does not judge. We have a butch/femme dykes' dinner of 1953, where the womanly women go off to investigate the kitchen while the manly women light each others' cigarettes. Women are consistently referred to as girls. Men have major parts in the narrative and are usually vile. The main emotional drama is between women; but the men are ever-present on the rim, waiting to have sex with whomever will let them into the action of the novel. There is even one entirely emblematic character: Christopher Marlowe Smith, who preaches creative morality, rubs his hands and steals. Esther, the narrator's unpossessed beloved, becomes his mistress. Within four pages she is talking exactly like him. This is well observed. Women who want to please men either become as exactly like them as they dare, or mouth their opinions. By viewing heterosexual characters from a Lesbian perspective Rule can easily challenge and criticize, without overt polemic. What is evident for Rule's method, first-person confessional narrative (of which she encourages us to be suspicious), is that suppressed sadism can easily be passed off as a great moral choice. The beloved Esther eventually marries a maniac, who goes for her throat every time she tries to have sex with him, so she gives up all hope of capturing Kate, the heroine-narrator, and chooses God·instead. Her life is blighted, thwarted, suppressed; because Kate never acknowledges and therefore never returns her love. I wonder, however, whether a heterosexual reader would understand this differently and perceive Kate's denial as a noble sacrifice and great moral choice. I have heard one married woman, commenting on the fate of a Gay colleague who had come out to her in a fit of deep misery, that she thought he was wonderful because he was fighting his desires and trying to suppress them. So far as the heterosexual world is concerned it is often more effective if we suppress ourselves and save them the trouble.

Rule's world is populated by successful professional women, living alone or with husbands they can control. All the narrator's friends seem to accept her bisexuality, or preference for women, quite cheerfully. They give her dinner parties and meet her off planes. Other women fall for her at once. So it becomes very hard to see what Kate imagined she was saving Esther from.

What is worse is that Kate makes the decision that Esther should never live as a Lesbian for her; Esther herself has little choice in the matter. She is thoroughly and carefully policed. 'I watched you, thinking, you are not to spend yourself on a Sandra Mentchen. I haven't saved you from myself for that' (p. 43). 'Leave her alone . . . It's just not her world, not her sort of thing' (p. 52). There are many good reasons why living as a Lesbian in the 1950s was a tricky enterprise; but Rule does not enlarge upon them. It takes a Lesbian feminist writer, Anna Wilson, to argue that case, in prose as subtle and understated as Jane Rule's own. But it is not necessary to argue explicitly, across page after page, that Lesbian love can be not only liberating but empowering, or that a political decision about our sexuality is involved in the way we live our lives. If that is the perspective of the writer, then her view will illuminate her material. Rule suffered from a vision of militant Lesbians, banging simplistic authoritarian drums and disturbing the silent Realm of Art. But there are some points upon which she neither recants nor retreats. 'As a lesbian, I believe it is important to stand up and be counted, to insist on the dignity and joy loving another woman is for me. If that gets in the way of people's reading my books, I have finally to see that it is their problem and not mine.'[33]

Jane Rule's refusal to write for The Cause is, to some extent, conditioned by the sexual politics of her generation. Rosemary Manning, also a lifelong Lesbian, whose coming out was only possible in the context of contemporary feminism and Gay liberation, explicitly refused to write for The Cause.

> I could not join an army of lesbian Joan of Arcs gripping a spanner in one hand and a copy of The Ladder in the other. I was urged to wield my pen in defence of the cause. I refused . . . The women . . . felt an insecurity that made it imperative for them to wear a uniform, to feel themselves a regiment, speak a private language, adopt a ritual behaviour which gave them coherence and strength against the heterosexual world which they affected to despise.[34]

This is accurate, but unsympathetic. Manning's own insecurity was both masochistic and self-destructive. She turned the anger and despair which made her life unliveable upon herself, not outwards against the heterosexual world which was, and is, the fundamental cause of the feelings. The scorn she expresses, and her military terms – 'a uniform,' 'a regiment', 'a private language', 'ritual behaviour' – all suggest conformity, introversion, the secret society of the ghetto. But Lesbian writing, even Lesbian feminist writing, has never reflected a narrow, land-locked world. The disturbing radical edge of Lesbian feminism has been its insistence on the community of women, all women, and its refusal to accept a split between the women of the ghetto and the women of the heterosexual world. This is why Lesbian feminist writing has usually been confrontational, contradictory, revealing a witty grasp of the bizarre.

Anna Livia's fiction overturns Manning's assumptions about the necessary 'crusading spirit' inherent in the work of women who write for The Cause. For 'the crusading spirit' implies an unhesitating march forward into paradise, on clear, straight roads, over somebody else's dead body. Livia's dialogue with feminist and Lesbian politics makes it clear that the road is anything but straight. She is typical of one phenomenon within feminist and Lesbian feminist writing: the return of the writer who insists on the relevance of her personal experience. Novels by women and men that have developed upon traditional, masculine literary values have increasingly come to be produced by academics. They are often also about academics. Literary work is now often described as 'well-researched'. The literary historical novel is making a comeback. Livia's not entirely serious biographical notes tell us that she has lived in Africa, conducted the No. 41 bus, been a teacher, been to university, lived in Stockwell. Feminist writing has revived the social novel; the novel of protest, political process and community. Attending university is just one of the things that Livia has done in her life, and it is not necessarily the most important.

Livia's first novel, *Relatively Norma*, is an Australian feminist soap-opera, a coming-out story.[35] Coming-out stories are always about being a Lesbian in a straight world. They are often family dramas. Livia's narrative is no exception. But it is also about compromise and bloody-mindedness in the lives of very different women; about how everywoman can refuse to play the game. It is in fact, a feminist family album. All the men are called John; John T., John Boyfriend, John Johnson, John Husband, Johnny François. The reader realizes only gradually that this is deliberate. It emphasizes the fact that all men are theoretically interchangeable more deftly than any amount of impassioned polemic could do. And there is an Australian twist, in that the men bait the women by describing them as either Gins or Sheilas, according to colour. The women of the book work out their own destinies, with or without men. The heroine Minnie, and her foster-sister Laura, read most of the books behind the book in the course of the novel. These are all Lesbian books, books which present radically different versions of Lesbianism. There are 'ugly, masochistic women who couldn't get a man, like that Violette woman in the scruffy paperback that had been passed around in the Home' (p. 59) – which is, of course, Violette Leduc's *La Bâtarde*; *Le Corps lesbien* by Monique Wittig, which is French Lesbian eroticism of a very sensual and intellectual nature; and Anna Wilson's *Cactus*, the novel Minnie takes to read on the plane home.

Not only books, but also the representation of Lesbians within films are the reference-points for Livia. The character of Nora in *Prisoner* is mentioned several times as the male version of a predatory Lesbian. And there is an important scene where the entire family watches the film version of D. H. Lawrence's *The Fox*. Lawrence was so threatened by what he described as 'clitoral women' that he had to despatch them by falling trees. Moira, one of the young women watching, is 'anxious to show Boyfriend her orthodoxy . . . ' and shrieks, 'Oh it's horrible, it's disgustin'! Two women kissing, I can't bear to look . . . ' (p. 20), thereby reducing Minnie, who is sitting there in the closet, to trembling fury. Livia specializes in making everyday homophobia and Gay-bashing painfully visible. She also points out the embarrassed silence which immediately descends upon any of Minnie's indignant objections. 'Most of them did not mistake Minnie's tone but none wished to comment' (p. 21). Mariana Valverde comments on this constant, irritating stress which most Lesbians, in or out of the closet, have to endure every day of their lives. 'For lesbians, the most trivial daily occurrence can give rise to the ever-present dilemma of silent anger versus public confrontation, self denial versus risk.'[36]

Livia's narrative combines naturalism with a variety of disruptive alienation devices. The invisible narrator suddenly becomes visible in a pastiche nineteenth-century mode. 'A close observer would have noticed . . . No such observer was present, however, only me, and I wasn't looking. At a rough guess I should say that Laura's ontology (so what? I had to look it up too) . . . ' (p. 58). The comment in brackets jeers cheerfully at the anti-intellectual streak within radical feminism. The legitimate demand that writers should neither be elitist nor deliberately bully their readers with a terminology that is inaccessible does sometimes become simple fear, masked by aggression or, worse, the patronizing assumption that Lesbians have no intellectual curiosity. But this is a fine line to tread, in both theoretical and fictional writing. Livia uses the power an author always has, to let loose bizarre retributions upon her characters. John Boyfriend is crushed to a 'pulped, pathetic mass' by a heap of flying bicycles and an 'act of goddess' (p. 61). Fate proves to be a feminist, for, as the offensive John boasts of the women he has screwed, Gins or Sheilas, willing or otherwise, the women are avenged. 'A neat brown hand appeared from out of the sky bearing a trim toasting fork and directed a blast in the direction of the retching figure' (p. 64). These alienation effects do not always work, though, because they are not integrated into the naturalistic framework of the narrative at all. Livia does not create an unsettled discourse in which anything might and does happen. Instead the disruptive events appear as sudden fissures in the realist text. But one entirely successful moment is the departure of Beryl, the mother who grows out of her family. Beryl is easily the most compelling woman in the book. She makes a final public speech in demand of mother's liberation – which is, I think, the climax of the plot – and then sails away into the blue beyond. On another textual level she simply departs with John Present Husband, to look at all the areas of Australia she has not yet had the chance to visit, leaving her daughters to sort out their lives for themselves. Minnie's coming-out is largely irrelevant to the woman she expected to shock and alienate, her mother, and crucial to her foster-sister Laura and her younger sister Ingrid. Both young women, through meeting Minnie and, via her, Australian Lesbian feminism, begin to take their first tentative steps towards becoming free women. But not every woman, according to *Relatively Norma*, has to be a Lesbian to be free.

The tone has changed in Livia's second novel, *Accommodation Offered*.[37] This is a novel specifically about Lesbians who live outside their families. Livia draws together three very different women, from radically different class and sexual backgrounds. This is a Lesbian rather than a Lesbian feminist novel; it demonstrates the irrelevance of community feminism, as ritually practised, to many Lesbian lives. Kim, a bus conductor, has one brief experience of the Women's Centre. 'It said in the newsletter you weren't allowed to advertise for lonely hearts but failed to mention that the correct way of doing it was to say you wanted to start a discussion group' (p. 92). And yes, of course the public face of feminism changes; but in *Accommodation Offered*, change becomes decay. 'The pink triangles had turned into double women's symbols; abortion marches were no longer a must, but a concession' (p. 92). The Lesbian sex scene in *Relatively*

Norma is endlessly, comically deferred. Indeed, it never happens within the text at all, thus implicitly demanding that the reader understand that this is not all the story, at all, at all. *Relatively Norma* assumed a mixed audience, Lesbian and straight, and insisted that Lesbianism was important for all women and that motherhood, and the oppressive expectations all children have of their mothers, are issues for Lesbians. But *Accommodation Offered* is written on Lesbian territory. There are explicitly erotic sexual scenes, narrated with matter-of-fact candour. Honesty replaces the lyric clichés of the 1970s coming-out narratives.

> I put my hand on her breast, her stomach and whatnot but all I could think was 'goodness me, so that's what that feels like from the outside'. I didn't feel anything inside, just sort of interested. I mean I didn't think at last I'd come home or anything . . . Only then I started to worry about how you said that word 'clitoris'. Did it rhyme with 'liquorice' or 'walrus'? (p. 17)

Passion, muddle and difficulty are never far apart in Livia's narratives.

Her literary references are deft and not laboured. Polly and Sadie, two of the household in *Accommodation Offered*, walk in Kew Gardens and then proceed to recite Virginia Woolf's *The Waves*, talking past each other as characters tend to do in modernist novels. But this is a moment in the fiction where it is imperative that the two women should understand one another. Alienated modernism becomes at once comic and sinister. The other book behind the book is D. J. West's *Homosexuality* for nurses, which sounds too appalling a travesty of heterosexual homophobia to be invented. *Relatively Norma* never shirked the darker issues of incest and sexual violence, but the impulse behind it was aggressively optimistic. *Accommodation Offered* describes a grimmer world.

Livia's novels offer a fine sequence of obnoxious, violent, sexist men. Her portrait of Gerard, Polly's fake socialist husband in *Accommodation Offered*, is truly disturbing. His violence, which breaks the surface of middle-class discourse, emerges, appropriately enough, at a wedding. His obscene baiting of his wife and her lover assumes the Lesbian reader: heterosexuals might well find it too usual to be disturbing. The verbs Livia uses – 'leer', 'force', grab', indicate that his aggression has escalated beyond a simple slanging match even though the words never actually give way to physical blows. The scene of Lesbian-baiting in *Relatively Norma* happens in a hospital waiting-room where the clichés 'sounded like something from a text book for poofta bashers' (p. 86). In *Accommodation Offered* the clichés of male violence have become more sinister, manipulative, obliquely pornographic. The Lesbians are now beleaguered women, on the defensive. It is a more frightening book.

Livia attempts to lighten the mixture by an extraordinary fantasy of pure play: the *dei ex machina*. These are the Liberty Boddesses of Hortus who can metamorphose into plants, have meetings which parody feminist collectives with fearful accuracy and intervene directly when the problems within the realist plot become quite insuperable. I must admit to a personal critical difficulty here. There are some fictional games which undermine the seriousness of a narrative, and reduce the writing to *The House at Pooh Corner*. The

Liberty Boddessess filled me with a sort of cloying horror. Not so the apocalyptic magic of Sadie's smile, which transforms the gloom of the book's themes into a happy ending. 'And it was possible for Polly to finish her thesis, Sadie to paint her bedroom and for Kim to decide what feminism meant now that men were the enemy . . . And it was possible to speak now of terrible things that had been done to you, and to cry and to go on speaking' (p. 182). The household stays together, and fights on. The Lesbian solidarity is profound, moving and unidealized. But I remained haunted by a still more subversively radical moment in the hospital waiting-room of *Relatively Norma*. Here, a Blackwoman, a Gin, who has also been tormented and threatened by the drunken cream of Australian youth, saves the Lesbian Sheilas from being beaten up. The potential solidarity of all women across class, race and sexual expression remains the central political tenet of radical feminism. It is good to read about and worth fighting for.

It is true – I am afraid – that any fiction which does not represent Lesbian women as frustrated, predatory, suicidal and sex-obsessed perverts simply because they are Lesbian, always serves The Cause. There is an emerging school of fantastical, non-naturalistic Lesbian writing which does not represent Lesbian women within the world as it is; a textual tactic which always involves recognizing our marginality. Instead, we present ourselves as either central in a predominantly Lesbian context, or as characters calmly taken for granted by their fictional colleagues. Alison Ward's novel – or novella, for it comprises a spare, well-turned ninety-two pages – *The Glass Boat* is one of these texts.[38] The book enacts a confrontation between the residue of the 1960s and the consumerist individualism of the 1980s. Our heroine is a well-heeled city architect, the woman who has made it in a man's world, in the way women usually do – by sleeping with the Cheque Book Man. She meets a group of imaginative squatters, who are not yet too drug-ridden to make sense, in a haunted, magical wharf, where they lead an Extraordinary Life Style. Ward constructs a textual argument between these two groups of people, between two interpretations of the world which are mutually exclusive. One of them must be wrong; and Stéphane, the heroine, has to choose between them. The magic woman lover she desires is the androgynous Dasha, star of the Honourable Nancy's Rich Hippy Videodramas. But Lesbianism appears as a concept only in the minds of men. Here is Stéphane's business partner, speculating on her sexuality.

> She spent too much time in the artificial light of conference rooms, and, as he suspected, glittering basements where women charmed each other fleetingly in dark mirrors, playing some soft fragment, wistful pretence at loving. He knew all that because he had read about it in paperbacks from airport bookstalls. He wondered if Martin knew what Stéphane got up to. Probably he did know, but so long as he was in control of a thing, he never saw any harm in it. (p. 10)

This is Lesbianism defined, interpreted and stage-managed by men; the fantasy in men's minds. And the word Lesbian appears only as an insult in the mouth of the Abandoned Cheque Book. Our heroine doesn't flinch.

He accused her then, in a very quiet voice, of being a lesbian.
No, she didn't accept that.
He wasn't surprised. It was an ugly word. Anybody would be ashamed to be called that.
'I'm not ashamed of it, Martin. It's not an ugly word, it's just irrelevant.' . . .
'Yes, I love that woman at the wharf. But that's a whole different point of view from yours. I'm not going to ring it round with one word, so that you can just write it off.' (p. 82)

This is a refusal of male definitions; but it is also sidestepping the issue. *The Glass Boat* is a beautifully written parable, which builds up two opposing sides in an abstract struggle for meaning: on the one side, heterosexuality, money, BMWs, regular paid work, leering sexism, the DHSS and a prison of capitalist greed; on the other side, the wharf, a world of the imagination, occasional drugs, sexual ambiguity, cosmic perception and liberty. This is not a naturalistic novel; it is a game, a debate. And Freedom is the prize, for that is what can be seen from the glass tourist boat under the bridges of Paris, the tiny replica of the Statue of Liberty.

The Glass Boat is also an essay in nostalgia, given that freedom is presented as the anarchic political imagination of the 1960s, limping on into the 1970s. It must be twenty years at least since I leaned back in a drug-filled haze and declared, 'There is no world.' But anarchist political idealism does not cease to be relevant as an alternative politics when the times change, it merely ceases to be fashionable. And the imagination still needs to be paid for by someone. In this case the DHSS foots part of the bill for the Gay Fantasts who inhabit the wharf; the Honourable Nancy, who produces the Cosmic Videodrama of Xanadu, lives on inherited wealth. And Dasha must be earning enough from her photography in Paris to afford the air fare. Even our heroine has a family chalet in the Tyrol to which she can retreat at the end of the novel and find herself. The economic base of every fiction always haunts me as being crucial simply because liberty is both so priceless and so expensive. Freedom and money, the two things women do not have, are of course intimately connected. *The Glass Boat* longs for a world in which the hard oppositions of women and men, power and poverty easily dissolve before originality and fearlessness. Stéphane's educator is not her Lesbian lover, but the Gay Fantast, Asmodus. And while it is still wonderful to hear 'a brilliant attack on outmoded duality concepts: peace and war, freedom and equality, men and women, all that worn-out rubbish' and to be told, 'It was an utter waste of time, creating opposites and then trying to reconcile them. You had to transcend them, then they wouldn't exist' (p. 51), the book demonstrates the crushing destructiveness one opposite exerts over another. Patriarchal power arrives to develop the wharf and evict the imagination, which slips away in a boat, retreating, but not defeated.

Women's imagination and womynmagic are all undefeated in Ellen Galford's fantastical frisk on a not-so-imaginary Scottish island. Galford eases the problems of heterosexuality out of the picture as far as possible by making all the central characters powerful, charismatic Lesbians. *The Fires of Bride* is a yarn in the magic island tradition.[39] The problems of this world are transported to another world where the power balance is in our favour, so that the patriarchal targets can be picked off one by one. The enemy is the Reverend Murdo MacNeish of the Second Schismatic Independent Church of the Outer Isles. But this is a text which reassures its readers that the women, with the Goddess on their side, will always win. Even the Americans, in the form of multinational exploiter Scotty McCrumb, can be bought out by radical politics if it proves to be a commercial enterprise. This is magical, consumer-friendly Lesbian fiction which includes a jolly sexual merry-go-round of successful, independent professional women: doctor, artist, archaeologist. It is fiction which pokes fun at hypocrisy, religious bigotry and patriarchal politics. There are no problematic, explicit sex scenes and no one turns really nasty as they often do in small, inward-looking communities. The dykes always hold the cards which count and always get the best lines.

> 'Murdo,' says Catriona pleasantly, as they sit in the Cailleach Hall waiting for the Community Council meeting to begin, 'did it ever occur to you that Christianity as we know it might be based on a typographical error? . . . with a mere change of a couple of letters in the original text,' she continues brightly, 'the Son of God could, in actuality have been a daughter.' (pp. 197–8)

This is, indeed, a wonderful thought, as is the fictional 'Book of Bride'.[40] Galford's text is Lesbian feminist fantasy to make us all feel good; it is rather like eating carob chocolate or healthy junk food. This kind of fiction serves a function; the content may not follow a formula, but the mode does. It is the fiction where the Good Gals Always Win. I must declare an interest here: I am not an addict of escapist fantasy and never read myself to sleep with thrillers, predictable science fiction, or romance pulp. I prefer fiction which directly confronts difficulty rather than evades it, and usually read sitting upright. Fantasy is never harmless, nor is it ever utterly detached from reality. Cailleach, the magic island, does not exist, however much we might wish it did; the patriarchal God is still safe in the hands of the priests; and not every dyke has a quick retort or a trump card handy when the clerics or the neighbours turn very nasty. There is always a danger, too, that this reassuring fantasy leaves heterosexual readers with the impression that all manner of thing shall be well with the Lesbians, and that they need not ask themselves any more difficult or embarrassing questions. On the other hand, it is bad for anyone's morale to be represented as a perpetual victim or social outcast. But there is a real world where women are making lives for themselves; and there are real victories to be celebrated. Cheerful, jeering comedy always boosts the morale of the underdog, but does not always reduce the scale of the threat; and very few Lesbians are received in the world with cosy, liberal, sentimental tolerance.

I find that my unease with optimistic fantasies is shared by Maud Sulter, who, writing about the representation – or rather, the misrepresentation – of Blacklesbians in films, has this to say about Lizzie Borden's revolutionary fantasy, *Born in Flames*, in which women of every colour work together. 'Blackwomen are being shot, raped and murdered in Britain today. I don't witness these spontaneous waves of white women uprising against it. The struggle is not that easy, pretending that it *is* easy don't make it come no faster. In fact it could be said it hinders it.'[41] I agree. And in considering Lesbian writing I do not forget that living as a Lesbian is not an option that is equally open to all groups of women. The Lesbian couples or coteries whom we have been able to celebrate in history have nearly always been rich. The women who lived in Paris during the first part of this century – Natalie Barney, Romaine Brooks, René Vivien and company – all had the money to live as they chose and sleep with whom they pleased.[42] They were all white and upper-class. For Blackwomen and working-class women within European culture, both the experience and the story of that experience will be utterly different.

Barbara Burford's collection of stories containing her long novella of the same title, *The Threshing Floor*, articulates some aspects of that experience.[43] So far there are no other texts which can tell us what it is like to be Black in south-east England where a good many of the inhabitants vote Tory and stride through the grass with their labradors, brandishing copies of the *Daily Telegraph*. Hannah is a Blackwoman who has lived with her white lover for twelve years in a rural part of Kent. The lover is a poet of great genius who dies of an interesting (unspecified) cancer. The novella is about grief, Hannah's eventual recovery, and her discovery of a new lover, Marah, another Blackwoman.

Every woman in the story is magnificently creative. Burford describes a pseudo-medieval world of ancient crafts, poetry, glass-blowing, weaving, music, from which everyone makes a decent living. I cannot say that I found this at all convincing. Hannah is a glass-blower, and easily the finest section in the novella is the glass-blowing sequence which does superbly well what the novel can do: transmit information in a way that is dynamic and absorbing. It is in any case, a Hallelujah moment in the narrative, when the heroine regains her artistic power, and the cumulative detail telling us how she does it is the more moving because it is done through technical, unemotional, exact description. The rhetoric which insists on skill and craft carries more weight than the clichés describing 'the wellspring of her creativity' (p. 142). The analysis of institutional racism is thrown up by the very situation described in the story: a Blackwoman and her white lover settled in white rural England. The locals refer to 'Jenny Harrison and her darkie woman' (p. 109). Anti-Lesbianism is more complicated to articulate than racism, because homosexuality is sometimes invisible when women either can, or wish to, pass as heterosexual; and anti-Lesbianism involves admitting that Lesbians exist, something which every culture on earth finds hard to do. But in the case of Hannah and Jenny racism can, swiftly and effectively, deny their lived reality. In the eyes of white racists, their shared existence as the 'equals . . . they had become' (p. 109) in their private lives is repudiated by the reduction of Hannah to the status of a nameless adjunct. Jenny Harrison is the subject, her 'darkie woman' becomes the shadow; and this is a village where everyone would know her name. The rejection is brutally painful and goes home with them, 'clinging like slime to their minds' (p. 109).

Judith, Jenny's mother, uses overt racism as her weapon against Hannah. Her motive is simple jealousy, but anti-Black racist discourse slips easily out of her mouth because it can be integrated into ordinary white conversation without the slightest breach of white good manners. I was very struck by the Englishness of this smug nastiness; an encounter which begins with, ' "Hannah, my dear . . . why don't you come and have breakfast with us? We've hardly seen you lately" ' (p. 110) ends with a comment on a pair of black stockings, loaned for Jenny's funeral: ' "You didn't seem to have any at all, let alone black ones. But then I suppose you don't really need them do you? Not with having a tan all year round." Judith smiled sweetly up at Hannah' (p. 111). Bigotry, cruelty and venom are often superbly packaged by the white British middle classes. Good manners, the very ways in which the social context is manipulated so that should the victim object, she is the one to cause a scene, shout, behave badly – all this acts as a form of racist social control. In order to be effective, racism – and sexism, anti-Lesbianism, all such prejudice – must appear usual, normal, part of the natural order. And insults must be delivered with a smile.

Racism is not too central a problem within Hannah's glass-blowing collect-ive, but emotional entanglements and sexual desire are. By the time Hannah gets back to work a barrage of erotic difficulties have built up. Burford writes perceptively and well about the fears, angers and unreasonable resentments which are released by someone's death. Her portrayal of Hannah as a woman who is capable, powerful, commercially successful, artistically gifted and sexually desired emerges not through direct authorial comment, but through the responses of other women in the fiction. The closeness between the Blackwomen at work, Hannah and Caro, becomes an interesting complicity. Hannah has known the white women longer, but it is to Caro that she turns, and to whom she always feels a sense of responsibility. 'Caro had a right to be angry. I was thoughtless and selfish – we all were – but it must have been worse coming from me. She has a right to expect support from me, not the same sort of carelessness that she gets from the others' (p. 174). And it is to other Blackwomen that Hannah commits her future. The usual network of emotions – jealousy, pain, anti-Lesbianism and empowering love – emerge from their connection. Burford does not idealize the relationships among the women of her community, but she does insist on a solidarity which would never be so self-evident now among white women. For white women are not so radically at odds with racist Britain: and there are more places to hide. A Blackwoman is always visible and invisible, at the same time, among whites. Only among other Blackwomen can she be comfortably acknowledged and at home.

Hannah's new lover, Marah, is a weaver. Hers is a woman's skill, passed on from the women of her family: 'My grandmother taught me . . . I'm hoping that she and my mother will come over for the exhibition' (p. 177). And here is the Black triangle, which Audre Lorde so triumphantly described in *Zami*, the Blackwomen's triangle of grandmother, mother, daughter, which reproduces itself within a continuum. 'I have felt the age-old triangle of mother father and child, with the "I" at its eternal core, elongate and flatten out into the elegantly strong triad of grandmother mother daughter, with the "I" moving back and forth flowing in either or both directions as needed.'[44] The community of Blackwomen in Burford's writing answers a physical need. 'When I first moved down here, I used to have to go to London every now and then, just to see and be with other Blackwomen' (p. 153). In one of her short stories in the same volume as 'The Threshing Floor', a subtle, funny tale called 'The Pinstripe Summer', it is the arrival of a Blackwoman called Willoughby, hair beads clinking like those of the Zulu warriors, which inspires Dorothy to realize her dream. The power and connection between the women is a reality which includes, but is not bound by, the word Lesbian. Burford's writing bears out Lorde's declaration that 'there have always been Black dykes around – in the sense of powerful, woman-oriented women – who would rather have died than use that name for themselves. And that includes my momma' (p. 15).

The women of Caeia March's *Three Ply Yarn* do actually discover that, before her marriage, their mother had a woman lover, whose letters she had kept. ' "But why keep them afterwards if she knew we'd find them?" "It's a message," I said quietly.'[45] For a working-class woman, Black or white, the obstacles to leaving any message, let alone a mark on British culture, are enormous.

> It's reasonable to want people to read what you write; but even if you manage to write it (and it should not be necessary to go on at great length about the material obstacles of time, overcrowding, fatigue, anxiety, other priorities; also the cultural problem of underrating yourself; the lack of acceptability of what you are capable of or want to write, language snobbery and more serious oppression of your language and thought; disbelief by the gatekeepers of the published culture; the tourist approach to poverty and working class life) what chance is there that you will find anyone to whom you can show your work in the expectation that it will be read, understood, supported, answered, propagated and built into culture, without being in some measure stolen from you and from the world that gave rise to it?[46]

In *Three Ply Yarn* the 'unheard truth' of working-class Lesbian experience is constructed through private modes of writing – letters, diaries – and through the device of fictional oral history. Both Lesbian experience and working-class experience are subject to censorship within ordinary public discourse. Our lives as Lesbians and as working-class women cannot be written about or described without breaching every cultural norm. This is why a good deal of working-class writing and early feminist or Lesbian writing is autobiographical, breaking the absolute silence imposed on a life lived. March gives us social history, following the lives of three characters and their friends during the post-war period. Two of the first-person confessional narratives, those of Dee and Lotte, are supposedly spoken, recorded and transcribed, so that they are written within the illusion of the spoken voice. The third narrator, Essie, uses her diaries and constructs the fiction. This, then, is fiction as testimony; the women speak as witnesses to history. There is, of course, no common working-class culture, any more than there is any single 'women's experience'; but there are no connections, bridges, shared perceptions, and it is with these links that March is concerned.

Easily the most distinctive and intriguing narrative among the three voices is that of Lotte, the working-class woman on the make. She breaks from her background by selling the only thing she has to sell, her body. She marries out, into the middle classes; but she never loses her perceptions of the ways in which class works. She knows that class is not only where you were born, but also money, manners and privilege. And she plays to win. 'The ranks of silver soldiers were no threat to me by then and I'd learned long ago to call bacon and egg pie *quiche lorraine*. I found that keeping my accent was working out all right. Everyone liked me. I was a bit different' (p. 77). Lotte's story, written with a disarming honesty, demonstrates the process of consciousness-raising. She works her way through every sexist ideology with conviction and candour. Society dictates that she must want children; so she does. 'The longings were coming through to me very intensely. I couldn't go on ignoring my body' (p. 79). The infantilization of women within heterosexuality is also deftly described. Husband James puts her down by dismissing her opinions under a mask of affectionate, diminutive pet names. And this has the required effect. 'I didn't have the same level of confidence in myself that I'd had before I met James' (p. 80). One of the great lies of liberal feminism is that men are unable to express their emotions. This is not the case. It is simply that the narrow range of emotions men choose to express are less than helpful to the cause of women's liberation. March knows this. Here is what happens when Lotte gets a job. 'There's a first time for everything, isn't there? James Junior knocked me from one side of the bedroom to the other when he found out . . . James showed many emotions, from fury that I'd gone behind his back, to weeping that I didn't love him' (pp. 87–8). This marriage, like most marriages, is about power and control. James married a working-class woman on the assumption that he could control and patronize her – and that she wouldn't mind reading the pornography he gives her to read. Feminism is not an option Lotte considers. At one point she reads *The Female Eunuch*. 'But I didn't want to be a revolutionary or a single woman, and I wouldn't want to live on my own, at all' (p. 84).

Lotte's conversion to Lesbianism is, alas! the least convincing moment of her narrative. She meets Dee, the ravishing older dyke, who, in a flurry of romantic clichés, sounds a bit like a racehorse, 'lean with a grace and beauty deep in her eyes' (p. 115). They fall into one another's arms, and once again – there we are. And yet, when I reflected upon this unlikely encounter I realized that there was a truth buried there; someone whose emotions have worked their way through every known sexual cliché might well fall in love in precisely this way. And would only fall for an older woman.

Neither Dee nor Lotte would think of herself as a particularly creative or articulate woman. March constructs their narratives as spoken speech; short sentences, grammatical liberties and the casual interjections of oral story-telling. Essie, the grammar-school girl, is more literary but less convincing than Lotte. Yet she too is a phenomenon of post-war social history: the working-class woman who is uprooted from her community. 'Fill you with their arty farty ideas, and set you apart from the likes of your people here, living like we do' (p. 104). The 'swot-rot' which besets Essie becomes the thinking disease which eventually leads her to feminism. One of the books behind this book is Marge

Piercy's *Woman on the Edge of Time*, which inspires Essie's utopian dreams.[47]
'My dreams became a jumble of hopes and fears about women, mental hospitals
and sexuality' (p. 178). But unlike Piercy, March's character dreams of a
separatist women's community. Explicit debate, with two voices in the fiction
taking up opposing sides, is a recurring feature of feminist writing. Essie's lover
Chris is a doctor who wants to become a psychiatrist. Chris is also working-
class and has fought her way into her profession. She refuses to challenge the
foundations of the career in which she has battled to succeed. Essie is a teacher,
and is busy asking all the unpleasant questions. They have a claustrophobic and
very interesting quarrel about Freud in an Essex cottage. But when the affair is
over, March gives Essie a very wise reflection. 'I feel as if her survival methods
are merely very different from my own. I still think she's completely up the
creek about Freud and male psychiatry . . . Our betrayals were mutual and
complicated. Just because she's a survivor in a man's world doesn't make her
bad' (p. 184). Well, it doesn't make her bad, but it does mean that she is
implicated, by whatever she does within the province of male psychiatry, in the
evil which that profession hands out to other women, especially other Lesbians.
The consequences of this are spelt out in the book. Dora, Dee's first lover,
spends years in a mental hospital.

> She had been one of their experiments for the new drugs for almost seven years.
> As far as I know, they did not drag out of her the truth about having been gay. It
> was hidden to Dora herself, and it's my view that the drugs finished off the
> cover . . . The official cause of Dora's death was heart failure. I know she died of
> terror when men came at her with their cables and electrodes. (pp. 52–3)

How far any woman is prepared to compromise with the institutions of
patriarchy will depend on her political analysis of her position as a woman, and
on her access to those institutions in the first place. But the decisive factor will
be whether she perceives the situation as appalling or as merely unfortunate;
and that will depend upon her own experience at the hands of men.

 This is an important argument within any revolutionary movement: whether
to infiltrate the establishment and to push from within, or whether to settle for
confrontation from outside, thereby unpicking the master's house with our own
tools. I do not think there can ever be an absolute commandment as to which is
the better course of action, but it is not a struggle in which anyone can claim to
have clean hands.

 Concern with Black issues, racism and the freedom of post-imperial
countries is crucial in March's fiction. Essie's best-loved friend from her
childhood is a Blackwoman called Laura. Dee raises her first lover's Black
daughter. March always writes from a white woman's perspective and never
presumes to trespass on the inwardness of Black people's experience. Racism is
a white problem; and March makes that clear. When Dee tells her old friend
Nell that her lover's child is Black, she is faced with a torrent of racism.

> 'I mean how brown. That's what. You shouldn't have kept it. You should send it
> back. Back where it came from.'

It. How could she say 'it'? It had a sex. It had a name. How dare she call Izzie an it. Because Izzie was brown. She'd not have itt-ed it if Izzie had been white. (p. 34)

This is the classic pattern of racism: deny your own community or connection with the person concerned, transform her into an object, and then reject and despise her reality.

March shows her characters learning and unlearning their fears; about other people, about themselves. Laura, the Blackwoman, becomes politically involved in Black youth work and eventually marries a Black man. She gives Essie some good advice. 'Don't get muddled up by guilt Essie. Just get on with the work, okay?' (p. 142). It is advice all white women would be wise to take. Guilt always has the effect of making the person who feels guilty central once more. They can then become paralysed by their own inadequacy, and politically useless. Laura's demand on Essie is to work, read, think, change. Laura in her turn has to re-think her attitudes concerning Lesbianism. When she is confronted by Essie's declarations her first response is one of the classics in the Grand Anti-Lesbian Repertoire: 'Keep away from my daughters.' This is what she says, ' "It's not a possibility in their lives . . . I have thought about it, you know, Essie. It's not simply my gut reaction. It's how Joseph and I both feel, and it's about what we want for Melody and Sophie and their futures" ' (p. 142). Dictating to their daughters is something all parents do anyway. Fortunately, children very seldom do fulfil their parents' demands and expectations. March's argument is that Lesbianism is a possibility in every woman's life; the central theme of her novel is coming out, and the effect it has on other people; and so there is a good deal of shouting, disruption, and tears.

Ordinary, unemployed working-class dykes in 1980s London become the heroines in Rebecca O'Rourke's *Jumping the Cracks*.[48] The book is marketed by the publishers as a thriller. Linda Semple, in an article on Lesbians and crime fiction, has this to say about it. 'Her heroine is an ordinary dyke who gets caught up in a murder and is more or less powerless, as any of us would be in a similar position. What many have seen as a banal and unsatisfactory solution, is, I suspect, simply the way such things would turn out for any of us in real life.'[49] But good thrillers never represent 'real life', whatever that might be in terms of writing fiction; verismo details should provide local colour and painted backdrop – and should never interfere with the plot. The murder intrigue in *Jumping the Cracks* is in fact painfully bad. The stage villain in his Rolls-Royce is named after various US medium-range missiles (now locked in a cupboard waiting for the next Cold War) and sports an American accent, just in case we have missed the point. But what the book does present well, in morbidly miserable detail, is the effect marginalization, rejection and unemployment have upon a woman's morale. It is a book about stasis and gradual awakening. Thrillers, even psychological thrillers, need action, reversals and change. Rats, the heroine, has thoroughly internalized a sense of her own powerlessness, which finds its external symbol in inner-city blight. She goes to bed for days on end, drinks 'herself into a stupor on the nights her dole cheque holds out' (p. 5). Rats does turn to the Lesbian life of London for support, and finds none.

'Usually she spent the night propping the wall up, too shy and intimidated by the other women who all seemed to know each other, to make any kind of move towards them' (p. 51).

Rats comes from Hull, from a working-class Catholic family who throw her out when they discover that she is a Lesbian. 'She had sinned against the Holy Virgin Mary and all the saints and martyrs of the Catholic Church. But her greatest sin was against the family, the Holy Family and her own' (p. 79). The book is about structures, institutions and individuals that reject and exclude Rats and yet manage to control her existence. Where she does find support is in the anonymous goodwill of the pub culture she normally inhabits. 'The pub carried on drinking, seething with the weight of the week's work being sloughed off' (p. 131). Here, no one is trying to change the world, and a man can be described as living 'in the cemetery and on a doorstep, one of those disused houses on Manor Road' (p. 134), as a matter of fact, without horror, righteous judgement or moral outrage.

Rats' lover, Helen, bristles with intelligent dynamism and becomes involved with various housing campaigns. The text makes clear that Rats' negativity is caused not only by her marginal situation, but also by her defeatist attitudes.

> She understood the power relations instinctively. For Rats, knowing that power was knowing its effects on your life, its ability to structure and control, intimidate. To Helen it was a challenge. To know power was to know its weaknesses as well as its strength. Where it didn't control you as well as where it did. Helen saw the possibility of change. Rats saw only accommodation. (p. 146)

These are two different political responses to powerlessness. I must say at once that O'Rourke is not advising unemployed Lesbians to brace up, mount their bicycles and build a better future for Britain. The daily experience of living as a working-class Lesbian does not throw up one catastrophic trauma after another – although these do also happen – so much as present a continuous, demoralizing, irritating string of difficulties which come from the refusal to fit into the straitjacket categories of a white man's world.

There are some passages in *Jumping the Cracks* that are genuinely devastating in their undramatic economy and clarity. The breach between Rats and her family is terrifying to read.

> That final beating had been unwitnessed and unrestrained . . . The kitchen was too small to evade him for long, his fury too powerful for her to resist. And instead of a terse, 'You are a great disappointment to your mother and me, Geraldine, a great disappointment,' it had been a string of curses that echoed every dockland bar her father had ever got drunk in . . . Rats had to stay away from work until the bruising went down. She lost her job. (p. 80)

The terse final sentence calmly marks the fulfilment of her father's hatred in the rest of the world. But the writing is not consistently sharp. We are also treated to rows of florid clichés, 'the new hospital', for example, 'casting a grim shadow of ill-fortune over the mean streets it stood amongst' (p. 73), which makes the hospital sound like Dracula's castle. Occasionally, too, working-class culture begins to sound implausibly cosy. 'Al's was a no-nonsense, steamy hub of warmth . . . men of all ages in the drab serviceable clothes of heavy work. A pall of smoke rested on the steam from the urn and the roll-up tins were passed around as easily as the newspapers' (p. 74). The problem arises from the patterns of double adjectives – 'no-nonsense, steamy', 'drab, service-able' – which weigh down the prose and wreck the book as a thriller, quite apart from the weakness of the plot. Good thriller writers use adjectives like bullets, sharp, fast and economically; their force comes instead from strong verbs.

It is the experience of seeing a corpse in the back of a Rolls-Royce and asking one or two questions about how it got there which gives Rats a sense of her own worth. This is because she is the one who asks and acts; she is no longer being battered by everyone else. At last, she is able to take charge of her own life and make her own decisions. 'She no longer felt at the mercy of the world' (p. 149).

The mainstream press is now moving into the Lesbian market – and a good many writers who began their careers as feminists are making for the mainstream. Nicci Gerrard thinks that this is a good thing.

> The most triumphantly feminist literature of the last decade is that which has been occupied rather than preoccupied by feminism; shaped and permeated by a feminist consciousness, rather than trapped within an inherited feminist structure . . . so many women writers, who welcome the adjective 'feminist' for their personal lives, react with a kind of horror at the suggestion that they actually write 'feminist novels'.[50]

One would have thought that Lesbianism was rather harder to assimilate into the conservative world of commercial publishing. Not so, it seems, so long as the political terms are carefully policed, and the sexual product elegantly re-packed. Elizabeth Wood's *Mothers and Lovers* comes beautifully published and packaged in hardback by Bloomsbury. Wood is an Australian now living in New York and her book is a Lesbian *Bildungsroman* of the How-I-came-to-be-what-I-am variety, written as a first-person confessional realist narrative. This is a broken-backed book; the excellent, beautifully written first section on childhood and adolescence suddenly sags into an often-told story of middle-class marriages dissolving in suburbia.[51] I felt that the novel died on the page simply because the silences in the text gaped like open wounds. We are treated to one appalling scene of rape and heterosexual abuse under hypnosis. Lesbian sex, however, is discreetly veiled, apart from a married voyeur bringing out a copy of *Playboy*.

> 'Is this what you and Jenny Murphy do?' she grinned lopsidedly.
> They wore the usual pornographic trappings – leather and whips and scanty lacy underwear, with lascivious baby-doll pouts and drowning eyes – and I abruptly changed the subject. I was furious with Pamela. (p. 192).

We are told that the heroine becomes a feminist. We never see her doing so. We are told that she produces a feminist theatre review which is unlike 'any theatre experience before' (p. 197). But we never see it happen. Feminism is narrated; the real subject is marriage and motherhood. Even here, there are blanks. The most disturbing blank of all is the heroine's husband. She is attracted to him because he is opaque, and opaque he remains. 'I can't ask questions. I don't have answers. Duncan's missing from my text. I don't recognize him anywhere' (p. 259). I didn't either. There is a strong, objection-able, silent, hairy slab of male flesh moving around in the novel; but the sign – husband – remains quite blank. And this is not a sinister, speaking silence, but simply a failure to analyse masculinity – which would be, I assume, an important element in a text that proposed to describe heterosexual institutions. Amazingly, *Mothers and Lovers*, in the last section, suddenly rises from the page and out of a grim torpor of cliché to become a thriller as our heroine fights a Lesbian custody case. As I have said elsewhere, courtroom fiction is always intrinsically dramatic. The narrative is tense, revealing, painful and heartrending. And yet, and yet . . . 'Lesbian. Why do I feel that no one has really dealt with this? . . . it is the one subject that everybody skirts around and hopes to shelve' (p. 296). She said it, sisters, I didn't. But I suspect that if Woods had dealt with Lesbianism as anything other than an unconventional sexual preference, the straight press would never have published this book. In the excellent opening section two dykes called Winnie and Gayle declare war on society and depart from the novel. ' "War!" Winnie shouted to the treetops. "War, comrades, sisters, into battle against society." She linked her arm in Gayle's and began to march off down the road' (p. 75). The politics of sexuality depart with Winnie and Gayle. I think that the two substantial silences surrounding the sign HUSBAND and the sign LESBIAN reflect each other. Woods's real subject was marriage and the politics of heterosexuality. Lesbian-ism was incidental. And yet *Mothers and Lovers* does not even deal with the levers and clamps of male power within marriage. Why did she marry him? Some mysteries are universal. Very few woman ever know quite why they marry, or why they married that particular man.

The question of Lesbian identity remains vexed – and plural. There are many ways to express the meaning of Lesbian. Even the parameters outside our lives are changing.

> Who can imagine, their mind half closed down, what a lesbian might be like in a non-hostile environment – we know as little about it as we know of the effect on plants of the absence of gravity.
>
> We are all in retreat, trying to merge with the wallpaper, get jobs, say nothing. Danger distracts one from abstract thought. I have to keep thinking. Dare I write another lesbian novel? What shall I live on if I do? [52]

The conditions under which a woman decides to live as a Lesbian, or to write as a Lesbian, have changed a great deal in the sixty years since *The Well of Loneliness* was prosecuted for obscenity. But even as I write now, I know that each fragile gain can be clawed back. I have already watched much of what we fought for in the 1970s being repossessed by a society riddled with hatred for anything or anyone who challenges the established structures of power.

Rosemary Manning's second autobiography, *A Corridor of Mirrors*, roughly spans these sixty years. Manning writes of her years in the closet – she first came out at the age of seventy in 1980 – as the 'years of dishonesty' and as 'the habit of secrecy'.[53] The mask of lies and the world which forced her to live in disguise almost destroyed her life. *A Corridor of Mirrors* often sounds like an end-of-term sermon, indicating where the girls have done well, and where they have not lived up to expectations. Unfortunately, there is no next term in which to do better. I believe profoundly, as Manning does, that this life is all we have. And her life, with its pain, despair, suicidal unhappiness, makes harrowing reading. She is unwilling to blame her misery on the world outside herself; yet her own story forces her to do so. 'The necessity to keep silent in public about being gay put a strain on me that young gays today have no conception of ' (p. 162). And it is also painfully clear that, for her, coming out at seventy was the assertion of freedom, which is 'just another name for nothing left to lose'.

Manning's attitude to writing is very much that of the old school, based on inspiration and creativity. She also maintains that her enforced habit of secrecy about her sexuality did not affect her writing. She writes, 'It is not necessary to write about gays because you are gay yourself, anymore than you would feel compelled to write about hunchbacks because you were so deformed' (p. 167). Even that sentence is a tangle of self-hatred; why equate Lesbianism with deformity? Or indeed, having a hunchback with deformity? She goes on to justify herself: 'I am quite simply interested in people and their motives, and the circumstances which make them what they are . . . ' (p. 167). This too is an attitude of the old school of privilege; the fallacy of liberalism which supposes that we can simply be interested in people as people regardless of whether they are women or men, Black or white, straight or Gay, as if these things did not, in some fundamental way, structure their lives. To be a 'person' then becomes some strange, detached, eternal, extra dimension. Even human being cannot be claimed with equal conviction by each one of us, when women and Black people have for centuries often been treated as sub-human. Lesbians are Lesbians twenty-four hours of the day. And Manning's whole poignant life bears witness to the fact that her hidden sexuality – to which she often refers as her proclivities, or her predilections, as if women were chocolates – marked her entire existence and nearly destroyed her.

Sex, sexuality, racism; these are political questions, and in our writing we should confront them with an open, informed political consciousness. Janice Raymond, interviewed by the radical feminist magazine *Trouble and Strife*, insists on the price tag attached to living as a Lesbian. 'You pay a price for being a lesbian, a political price. And at some point, politically speaking, I think you make a choice to be a lesbian. Although I have never been anything but a lesbian I still think that at some point I made a very conscious choice . . . '[54] And of course, what or who a Lesbian actually is, is still very much a matter for debate, since, especially within the women's movement, there are women who will cheerfully and honestly write, 'I believe in sex and have been empowered by sex with both men and women . . . '[55] Recent interest in butch/femme roles and even the Great Lesbian Sado-Masochism Debate are, I believe, bound up with the retreat from feminism within many Lesbian communities.[56] But there are also radical Lesbians like Julia Penelope, who have ceased to call themselves feminists because for them the word has dissolved into a wash of reformist liberal humanism.

But would the political price tag attached to living as a Lesbian necessarily involve any kind of commitment to other women who decide that they are not Lesbians and prefer to take their chances with men? Perhaps only for women who name themselves as feminists and use the word with all its original angry force. One fictional answer comes from Anna Wilson's *Altogether Elsewhere*. This novel is a portrait of a group of women at war; women whose solidarity extends across race, class and sexuality. Their energy is turned outwards against their enemy; they defend other women, all other women, against violence from men. Lesbians are just as vulnerable to this endemic violence as any other women; sometimes more so if we are unable or refuse to pass as heterosexual. Wilson's terse, elegant and frightening prose describes a violence that is not personal, that is in itself the system of woman-hating, an intensification of the conditions within which we all live. 'There is a detached quality to their actions as they press her against the wall . . . He stands so close to her, almost touching, a deliberate intimacy of violence.'[57] It is Lesbian radical feminism which recognizes women, all women, as a people at risk. Our hope for change lies therefore in necessary alliances and collective action. And that really does involve a political analysis which understands Lesbianism to be more than a personal preference. Writing Lesbian then becomes a place on which to stand and from which to understand the world. And for all of us, I want Rosemary Manning's wonderful, unexpected, Hallelujah ending: ' . . . My friends and I, in a final gesture, toast our loves and toss our champagne corks into the river at our feet.'[58]

Notes

1 For a discussion of the meanings of 'Lesbian' in the period 1880–1930 see Sheila Jeffreys, *The Spinster and Her Enemies: Feminism and Sexuality 1880–1930* (London, Pandora, 1985), esp, ch. 6. In France a lot of work is being done on this period by Lesbians and Gay men. I was at an international seminar on homosexuality and Lesbianism at the Sorbonne on 1–2 December 1989 and heard there an especially interesting paper by Brigitte Lhomond, a researcher with the CNRS in Lyon. She works on the ways in which Lesbians and Gay men understood their own identities in the early twentieth century.

2 Esther Newton, 'The Mythic Mannish Lesbian: Radclyffe Hall and the New Woman', in Estelle B. Freedman et al. (eds), *The Lesbian Issue: Essays from* Signs (Chicago, University of Chicago Press, 1985), pp. 7–25: p. 10.

3 See Newton's brief but helpful comments. The advantage of the innate biology theory is of course that no one can be morally blamed for being born deviant. See also Celia Kitzinger, *The Social Construction of Lesbianism* (London, Sage, 1987). On Radclyffe Hall and various theories of inversion, see Michael Baker, *Our Three Selves: The Life of Radclyffe Hall* (London, Hamish Hamilton, 1985) and Rebecca O'Rourke, *Reflecting on The Well of Loneliness* (London, Routledge & Kegan Paul, 1989).

4 Judith Fetterley, *Gay Studies Newsletter*, vol. 14, no. 1 (March 1987). The full text of her talk 'Writes of Passing' is reprinted in *Gossip: A Journal of Lesbian Feminist Ethics*, no. 5 (Autumn 1987); this quotation appears on p. 25. *Gay Studies Newsletter* is available on subscription from the Department of English, 7 Kings College Circle, University of Toronto, Toronto, Ontario, Canada M5S 1A1; *Gossip* is available from Onlywomen Press, 38 Mount Pleasant, London WC1X 0AP. A Gay and Lesbian Academic network is just beginning in Britain. For more information write to: Ford Hickson, Department of Social Science, South Bank Polytechnic, London Road, London SE1 0AA. The first issue of the *Newsletter* came out in April 1991.

5 Fetterley, *Gossip*, no. 5, p. 25.

6 Catharine R. Stimpson, 'Zero Degree Deviancy: The Lesbian Novel in English', in E. Abel (ed.), *Writing and Sexual Difference* (Brighton, Harvester, 1982), pp. 243–59: p. 244.

7 Lillian Faderman, *Surpassing the Love of Men: Romantic Friendship and Love Between Women from the Renaissance to the Present* (1981; London, Women's Press, 1985), p. 400.

8 Gertrude Stein, quoted by Faderman, *Surpassing the Love of Men*, p. 405. And see Stein herself in a little-known, very erotic poem *Lifting Belly*, ed. Rebecca Mark (Tallahassee, Fla, Naiad, 1989).

9 Marguérite Yourcenar, *Memoirs of Hadrian* (1951; London, Penguin, 1982).

10 Marilyn Frye, 'To Be and Be Seen: The Politics of Reality': the title essay in her excellent collection of philosophical and political essays, *The Politics of Reality: Essays in Feminist Theory* (Trumansberg, NY, Crossing Press, 1983). Quotation taken from p. 172.

11 Marguérite Yourcenar interviewed by Ronald Hayman, *The Observer*, 29 April 1984.

12 Arnold Bennett, *The Old Wives' Tale* (1908; London, Pan, 1964, 1975), preface, p. 24.

13 Stimpson, 'Zero Degree Deviancy', p. 254.

14 Sara Maitland, *Virgin Territory* (London, Michael Joseph, 1984), p. 106.

15 Mary Daly's pioneering work has been very influential as a feminist critique of traditional Christian theology; see her *The Church and the Second Sex* (1968; Boston, Beacon, 1985); *Beyond God the Father: Towards a Philosophy of Women's Liberation* (1973; Boston, Beacon, 1974); *Gyn/Ecology: The Metaethics of Radical Feminism* (1978; London, Women's Press, 1979) and *Pure Lust: Elemental Feminist Philosophy* (London, Women's Press, 1984). For women remaining within the Church there is Maitland herself: *A Map of the New Country: Women and Christianity* (London, Routledge & Kegan Paul, 1983; the title is a little misleading – the book is about reformist feminist interventions in the western church). On Christian origins I recommend Elizabeth Schüssler Fiorenza, *In Memory of Her: A Feminist Theological Reconstruction of Christian Origins* (London, SCM, 1983) and Letty M. Russell (ed.), *Feminist Interpretation of the Bible* (Oxford, Blackwell, 1985). All of this indicates a vast bibliography for further reading. On the other side of the fence I have been immensely interested by Luisah Teish's *Jambalaya: The Natural Woman's Book of Personal Charms and Practical Rituals* (San Francisco, Harper & Row, 1985) – but these are simply starting-points, and the list is potentially endless. Women's spirituality and critiques of patriarchal religious systems have engaged a good deal of feminist energy in recent years.

16 Mary Wings, *She Came Too Late* (London, Women's Press, 1986).

17 Verena Stefan, *Shedding* (1975; London, Women's Press, 1979), p. 25.

18 Dacia Maraini, *Letters to Marina* (1981; English edition, translated from the Italian by Dick Kitto and Elspeth Spottiswood, London, Camden, 1987), p. 25. The

passion for men comes, according to Maraini, from our longing for our fathers and our sons. 'First my heart-breaking and defenceless love for my fair-haired athlete father with his slanting features who shunned me and whom I pursued over land and sea regardless of myself and my mother and my sisters. Then my all-consuming love for my lover sons.'

19 Violette Leduc, *La Bâtarde* (1964; London, Virago, 1985).
20 Simone de Beauvoir, preface to *La Bâtarde*, p. xxi.
21 Jo Jones, *Come Come* (London, Sheba, 1983).
22 Jeanette Winterson, *Oranges Are Not the Only Fruit* (London, Pandora, 1985). Ms Winterson's rise to stardom has been pleasingly meteoric. In *Oranges* she makes it clear that she was a Star from the beginning. The book has now been metamorphosed into a three-part television film.
23 Rita Mae Brown, *Rubyfruit Jungle* (1973; New York, Bantam, 1977; reprinted nine times by 1983).
24 Barbara Deming, *A Humming Under My Feet: A Book of Travail* (London, Women's Press, 1985), p. viii.
25 Jane Gapen, from the introductory preface to the section 'A Book of Travail – and of a Humming under My Feet', in Margaret Cruikshank (ed.), *New Lesbian Writing: An Anthology* (San Francisco, Grey Fox Press, 1984), p. 161.
26 Sheila Shulman, in *Love Your Enemy: The Debate between Heterosexual Feminism and Political Lesbianism* (London, Onlywomen, 1981), p. 65.
27 Claire Morgan, *The Price of Salt* (1952; Tallahassee, Fla, Naiad, 1984), p. 278.
28 Anna Wilson, *Cactus* (London, Onlywomen, 1980), p. 11.
29 Jane Rule, *Desert of the Heart* (1964; London, Pandora, 1986); *This Is Not For You* (1970; London, Pandora, 1987).
30 Jane Rule, *Lesbian Images* (1976; Trumansberg, NY, Crossing Press, 1982).
31 Sibyl Grundberg, 'Deserted Hearts: Lesbians Making it in the Movies', *Gossip: A Journal of Lesbian Feminist Ethics*, no. 4 (1987), pp. 27–39: p. 37.
32 Jane Rule, 'Lesbian and Writer: Making the Real Visible', in Cruikshank, *New Lesbian Writing*, pp. 98, 97.
33 Rule, 'Lesbian and Writer', p. 99.
34 Rosemary Manning, *A Time and a Time* (1971; London, Marion Boyars, 1986), p. 137.
35 Anna Livia, *Relatively Norma* (London, Onlywomen, 1982).
36 Mariana Valverde, *Sex, Power and Pleasure* (Toronto, Women's Press, 1986), p. 92.
37 Anna Livia, *Accommodation Offered* (London, Women's Press, 1985).
38 Alison Ward, *The Glass Boat* (London, Brilliance, 1983).
39 Ellen Galford, *The Fires of Bride* (London, Women's Press, 1986).
40 Women have never had the opportunity to imagine our own religion. Fiction is the ideal place wherein to do it. But that *The Fires of Bride* is a fantasy to make us all feel good is an estimation of her own work which Galford accepts. Interviewed at 'SATISFACTION: The Second Symposium of Lesbian and Gay Writers living in Europe' (Rotterdam, 17–22 October 1988), she said: 'Of course it's fantasy. Because the women win.'
41 Maud Sulter, 'Black Codes: The Misrepresentation of Black Lesbians in Film', *Gossip: A Journal of Lesbian Feminist Ethics*, no. 5 (1987), pp. 29–36: p. 31.
42 For more information on lesbianism and modernism see Gillian Hanscombe and Virginia L. Smyers, *Writing for their Lives: The Modernist Women 1910–1940* (London, Women's Press, 1987) and Shari Benstock, *Women of the Left Bank: Paris 1900–1940* (London, Virago, 1987).
43 Barbara Burford, *The Threshing Floor* (London, Sheba, 1986).

44 Audre Lorde, *Zami: A New Spelling of My Name* (1982; London, Sheba, 1984), p. 7.

45 Caeia March, *Three Ply Yarn* (London, Women's Press, 1986), p. 226.

46 Dave Morley and Ken Worpole (eds), *The Republic of Letters: Working Class Writing and Local Publishing* (London, Comedia, 1982), p. 11. Also very relevant here is Tillie Olsen's *Silences* (London, Virago, 1981). See also June Burnett et al. (eds) *The Common Thread: Writings by Working Class Women* (London: Mandarin, 1989).

47 See my discussion of Piercy's novel in chapter 4 above, 'On Genre Fiction'.

48 Rebecca O'Rourke, *Jumping the Cracks* (London, Virago, 1987).

49 Linda Semple, 'Lesbians in Detective Fiction', *Gossip: A Journal of Lesbian Feminist Ethics*, no. 5 (1987), pp. 47–52: p. 51.

50 Nicci Gerrard, *Into the Mainstream: How Feminism has Changed Women's Writing* (London, Pandora, 1989), p. 106. I disagree with most of what Gerrard has to say. Her knowledge of the publishing industry is clearly that of an insider. Her account confirmed my fear that the worst things I hear about it are all true.

51 Elizabeth Wood, *Mothers and Lovers* (London, Bloomsbury, 1988). But see Linda Semple's review in Silver Moon's quarterly bookshop review, no. 6 (Spring 1988): 'This part of the novel is extremely convincing; the slow collapse and eventual complete breakdown of Morgan's marriage and her realisation, through meeting and falling for another lesbian, are cleverly written.'

52 Anna Wilson, 'On Being a Lesbian Writer: Writing Your Way Out of the Paper Bag', in Lesley Saunders (ed.), *Glancing Fires: An Investigation into Women's Creativity* (London, Women's Press, 1987), p. 145.

53 Rosemary Manning, *A Corridor of Mirrors* (London, Women's Press, 1987), p. 3.

54 'The Politics of Passion: Janice Raymond talks with Suzanne Kappeler, Liz Kelly and Kathy Parker', *Trouble and Strife*, no. 11 (Summer 1987), p. 40.

55 Pat Gowans, 'Womb Oppression and Sex as Power', *Off Our Backs*, vol. 17, no. 8 (August–September 1987), p. 24.

56 Two relevant articles in *Gossip: A Journal of Lesbian Feminist Ethics*, no. 5 (1987) are Anna Livia, ' "I would rather have been dead than gone forever": Butch and Femme as Responses to Patriarchy', and Sheila Jeffreys, 'Butch and Femme: Now and Then'.

57 Anna Wilson, *Altogether Elsewhere* (London, Onlywomen, 1985), p. 108.

58 Manning, *A Corridor of Mirrors*, p. 234.

7

Writing Against Racism

On Hurt

Hurt?
Who me?
Hurt?

Don't kid yourself.
I'm not hurt.
Just mad
at your middle class
pain in the ass
self-righteousness.

Meiling Jin, from *Watchers & Seekers*

Throughout this book, my autobiography of reading, I have refused to write the conventional division between myself as writer and my subject – my reading. I have not been the outsider who observes, comments and remains detached. I have been part of my own narrative. I have always written I/We. But here I write as an outsider. I read as a white woman looking inwards on a knowledge and an experience which I can struggle to imagine but can never know in my own flesh: that of being Black. And I am aware that, when I read the work of Afro-Caribbean and Asian women who live in Britain, or who have been part of the numerous migrations of Black people, forced upon them by white capital, that I read in different ways from the ways in which I read fiction by white feminists or white women. This is not a question of having less exacting critical standards from those I would use to comment on writing by white women, nor even necessarily different ones. Either would be both patronizing and racist. Rather, it is a question of reading within different traditions: traditions which are not white, which have different priorities, different literary foremothers, different male echoes, different rhythms – and, above all, a different relationship to oral story-telling. Sometimes white western writing is answered back by Blackwomen, from their own perspective: for a Blackwoman's connections or confrontations with the white woman's or the white man's words will be different from those of a white woman. The most important thing for me to do, as a reader, is to listen for those differences.

A good many supposedly creative misreadings of Black and Asian writing by white women are simply the results of ignorance, arrogance and prejudice. Barbara Burford, in an article about Blackwomen's reading, writing and publishing in Britain, warns against white voices 'that seek to describe us'. She points out: 'We will see that any white voice seeking to describe us is describing their own drives and consuming desires.'[1] In fact, all political critical reading will – necessarily – reflect the desires of the reader rather than those of the writer. And writers are not always in control of their own meanings. I am, however, of the school of writers and readers who believe that some readings are more appropriate and intelligent than others. I have a great deal of sympathetic understanding for Amryl Johnson when she writes of the critics: 'What comes over a lot of the time is that they do not even understand what you are trying to say. This is the annoying part. In some cases they do not even come *close* to comprehending.'[2] I am sure she's right. In the case of a white woman reading Black and Asian writing the consequences of that non-comprehension can be to reproduce the clichés of white racism. The title of this chapter, therefore, 'Writing Against Racism', not only describes the political intention or effect of the work I read but is also a challenge and a reminder to myself as a writer. Writing, all writing, can be a weapon for change; equally, it can reinforce the existing status quo. Very well then, I have been warned. And noted the warning.

All reading, my own included, is a sequence of encounters: with a text, with another mind, with a new way of seeing. Some of these encounters result in a rueful sense of recognition; some in fear, shock, alarm, anger, or the acknowledgement of an Otherness which I have never touched before and from which I can only learn. There is no correct way to read. Nor is any reading ever innocent. Throughout this essay I have been committed to an anti-racist politics of reading. But I am part of the wider audience for Black writing, an incidental reader. Most of these books were not written for me, but for other Black-women; and this would remain true, even if the majority of the readership were white.

The experience of 'unbelonging' is eloquently charted by Black British writers of fiction and poetry, and is the title of Joan Riley's first novel, *The Unbelonging*.[3] Unbelonging can be an abstract noun, describing a state or a condition, and it can also be a concrete subject, a person who is stateless, rootless, alienated. Adjoa Andoh thanks Riley for her words and tells, in verse, another version of the same title.

> i don't have the right accent to even pronounce my own
>   name properly.
> no – not ghanaian.
> english?
> look at me, i'm black, i'm not white,
> don't tell me i'm english, i've heard too many wogs and
>   niggers and go back where you came from.
> where's my heritage?
> you don't just pick it up where you can, you grow up with it,
>   you absorb it,
> i have absorbed no one's land.[4]

Again and again, Black and Asian writing reflects the uncanny, exhausting experience of being both visible and invisible, at once present and absent, harassed and ignored, perpetually insecure in white, racist Britain. White Lesbian women, if they wish or are able to pass for straight, can vanish into a privileged social category to evade censure, violence or discrimination. Black and Asian women never can. The perpetual white question, 'Where do you come from?' followed by, 'I mean where do you really come from?' insists on the fact of unbelonging. But out of the Black analysis of unbelonging come the powerful Black meanings – of identity and community.

But of course there is no such thing as 'Blackwomen's writing': no homogeneous block of work which necessarily has the same concerns, obsessions, assumptions, shapes. There are the Blackwomen who live, work and write in Britain, some of whom would describe themselves as British and others who would not. Women's writing from India, as well as the writing by Black Afro-Americans, have been and continue to be an inspiration to Blackwomen in Britain. 'They have acted as a catalyst for discussion, and reaffirmed that similar kinds of consciousness were being explored. Always with an appreciation that "although it speaks directly to our experience in Britain, it does not speak directly of it".'[5] The first conference for Blackwomen in Britain, for women who define themselves as Blackfeminists, was held in 1984; significantly, the women entitled the conference 'We Are Here'. This proud and defiant self-definition indicates that Blackwomen are not only here, present in Britain, but also visible as an autonomous Blackwomen's movement – here for each other. There has, of course, been a Black presence in Britain for at least 400 years. 'We are here, have been here for a long time and are here to stay. Yet our voices and histories are suppressed in order to maintain the lie that we are going back or will be sent back.'[6]

In 1987 the first Blackwomen's publishing group, Black Womantalk, published their first anthology, *Black Women Talk Poetry*. The collective editorial statement in their text outlines their struggle to appear in print against all the odds. And the odds – economic, emotional, political – were enormous. They were certain that the work was being done, but they knew that they had to go searching for it. 'Blackwomen are not used to their writing being taken seriously, and we realised early on that it wouldn't be a simple case of advertising for poems! We held several open readings for Blackwomen and slowly they were persuaded to part with their writings.'[7] The members of the Black Womantalk Collective come from a variety of different ethnic backgrounds. One comes from the Chinese community. Some Blackwomen activists prefer to use the term 'Black' only to refer to women of African origins – and certainly there are vast cultural differences between the two largest non-white communities in Britain: the women from south Asian and those from Afro-Caribbean cultures. On the other hand, there are women who see 'Black' as a political term, as a unifying force. Savitri Hensman writes in her poem 'Black is Not a Skin Colour',

> Black
> Is not the colour of a skin
> Black cannot ride in posh cars
> Or look with contempt on the poor

> The hand is black that wields a machete
> Cutting sugar that others may grow rich . . .
> Black grips the guns and the knives
> To bring down the well-off and mighty
> Black is the colour of a heart.[8]

Hensman was born in Sri Lanka, came to Britain at the age of two and has been brought up and educated in London. Jamaican writer Elean Thomas takes a similar position in 'Of Colours and Countries':

> White is not a colour
> It is an attitude
> A certain behaviour
>
> Black is not a colour
> It is a statement
> of a shared past
> a present reality
> a future intent[9]

The migrations and the displacement of populations during the colonial period have bound people from the West Indies, Africa and the Indian sub-continent together. Many of the Asian people who now live in Britain come from East Africa – Tanzania, Kenya, Uganda – and knew no country other than Africa. Their experience of Africa has been that of an immigrant community, as is their experience of Britain. The migrations caused by British colonialism also created Asian communities in the West Indies. Black, in many women's writing, therefore becomes a political category – and an assertion of proud resistance to white racism. For British racists are not in the business of making fine distinctions in the matter of historical traditions and realities. Racism, in all its forms, both subtle and brutal, is endemic in every structure of this society, and affects both groups of women. Thus, racism is one parameter of Black existence. Mumtaz Karimjee, the Black/Asian photographer, writes in *Mukti*: 'In the final analysis I feel that it is this racist society and its hostility to my and the existence of all Black people which forces us to continually question who we are, where we belong and why. It never allows us the security to just sit back and be who we are without justifying our existence.'[10] And of course there will be tensions between Afro-Caribbean people and Asian people living in Britain.[11] Buchi Emecheta, in her autobiography of survival, *Head Above Water*, makes it clear that 'us, the Blacks' means Africans and Afro-Caribbeans. In her job as a teacher in a large London comprehensive she has an encounter 'with someone of Asian origin, one Mrs Patel.'

> At first she sat with us, the blacks, and we talked about our work, our backgrounds, and our families. I came to know her very well and thought she was a friend. Then suddenly she stopped sitting with us, and wouldn't even answer my 'Good morning'. I kept staring at her, not knowing what we had done. A few days later she walked over to Mr Enenmoh and myself and said that she wanted to be an established teacher and she would rather be seen to be getting on with the

white teachers ... We laughed about this throughout the team and I personally admired her frankness.[12]

It is Mrs Patel, in this case, who excludes herself. And, as in this passage, the tension or resentment between Asians, Afro-Caribbeans and Africans must always be read in the context of white racism and the history of British imperialism. Divide and rule has always been the most universal, and most successful, policy used by the powerful to maintain their position. Whites have used this method against Black communities, men have used it against women. Nevertheless, to counter and defeat white racism it is crucial to analyse and understand different cultural inheritances, different historical memories.

There are religious contrasts between women of Asian or Afro-Caribbean descent. Asian women are likely to make the system of arranged marriage more central to their narratives and concerns,[13] whereas the experience of polygamy is important in African writing, both by Moslem women and by women living within traditional African religious structures where polygamy is practised. (It will not be so for Afro-Caribbean women living in Britain.) Family, community, motherhood; these things will be shaped and experienced in different ways. The security and the torment encountered within traditional institutions have different forms and implications. Yet the abuse of women appears to be remarkably constant within every community. The same patterns emerge: sexism, male violence and the persecution of Lesbians. Both communities have had the historical experience of British or European imperialism and the consequent disruption or destruction of culture and values, the migrations, exploitation, oppression; but only Black Africans and their descendants have had the experience of slavery.

Every Blackwoman is an expert on white racism. 'As for working in this country, there is always a doubt in people's mind whether an Asian woman in a sari is capable of doing a job which requires intelligence.'[14] Questions of language, dress, identity, tradition therefore become critical in the work of British Blackwomen. If, like the novelist Buchi Emecheta, you are a Blackwoman writing not in your mother tongue but in your fourth language, then your relationship to that language and its history will be complicated and oblique. Many Blackwomen come from cultures that have a far closer relationship to a great oral tradition of story-telling, recitation and song than that of white British writers working in English. Emecheta dramatizes this in *Head Above Water*. The story of her birth is told to her by her mothers, and within her own text, her oldest mother, that is, her father's eldest sister, tells the story to the children. 'She had succeeded in rousing our curiosity and expectancy and she knew it. She closed her eyes and slowly drifted into one of her story-telling trances. And when she opened her mouth to speak, the voice that came out was distant and mesmerizing ... ' (p. 8). Many Blackwomen writers working now in Britain write both poetry and fiction. Barbara Burford, Merle Collins, Grace Nichols and Amryl Johnson have all published both poetry and fiction (or prose autobiography). Black writing often draws on the rhythms of oral narrative or spoken speech. The testimonies by Sistren in *Lionheart Gal: Life Stories of Jamaican Women* are largely written in Jamaican

Patwah and, ideally, should be read aloud. Many of the narratives were originally taped from the spoken voice.[15] Poetry forms much of the creative work by Blackwomen in Britain which has been published: and here, the link between song and oral tradition becomes explicit. At the afternoon 'In Aid of Azania/In Celebration of Audre Lorde' on 6 December 1987 at the Shaw Theatre, London, Iyamidé Hazeley read her poetry; her last poem became a chant and a song. She taught us the chorus and we joined our voices to hers, thus creating the community of shared perceptions, shared resistance to oppression. Poetry became performance, and then the possibility of collective action. When Blackwomen have been unable to write, they have still answered back, they have still fought back – in song.

> The important roles of music and dance in Black culture have historically been influential in the sexual socialization of young Black females. Traditionally music – spirituals, gospel, blues and jazz – has figured prominently in the lives of Black folks. The blues dealt with the real stuff: there's no escaping from the hard, bitter, day-to-day struggles.
>
> Females blues singers were unique in recording Black women's history and struggles via song.[16]

For many Blackwomen, either Afro-Caribbean or Black American, the song is the gospel song and the Black community who sings is the church. The church becomes a character, a presence, in Maya Angelou's *I Know Why The Caged Bird Sings*.[17] The meaning of Christianity, and particularly of radical protestantism, is very different for Black and white communities. For a people who have a historical memory of slavery, the story of Exodus becomes the liberation tale of a people in chains, and the God who fought on the side of the oppressed, the Lord who set them free. The reggae versions of Psalm 137, 'Waters of Babylon' are a dramatic reminder of the roots political desire has in the Bible. Babylon becomes the pitted dirt tracks of Trench Town, Kingston – or the streets of Brixton; the song continues, the dream is never forgotten and the fight goes on. The song makes a guest appearance – at a student party on campus in Jamaica – in Merle Collins's *Angel*. And when the D. J. plays 'Version', the flipside of 'Babylon',

> Bring back Macabee Version
> It belong to – de black man!
>
> Give back King James Version
> Dat belong to – de white man!

Angel cries out ' "Come! Lewwe dance dat!" she pulled Edward to his feet. "We caan siddown for dat." ' Hear the song again from the Carnival Bands in Trinidad in Amryl Johnson's *Sequins for a Ragged Hem*.[18]

For many Blackwomen, whether Christian, Moslem, Hindu, Sikh or Jew, religion has been an ambiguous force in their lives, either constricting their freedom or providing the arguments for their own self-determination. Tasneem, a Shia Muslim from Zanzibar, was lucky enough to have a feminist grandmother. 'She was a talented woman who did a lot of religious studying herself. She used to write articles and religious poetry and a lot of her work was on the rights of women in Islam. Often she did not agree with the men at the mosque. But she couldn't challenge them directly, so she challenged them through articles.'[19] When Tasneem was under pressure from her family to wear a Burkha (the Moslem headdress), her grandmother came to visit. 'She did not think I should wear Burkha. She had an orthodox way of looking at it. She said, "If you wear it now and you marry a modern husband and he makes you take it off, then it is bad." So I managed to get rid of that' (p. 150). Tasneem's grandmother showed her the way to argue back, using the religious language of Islam.

I described Tasneem's grandmother as a feminist, and in every sense of the word, so she was. She stood up for herself as a woman and she defended other women. But many Blackwomen, understandably enough, have been unwilling to name themselves feminists, for they have encountered both racism from white women within the women's liberation movement and hostility within their own communities. And of course, the priorities of white feminists are not necessarily those of Blackwomen. 'Feminism is often perceived as a "white-girls-thing". Something that is synonymous to lesbianism. Blacklesbian feminists suffer from another oppression. Not only are they into a white woman thing they have also caught the white woman's disease.'[20] So Blackwomen have chosen other words for themselves. Some have adopted Alice Walker's proposition, 'womanist' – a word that has its roots in Black communities – or Audre Lorde's 'Zami' – a proud, warrior name for Blacklesbians. Lorde and Walker are both Americans, and their relationship to their country is radically different to that of Blackwomen living in Britain. 'If British Blackfeminists have more links with the so-called "third world" it is perhaps due to our "Commonwealth history". Also the fact that some of us are only first or second generation in this "motherland". In the United States, Blackwomen see themselves as a firmly rooted, integral part of that society.'[21] The experience of literal displacement to another, very different, country, or of being born into a British culture with the sense of that displacement as your inheritance, haunts the writing of Afro-Caribbean and Asian Blackwomen. This is a fiction of displaced persons, a fiction rooted in radical insecurity. Joan Riley's heroines move from the West Indies to Britain, west to east; Sita, the speaker of *The Scarlet Thread*, Sharan-Jeet Shan, and the women of Bharati Mukherjee's novels move from India to Europe or the Americas – from east to west.[22] Buchi Emecheta came from Nigeria to Britain, south to north; the heroine of Myriam Warner-Vieyra's extraordinary novel *Juletane* travels from the Caribbean to Paris, then from Europe to Africa.[23] The substance of much of this writing is the collision of cultures, the sudden experience of being alien, different, Other; of being forced to justify and explain things you have always taken for granted, of having no language in common with the people around you, of being seriously misunderstood. Tasneem describes her early difficulties in Britain.

> I was naïve enough to think that British people were homogeneous, all speaking the same sort of language. I was surprised I couldn't understand my landlady who

was a cockney. When I spoke to my landlady I would look down, I would never look her in the eye . . . We discussed it all and I told her that in my culture we don't look anyone, and particularly an older person, in the eye. She told me 'In our culture if you don't look into somebody's eyes that means you are telling a lie . . .'[24]

At least they discussed it all, and put matters straight.

For many Blackwomen the encounter with Britain can be their first experience of racism. For Asian women coming from close-knit communities, the confrontation with British culture can be liberating, but can also lead to an even more profound sense of alienation and rootlessness. Some women decide to refuse the family's demands – arranged marriages, religious traditions, manners, customs, clothes. But others either withdraw defensively or proudly re-assume their customs and religions as an assertion of Black identity. This differing response to Britain can cause conflict within the communities. Surjeet, one of the contributors to Amrit Wilson's *Finding a Voice: Asian Women in Britain*, tells of her arranged marriage to a man from a less liberal Sikh family in a terrifying narrative of oppression and escape. Her first night with her husband, a complete stranger, results in a brutal sexual assault. 'All I can say is I was attacked and I screamed. First I tried fending him off but I was so scared I screamed, I just screamed . . .'[25] Surjeet has no defence under British law, either, for rape in marriage has never been a crime in Britain: a woman's body is her husband's property. Surjeet's parents welcomed her back. Other women are not so fortunate. Their unhappiness may be regarded as their shame and as a disgrace to the honour of their family. Amrit Wilson, in her acknowledgement to *Finding a Voice*, makes the point that speaking truth is a dangerous business. 'Most of the women who helped me did so at their own risk and their names must not be mentioned' (p. viii). To be a Blackwoman in Britain and to transgress the bounds set by family and community is to make yourself doubly vulnerable, for outside those bounds there is only the white racist state. Sharan-Jeet Shan, in entitling her autobiography *In My Own Name*, is a very brave woman indeed.

Let me here declare an interest which will perhaps explain the ways in which I read this writing. I too had the experience of coming to Britain from another country when I was a girl in my teens. My perception of this country, after a childhood spent on an island in the Caribbean, was very similar to the experience of displacement described and analysed in the writing of many Blackwomen. But because I am white I could, and did, busily set about becoming British with a vengeance. The first thing to vanish was my Jamaican accent. Now, when I am asked, 'Where do you come from?' I can, and do – if I want to avoid lengthy true-life confessions – easily lie and say 'London', knowing that I will never be asked the pernicious second question. 'But where do you really come from?' I applied for British nationality after five years' residence: still, my birth certificate and my other passport record the truth of my other identity, as a Jamaican citizen. Within myself, I know I have no country. The Blackwomen writing, who remember and re-vision the West Indies, or who articulate that narrative of exile and voyaging, write a memory which is, for me as a reader, electric on the page. It is not, nor ever will be, my story too. But it is a story with peculiar echoes, a sort of haunting, a door opening into the past.

A good deal of intellectual expertise over the past years has gone into unpicking the feminist notion of 'women's experience'. Does feminist writing represent 'women's experience'? And is it possible to represent authentic experience within the conventions and determined meanings of literary structures? What is authentic experience anyway? Blackwomen writers often call upon the concept of experience. 'I write from deeply felt experience,' says Maud Sulter; and Amryl Johnson, in her book of memories *Sequins for a Ragged Hem*, explains that her work is 'not a travelogue nor is it a guide for those who wish to visit. I am writing about my own experiences on the island.'[26] What is intended here is experience in the flesh, blood, body, breast and bone – the word as testimony. But of course the origin of the word which gives flesh to the experience is never simple, as feminist writers have argued again and again. Who owns the words and controls their meanings is endlessly problematic, contradictory, and an area of struggle in itself. Re-making the word is part of the project of Blackwomen writing. Here is Fyna Dowé's word:

> The Word
>
> Black is a political word
> This I now overstand.
> If I don't use the word,
> I said if I don't use the word . . . Black!
> It makes me no less a woman than I am.
> But brings me closer to my Home Land,
>   Closer to my Home Land.
> Afrika!
>   Afrika!
>   Afrika
> Afrika![27]

Merle Collins's poem 'No Dialects Please', written in Grenadan Creole, exposes the racism and idiocy of a poetry competition which demands NO DIALECTS PLEASE as part of the rules of entry.

> Well ah laugh till me boushet near drop
> Is not only dat ah tink
> of de dialect of de Normans and de Saxons
> dat combine an reformulate
> to create a language-elect . . .
>
> Make me ha to go
> an start up a language o me own
> dat ah would share widme people . . . [28]

And so she departs to re-make the word and the world. Only her language, her word, can tell her experience.

Language creates community. Here language and experience bind together; for the experiences of Blackwomen often disrupt the conventional literary meanings of standard English. The clash of two cultures and the experience of a Blackwoman cracking open the alien languge of imperialism can be intriguing, extraordinary, and can often emerge in subtle ways, pushing through the surface of a text. Buchi Emecheta describes the British Museum's Personnel Board, agreeing to her three months' maternity leave: 'the pillars of the establishment nodding in agreement like lizards'.[29] Her African image, the observation of lizards in the sun, married to the cliché phrase 'the pillars of the establishment' suddenly sharpens the prose. Instantaneously the Board becomes bizarre, grotesque and silly.

I have also heard it argued, by Indians, that English should be regarded as an Indian language, to be used in the dance of writing whenever it pleases Asian Blackwomen to do so. Language, at least, need not determine the meaning of experience. But as women we have to fight for our own meanings: for there can be no unitary experience, no final bedrock guarantee of authenticity, no one meaning of what it is to be a woman. But there is what Dorothea Smartt calls 'the collectivity of our experience'.[30] Many of the women in the anthology by Black British-based writers *Let It Be Told* speak about their writing in intensely physical terms. Amryl Johnson, writing about the composition of the title poem to her collection *Long Road to Nowhere*, has this to say: 'I would need to relive the experience, retrace my footsteps. I had the idea of a form far simpler, words less torrid than what came. It came like a vomit, in a torrent of uncontrollable tears. Blood and tears' (p. 45).

Marsha Prescod, author of *Land of Rope and Tory*, unforgettable satirical poetry, comments, 'Above all, I try not to write things I don't feel . . .' (p. 112).[31] All the Blackwomen in this anthology insist on a common perspective, whatever the form of the writing. Julie Pearn, commenting on Amryl Johnson's work, writes, 'Such feelings are rooted in the actual experience of black people, both historical and contemporary' (p. 46). Marsha Prescod says of her own sense of responsibility towards the Black community, 'As for what might be called moral compulsions involved when I write . . . [I] try not to let myself down or to let Black people down by writing anything that is sensational in a scandalous way, or distorts or damages our experience' (p. 107). I do not think that this is a case of towing a political line determined elsewhere, but a genuine honouring of a community that is in constant danger. And so far as the 'collectivity of our experience' is concerned, Prescod argues that 'We'll find certain experiences shaping our writing whether we like it or not' (p. 108).

Deep feeling, vomit, blood and tears; this emphasis on the physical is not a coincidence. When the words of a people have been silenced by violence, censorship or illiteracy, then their joy, anger, mutiny and grief can only be expressed in the body. So the collectivity of Black experience is a physical thing; a fact which will show, visibly, both in the writing and in the reflection upon that work. But Blackwomen are not, indeed refuse to be, long-suffering victims. Not every woman is strong, but not every woman is a silent piece of trodden carpet either. Grace Nichols, the Black Guyanese poet and novelist, who now lives and works in Britain, firmly refuses the stereotypes and ideologies massed about Blackwomen's lives.

                    maybe this poem is to say
                    that I like to see
                    we black women
                    full-of-we-selves walking . . .
                            crushing out
                            with each dancing step
                    the twisted self-negating
                    history
                    we've inherited.[32]

Blackwomen's writing inevitably exposes the values encoded in the Great Tradition of the white men's literature. Who or what is eventually published, or not published, reveals the hostile edge in British culture towards writing which refuses to endorse those values. Lauretta Ngcobo's fine analysis of how racism works in Britain yields the following insight.

> Their power to subordinate us operates just below the surface of things. By and large, parliament is even-handed. Neither the legislature nor the executive departments can be accused of open prejudice, particularly by comparison with the extremes of South African apartheid. The exception remains the Commonwealth Immigration Acts (1962–1983), in many clauses clearly drafted against Afro-Caribbean and Asian people.
> . . . the underhanded operation of discrimination is left to individuals and bodies and institutions. It is the fault of a particular bank or private concern, not banking law; it is the solicitor, not judicial law; it is the teacher, not the education authority. Yet one senses distinctly that this is not a matter of random prejudice; it seems officially sanctioned.[33]

This is the invisible consensus of white racism, what Ngcobo describes as 'a pervading sense of separateness' (p. 19) – the assumption that Blacks and Asians must be excluded, blocked. Often nothing needs to be said; the whites act as a single consciousness. White women who like to think that they are not racist will rarely ever see this process in action, unless they have Black husbands, Blackwomen lovers, or Black friends. One of my Asian Blacklesbian friends was telling my mother and myself how she had been verbally abused as a 'Lezzie' in Camden Town. We were righteously indignant. She laughed at us and said that she had been rather pleased. Usually, she said, I'm called a 'Paki'. And she makes it clear that she is Asian whenever she answers advertisements; so that she does not waste her time watching white people making up their excuses or reasons why she is unsuitable for them.

Black people's struggle to re-possess their languages, their history and the soul of their own experience becomes a crucial imperative within a host society which remains largely locked against them. In the 1980s this is a proud rejection of what Ngcobo calls 'the politics of assimilation'.

> The Black community has no option but to recover what it can of its identity. The host society has not always been sensitive to the urgent need for cultural identity as a vital component, a prerequisite for success in the education of each child. For

years they did not realise that the policies of assimilation were undermining the value of each child and reducing that child's capacity to learn. (p. 22)

Rashda Sharif, speaking on the theme of British racism at the 10th Jewish/Christian/Moslem Women's Conference in Bendorf in November 1986, spoke of her despair at the situation in Handsworth, Birmingham, where she works as a teacher; a despair mitigated only by her perception of the way in which young Asian people were returning with pride to their cultures, languages and religions. She also linked contemporary white racism very firmly to the history of British imperialism. 'British colonialism is ritually referred to by politicians and others as a golden age to look back to with nostalgia and as a model on which to base the future. For Britain's black population this "age of glory" was an age of oppression when their lands were occupied by foreign powers.'[34] A significant part of Blackwomen's writing addresses that history, writing the story that the whites ignored, suppressed or distorted. The opening chapters of *The Heart of the Race: Black Women's Lives in Britain*, by Beverley Bryan, Stella Dadzie and Suzanne Scafe, re-write that history of colonial exploitation from the Black perspective.[35] Merle Collins's saga of Grenadan history, *Angel*, tells her island's history through her people and through her Creole language, with all the intense particularities and muddles of fiction. For fiction is never pure polemic, and can therefore tell dangerous truths.

There is always a danger that the Homeland, the remembered, imagined or reconstructed country of origin – Africa, India or the Caribbean – can become an ideal dream, untouched by history, conflict, poverty or corruption. This is one theme in Joan Riley's *The Unbelonging*, where Hyacinth Williams's memory of her Caribbean childhood becomes a Fall from Paradise which dominates her life. Riley has the courage to say difficult, often unacceptable things. When Hyacinth returns to Jamaica it is to confront the violence and poverty of the slums of Kingston. *The Unbelonging* has been criticized within the Black community for dwelling too much upon the powerlessness of Blackwomen. 'The book is marked by a total absence of protest. It vividly depicts the victimisation of a young Black girl and exposes the ravages of sexist violence in the community.'[36] Sexist violence is one aspect of male power which exists within every community; among Asian and Afro-Caribbean Black people as well as among white men who are in no sense victims of society's injustice. To pretend that it does not is to connive in the lies which mask that fact and is no basis for freedom of any kind. I found *The Unbelonging* a meticulous, passionate and devastating book, shot through with a protest no less effective for being carefully argued and constructed within the terms of the plot rather than through overt polemic. Hyacinth's college friends, Perlence and her comrades, are radical, articulate Blacks, engaged in political activism. Their painful failure to reach Hyacinth in her isolation and 'unbelonging' never puts either their radical intelligence or their committed protest in question. The psychological effects upon Black women of sexism and white racism are central issues in Riley's fiction, and, as a writer, she never hesitates or flinches in confronting difficulty.

The collision of two cultures produces the communities of those who do not belong. Many other Blackwomen writers take up this theme. This is a fiction of displaced persons, a theme that disrupts any easy analysis of either culture and confounds both prejudice and facile expectations. It is also a theme that disrupts the priorities of white feminism. The structure of many of the early white feminist campaigns around abortion and reproduction, for example, alienated Blackwomen in Britain whose predicament was very different. Indeed, 'Abortion on Demand', for a Blackwoman whose right to bear a Black child is so often abused and denied, and for Blackwomen who may even suffer enforced sterilization within the NHS, is a particularly offensive slogan. Of course, in the so-called 'Third World' the situation will be different again, depending on the country, the cultural customs and the predicament of women within that culture. Maud Sulter's fine prize-winning poem 'As A Black-woman', takes up the argument of motherhood, and who has the right to bear children.

> As a blackwoman
> the bearing of my child
> is a political act
>
> I have
> been mounted in rape
>   bred from like cattle
>   mined for my fecundity
>
> I have
> been denied abortion
>   denied contraception
>   denied my freedom to choose
>
> I have
> been subjected to abortion
>   injected with contraception
>   sterilised without my consent[37]

Here, Sulter takes the sign 'Blackwoman' to mean the Black women living in the West, the Americas, Africa, Asia. She extends her writing through 'the collectivity of our experience'; she writes the links.

Even the questions of men's sexism, misogyny and Black men's power have to be tackled in different ways from those of white feminists, simply because Black male sexism is articulated within the context of an unequal, racist society. White feminists must not expect Blackwomen's portrayal or analysis of sexism and male violence or even the social control of women within the family to be drawn in similar ways. Indeed, it is only when the particularities of our cultural differences are made visible, discussed and understood, that we will be able to find our common ground. Separatism, ferociously contested among white feminists, will assume a different complexity within the context of Black-women's politics.[38] Some Blackwomen are ferociously and openly angry at Black men's sexism. Iyamidé Hazeley's poem 'Political Union' sets her conditions of agreement to the contract between Blackwomen and men.[39] Millie Murray's story 'The Escape' tells the tale of a Black mother resisting domestic violence and fighting back, with a little help from her Blackwomen friends. The overt criticism of Black men by Blackwomen in print has led to some public disagreement. Maya Angelou had this to say to the whites: 'I'm always quite leery of this theme because I'm reminded of the Machiavellian theory, separate and rule; divide and conquer and I refuse to be a gladiator for the express delectation of people who don't give a damn about my life – about our life.' And she says this to Black men: 'This ninny [referring to one particularly hostile Black author] implied that *The Color Purple* would absolutely destroy black Americans. But it's interesting that we've survived rape, slavery, ridicule, abuse, discrimination and you tell us we are so weak that a book is going to destroy us. Please.'[40] Maya Angelou questions the motives of both groups of people, both white people and the jealous Black men. I think she is right to do so; but it is Blackwomen's business to pose those questions.

The problems of commenting upon or attempting to reproduce Blackwomen's experience from a white perspective are inevitably illustrated by Marion Molteno's short stories, *A Language in Common*.[41] Molteno is a white South African, engaged in anti-racist community work in Croydon. She teaches English as a Second Language (ESL) to Asian women. The Women's Press breached their usual rule of not publishing work by women writing about women of another racial or cultural community in order to publish this book. It is intended to be a bridge of understanding between white consciousness and Asian tradition, initiating the search for a common cultural language. The impulse behind the book, that of celebration, friendship and solidarity, is of course to be welcomed. But the text itself left me uneasy, confused and enraged. For Molteno falls into the inexorable trap which awaits all well-meaning middle-class liberals who try to understand and explain other groups: perceiving the Other as alien. Wordsworth's researches among the rural poor of late eighteenth-century England, recorded in *Lyrical Ballads* (1799, 1800), produced precisely the same problems.[42] In Molteno's stories, as in Wordsworth's ballads, the writer is the subject, the questioner, the Asian women are the objects perceived, however spirited, individual and unique they appear to be. They are narrated, described, encountered as the Other, not the Self. The result is both patronizing and sentimental. Difficult questions are left unasked, unanswered.

The first story, 'The Uses of Literacy', tells of the narrator's encounter with Mr H. S. Ramgarhia, 'A tall, immensely dignified, heavy-shouldered old man' (p. 1). He emerges as a kind of saint, sensitive to the women whose class he has insisted on joining. Why the class should have been women-only in the first place is never explained or examined; the need for a women-only class is simply assumed. This is disturbing, because it undercuts the whole point of the story. When the noble old Sikh dies the ESL teachers discover that his wife, who neither speaks nor writes English, is hidden away in his home. For whatever reason, sinister or otherwise, his wife never came to the women's class while he lived. Mr H. S. Ramgarhia is articulate, gracious, impressive. His old wife learns only copying; graceful and charming she may be, but she never progresses beyond the first reading book. The one sentence she learns is that which proclaims her identity – as a wife. Thus the infantilization of an old woman is complete. I personally do not share the traditional respect many Asians show towards old people. As I have pointed out elsewhere, a lifetime of experience can also be a lifetime of brainwashing. Molteno's anxiety to present tiny steps as great achievements diminishes what can be imagined possible. Is it racist or culturally prescriptive to want freedom of movement and access to education for all women, for Asian Blackwomen just as much as for white women? There is a big difference between a class that is women-only because the women have decided to exclude the men and a class that is women-only because if it were not the men would not allow their wives to go.

The Women's Press has always been a feminist press. Molteno's stories are written from a feminist awareness, but not with a feminist analysis. This is clear from 'The Abyss', a disturbing, infuriating story about violence against women. Farida, the object of the narrator's concern, is caught in the downward spiral of poverty and domestic battery. All the usual contradictions in women's responses to male violence emerge in the narrative. All the usual excuses and explanations are dug up for Mr Malik, Farida's husband. He is unemployed; 'his anger was vented on the only people under his control' (p. 12). There is a paragraph appealing to 'the moments of physical fear' (p. 14) every woman feels, which never explicitly says that what women fear is men's violence. Finally, Mumtaz, the narrator's Asian colleague, advises Farida to stay with her husband, because 'he is the father of her child. Her duty is to him . . . I told her that God will give her strength' (p. 16). And, justifiably, the narrator is angry and confused. The problem here is simply this: the critique of Mumtaz which remains implicit in this story is not given a context, so that the effect is both racist and sententious. We have an 'enlightened' white woman listening to quite appalling advice about shame, duty and God, coming from an Asian Black-woman. There are plenty of white women who can and do take the same line as Mumtaz when talking to battered women: if a man attacks and rapes you, it is your shame and your fault; if your husband batters and abuses you it is your duty to go on loving him. The dubious dishonesty in this text arises from the limitations in the narrator's political perspective. For, yes, Asian women do face almost insuperable problems within British culture, but very often they have not fled from a sun-drenched paradise. Molteno describes East Africa as a place 'where it is warm all the time and children can run outside and yell and let off energy without terrible things happening' (p. 17). I was under the impression that very terrible things did indeed happen in East Africa and it was because of them that many Asian people came to Britain. But in any case this is a risky sentence to send out into a context where there are many white people anxious to send Farida and her community straight back to wherever they used to live.

The difficulty with books which describe the meeting of two communities from the perspective of the more powerful community is that the centre of awareness and change always remains with the white narrator. In the story 'Someone Else's Clothes' the narrator wears a sari for the first time to dance for Navratri, the nine nights before Diwali. It is all very sensuous and exciting when the teacher becomes part of the class. But the next lesson she has to unlearn is

Stereotyping the Sari. She goes down the street unintentionally still wearing the sari. 'I skirt the group of young men hanging around the betting shop, painfully aware that I cannot run, that in this garment I cannot answer back with perky confidence if they make quips – some limit in me is defined by what I wear' (p. 46). Sexism and racism are confused in this passage. The streets are public space, still controlled, owned and policed by men. No woman is able to escape sexual harassment, here described as 'quips'. And yes, Asian Blackwomen are more vulnerable to what would be racist as well as sexist aggression. But women wearing saris can and do still fight back. And of course, given the existing power structures in Britain, educated white middle-class women might find it easier to tell the boys where to get off, whatever they happen to be wearing. In the second part of the narrative Molteno tells the story of Santosh, an Indian woman who is told by her husband that she must start wearing western clothes, obeys, and comes to feel at home in them. She still wears shalwar khameez for special occasions. 'Perhaps it is my imagination, but it seems to me that she carries her body in a different way on days like that; as if it is easier to express her natural energy; as if she is speaking her mothertongue' (p. 49). This is a beautifully written sentence, and the metaphor of a woman's body speaking through her clothes is apt and striking. For clothes are our advance guard in the world, they speak for us before we do. For a white, European, middle-class woman trousers would have been a firm political statement in the 1900s; not now. For an Asian Blackwoman, trousers can signal to her community that she is 'westernized'. This does involve some measure of social tolerance from the British, tolerance; not acceptance. It is also a statement to her community, and might, in some quarters, still be met with a response such as 'These are men's clothes' or 'This is not modest.'[43] But no easy comparison can be made between a white woman wearing a sari and an Indian woman who wears western clothes. This is not common ground, and so far as trousers and saris are concerned, there is no common language. The experience of Santosh, a fictional character, must be understood as particular, not representative. For there is no universal general response Asian women might have to wearing western clothes. Marks and Spencer sweaters might indeed change something irrevocably inside another Asian woman. And western clothes might also be, in some cases, liberating, not 'a destruction of some area within herself, a painful acquisition of unwanted new parts' (p. 48).

Molteno's narratives have the effect of fixing cultural differences. For there are many Asian Blackwomen who would quarrel with Mumtaz, challenge male power within the extended family, and take what they want from western culture, including trousers.[44] Some Blackwomen regard themselves as British, and see their culture as British. And not every Asian woman's life revolves around her husband, family, children, religious festivals, food, the gas bill or learning English, which might in some cases be her mother tongue. Some Asian women are making fine, independent careers for themselves, earning good money. Some are atheist, some are Lesbian; some are revolutionary feminists. From the collective portrait in Molteno's book, this seems impossible. In fact, throughout these stories, again and again, the current which breaks the surface is absence, visible absence, what is not there, what is left unasked, unanswered, what is not said. We have too little writing published by Asian women about their own experiences; and we need to hear from them first.

It is too easy for white women to slip into the political traps set by the white racist state. I have often heard white feminists denouncing the system of arranged marriage. But in fact, Asian women are often forced into legal dependency upon men by the British immigration laws. Parita Trivedi explains: 'Because certain immigration legislation allows women entry to Britain only as dependants of a male worker, their dependency upon men has been entrenched and perpetuated.'[45] The ban on male fiancés entering Britain is a mask for the real intention of British institutional racism, namely, to exclude Black workers seeking entry to the UK. Instead of openly stating this aim, the authorities vilify the arranged marriage system and purport to be coming to the rescue of helpless Asian maidens. Asian family networks can often be an informal system of social security, providing employment, finance and care for the elderly. The business of transforming those networks so that they are not oppressive to women is part of a centuries-long historical struggle on the part of Asian Blackwomen. But it is those very networks which are under attack by the state. Trivedi gives us uncompromising clarity on this point.

> Whether some of us decide to marry at all, let alone have an arranged marriage, is an issue we define and act upon autonomously of the state. We do not require the racist state to intervene on our behalf. To ally and collude with the racist state in a pseudo-feminist struggle would be crass and misguided. This has been one issue in which we have had to be clear about how the two areas of oppression – racial and sexual – operate. (pp. 46–7)

Given the attitude of the British state, the question of audience for Black writing which deals with sexual abuse within the community is particularly sensitive. Blackwomen's truths are vulnerable here; they can be seized upon and exploited by racists, who are anxious to ignore the same abuse in white communities. Sita, the narrator of *The Scarlet Thread*, describes, without bitterness, the structure of social relationships in her home village. 'This was always the way in the village; to be unmarried was unthinkable. A woman without a husband was not a person at all. And this is how even a widow is considered. For the rest of her life after the death of her husband she is a person of no importance' (p. 26). Sita's story of marital violence and eventual escape is the story of a woman who becomes unmarried, stands up for herself and remains a person of immense importance. She says, 'No woman should be treated as I was treated and left to suffer, beaten, terrified and alone' (p. 142). The audience she addresses directly are her own people, not the whites among whom she lives; but her story is the story of all women, of every race and class, who have been battered and abused. Domestic violence bears witness to one of the universal patterns of male domination; but this does not necessarily mean that the men within different communities, collectively or individually, can be challenged and resisted in the same ways. The fundamental issues which affect and shape the lives of Blackwomen and white women are often the same; but the cultural and historical context will always be different – and so too will be the appropriate analysis, strategies and solutions.

Sometimes the same gaps, silences and anxieties which are visible within white feminism emerge in Blackwomen's writing.[46] Loretta Ngcobo's essay on Blackwomen writing in Britain, which introduces the articles in *Let It Be Told*, is occasionally equivocal on the subject of Blacklesbian writing. She says that 'there have been for some time among us women making a radical choice against traditional relationships with men . . . These women constitute a small minority, but they are there and their numbers are growing. What is undeniable is that they have a voice that will not be silenced.'[47] I notice that Ngcobo describes Lesbianism as a negative choice against men, rather than a positive choice for women. But in her comments on Barbara Burford's collection *The Threshing Floor* she declares that the title novella is 'a universal story of love and pain', so that 'the lesbian element is unimportant'.[48] Given the anguish that Burford's Blacklesbian heroine suffers at the hands of her dead lover's family, and the ambiguous treatment she suffers as a bereaved *woman* partner, I would have thought that 'the lesbian element' was urgently relevant, indeed, the subject of the narrative. Often, when a Lesbian woman dies, a family who may have grudgingly tolerated her sexuality while she lived turn very nasty indeed as soon as she is dead. The dead become saints. The surviving woman may even be accused of leading her dead lover astray. Or told, 'You may be a Lesbian, but she wasn't.' All their joint possessions may be seized by the vindictive relatives. In Burford's narrative, Mrs Harrison, the mother and vindictive relative in question, begins sabre-rattling about who owns the house. Burford's heroine stands firm and finds support elsewhere among her dead lover's family. Outside fiction this sometimes does not happen. One moral is: if you are homosexual, make a ferocious and watertight will. Apparent family tolerance may well disguise submerged and bitter resentment.

Ngcobo analyses Burford's method of decentring heterosexuality and the family, then declares that the text 'is a view of life through the lesbian monocle' (p. 32). This is an open piece of creeping anti-Lesbianism. Lesbians see the world perfectly clearly, and with both eyes open. Indeed, seen from the rim of the circle, power structures can usually be analysed and criticized rather more incisively than they can from the centre. But Lesbians do see a different world. This is not the official version.[49]

Becky Birtha, an American Blacklesbian writer, takes the same theme of love and loss as the subject for one of the stories in her collection *Lover's Choice*, but removes the family entirely. Family becomes Lesbian community. Jinx and Gracie have been 'In the Life' all their lives. They are a butch/femme Blacklesbian partnership which has had its own rhythm, a long life of hard work and real love. The narrative voice is that of Jinx, haunted by memories of her dead lover, affirming their life and the Life. The tone is delicate, comic, just the right side of sentimental. The old Blacklesbian woman observes her younger sisters in the Life, mystified by their version of Lesbian community as political rather than social. 'When I first heard about this club she in, I was kinda interested. But I come to find out it ain't no social club, like the Cinnamon &

Spice Club used to be. Yvonne call it a collective. They never has no outings or parties or picnics or nothing – just meetings. And projects.'[50] I laughed out loud when I read this. Lesbianism as politics can often seem that we study rather than enjoy each other.

Birtha's stories form the critical links between the experiences of living on the boundaries of social existence, as Black/Lesbian/Woman: she argues for the necessary connections. In many of the stories Blackwomen as mothers struggle to understand and engage with their children. The finest stories are dramatic monologues. Jinx, talking to Yvonne's tape-recorder, also speaks to us, telling us her version of Black Lesbian herstory. Cecily Banks, driving the South Street Line; Leona Mae Moses, keeping her children warm and dry on Route 23; Johnnieruth, having a formative early experience of two women kissing one another; all the voices demand attention, sympathy, an audience. Leona Mae Moses talks to another passenger on the bus as well as to her children. Thus Black experience is presented and represented directly, not analysed, explained or revealed by an external narrator. The political effect of this is to insist on the centrality of a Blackwoman's vision of the world; it is the woman's voice which decides what is important, what matters. Sexism, and anti-Lesbianism within Black communities, are unequivocally described. No one – neither Black men nor Black families – gets off the hook.

Several of Birtha's stories are set within the American multi-racial Lesbian community. 'Her Ex-Lover' is one of the most intriguing of these stories, dealing as it does, with the particular tensions of inter-racial love.[51] The speaking voice, Shirley, is a Blackwoman whose Black lover, Ernestine, maintains a tenuous and uneasy relationship with 'Lisa. Her last lover. Her white lover' (p. 80). These two elements – the last lover, the white lover – are interestingly confused by Shirley's jealousy.

> 'Don't you see,' I'd insist, 'why you love her, or think you love her? It's power you're in love with. Privilege. You don't want her. You want to be her.'
>   Once she cut me short, asking 'Shirley, if I felt like that, would I bother with you?' (p. 87).

Through these brief exchanges Birtha asks us, not to mistrust the speaking voice, but to hear her critically; to listen to the gaps, omissions, fears. Jealousy, insecurity and a just perception of a white woman shifting her ground are inter-connected. Lisa learns a lesson, but she doesn't learn it from Shirley. She learns from her ex-lover. I discussed this story with a Blackwoman who had just read it and she asked me what I thought. I said that I had loved the way the story made me prickle, got under my skin. I was irritated by the narrator's assertion that western music was exclusively 'white culture' when I had heard Jessye Norman, Shirley Verret, Kathleen Battle, sing dozens of white sopranos right off the stage, thereby proudly taking possession of western classical music for themselves. But Shirley's point was about cultural imperialism, and the way in which Lisa had imposed her values upon Ernestine. And I recognized myself in Lisa; the white woman who studies Black history, reads Black writing, anxious to educate herself. I asked my friend what she thought. And she pointed to the silence at the centre of the story, Ernestine. This is the Blackwoman who 'looks hard for what she likes in people, and won't let the things she doesn't like keep her from loving them' (p. 87). Then my friend said, 'My money's on Ernestine every time.' Appropriately, this story was first published in an anthology entitled *The Things That Divide Us.*[52] It should be required reading for every white Lesbian.

None of Birtha's stories offers easy answers or shirks dificulty. The narratives deal with breaking-up, separation, loss, poverty, sexual temptation, the problem of maintaining emotional commitments, defending our children, holding down our jobs, the difficulty of loving each other.

On 19 November 1987 the Polytechnic of North London's Centre for Caribbean Studies held a Women Writers Forum. In her account of that evening Jaqui Roach points out, 'It is important when thinking of the Caribbean to remember that the history of the region is a vast and diverse one full of people of various "ethnic" origin.'[53] On that very evening there were women present from many different countries: Grenada, rural Guyana, St Vincent as well as British Blackwomen of Caribbean descent. The Caribbean does not have a homogeneous culture, nor a single language. The islands were occupied at different periods by different colonial powers. In her Caribbean odyssey Amryl Johnson comes face to face with the peculiar results of history.

> I would later come to understand the division between the inhabitants of St Lucia, Martinique, Dominica and Guadeloupe more clearly. I already knew of the long and bitter battle fought between the British and French for possession of these islands. One of the islands had changed hands thirteen times. St Lucia and Dominica remained with the British. Martinique and Guadeloupe were departments of France making the inhabitants French. This did not register until I arrived in St Lucia and later Dominica. It always seemed strange to hear the Martiniquians and Guadeloupians referred to as French.[54]

Blackwomen of the Caribbean have written and are writing both in the languages of those invading cultures and in their own – originally oral – languages. Merle Collins' *Angel* is written both in Grenadan Creole and in standard English. Sistren's *Lionheart Gal* is written largely in Jamaican Patwah. Myriam Warner-Vieyra, who is from Guadeloupe, and has lived for many years in Senegal, writes in French. Her novels, *Le Quimboiseur l'avait dit* (1980) and *Juletane* (1982) have both been translated into English. The Caribbean is not only a place where Black culture encounters and answers European culture, appropriating, transforming and re-making western literary traditions; it is also the place where Africa is the powerful structuring force. Africa, in Caribbean writing, is history, myth and dream. In a French television documentary[55] Aimé Cesaire, the poet and dramatist from Martinique, said that his unconscious mind, in his life and in his art, was Africa. Thus, the Caribbean is often a point of contact between Black Afro-American writers, women who live and work on the islands, and British Blackwomen who see the Caribbean as their source, the cultural root in their lives. Amryl Johnson observes, 'The island where you were born was always with you in spirit.'[56] This is true both for British Afro-Caribbean women and for Afro-Caribbean Americans.

In her collection *Our Dead Behind Us*, Lorde's poem 'Equal Opportunity' unmasks the political double-dealing of imperial 'Amerika', the state which employs Blackwomen yet orders the invasion of Grenada.

> The american deputy assistant secretary of defence
> for Equal Opportunity
> and safety
> is a home girl.
> Blindness slashes our tapestry to shreds.
>
> The moss-green military tailoring sets off her color
> beautifully
> she says 'when I stand up to speak in uniform
> you can believe everyone takes notice!'
> Superimposed skull-like across her trim square shoulders
> dioxin-smear
> the stench of napalm upon growing cabbage
> the chug and thud of Corsairs in the foreground
> advances like a blush across her cheeks
> up the unpaved road outside Grenville, Grenada . . .[57]

Lorde's family comes from Grenada; her mother is from Carriacou. That rural landscape, the crops destroyed, the people terrified, appears again in Merle Collins' *Angel*. Collins, a Grenadan poet, novelist and performer now living and working in Britain, describes the American invasion of Grenada in the closing pages of the novel.

Angel is a *Bildungsroman*, the political, rather than the sentimental education of one young Grenadan woman. It is also a novel of mothers and daughters; Ma Ettie and Doodsie, Doodsie and her daughter Angel. Fiction which traces the links, not only between generations but also between specific political movements, acts of Black resistance to imperialism, is particularly important within Black writing. This is a fiction which traces a heritage left invisible by white history; a fiction which creates both continuity and community. Fiction and Black history interweave. The New Jewel Movement in Grenada, which led to the bloodless coup of 13 March 1979, ended twenty-nine years of Sir Eric Gairy's regime. Collins transposes a particular political history into an archetypal pattern. The politicians represent rather than embody that history. This shifts the centre of interest from personalities to actions, from controlling demagogues to the people. *Angel* is not a Black history book, but a fictional interpretation of Black history. And necessarily, when the interpretation of history is especially contentious, there will be substantial disagreement among her readers about the meaning of events, or even the events themselves. The excitement of a people's revolution, the confusion and fear which ended in the American invasion of October 1983, are carefully evoked and described. The sympathy of Collins' narrative is always with the people: championing their autonomy, representing their contradictions. There are no easy simplicities.[58]

Collins uses the oral traditions of her language in her writing. Much of the action is carried forward through women's forms: domestic letters, visits, gossip, reminiscences, family quarrels and household conversations. The women talk, exchange ideas, information, argue with and support one another. The effect of this is, first, to place a powerful value on that which is usually marginal in history and in literary fiction: domestic dailiness. Secondly, Collins' method establishes a women's continuum that is a continuum of change. Angel refuses to put up with what her mother endured from her husband, Angel's father. She challenges them both at every turn. In the middle of a bitter family row the following analysis of Doodsie's economic situation emerges naturally from the shouting. Doodsie argues, ' "Is the man house you know. When dey cut up de estate an dey sellin out to who want lan, is he dat had money to buy piece wid house on it, not me!" ' To which Angel replies, ' "How you mean is the man house? You not livin in it? Is the man sweat an blood alone that keepin this house goin? Mammie, for thing you tell me, ah don understan you" ' (p. 188). The subordinate status of women and the brutal mechanics of male power never go unchallenged or unquestioned by Collins' text. Angel herself is in no hurry to be married or pregnant. Her passion is politics. And womanist politics are always seen within the context of the social and political revolution. Doodsie fights for her daughter's education, but then finds it hard to see all her assumptions called into question. The political shift within the novel, from acceptance to resistance, is inexorable.

The book opens with the expectant workers watching the burning estates of the wealthy landowners. Even after the intervention in the Grenadan revolution by the Americans in the last pages, Collins refuses to end her narrative on an elegiac note. Her narrative, because it is rooted in history, will continue beyond the text. Instead Angel lights a candle for the spirits of the old cane mill down by the river. 'She looked at the flame. She smiled as it remained steady in the still cool morning . . . the spirits gone, you know. The candle not goin out. They either gone, or they sympathetic. Nothing to fraid' (p. 291). As the narrative moves momentarily inside Angel's mind the Creole language takes over from standard English; 'Nothing to fraid'. Collins uses Creole to represent direct speech, but the interpreting contextual language is standard literary English. The effect of this is to hold the spoken language at a little distance, but also to teach it to the reader. A great deal of the text actually works like drama as we hear the Creole language in domestic and political action. The section headings within the chapters interpret each scene in short fierce or reflective Creole phrases, used as traditional proverbs.

> Don play de ooman wid me.
> Vini ou kai vini, ou kai wè. (We are coming, you will see)
> We ha to hol one another up.[59]

Thus, the overall directive meanings – or guidelines for our interpretation of the text – are given in Creole. And, at one critical moment in the novel, when Doodsie is writing to her woman friend, Ezra, she begins in 'school book ting' – that is, standard English: 'Dear Ezra, How are you? I hope fine' then turns the page and begins again: 'Dear Ezra How's tings, girl? . . . ' (p. 206). And so the Creole language is thought, spoken, written; at last, utterly possessed and used to celebrate a community and a people. In this language the numerous Caribbean migrations, people seeking work, education or adventure, are reflected in the changing language. A word like 'hefe', meaning chief, comes from the Spanish 'jefe'. Collins' glossary suggests that this was probably taken into English through workers on the Panama Canal. Some words have their origins in Africa. Some phrases, such as 'gardé bèt-la' (*regardez cette bête-là*) clearly have their origins in French.

Needless to say, the Creole language was neither taught, nor used in school. The ludicrous, inappropriate education served up to Angel and her brothers is deftly criticized through Collins' dialogue and children's voices.

> 'Angel, what is an apple?'
> 'Ent you know is de ting in de ABC card!'
> 'You could eat it?'
> 'Yes, is like a mango.'
> 'So A is for mango too?'
> 'No. A is for apple. If you want you could aks Mammie to buy an apple for you.'
> 'Ah aks her arready. She say it too dear.' (p. 64)

In my own childhood I can remember wondering why A didn't stand for Akee, the national fruit of Jamaica.

Angel has to learn all the Kings and Queens of English history for her A-Levels. She fails her West Indian history exam ('. . . an dose long slave reports well borin! Who could study dat?' (p. 121)) but then goes on to take part in shaping the history of her country and her people. She no longer learns other people's history, or their interpretation of her own; she goes out to make history. But not all European culture is racist or irrelevant, as Angel's friend Kai discovers: 'I've discovered that there are sides to people like Shelley that are really quite exciting and thought-provoking, which is no doubt why they were never introduced to me' (p. 252). And of course, he is right. They are not often introduced to children in British schools either. Collins' text uncovers the more problematic aspects of politics, literature and history. The historian C. L. R. James has always argued for the appropriation of European radicalism by Black activists. I have seen an extraordinarily moving television sequence of Michael Smith reciting Shelley's 'Song to the Men of England' in Poet's Corner at Westminster Abbey. And yes, the radical dissidents of every tradition do speak to one another. But what could Shelley say to a radical Blackwoman? He was a nineteenth-century aristocrat, whose sexual politics were, in effect, no different from those of other men of his class. He may have preached free love, but in fact the consequences for his women were utterly conventional: oppression, exploitation, pregnancy and financial dependence.

Collins' *Angel* makes it perfectly clear that the struggle to possess ourselves as women, as the doubly disinherited without our communities, must remain in the foreground of every revolutionary struggle. A woman's analysis always challenges radical socialism when liberty, equality and fraternity are demonstrated to be for men only. As the old slogan has it, the people are not free until the women are free. For the Black peoples of the Caribbean that struggle must take place in the streets, in the fields and in the kitchens, in the classroom and on the page. Angels are God's messengers. And *Angel* is a marker, a way, the story of the dispossessed, coming back into their own.

The Blackwoman's word as testimony[60] is the basis of the collective self-portrait by Sistren in *Lionheart Gal*. Sistren are a mixed group of middle- and working-class Jamaican women who came together as a women-only theatre collective in 1977. The thirteen women were all originally part of the Manley government's Impact Programme, which was a desperate attempt to reduce unemployment. Since then Sistren have become an international theatre company, touring widely, producing their own cultural work: workshops, silk-screen designs, a magazine. Their life stories, which form the text of *Lionheart Gal*, are not individually signed. Thus the group, not single voices, takes responsibility for the word. Many of the stories are consciousness-raising narratives; about growing up, becoming politically aware, learning and unlearn- ing the social construction of Black womanhood. Most of the stories by working-class members of the collective are written in Jamaican Patwah. These were transcribed from tapes. Patwah is traditionally an oral language. The spoken word, with its particular oral rhythm, is therefore primary. Honor Ford Smith, Sistren's artistic director and the editor of the volume, carefully describes the process of making the book. This was, essentially, the same method the group uses in the development of their theatre projects, from the idea through to the finished performance. Collective discussion shapes and develops each individual contribution. Ford Smith's passionate argument for written Patwah is based on the perception that 'language is central to all power relations' and that 'not to nurture such a language is to retard the imagination and power of the people who created it.'[61] Ideally, of course, Patwah should be spelt phonetically, to break the imperial link with standard English. The entire book was read through and agreed by the whole collective. 'In long meetings we decided on the title of the collection from those proposed, how the authorship credits would go and how money from the book would be used in the collective' (pp. xxiv–xxv). It is this process, Sistren's control over the means of production and the wealth generated, which is democratic, exhausting, time-consuming and feminist.

Violence, male violence, sexual violence, parental violence, political violence; violence in all its hydra forms is the central theme of *Lionheart Gal*. 'Rebel Pickney' makes the connection between parents savagely beating their children and the treatment meted out to Black slaves in history. 'Inna slavery dem use di murderation in di plantation and den our fore-parents, when dem lef out a slavery dem believe di only solution is beating. Me no beat my pickney' (p. 17). 'Veteran by Veteran' tells of the political gang violence of the 1970s. 'Ava's Diary' is about domestic violence by men against women and women's collective action in our own defence. 'When we got back to Cross Roads station all of Sistren were sitting or standing outside the police station. They stayed there until they were sure he was spending the night in jail' (p. 279). Ava's man, Bertie, becomes violent because he fears that the money Ava earns with Sistren will set her free from him. He demands her money. When she will not give it to him, he hits her. This is the eternal argument about women as property; the property of men, both our labour and our bodies. Whenever a woman claims her own life, her own income from her own labour and her own freedom the male response is violence. Not that the women of *Lionheart Gal* are ever tepid in their response. This is not a book about victims. One woman's mother married a man called Mr Jimmy. When he abused her ' . . . she just tek di chair wid him and him felt hat and bend-mouth walking stick, and throw him a gully. Him and di chair roll down deh and me madda not even look pon him' (p. 45). So much for Mr Jimmy.

The other theme which recurs throughout these narratives is the evil of sexual ignorance. The writer/speaker of 'Exodus a Run' bitterly points out women's collusion in their own oppression with the refusal to tell the explicit truth about sex and about men. 'Dem always a tell yuh seh baby drop out a sky, and come inna plane and all dem someting deh' (p. 22). Many of the women telling their stories became pregnant while they were still schoolgirls. 'Mama never really reason full wid me about sex . . . A must coward lick me mek me get pregnant, for me never so keen on di sex business' (p. 264). There is the usual catalogue of betrayal, exploitation and treachery which women, all women, produce whenever they write about men. 'Me did have one man friend dat was me good good friend till him go a England wid me eighty pounds . . . ' (p. 82). But among the massed ranks of seducers, scroungers, liars and batterers there are one or two signs of hope. There is Negus, a beautiful Rastafarian brother who sold snowballs from a handcart. Negus clears up his own mess and gets himself organized around the issue of food. 'Negus made the point that food was important. The other brothers would rather starve than prepare it for themselves . . . Negus was my first example of true working-class brotherhood' (p. 229). Mine too. Never in all my days as a revolutionary socialist have I ever seen one of the brothers making the sandwiches.

The narratives of *Lionheart Gal* often articulate bitter conflicts between women of different generations. There are mothers who betray, abandon or reject their daughters. The grandmother in 'Grandma's Estate' spends sixty years haunted by the supposed stigma of her mixed race, bastard status. The hierarchy of colour politics in Jamaica, another legacy of white racism, is unflinchingly described. One mother begins shrieking when she discovers that her daughter is pregnant by a black Black man. ' "Me tink seh di gal would a look up off a di ground. Instead di gal not even raise up him head, him hold it down. A black man! Wid rolly-polly black pepper head! Me no waan dat deh pickney. None at all. . . . OH MY GAWD!" She definitely feel seh if yuh hair no straight, yuh nah gwan wid notten' (p. 52). But none of this goes unchallenged. The social backdrop for these narratives is the submerged social history of Jamaica since independence in the 1970s and 1980s. Politics is viewed from the belly-side, from its effect on working-class people. Naturally, there is a good deal of cynicism. 'From me know myself, politician keep dem meeting and a tell we seh we fi vote fi dem, cause we need new toilet and bathroom. Up to now, no new toilet no build' (p. 266). But *Lionheart Gal* begins to re-define politics from a woman's perspective. This is one of the most searchingly radical texts by Blackwomen that I have ever read, because Sistren ask every one of the unpleasant questions. Why indeed, do the reggae and calypso lyrics which protest so strongly against the injustice done to Black people and demand freedom for Black men continue to denigrate and abuse Blackwomen? 'I wondered why lyrics that were so original and so immediate about one set of social injustices could be so blind to another' (p. 190).[62] Precisely. And Sistren speak for every woman who has ever wondered – and then begun to act upon her analysis of that contradiction. All the narratives are about women changing, growing up, taking control of their own lives, living differently.

Among working-class West Indians the 'yard' is usually the social unit; the centre of action, the place where opinion is formed, scores settled, rows negotiated, support given and taken, vendettas pursued. The yard is usually a women's space, dominated by women and their children. During my childhood the yard was adjacent to the three separate kitchens in the house. It was the safe space to play cricket. The yard dominates another Caribbean childhood narrative, published in the mid-1980s; Grace Nichols' *Whole of a Morning Sky*. This is a woman-centred rather than a feminist novel, but, like many other Blackwomen's texts, the political situation of women forms the core of a more general social analysis. The subject of Nichols' novel is memory; and the relationship between memory and imagination. Her elegant realist narrative is broken by lyrical passages where the sentimental consciousness of an adult re-invokes the naïve consciousness of a child's world. These passages, sensuous, lurid with detail, where events are inexplicable, sudden, out of scale, are laid alongside the third-person narrative which analyses and explains. Her material is political in conventional terms, dealing with the racial politics of Guyana at the time of independence – another complex, dangerous legacy of imperialism. The racial conflicts between the Blacks and the East Indians – as Asians are usually described in the Caribbean and the Americas – are set within a historical perspective and within the daily experience of one family. The Walcotts are educated, middle-class, critical of incendiary political discourse. They refuse to relinquish an active liberal politics which they share with their working-class neighbours in the yard behind their house. They are Blacks, but they celebrate Deepavali (*sic*) with their East Indian neighbours, and on the night when the Ramsammys' house is threatened by fire the entire yard turns out to defend them, albeit in self-interest. 'For if the Ramsammys were burnt out, everyone knew that the entire yard of close wooden houses would be gone, especially with all the rum and spirits around.'[63]

The community organizes around the yard. The women, in Nichols' text, are defined by their place in that community. Yet their experience is central to the text. She celebrates the inevitable sympathy between women, 'Clara missed Rose . . . the belly laughs, the one-to-one fullness whenever she and Rose were together. Not having Rose come over to see her nearly every day, or she going across to see Rose was like having a piece of herself damped out' (p. 85). None of the women Nichols represents are victims. One way or another they all fight back. 'Mrs Ramsammy, who had been hoping for a submissive daughter-in-law, was bitterly disappointed. Whenever her husband tried to beat her, Zabeeda would fight back, her wiry body clawing and scratching' (p. 124). But there is no place for Zabeeda outside that house where her husband has the right to beat her – unsuccessfully. Nichols describes a world where men beat their wives, withhold money from them, humiliate their mothers, pursue women in the street threatening rape and murder. For in the real world that is what men do. But she never explains or analyses, she simply describes. Feminism makes the real world, in all its dailiness, unforgivable and intolerable; and this would disrupt the surface of lyric narrative.

What is really original in Nichols' *Whole of A Morning Sky* is not the method, nor the style, nor the writer's implicit perspectives, but the material itself. And this is a factor which emerges again and again in writing by Asian and Afro-Caribbean Blackwomen. This story has – quite simply – never been told. The shift from description to analysis is the shift from a concern with women to the feminist demand for a fundamental change in the world. Honor Ford Smith says of Sistren's theatre work that it is 'not a reflection of life but a demystification of it'.[64] While we are involved in this process of demystification we will inevitably be attacked and insulted by everyone who has a vested interest in maintaining the mysteries. I was amused to note that the abusive insults meted out to Sistren – that they are 'communists' and 'lesbians' – are exactly the same as those flung at feminist activists in Britain.[65]

> On the street we have been labelled 'communist' (a word guaranteed to generate much hysteria though few are clear on exactly what it means), or 'lesbian' (the assumption being that to be so labelled is to be so damned that nobody would listen to your 'perverted' insights, let alone take them seriously, as social criticism). The middle strata accuse us of promoting 'raw chaw' and vulgarity. Finally and worst of all, we fail in our work to recognise the contribution of the middle class to our society . . . For these things our work has been censored by local media and our performances sometimes attacked violently.[66]

But they have gone on with their work, dismantling other received opinions. 'There is a kind of prejudice that says that because they drudge, women from the labouring poor have no imagination. We wanted to show that this was not only a lie, but that, in fact, women from the labouring poor often have better imaginations and more poetry than bourgeois actors.'[67] Amen.

The diaspora which has uprooted so many women from their original countries and cultures has produced not only classes but cultures in collision. What does it mean to be Indian in Britain? How does one culture translate into another country, another language? How does the shift in authority, when customs and traditions refuse to root in a strange land – or grow into different shapes – affect the women of the first, second and third generations? 'What is it this country does to our young people?'[68] Who are we now? And what do we wish to become? There are no books behind the experience narrated in Ravinder Randhawa's extraordinary social odyssey *A Wicked Old Woman*, no texts against which to write. And so, in her own text, everyone is writing their version, as screenplay, theatre, social documentary, sociological analysis. Anup is writing *The Invisible Indian*, 'his plans for a book charting the Indian contribution to England's economy and society' (p. 99). Satwant Singh is making his 'notes on the Life and "British" histories of the men who come to this club. "Some of these men have lived their lives on three continents, India, Africa and now Europe" ' (p. 155). Sonia writes the leaflet; Shazia runs the whole story in her news-sheet. Maya has her first ideas stolen by her lover, who then produces an Asian farce, *Laying the Blame*. But that is in fact what the text of *A Wicked Old Woman* does – lays the blame at the right doors, and then lays the blame to rest. Eventually Maya writes her own screenplay, where the community of the novel is gathered together, to tell their story to the small white screen and to the reader of Randhawa's text.

A Wicked Old Woman is not a social realist text but a quilt of dialogues and voices; scenes from an Asian soap opera with Kulwant as the link, joining woman to woman and generation to generation. Every single stereotype of Asian life is invoked, examined, jeered at or critically affirmed. All the variety of responses to England are thrown up by the pattern on the quilted text: the marriages which collapse, the girls who run away from home, the racial mixes, inter-racial friendships, peculiar connections. All the sets in the theatrical text are visible, in every British city: the garages, the vegetable shops, the decaying inner-city churches, the Labour Party meetings. Randhawa argues for the importance of what at first appear to be unlikely links: the friendship between Shazia and her Blackwoman friend Angie, an expert at making samosas, the connection between Ammi and the Greenham women who interfere with her dreams, between Anup and the old Sikh men sitting on the wall beside his garage, between Kulwant and her white woman friend Caroline, between Rani, the runaway, and every character in the fiction. For it is Rani's homecoming which draws all the women in the fiction together. Many of Randhawa's fictional names are of Sikh origin; but religion, any religion, as a serious shaping influence on Asian lives, is not present in the text at all. Religion is usually a source of division and has been a terrible one in Indian history. The nightmares in the book, often Ammi's nightmares, are about isolation, separation, division, loneliness. One of the worst, is the memory of Partition. 'Partition: a people torn apart, families ravaged, homes destroyed, enemies where there was friendship, hate come to stay' (p. 164). Partition, in the bleak grey of England, is an evil which can be unmade, undone. Hate can be driven out; homes rebuilt. The acceptance of Kurshid and her child, who are outsiders, un-people who have disgraced the honour – izaat – of family and community, is crucial to the re-making of the past and the impetus behind Randhawa's writing. For Randhawa, even by deliberately stepping on other people's sensibilities and preconceptions with comic irreverence, argues for unity, community, solidarity. 'People are so thicko, I do despair sometimes. Even if we linked our little fingers we'd change the world' (p. 197).[69]

The core of the novel, where the writer's brazen, abrasive tone changes completely, is the scene entitled 'Tandoori Nights'. This section describes a racist petrol attack upon an Asian household. Randhawa gives the family a context, problems to deal with, an extravagant bright wallpaper which makes their happiness and writes their presence on their house. But she gives them no names, for 'any one of us could have been them' (p. 134). At one end of the white racist spectrum stands Blonde Hair and her torrent of ignorance, insults and abuse.

Kulwant was transfixed with fascination. It had been a long time since she'd heard this kind of talk, she'd actually begun to wonder whether racism was on the ebb. Blonde Hair had restored her faith in the brutality of humankind. 'Don't know what you've got to grin at,' complained Blondie. 'One day, someone'll make hari-kiri curry out of you . . . ' (p. 125)

And within five pages the suggested link is made, and an entire Asian family are murdered by white racists. It is this event which smothers Kuli's energy and hope. Words become flames.

Kulwant's force and power return to her when she pulls her family together. That family is imagined in its most extended form; the Asian community and associated supporters, rising to the defence of one of their daughters. Randhawa refuses to sentimentalize that gesture when Maya snaps at Rani, the returning runaway: ' "Don't imagine it's just for you! . . . and don't imagine that you're unique . . . That skin of yours means we all go in the dock with you. Understand?" ' (p. 204). What the book imagines, through very different voices, overheard and written down with accuracy and energy, is 'the old weatherbeaten framework of family, friends, and social pressures' (p. 63) breaking down and then re-grouping. Randhawa's tone is hilarious and unexpected because she is revealing a community in transition. None of the women she describes is domestic, static or passive. Even as the lovers of men, they are independent women. The 'kind country of exact relationships'[70] is re-built on different terms in another country. Randhawa's conclusions are uncompromising. Unite. Fight.

The narratives of Black and Asian migration, displacement and re-settlement describe two kinds of culture collision: either the unease of a community uprooted and reshaping itself in the west; or the narrative of return, the stories of immigrants who re-visit their countries of origin or explore their inheritance for the first time, measuring their own distance from their parents' or grandparents' past. Bharati Mukherjee's fiction addresses both these territories. Her writing is lucid, aggressive and unsentimental. Caste, class, racism and male power – even the counter-culture of the 1960s – are all anatomized with sardonic, unhesitating acuity. Mukherjee's satire cuts both ways: because she uses each culture, and each set of values, western and Indian, each community's preconceptions and expectations, to dissect the other.

Her first novel, *The Tiger's Daughter* tells the story of Tara, who returns to Calcutta after seven years in America where she has 'arranged her own marriage', as one of her friends puts it, to a white American.[71] Tara becomes a perpetual foreigner, an outsider in both cultures, able to perceive the inevitable disintegration of her childhood world, to see her parents as part of a doomed class. The book develops as a picaresque voyage; each scene unfolds before Tara, as both India and the west become unintelligible and remote. The milieu Mukherjee takes as her central point of reference is that of the wealthy upper classes of Bengal. She stands outside her own narrative, a sardonic, querying voice. The question this text asks again and again is the most simple and unanswerable of all: 'How does the foreignness of the spirit begin?' (p. 37). It is the narrator's voice, everywhere present in Mukherjee's writing, which assesses, judges, condemns. That voice, merciless against ignorance, pretentiousness and corruption, becomes elegiac, the voice of grief and loss, when she describes Tara's alienation from her religion in her mother's prayer room. Abandoning her usual punitive irony, Mukherjee describes the ritual in detail and with great love.

> When the sandalwood paste had been ground Tara scraped it off the slimy stone tablet with her fingers and poured it into a small silver bowl. But she could not remember the next step of the ritual. It was not a simple loss, Tara feared, this forgetting of prescribed actions; it was a little death, a hardening of the heart, a cracking of axis and center. But her mother came quickly with the relief of words.
> 'If you've finished making that thing, dear, why don't you just go ahead and bathe Shiva.' (p. 51)

That forgetting should be a 'hardening of the heart', a refusal of sympathy and of the past, means that forgetting is also a breach between people. The mother's gesture of love towards her daughter is subtly drawn; there is no unease or embarrassment, only delicacy and grace in her reminder. But the loss is not simple, because it is an eternal forgetting.

What characterizes the white westerners in Mukherjee's narrative is not just their mindless racism, but their gracelessness. But it is not the whites alone who cause chaos. The two Americans who march tactlessly through the book are representatives of a culture. One is Black: Washington McDowell, a far-out cool cat, into Black Power and beads. Washington McDowell arrives at the airport during a riot. 'His hair grew in a foot-wide halo around his face. Tara tried to whisper the word "Afro," but Reena's family was too stunned to listen' (p. 140). McDowell, fresh from student uprisings and Black Power demonstrations in California, brushes aside his host's mad apologies for the riot. With the fearlessness of the revolutionary 1960s, Black Power confidence and courage, and wonderful ingenuity, he disarms the barricades.

> . . . he walked around the Fiat and shook hands with everyone. 'Now you cats gotta get with it! I want some noise. I want some chanting, man. You guys gotta get a little class in your riots or else you ain't gettin' nowhere.' He taught them to raise clenched fists and shout 'Brown is beautiful!' He read them jokes from his sweatshirt and jeans and he was hysterically applauded.
> 'Right out!' the boys shouted.
> '*On*, man. *On*,' said McDowell. (pp. 142–3)

McDowell eventually vanishes into the urban revolution of Calcutta, but not before he has wreaked havoc among the wealthy Indians of Carnac Street. They try to welcome him as one of them – despite the fact that the servants run screaming at his approach. It is the politics of class and race that are at stake in this comic, disastrous encounter. Reena's mother is anxious to give McDowell a chilled cocktail; he wants to know 'Don't people here use any deodorants?' (p. 148). The two are hopelessly, helplessly, at odds. *The Tiger's Daughter* insists on the pain of schism and absolute division. It is this division that the kind, wealthy, open-hearted and generous Bengalis find it hard to acknowledge. There is an unbridgeable gulf between the slum housing, the 'bustee', which

Tara visits and the terrace of the Catelli-Continental, where her friends sit drinking coffee: just as there is between east and west. Tara attempts the task of constructing bridges; her country defeats her. For the characteristic of Mukherjee's India is blur, muddle and confusion.[72]

The other visiting American is the appalling Antonia Whitehead (an entirely symbolic name), who comes armed with her Instamatic camera. She arrives bearing the gospel of sexual liberation. After a visit to a local woman guru in Darjeeling, Antonia Whitehead declares that confusion is the enemy. Mata Karanbala Devi, like many religious leaders and prophets, says and does more or less nothing, but what is important are the emotions she inspires; the unity and love between her followers. That love binds people together, amidst the confusion. However,

> Antonia Whitehead had not been impressed. She said clearly and rather loudly that she had witnessed a depressing performance. What India needed, she exclaimed, was less religious excitement and more birth-control devices. She hated confusion of issues, she said. Indians should be more discerning. They should demand economic reforms and social upheavals . . .
> 'You're making fun of us,' Arati interrupted 'What do you know of the beautiful feelings I had in that room . . . ' (pp. 174–5)

Antonia's overbearing, insulting racism reveals the extent to which the two cultures talk at cross-purposes, past each other. The most hilarious and extraordinary sequence in the book is Mr Patel's Beauty Contest at the Kinchen Ganga Hotel, where Antonia demands that the women abandon saris and modesty for the candour of revealing swimsuits – something more in line with western traditions. The judges, including Tara, are a comic cross-section of the Indian middle classes. Antonia takes off her dress, 'till she was revealed to the world in her body stocking: an immense column of white flesh' (p. 188). Mukherjee is writing parables rather than realist prose. The sexual liberationist of the 1960s suddenly becomes raw, white, female meat; like a blank white mark in a situation where traditions, codes, chartered feelings, are wrenched into confusion and complexity. The American body says one brash, simplistic thing against the Indian fog of manners, conventions and uneasily accepted change. Mukherjee uncovers muddle and confusion with unyielding, unhesitating precision; for while Mr Patel's Beauty Contest collapses around them, the band plays on. 'The band, caught up in the beauty of its own music, remained totally calm in the face of such hatred. It sat like a tropical island, solid though buffeted, and played "I Feel Pretty" with touching recklessness' (p. 187). The narrator's eye is always outside the confusion; but it is never ungenerous. The idiocy of the band becomes their courage, their ignorance an oasis of tranquillity. The band is both ludicrous and moving, a dignified folly in the midst of chaos.

The violence that simmers in the text, and which is accepted as a fact of life by all the *dramatis personae*, comes to a climax in the rape of Tara by a corrupt politician and the riot outside the Catelli-Continental. Mukherjee takes two older men as representative of two aspects of India. Joyonto Roy Chowdhury tries, courteously but ineffectively, to protect Tara. His grasp of India, interpreted through European culture, is disintegrating into madness. The new man is Tuntunwala, intent on reforming India. 'We can put a T.V. set in every hut if I'm elected' (p. 195). As an outsider to Mukherjee's culture, I am unable to grasp all the weight and significance of her comments on caste and class destructiveness in the text. When Mr Tuntunwala rapes Tara, Mukherjee abandons his personal name for the name of his tribe. 'The Marwari sat on the arm of Tara's sofa, looking most unhappy. Then slowly disappointment paled and was succeeded by dull anger' (p. 98). I can hear the shift in meaning but I cannot measure the writer's intent. 'In a land where a friendly smile, an accidental brush of the fingers, can ignite rumours – even lawsuits – how is one to speak of Mr Tuntunwala's violence?' (p. 199). Tara is silenced. And Mukherjee makes no further comment; her method as a writer is to uncover, not to argue or explain. Her text cannot begin to answer all its own questions. The formality of address, the impersonal use of 'one' in that last sentence extends the question beyond Tara's appalling situation. The insidious violence of men against women lies hidden behind good manners and elaborate proprieties; it cannot be spoken, thus leaving the woman with her 'unforgiving bitterness' (p. 199).

Joyonto Roy Chowdhury, now quite insane, but speaking fragmented truth, tries to save Tara from the rioters. His speech, from the entrance of the Catelli-Continental, is made up of the already fragmented texts of T. S. Eliot's *Gerontion* and *The Waste Land*. At last 'The Thunder Speaks'. East and west come together in apocalypse. Tuntunwala explodes. 'I weritably believe he's been sent by the other side' (p. 209). And in a sense, he has. For Joyonto Roy Chowdhury holds the incoherent vision of holiness, the union of west and East as both shiver and collapse, which he has tried to pass on to the woman standing astride two cultures, passing from old India into the modern world.

Mukherjee's second novel, *Wife*, answers some of Joyonto's mad questions from Eliot's *Gerontion* – 'After such knowledge, what forgiveness?' It is also an extraordinary study, both of a Bengali community in America and of marriage. Dimple Dasgupta believes – as many women in many radically different cultures have done, do, will do – that pre-marital existence is a kind of dress rehearsal for real life. Dimple gathers all her information and imaginative resources to become a modern wife from Indian films, women's magazines and the ideal of Sita in Hindu legend, 'who had walked through fire at her husband's request. Such pain, such loyalty seemed reserved for married women.'[73] Few women bent on marriage ever look hard at the marriage under their noses, that of their parents. Dimple's mother, Mrs Dasgupta . . . had been brought from the sickbed for her orthodox ceremony, and had promptly returned to it when the ordeal was over' (p. 6). Dimple, though, ' . . . was sure love would become magically lucid on her wedding day' (p. 9). Dimple Dasgupta is a Bengali Madame Bovary, with less room for wickedness and a far more astute assessment of how her life has been curtailed and herself reduced to a state of alienated insanity.

Like a *leitmotiv*, all through the book, are the burning wives. When Dimple is in hospital she hears the screaming. ' "A human torch!" the nurse said. "Would you believe it, she set fire to herself!" ' (p. 6). They follow her through the fiction. Marooned in New York she hears of another death. 'Setting fire to a sari had been on of the seven types of suicide Dimple had recently devised' (p. 115). The fact that other people – husbands, families – may be implicated in these women's deaths is never explicitly stated. Dimple's husband, Amit Basu, refuses to look at the reality of either women's despair or women's destruction. He has this to say: ' "Rule number one," Amit shouted from the living room . . . "Never wear anything but *cotton* saris while cooking. Synthetic fibres are dangerous" ' (p. 116).

The following letter was published in *Manushi* in 1988.

> On May 26, Vanita Khera, a Gujarati lawyer, aged 31, died of 95 per cent burns incurred in her husband's house. The police declared her death an accident. Only after a campaign was organised by the local Gujarati community, women's groups and lawyers, did the police register murder cases against her husband Kishore Khera, brother-in-law, advocate Bharat Khera, mother-in-law, Shantabai and father-in-law, Harijiwan Khera. The accused have been granted bail . . .
>
> According to the Kheras, Vanita got burnt while heating water for her bath on a kerosene stove in the bathroom. This sounds absurd, since it was the height of summer, and secondly, the Kheras have a gas stove in their kitchen. The Kheras are an influential business family, which probably accounts for the police having delayed investigation for two days, giving them plenty of time to tamper with evidence.
>
> Which way the case will go is to be seen. But one can say that Vanita's death is a direct result of our society's notion that a woman's existence is vindicated only if she is a wife.[74]

Dimple's husband is not drawn as a monster. In the world's eyes he is a responsible man, a good catch. He never beats his wife, nor does he abuse her openly. He simply crushes the life out of her by annihilating all reason for her to exist. And he does not do this because he, Amit Basu, has any particular personal animus against women. He does it because he is a husband and she is his wife. Mukherjee is engaged upon an analysis of what happens to women when they have no identity beyond the role they had no choice but to accept.

Not that breaking out and 'finding oneself' in the time-honoured tradition of American individualism provides any kind of a solution. One of the Bengali wives, Ina Mullick, joins the women's liberation movement and discovers why she is unhappy. But she goes on being so. In a hilarious, bizarre and heart-rending sequence she thrashes out her problems with her girlfriend, the appalling Leni Anspach, in front of the uncomprehending Dimple. Mukherjee's black comedy comes from the absolute clash of values, manners, assumptions. Leni and Ina scream abuse at each other, then, in passing, at Dimple. 'But Leni Anspach . . . screamed that Dimple was a coward, that she had no right to worry about the rug and housework when she, Leni, was laying bare her soul to Ina' (p. 148). Leni is of the Reveal All and Be Damned School of American Therapy. By the time Dimple returns with the tea and her 'pretend serenity' Leni is denouncing the artificial mask society forces upon her through her dentures. 'The moment I stopped wearing them in public I became a new woman' (p. 151). She then declares Universal Freedom from Dentures, and ' . . . detached two rows of teeth, which she dropped with a clatter between the sugar bowl and the teapot on the tray. ' "So there," she said, baring her gums . . . Then, after two false starts, Leni and Ina fell into each other's arms' (p. 151–2). The entire scene demonstrates how the personal and the political can part company in a great torrent of theatrical self-indulgence. Dimple's inarticulate desperation passes unnoticed by the two women's group veterans.

Dimple's sense of herself is rooted in performance; and therefore in other people's approval of her presentation. Talk about 'sexism and day-care centres' (p. 146) means nothing to her. She wishes only to please and to be certain that her role as a hostess and a wife has been properly executed. Yet, despite her almost completely submerged personality and her catalogue of suicide methods, Dimple turns her violence outwards. While she is still in Calcutta, waiting for her immigration papers to arrive, she becomes pregnant – and therefore public property. Her body is owned by the Basu family. 'They looked on the unborn son as communal property and were very solicitous of her health. They laid down rules . . . ' (p. 33). Her husband is convinced ' "It'll be a boy . . . He'll be a doctor and mint money" ' (p. 33). Dimple rebels. She breaks through 'her fortress of politeness' (p. 34). Her anger is murderous. The first victim is a mouse, the second is a goldfish. Then she begins to slaughter the cockroaches. 'If the roach was slow she hit it with her broom until the hard shell broke and the whitish liquid splattered' (p. 41). Finally, she kills the foetus by inducing her own miscarriage. Dimple's sense of self returns to her in violence. Women usually absorb the violence done to them and turn it on themselves. And there is, usually, only one solution: the death of the woman. A sort of inner rot brought on by rape does for Clarissa Harlowe, desperate fever for Catherine Earnshaw, arsenic for Emma Bovary, the railway lines for Anna Karenina, the river for Virginia Woolf, the gas oven for Sylvia Plath. Mukherjee proposes the hitherto unthinkable other solution.

In fact, the only simple aspect of Dimple's situation is her solution. Mukherjee specifically places the experience of a wife's alienation, the nature of the abuse that is described generally early on in *Wife* by a magazine editor. 'Abused wives, a category embracing perhaps twenty crore women in this country, need political power' (p. 28). Dimple has no power. And so . . . 'She sneaked up on him and chose a spot, her favourite spot just under the hairline . . . and she drew an imaginary line of kisses because she did not want him to think that she was the impulsive, foolish sort who acted like a maniac' (p. 212). This reader is very far from thinking that Dimple acts like a maniac. In fact, it is not true to say that she has lost touch with reality: for there was nothing sane about the patterns for living which Dimple had absorbed and desired. She had accepted the life prescribed to her, 'her life had been devoted only to pleasing others, not herself' (p. 211). When Mukherjee's text moves into Dimple's mind it is to perceive, at last, the real meaning of her life as Mrs Basu.

> . . . the birdcage was there and now it had a small thing suspended from its wing, a hairy thing with a baby face; she could not be sure whose face since all baby faces

were the same. She had to get out of there; she had to save herself. Not that it was uncomfortable: there was a bowl of water and bird seed and the swing was a lot of fun, if you liked to swing, and she could remember having been happy in spite of the striped shadow of the bars because happiness was mostly a shadowy place and sleep. (p. 210)

Marriage to Amit Basu is the gilded, comfortable cage. And here again are T. S. Eliot's 'bats with baby faces'. But this time, in this text, they are not helpless; they have teeth, and knives in their hands. Mukherjee's dedication – to a row of men, one of whom wondered about Bengali wives – begins to look wonderfully sinister.

In the introduction to her first collection of short fiction, *Darkness*, Mukherjee describes her own voyage as one of the travellers in the Indian diaspora, both as a writer and as a private person. She charts the change from the condition of expatriate to the status of immigrant. Indianness becomes metaphor, a way of perceiving. She writes, 'Instead of seeing my Indianness as a fragile identity to be preserved against obliteration (or worse, a 'visible' disfigurement to be hidden), I see it now as a set of fluid identities to be celebrated.'[75] Mukherjee now makes her home in the USA, where money, I'm told, can put a more comfortable gloss on the endemic racism. Canada boasts more shut doors and overt white racism. It is a predominantly white country which has never had a strong, visible, indigenous Black civil rights movement.[76] In all Mukherjee's short stories, both terrifying and hilarious, the immigrant comes from a real world where war, poverty and pain make human life cheap, where the great metaphysical questions are reduced to survival tactics. Against this nightmare of pain, North America, Canada and the USA emerge as a kind of Disneyland, gripped by insanity and trivia: a land where too much wealth is concentrated in the hands of the innocent, the arrogant and the blind. Sometimes Mukherjee's method is bitter and comic, her irony a knife at the throat of the west. 'Mrs Beamish was brave, she asked the dentist about his family and hometown. The dentist described west Beirut in detail. The shortage of bread and vegetables, the mortar poundings, the babies bleeding.'[77] Sometimes her commentary on the experience of the Indian immigrants in America has a haunting, bizarre pathos. 'Dr Menzies doesn't care for basketball . . . The trivia, the madness, elude him. He approaches the New World with his stethoscope drawn; he listens to its scary gurgles.'[78] For Indian women the USA can appear to be the door out of Indian patriarchy. Both mother and daughter in her story 'A Father' begin to evade his rule with the help of Mastercards and AID sperm donor services. Yet it is through the ghost of Indian culture, the cult of Kali-Mata, the goddess they neglect, that they are eerily assaulted. The daughter, Balbi, decides to have a baby on her own through AID. ' "Who needs a man?" she hissed, "The father of my baby is a bottle and a syringe. Men louse up your lives. I just want a baby . . . " '[79] The father's violence erupts as he sees his power and paternity dismembered and repudiated.

Several of Mukherjee's stories describe illegal aliens, who survive as unpersons, unaccepted, unregistered, hunted, hidden on the rim of the black economy. The status of alien – legal or illegal – becomes a metaphor for an underground of otherness in western culture. Some of the people she describes have always been refugees, displaced, permanent aliens. One of the recurring memories within the Asian diaspora is of course the memory which also haunts Ravinder Randhawa's *A Wicked Old Woman*: the memory of Partition. In Randhawa's text and in Mukherjee's texts, division, the loss of homes, lands, lives, the story of displacement, is told by the older generation to the younger. The story lives on within cultural memory. In Mukherjee's story 'The Imaginary Assassin', it is the grandfather who tells to the immigrant child the tale of despair, destruction and murder; the tale that is, however horrible, still part of his inheritance.

As an analyst and observer of western culture Mukherjee is unsurpassed. The clearest, sharpest insights into any given culture are often produced by outsiders whose status within that culture is ambiguous and subordinate. Conquerors can very seldom offer just perceptions of the places they invade. They are too busy imposing their own values, too anxious to dominate and subdue. The immigrant has a marginal status, and a shifting claim upon the society she chooses to inhabit and understand. She watches the host culture carefully – because it is dangerous not to do so. Mukherjee uses the position of watcher to her own advantage; it is at the root of her prose.[80] All Mukherjee's stories to date are about recent immigrants rather than long-established immigrant communities – second and third generations growing up in a country which continues to resist and deny their presence, their rights, their gifts. This is Joan Riley's fictional territory. Riley, originally Jamaican, was educated in Britain, and works here now. Her subject has been the post-war Black community in Britain, the changing experience of immigrants and their children over four decades.

Riley's recurring question throughout her first three novels, *The Unbelonging, Waiting in the Twilight* and *Romance*, is simply this: how are Blackwomen to live their lives in the awareness of truth when that truth is impossible to bear? The question is one of survival, and a theme which unites Caribbean women writers.[81] Riley's concern is with the destructiveness of illusions and self-deception. All Afro-Caribbean Blackwomen writers are concerned with history, a history that is unwritten, unspoken, masked, denied.[82] Riley's history is the history of the women who came to make their lives in Britain. *The Unbelonging* speaks to the experience of Blackwomen becoming alien everywhere, within the family, within society, within Britain, re-visiting Jamaica. *Waiting in the Twilight* is about the destruction of hope. Adella abandons her illusions about England, about whites, about the police, about the NHS. The only hope she will not and cannot abandon is her belief in her husband's love. Here Riley is engaged on an unflinching, remorseless removal of one comfortable promise of security after another. Adella is stripped psychologically naked. There is a clear continuity of theme and style between the Afro-Caribbean Blackwomen writers I have read. The Jamaican section of Riley's narrative, which describes Adella's seduction by a sweet-talking policeman, exactly parallels the Sistren narratives of adoration and betrayal. Riley uses Patwah as spoken dialogue framed by a narrative written in standard British literary English, just as Collins does in

Angel. But Sistren and Collins write from an explicitly political position, committed to transformation and change. Riley's territory is also women's lives; but her proposals for change are rarely explicit in her text. There is always a woman's voice in Riley's fiction which counsels rebellion, even if that voice is not central to the heroine's decisions. Perlene in *The Unbelonging*: ' "Get your head out of your test-tube and take a look at the real world for once, Hyacinth . . . You better realise that it's Africans like you and me who represent Jamaica's future . . . why don't you admit what you are and be proud of it?' (p. 111). Lisa in *Waiting in the Twilight*: ' "Yu haffe start stan up to ihm, show ihm sey yu is no doormat. Yu haffe mek ihm gi yu more money. What ihm gi yu couldn't feed fly, let alone five pickney and pay bank loan too" ' (p. 60). Mara in *Romance*: ' "Don't try to intimidate me, John," she said coldly. "Is long time since I care one way or other what man like you and Winston think" ' (p. 61). But, as I said, the invigorating assertiveness of rebellious women is not central in Riley's fiction in either mood or theme. Depression seeps into the texture of Riley's prose. The gloom and cold of England become a metaphor for poverty of opportunity, dereliction of life, a defeat of the spirit. Here are the adjectives which surround Adella's homecoming after an ordinary day at work, taken from four consecutive paragraphs in *Waiting in the Twilight*.

> The wind blew icily
> grey January day
> bad leg dragging
> crippled hand
> yellow glow of artificial lights
> dense greyness
> cracked, dirt-streaked uneven pavement
> mouldy
> constant rain of winter
> big muddy gaps
> gloom of early afternoon
> last cold stretch
> gloomy street
> icy fingers
> biting cold
> cold seeping into her shoes
> plastic had split
> fingers stiff and numb
> crippled hand (pp. 5–6)

The problem with naturalistic writing of this kind is that it is almost unendurably painful to read. The climate of cumulative gloom, damp, rain, cold and misery becomes frustrating and enraging because it is being used, not just as an urban weather report, but as a metaphor for Black lives, diminished, curtailed and distressed. Riley's anger is certainly there: we must refuse to live Adella's life and we must refuse to allow other Blackwomen to sink beneath this terrible poverty of the soul. But at no point in the fiction does Adella rebel. Nor does she ever clearly point the finger at the real enemies: male sexism and brutality – and the racist, white British state. However, if Adella does not recognize the main enemy, Joan Riley does.

Even if she cannot or does not rebel, Adella is at least prepared to acknowledge the ugly facts of white racism: that she cannot buy a house in any area she chooses, that the police will not defend her, that she is economically expendable, that she will receive mediocre health care. But the one thing she continues to do is to acquiesce in men's judgements of women. Men can be excused meanness, infidelity, brutality. Adella blames other women. Her husband, Stanton, has gone off with her cousin Gladys. 'Stanton was not to know what a good for nothing the other woman was. She couldn't blame him for the weaknesses of the flesh. She knew men were always like that, they couldn't help it. It was the women who knew better' (p. 61). Certainly, Gladys has spotted a soft touch in a stupid man she can manipulate, and she has no sense of solidarity with her cousin. But Gladys will come to the inevitable bad end, the clichéd fate of the temptress. 'She had heard rumours that he was seeing other women, that he was getting tired of Gladys' (p. 134). However, to be exploited, mistreated and abused by men has also been Adella's fate. She never perceives the pattern in other women's lives, or in her own, and she dies clinging to her last illusion, that her husband loved her. Riley has spelt out her pattern for her readers; which makes Adella's refusal to face facts the more painful and frustrating to read. *Waiting in the Twilight* underscores the bitter self-deceptions and lies endemic in women's love for men.

Adella's drug of forgetting is provided by Westerns on the television. Here are the stories which save us thinking; where we know the good guys from the bad guys by the colour of their hats (the bad guy always wears a black hat) and where the good guys always win in the end. In Riley's third novel, *Romance*, Verona is addicted to white trash-Romantic fiction of the *Castle of Desire* variety. That is her drug of forgetting. The pernicious illusion of these texts is their mystification of male violence as erotic, whereas the reality for Verona was being raped by her sister's boyfriend at the age of thirteen. Riley does not often use the two texts, formula women's fiction and her own text, Black family drama, as counterpoints. But when she does the results are interesting. 'Maybe V. was right: maybe it was best to stick to a hero in a book. At least you'd never have to wash his dirty underpants, or grit your teeth when he rolled on you grunting like a pig because that was how he ended his evening out' (p. 106). Riley is committed to naturalism. *Romance* is a Black soap-opera, a slice-of-life domestic drama of birth, death, rumbling marriages and growing-up pains. Both Riley's earlier novels concentrated on an inward psychic drama of the delusions and self-deceiving lies with which we comfort ourselves. In *Romance* she sets her Black characters within a white urban context which visibly generates most of the internal upheaval and difficulty. John is constantly passed over for promotion because he is Black. Mara's son Jay is picked up by the police and accused of theft simply because he is carrying the money he saved to buy a leather jacket. Verona is framed and forced out of her job so that the firm can avoid paying her redundancy money. Thus, the anger generated by the text is turned outwards against the main enemy: the racist white world. Riley is writing for a Black audience; therefore the Black community is criticized with uncompromising clarity. At one awful political meeting, which generates a lot of talk and puffing up of the male ego, Verona explodes:

> 'Yeah, you big with me, ain't it?' Verona sneered. 'But that's through I'm black – you always was ready to attack black people, specially those that really doing something or don't 'fraid of white people. That's why you lot always quarrelling with everybody else and attacking all them black people minding their own business. If you too scared to do nothing about what's happening to the kids out on the street, why don't you just say so?' (p. 128)

Verona's analysis of the way in which action gets lost in theory, procedure and analysis is loud and accurate; but she is slow to absorb the lessons of her own experience. The first man who abused and raped her was a Black man; so she takes white male lovers after that, men she can imagine as part of the patterns in her white trash-fiction. And, of course, she is eventually seduced and betrayed, battered and abandoned, left pregnant with a white man's child.

> He was no different from those white people who were in the National Front. He's only wanted her because he was trying something exotic . . . It crossed her mind that the only difference between him and Ronnie was that Steve was white and that she was older. It hadn't taken long for him to show his true colours . . . 'I don't want no black bastard calling me Dad,' he had told her with cruel frankness . . . (pp. 213–14)

The cliché phrase – 'true colours' suddenly comes alive. Ronnie and Steve exploited her sexually because they are men. Steve's sexual violence becomes racist in its expression because she is Black and he is white. I asked a Blackwoman friend about the antagonism towards inter-racial relationships within Black communities. She pointed out that if a Blackwoman runs into trouble with a Black man the community can deal with it; but if, as in the situation described in *Romance*, the man is white, there is no redress.

In her critical comments on Joan Riley's work, Merle Collins took exception to Riley's portraits of Black men.

> Why are the men portrayed by Riley so abusive and uncaring? Since they do reflect some aspect of the reality of the Black man's attitude, is this a function of race, or class, or both, since capitalism and its vehicle, colonialism, has made of Black people a collective underclass? Whether Riley intended it or not, we cannot but wonder how much a part is played by wealth and comfort in the maintenance of decency.[83]

The one aspect of the Black man's attitude to Blackwomen which Collins does not confront is, of course, sexism. Do wealth and comfort make men decent in their behaviour to women? Not necessarily. Riley never lets the men off the hook. Here is Verona telling her sister a row of home truths. ' "All I can see is John wiping his foot on you, and you just sit there. I mean, I'm not a feminist and that, but what I can't understand is how you take so much crap from him when you won't take it from no one else" ' (p. 50). Desiree makes the usual excuses – 'John face a lot of racism at work' (p. 50) – and Verona retaliates. ' "Yeah, it's easier to take it out on you, ain't it? God, anyone would never think you face no racism in your life" ; (p. 51). The point here is the same one that Verona makes in the political meeting: it is easier to demolish your own people than to confront the main enemy. And here Riley answers Collins, but her message is to Black men. Pull together with your women. Don't pull them apart.

The community of Blackwomen in *Romance* spans the generations, from Grandma Ruby with her sharp, honest tongue and her unsentimental clarity, to Mara, who fights for an education, tells her husband where to get off and earns her own money. They are the agents of change in their own lives. The discarded book within the book will be the *Castle of Desire*. Verona now has another book to read as she learns to stand up for herself, 'a children's book by a black writer' (p. 229). *Romance* shows a Black community of women asserting themselves, supporting their networks – a Black luncheon club, a Black law centre – and fighting back. This is not middle-class fiction, where people step into Volvos or go on holiday in Europe. Riley's characters wait for buses, sign on, work shifts, negotiate the urban landscape of a hostile country. The strength of naturalism is precisely this: lives that are locked out from white culture are at last made visible, recognizable, are at last analysed, celebrated and understood.

The history of a people living within an alien culture is central to the writing of Asian and Afro-Caribbean women of the diaspora. The telling of that history always cuts both ways: it will tell of a people in exile, surviving, suffering, camouflaging themselves, building new lives, flourishing, fighting back; and it will also, always, tell us about the host culture, with a clarity and ferocity that is unique. I have learned new perceptions of Britain and North America from expatriates, immigrants, travellers; new rhythms in prose fiction, new patterns of feeling. And as the first generation gives way to the second and third generation a new culture is created and a new literature is being made. For Afro-American Blackwomen writing now the project is different from that of the Blackwomen working in Europe.

Two American texts which have influenced my thinking will make this point clear: Alice Walker's *Meridian* and Toni Morrison's *Beloved*. Blackpeople were transported to America as slaves at the same time as the European colonials began to take possession of the continent. Modern America was built with the labour of Blackpeople. It is that history which is addressed in the political fiction of these Blackwomen writers: a history of slavery, the struggle for freedom and the great shift in consciousness achieved by the civil rights movement. 'The legacy of U.S. slavery is racism. The Civil Rights movement changed some of that racist history. I didn't feel powerless and I didn't give up.'[84] But the situation in the USA is, of course, as complicated as it is in Britain. The Native American Indians have had to face many white and non-white groups inhabiting their country as each successive wave of immigrants has arrived. The racism and prejudice which these non-white groups encounter have their origins in the history of American slavery and the genocide of Native American Indians. Alice Walker's *Meridian* is a book of Black history; a novel whose subtle, difficult quilt confronts all the complexity and intermeshing emotional pain of racism and woman-hating.[85] It is a psychological account of the characters within the civil rights movement, written on inter-racial territory. Here the Blackwoman, Meridian, is the mean, the norm, the teacher; the woman who never gives way and never gives up. She is the guide for both Trueman Held, the Black man who both loves and rejects her, and for Lynne, the Jewish white woman who works for Black civil rights. Trueman Held's name – the True Man, the Hero, which is the meaning of *Held* in German – is entirely ironic. These are all flawed people, but their flaws are often the source of their power. Walker herself describes the novel as 'a crazy quilt', or a 'collage'. It is Meridian herself who holds the key to the pattern. 'Meridian's struggle is in this sense symbolic. Her struggle is the struggle each of us will have to assume in our own way. And Trueman will certainly have to assume his because his life has been so full of ambivalence, hypocrisy and obliviousness of his actions and their consequences.'[86]

Two aspects of this rich, difficult text have remained with me; two aspects which speak to all radical movements, both to the Black people's struggle and to the women's liberation movement. The first is the issue of political integrity. When the novel opens Meridian is leading a small party of Black children across a hot square in the deep South to see a fake dead lady show on the day they want to go and not the day designated by the white racists of the town who don't want to mix with Black folks. The town assembles to stop them with a threatening old tank, bought in the 1960s 'when the townspeople who were white felt under attack from "outside agitators" – those members of the black community who thought equal rights for all should extend to blacks' (p. 4). Suitably, for an emblem of white racism, they paint the tank white. Meridian raps the tank on the nose and leads the children in to see the fake dead body. The 1960s are gone. The era of the big marches, the voter registration drives, the protests, the non-violent demonstrations, the Black revolutionary underground, is past and gone. In this post-revolutionary period, many middle-class Blacks settled back on the territory they had won from the whites. Meridian makes a difficult political decision. 'I'll go back to the people, live among them, like Civil Rights workers used to do' (p. 18). Meridian is neither sentimental, sanctimonious nor self-righteous. She simply chooses to live according to her political beliefs, however difficult this proves to be and whatever the cost, long after the revolutionary bandwagon has rolled on. Her decision is a perpetual victory in the midst of a defeat. And a rebuke to compromise.

The second aspect of *Meridian* which is of infinite value to me is Alice Walker's refusal to shirk complexity. Blackpeople were not, and are not, the only Americans to suffer at the hands of the whites. Alice Walker never forgets this. She has this to say about her book. 'Another reason I think nobody has been able to deal with *Meridian* as a total work is the whole sublayer of Indian consciousness, . . . I had been working very hard, but not consciously really, to let into myself all of what being in America means, and not to exclude any part of it.'[87] Walker argues for the connections between the dispossessed, the Native American Indians and the Blacks. When Meridian's father discovers that his vegetable garden is on an Indian burial ground, he insists on giving the land back to its rightful owners. ' "But the land already belonged to them," her father said, "I was just holding it. The rows of my cabbages and tomatoes run right up along the biggest coil of the Sacred Serpent . . . Course, since it's a cemetery, we shouldn't own it anyhow." ' (p. 46). Meridian's father insists that Black Americans are part of the historical process that all but destroyed Native American culture and should be aware of that history. Walker is not recommending an outburst of guilt on the part of Blackfolk, which would be entirely inappropriate. White people were, and remain, responsible for the atrocities committed against the Native Americans. But Walker is against ignorance; the ignorance that refuses to acknowledge historical memory, and the responsibility that comes with remembering.

As white women in the women's movement have been slow to learn, even the most downtrodden among us still enjoy privileges that result from the fact of our colour.[88] Walker insists on examining the complicated interactions of racism and sexism. A Black man can think of a woman, of whatever colour, as an object, and despise her accordingly. In a painful chapter 'Of Wives and Bitches' Walker examines that aspect of Black male consciousness. Tommy Odds, appallingly damaged by white hatred, begins to hate in return, and makes his views clear to Trueman Held. 'He could read the message that Tommy Odds would not, as his former friend, put into words. "Get rid of your bitch, man." That was all. Getting rid of a bitch is simple, for bitches are dispensable. But getting rid of a wife?' (p. 133). Walker is interested in that process in the male mind, when wives become bitches; and in the way Black men perceive white women. 'They did not even see her as a human being, but as some kind of large, mysterious doll. A thing of movies and television, of billboards and cars and soap commercials' (p. 135). Trueman Held represents an attitude towards white women when he marries Lynne, his wife and his bitch. But when the political wind changes and it is fashionable to collect a 'shiny new black wife' (p. 134), he goes off in search of Meridian. The courage to confront complexity, to reject the secure simplicity of slogans, is the basis for all fine political writing. But the real achievement, both in politics and in art, comes in the refusal to be confused or compromised by complexity, to decide on political priorities, to act and to write on the basis of that decision. Walker sees Black separatism as an inevitable part of a process, the difficult process of recognizing and knowing the enemy.

Toni Morrison's *Beloved* is also a book about Black consciousness and about knowing the enemy.[89] Morrison's subject is slavery; not just the experience of slavery, but the meaning of that experience and its political consequences for Black Americans. Morrison takes the unspeakable, articulates it precisely, and yet still leaves the reader with the sensation that it is precisely that – unspeakable. The understanding of slavery developed by modern Black writers and thinkers, is, in Morrison's text, given back to the people who suffered, fought back against white brutality, and survived. Here again there is a direct and immediate link between Afro-Caribbean and Afro-American women writing. Grace Nichols' analysis of slavery in her poem sequence *i is a long-memoried woman* uses the same characters who appear in *Beloved*. The voice in 'I coming back' is the voice of Beloved herself, the Blackwoman butchered, vengeful, returning.

I coming back 'Massa'
I coming back

mistress of the underworld
I coming back

colour and shape
of all that is evil
I coming back[90]

Baby Suggs (holy), the old wise woman of Morrison's novel, stands in the poem
' . . . Like Clamouring Ghosts', even down to the detail of her twisted hip.

I see the old dry-head woman
leaning on her hoe
twist-up and shaky like a cripple
insect

I see her ravaged skin, the stripes
of mold where the whip fall
hard

I see her missing toe, her jut-out
hipbone from way back time when
she had a fall (p. 42)

Here is Morrison's text:

Resting on the handle of the hoe she concentrated . . . When she hurt her hip in
Carolina she was a real bargain . . . Because of the hip she jerked like a
three-legged dog when she walked. (p. 139).

Morrison's heroine, Sethe, appears in Nichols' poem 'Ala'. Ala is the rebel
woman,

who with a pin
stick the soft mould
of her own child's head

sending the little-new-born
soul winging its way back
to Africa – free

they call us out to see
the fate for all us rebel
women (p. 23)[91]

Ala may have had no choice but to murder her child; Morrison suggests that
Sethe can and does finally choose otherwise. Character proves not to be destiny
pre-ordained.

    The relationship between Morrison's novel and Nichols' poem sequence is
not a simple question of influence. Blackwomen writers are making a commun-

ity through their writing; these are the characters from a collective Black memory. Their stories are part of an intersecting web; a quilt of history.

Beloved is a lost child; the woman lost in the psychic and physical devastation of slavery. She returns to the mother who murdered her as a haunting, both as a psychological and as a textual reality in Morrison's fiction. 'But in what sense is Beloved really there?' asked one of my family who had just read the novel, spellbound. My view was that Morrison was using the differing levels of fictional structures – the sorcery of imagination – to suggest the ways in which our dead haunt our consciousness; and to indicate the ways in which the suffering of slavery remains with Black Afro-Americans. There are enough textual references to explain Beloved as a natural, rather than as a ghostly, sign in the fiction. But Morrison is using both a natural and a supernatural code in her construction of Beloved. Beloved is a voice, an echo, a memory. For the core of the narrative is, in any case, not the presence or absence of Beloved, but Sethe's act of violence; her attempted murder of all her children and her bloody slaughter of her crawling already? baby girl. Morrison's novel has an uncompromising unhesitating, fighting message. Simply this: it is always easier for a degraded, humiliated and broken people to turn their anger, not outwards against their enemy, but inwards against themselves. Know who your enemy is, and strike back.

Sethe did not attack the white schoolteacher, the white nephew, the white slavecatcher and the white sheriff, who, like the four horsemen of the Apocalypse, come to take her and her children. Instead she attacks her own best thing, her Black children. To acknowledge Beloved, in love and in grief, means knowing who was the real cause of her death: the white men coming. There is no space in Morrison's text for liberal whites, even those of the Sweet Home variety, slaveowners with a human face. Their brand of slavery, which makes Sweet Home both a sanctuary and a padded prison, is still slavery. Even as Baby Suggs answers Garner's catechism: Did she ever go hungry or cold? Was she ever mistreated? Was her son refused when he wanted to buy her freedom? with a row of obedient no, sirs, she thinks, 'But you got my boy and I'm all broke down. You be renting him out to pay for me after I'm gone to Glory' (p. 146). White folks are the enemy; the menace on the rim of this book. But, like Walker, Morrison insists on a complicated analysis of the pyramid of power. She sees where white women sometimes stand in the system. She celebrates Amy Denver, the white trash girl, also a runaway from oppression, who helps Sethe escape. She honours the Cherokee Indians who help Paul D and tell him to follow the blossoms on his escape north.

Beloved is, above all, a woman-centred book. Here again is Audre Lorde's triangle of grandmother (Baby Suggs), mother (Sethe), and daughters (Denver and Beloved). They can love one another only in freedom. 'Anybody Baby Suggs knew, let alone loved, who hadn't run off or been hanged, got rented out, loaned out, bought up, brought back, stored up, mortgaged, won, stolen or seized' (p. 23). Yet the fact that Denver and Sethe re-create Beloved, the desired child and lost sister, between them, is clearly perceived by Morrison as an unhealthy and terrifying sign of their alienation and isolation from the rest of the Black community. Paul D represents the necessary balance. Elsewhere,

Morrison cautions women against 'the absence of men in a nourishing way . . . That is the disability we must be on guard against for the future – the female who reproduces the female who reproduces the female.' Morrison subscribes to the balance of women and men in 'nurturing relationships'.[92] For me, this was one of the most heartening aspects of her fiction *Beloved*; the way in which Paul D nurtures Sethe, and all the shared suffering and love between them. But the fact remains that men do not, on the whole or as a group, nurture women. It is women who nurture and support men. In her advocacy of nurturing men, Morrison is being utopian rather than historical. Paul D is a different model for men, a different interpretation of masculinity. And I hope that all men will read him that way. Neither I nor any of the women I know, Black and white, Lesbian and straight, have ever met him in the flesh.

Religion is very often a powerful source of identity and energy in Black writing and in Black lives. For Baby Suggs (holy), the wise woman of Morrison's text, religion is simply the affirmation of the goodness and beauty of Black flesh. Slavery is the denial of human worth and human love. Loving God is loving yourself and loving each other.

> 'Here,' she said, 'in this here place, we flesh; flesh that weeps, laughs; flesh that dances on bare feet in grass. Love it. Love it hard. Yonder they do not love your flesh. They despise it. They don't love your eyes; they'd just as soon pick em out. No more do they love the skin on your back. Yonder they flay it. And O my people they do not love your hands. Those they only use, tie, bind, chop off and leave empty. Love your hands! Love them. Raise them up and kiss tem. Touch others with them, pat them together, stroke them on your face 'cause they don't love that either. *You* got to love it, *you*!' (p. 88)

Beloved's demand is to be accepted, loved, avenged. When Sethe at last defends her beloved ghost against the coming white men, Beloved departs forever.

There is a triumphant conclusion to this book. Not only does Sethe learn to confront the real enemy, but the community of Blackwomen, who had betrayed and abandoned her, come back to acknowledge her as one of their own. In doing so, they acknowledge their own responsibility for one another. At last, need is recognized, answered. Sethe is secure again from her past and her ghost, free to remake her life. And here Paul D reiterates Baby Suggs' visionary message to Blackpeople, when he says to Sethe, 'you your best thing' (p. 273). Love yourself. Love each other.

Beloved has gone. But she is not at peace. She is the loneliness that roams. For of course, the fact of slavery remains, and so, too, does the person 'disremembered and unaccounted for . . . Although she has claim, she is not claimed . . . Beloved' (pp. 275–6). History can be faced, acknowledged, remembered, understood, both on the page and in the flesh. But it cannot be undone. Blackwomen, as writers, activists, politicians, artists, commentators, policy-makers and agents of change, are at last forcing their entrance into British – and American – society. British Blackwomen bring with them 'the contradictions and legacies of Britain's past',[93] but they are going on to make a new and different future.

Feminism as a political consciousness, and the women's movement as a whole, is being transformed from within by Blackwomen's politics. But history is not an irresistible process sweeping us along, as some old-fashioned Marxists would have us believe. History is made with our bodies, our hands and our brains. Even as we are the resisters, there are those, women and men, who resist us. Blackwomen have been censured, silenced, ignored; the repressed in history, even in white feminist history. Blackwomen writing – speaking – change the terms of the discussion. But, as I have argued earlier, silence is not absence; silence is not consent. The last word on the subject of Black silence comes from Marsha Prescod.

> All de big shots were nat'rally upset,
> 'Why dese darkies so wicked?' dey cry
> 'We've tried so much good kindness for four hundred years,
> An dey still go an selfishly die.'
>
> De millions of black dead don't answer,
> Well, dey can't, tru der shackles an chains,
> But dey chil'ren an gran' children busy,
> Wid dey skills an dey guns . . . an dey brains.[94]

Notes

1 Barbara Burford, 'The Landscapes Painted on the Inside of My Skin', *Spare Rib*, no. 179 (June 1987), pp. 36–8.
2 Amryl Johnson, in Lauretta Ngcobo (ed.), *Let It Be Told: Black Women Writers in Britain* (London, Pluto, 1987), p. 44.
3 Joan Riley, *The Unbelonging* (London, Women's Press, 1985).
4 Adjoa Andoh, 'I'd Also Like To Say . . . ', in Black Womantalk (ed.), *Black Women Talk Poetry* (London, Black Womantalk Ltd, 1987), p. 31.
5 Dorothea Smartt and Val Mason-John, 'Blackfeminists Organising on Both Sides of the Atlantic', *Spare Rib*, no. 171 (October 1986), pp. 20–4.
6 Maud Sulter in Ngcobo, *Let It Be Told*, p. 64.
7 Black Womantalk, *Black Women Talk Poetry*, p. 8.
8 Savitri Hensman, *Flood at the Door* (London, Centerprise Trust, 1979), p. 4. But see Audre Lorde's meditation on this subject in *A Burst of Light* (Ithaca, NY, Firebrand, 1988), p. 67. 'I see certain pitfalls in defining Black as a political position. It takes the cultural identity of a widespread but definite group and makes it a generic identity for many culturally diverse peoples, all on the basis of a shared oppression. This runs the risk of providing a convenient blanket of apparent similarity under which our actual and unaccepted differences can be distorted or misused.'
9 From Elean Thomas's collection *Word Rhythms from the Life of a Woman*, quoted by the author in her article on Sistren, 'Lionhearted Women', *Spare Rib*, no. 172 (November 1986), pp. 14–19.
10 Mumtaz Karimjee, 'Black and Asian: Definitions and Redefinitions', *Mukti*, no. 6 (Spring 1987), special issue on racism and prejudice.
11 The issues here are very complex. See, for example, the article on 'Maids and Madams in the Natal Indian Community' by Lorna, *Mukti*, no. 6 (Spring 1987), and the response by Najma Kazi to the debate surrounding this controversial discussion published with the article.

12 Buchi Emecheta, *Head Above Water* (London, Fontana, 1986), p. 179.

13 See Sharan-Jeet Shan's extraordinary autobiography *In My Own Name* (London, Women's Press, 1986), discussed in detail in chapter 3 above, 'On Autobiography'.

14 Babli talking to Amrit Wilson in her study *Finding a Voice: Asian Women in Britain* (London, Virago, 1979, 1984), p. 133.

15 See Honor Ford Smith's introduction to Sistren, *Lionheart Gal: Life Stories of Jamaican Women* (London, Women's Press, 1986), pp. xxvi–xxxi.

16 Gloria I. Joseph, 'Styling, Profiling and Pretending: The Games before the Fall', in Gloria I. Joseph and Jill Lewis, *Common Differences: Conflicts in Black and White Feminist Perspectives* (New York, Anchor/Doubleday, 1981), pp. 182–3.

17 Maya Angelou, *I Know Why the Caged Bird Sings* (1969; London, Virago, 1984). See her hilarious but very loving chapter 6.

18 Merle Collins, *Angel* (London, Women's Press, 1987), p. 141; Amryl Johnson, *Sequins for a Ragged Hem* (London, Virago, 1988), pp. 51–2. For 'Waters of Babylon' listen to the version by the Melodians on the original soundtrack recording of *The Harder They Come* (Island Records, 1972).

19 In Wilson, *Finding a Voice*, p. 148.

20 Smartt and Mason-John, 'Blackfeminists Organising', p. 21.

21 Ibid.

22 Joan Riley, *The Scarlet Thread* (London, Virago, 1987); Shan, *In My Own Name*; Bharati Mukherjee, *The Tiger's Daughter* (1971; London, Penguin, 1987), *Wife* (1975; London, Penguin, 1987).

23 Myriam Warner-Vieyra, *Juletane* (1982; London, Heinemann, 1987).

24 Wilson, *Finding a Voice*, p. 151.

25 Ibid., p. 159.

26 Sulter, in Ngcobo, *Let It Be Told*, p. 57; Johnson, *Sequins for a Ragged Hem*, p. 2.

27 Fyna Dowe, 'The Word', in Rhonda Cobham and Merle Collins (eds), *Watchers and Seekers: Creative Writing by Black Women* (London, Women's Press, 1987), p. 112.

28 In Cobham and Collins, *Watchers and Seekers* pp. 118–19.

29 Emecheta, *Head Above Water*, p. 39.

30 In Ngcobo, *Let It Be Told*, p. 68.

31 Marsha Prescod, *Land of Rope and Tory* (London, Akira, 1985).

32 From her poem 'OF COURSE WHEN THEY ASK FOR POEMS ABOUT THE "REALITIES" OF BLACK WOMEN', quoted by the author in Ngcobo, *Let It Be Told*, p. 100. For the white feminists arguing about the issue of 'women's experience' see Toril Moi, *Sexual/Textual Politics* (London, Methuen, 1985), pp. 43–9, and an even more telling analysis from Jan Montefiore, *Feminism and Poetry: Language, Experience, Identity in Women's Writing* (London, Pandora, 1987), pp. 1–25. Montefiore challenges radical feminist poets for their 'unrecognized Romanticism', their assumption that female experience is 'unitary' and that there is an uncomplicated connection between the poet as woman and the poetry she produces. She also criticizes 'the ideal – or fantasy – of poetry as experience encountered at white heat' (p. 12). Here she parts company with Amryl Johnson. The debate goes on.

33 Ngcobo, *Let It Be Told*, p. 19.

34 Rashda Sharif, 'On British Racism', unpublished proceedings of the Bendorf 10th Jewish Christian Muslim Women's Conference, 18–25 November 1986. This conference is held annually in the autumn under the auspices of the Hedwig Dransfeld Haus e.v. at Bendorf-am-Rhein, Germany.

35 Beverley Bryan, Stella Dadzie and Suzanne Scafe, *The Heart of the Race: Black Women's Lives in Britain* (London, Virago, 1985).

36 Ngcobo, *Let It Be Told*, p. 9. For the same views discussed, see ' "Wild Women Don't Get the Blues": Alice Walker in Conversation with Maud Sulter', in Shabnam

Grewal et al. (eds), *Charting the Journey: Writings by Black and Third World Women* (London, Sheba, 1988), pp. 100–10, esp. pp. 104–5.

37 In Ngcobo, *Let It Be Told*, pp. 66–7.

38 See Valerie Amos and Pratibha Parmar, 'Challenging Imperial Feminism', *Many Voices One Chant: Black Feminist Perspectives*, special black issue of *Feminist Review*, no. 17 (Autumn 1984), pp. 3–19.

39 Published in *Many Voices One Chant*, pp. 76–7; see also her collection *Ripples and Jagged Edges* (London, Zora, n.d.).

40 Maya Angelou interviewed in *The Guardian*, 13 August 1987.

41 Marion Molteno, *A Language in Common* (London, Women's Press, 1987).

42 For an analysis of Wordsworth's ballads and their ambiguities see Heather Glen, *Vision and Disenchantment: Blake's Songs and Wordsworth's Lyrical Ballads* (Cambridge, Cambridge University Press, 1983).

43 These are genuine comments. For the information, my thanks to N. Kassam. She does also say that she feels things are changing in her community and that there is now a more liberal attitude towards trousers.

44 See Yasmin Alibhai and Pragna Patel, 'Afterword' to Riley, *The Scarlet Thread*, pp. 143–51; also Shaila Sha, 'We Will Not Mourn Their Deaths in Silence', in Grewal et al., *Charting the Journey*, pp. 281–91.

45 Parita Trivedi, 'To Deny Our Fullness: Asian Women in the Making of History', *Many Voices One Chant*, pp. 37–50: p. 45.

46 See 'Becoming Visible: Black Lesbian Discussions', Carmen, Gail, Shaila and Pratibha, in *Many Voices One Chant*, ' "Pushing the Boundaries": Mo Ross talks with Jackie Kay and Pratibha Parmar', in Grewal et al., *Charting the Journey*, pp. 169–187, on Black/Lesbian motherhood. There is a section 'Being a Lesbian . . . ' in Black Womantalk, *Black Women Talk Poetry*; and there are Black Lesbian contributors to Lilian Mohin (ed.), *Beautiful Barbarians: Lesbian Feminist Poetry* (London, Only-women, 1986) and Chris McEwan (ed.), *Naming the Waves: Contemporary Lesbian Poetry* (London, Virago, 1988). All this is just for starters – Black Lesbian writing is, happily, becoming increasingly available.

47 Ngcobo, *Let It Be Told*, p. 30.

48 Ibid., p. 31.

49 For an analysis of this very different version see 'Becoming Visible: Black Lesbian Discussions'.

50 Becky Birtha, *Lover's Choice* (1987; London, Women's Press, 1988), p. 148.

51 See also Ann Allen Shockley, *Loving Her* (1974; Tallahassee, Florida, Naiad, 1987).

52 Faith Conlon, Rachel da Silva and Barbara Wilson (eds), *The Things That Divide Us* (Seattle, Seal Press, 1985).

53 *Spare Rib*, no. 186 (January 1988).

54 Johnson, *Sequins for a Ragged Hem*, pp. 186–7.

55 *Océaniques*, October 1987.

56 Johnson, *Sequins for a Ragged Hem*, p. 211.

57 Audre Lorde, *Our Dead Behind Us* (London, Sheba, 1986), p. 16.

58 The Western capitalist media usually do deal in easy simplicities. I found the following atrocity by William Greaves in 'Postcard', *The Observer Magazine*, 10 January 1988: ' . . . the day when American liberation forces landed without warning and booted out a hated revolutionary government which had terrorised these friendly and peacable islanders since the late 1970s'. For a very different view see Audre Lorde, 'Grenada Revisited: An Interim Report', in *Sister/Outsider: Essays and Speeches* (Trumansberg, NY, Crossing Press, 1984), pp. 176–90.

59 See the glossary at the back of Collins' text, where all is explained to the uninitiated. A good deal of the language is familiar to me from my childhood and the poetry of

writers like James Berry and Louise (Miss Lou) Bennett. But the excitement of seeing West Indian languages used in fiction – major fiction, at that – is enormous. For further reference see Morgan Delphis, *Caribbean and African Languages: Social History, Language, Literature and Education* (London, Karia, 1985) and Hubert Devonish, *Language and Liberation: Creole Language Politics in the Caribbean* (London, Karia, 1986).

60 See Honor Ford Smith, 'Sistren Women's Theatre, Organizing and Conscientization', in Pat Ellis (ed.), *Women of the Caribbean* (London, Zed, 1986), pp. 122–8.

61 Sistren, *Lionheart Gal*, p. xxix.

62 See also Elma Reyes, 'Women in Calypso', in Ellis, *Women of the Caribbean*, pp. 119–21.

63 Grace Nichols, *Whole of a Morning Sky* (London, Virago, 1986), p. 140.

64 Ford Smith, 'Sistren Women's Theatre', p. 128.

65 See Steve Bell's cartoon 'If . . . ' in *The Guardian*. Bell had a running joke for years about the Greenham women as 'woolly-hatted lesbian Trotskyists' – but Mr Bell is, of course, on our side.

66 Sistren, *Lionheart Gal*, p. xxvi.

67 Ford Smith, 'Sistren Women's Theatre', p. 124.

68 Ravinder Randhawa, *A Wicked Old Woman* (London, Women's Press, 1987) p. 102.

69 See Randhawa's comments in an interview with Laxmi Jamidagni, *Mukti*, no. 7 (1987), p. 20, on the question of integration and friendship with the white community in Britain. 'We have to get on with living in England and inevitably, there's going to be all kinds of relationships between the Asian community and the white community . . . as long as we are confident of ourselves, and we're not ashamed of what we are, and as long as the relationships are based on mutual respect . . . '

70 Gillian Hanscombe and Suniti Namjoshi, *Flesh and Paper* (Seaton, Devon, Jezebel, 1986), p. 57.

71 Bharati Mukherjee, *The Tiger's Daughter* (1971; London, Penguin, 1987). For another exploration of 'foreignness of the spirit' see Leena Chingra's narrative of return to India in her novel *Amritvela* (London, Women's Press, 1988). This is a moving, woman-centred novel set among the upper classes of Delhi. The memory of Partition haunts the text. But her vision is gentler, less savage, less critical than Mukherjee's.

72 In this she resembles the earlier chronicler of India for the British, E. M. Forster. Mukherjee herself acknowledges this literary inheritance in her introduction to *Darkness* (London, Penguin, 1985), p. 3: 'The book I dream of updating is no longer *A Passage to India* – it's *Call It Sleep*.' Forster's novel was one of the books behind the book for Mukherjee.

73 Bharati Mukherjee, *Wife* (1975; London, Penguin, 1987), p. 6.

74 Letter giving details of the case of Vanita Khera, signed by Susan Abraham and Nishtha Desai, Maharashtra, in *Manushi: A Journal about Women and Society*, no. 47 (1988), p. 23. To subscribe to *Manushi* write to Manushi Trust, Manushi C-1/2-2 Lajpat Nagar, New Delhi 110024, India.

75 Bharati Mukherjee, *Darkness* (London, Penguin, 1975), introduction, p. 3.

76 This generalization is supported by Mukherjee in her introduction to *Darkness*, where she writes, 'In the years I spent in Canada – 1966 to 1980 – I discovered that the country is hostile to its citizens who had been born in hot moist continents like Asia; that the country proudly boasts of its opposition to the whole concept of cultural assimilation' (p. 2). Indian members of my family who have had occasion to visit both Canada and the United States agreed with Mukherjee's points. Apparently

racist abuse is much more overtly expressed in Canada, and the undercurrent of white racist disdain for Black people more forcefully felt.

77 Mukherjee, 'The Lady from Lucknow', *Darkness*, p. 27.

78 Mukherjee, 'Angela', *Darkness*, p. 17.

79 Mukherjee, 'A Father', *Darkness*, p. 72.

80 See her collection of short fiction, *The Middleman and Other Stories* (London, Viking Penguin, 1988), which circles around the immigrant experience. I await her third novel to be published by Virago with immense interest.

81 Joan Riley, *The Unbelonging* (London, Women's Press, 1985), *Waiting in the Twilight* (London, Women's Press, 1987), *Romance* (London, Women's Press, 1988). See Merle Collins' article, 'Women Writers from the Caribbean', *Spare Rib*, no. 194 (Summer 1988), pp. 18–22.

82 On the struggle to document and interpret that history, see Linda King and Jenny McKenzie, 'Unspoken Stories', *Spare Rib*, no. 196 (November 1988), pp. 20–4.

83 Merle Collins, 'Two Writers from the Caribbean: Joan Riley and Jacob Ross', in Kwesi Osusu (ed.), *Storms of the Heart: An Anthology of Black Arts and Culture* (London, Camden, 1988), p. 159.

84 'C.G.', part of the editorial statement, *Heresies*, no. 15, 'Racism is the Issue', 21 October 1982.

85 Alice Walker, *Meridian* (1976; London, Women's Press, 1982).

86 'Alice Walker: In Conversation with Claudia Tate', in Claudia Tate (ed.), *Black Women Writers at Work* (1983; Herts, Oldcastle, 1985), pp. 176, 180. I apologize to Alice Walker for not offering here as detailed and meticulous a reading of *Meridian* as she would like to see. She herself points out that 'The reviews I've seen have taken little parts of the book, never treating it in its entirety' (Tate, 'Alice Walker: In Conversation', p. 177). I refer the reader of this text to Barbara Christian, *Black Women Novelists: The Development of a Tradition, 1892–1976* (Westport, Conn., Greenwood, 1980).

87 Tate, 'Alice Walker: In Conversation', p. 178.

88 For encouraging developments to the contrary see the work of the US group 'Women Against Racism': 'Papusa Molina: Building Alliances Against Racism. An Interview by Becky Thompson', *Sojourner: The Women's Forum*, vol. 14, no. 3 (November 1988), pp. 16–18. *Sojourner* is available from 380, Green Street, Cambridge, Mass., 02139, USA.

89 Toni Morrison, *Beloved* (London, Chatto & Windus, 1987).

90 Grace Nichols, 'I coming back' in *i is a long-memoried woman* (London, Karnak House, 1983), p. 43. See also the video film and radio play based on the poems, directed by Frances-Anne Solomon, reviewed by Claudette Williams, *Spare Rib*, no. 218 (November 1990), pp. 20–2.

91 An important Blackwoman's narrative about slavery has been reprinted: Mary Prince, *The History of Mary Prince*, ed. Moira Ferguson (1831; London, Pandora, 1987). Prince tells her own story of cruelty and escape.

92 Toni Morrison, 'Rootedness: the Ancestor as Foundation', in Mari Evans (ed.), *Black Women Writers: 1950–1980* (1984; London, Pluto, 1985), p. 344.

93 Owusu, *Storms of the Heart*, introduction, p. 2. See especially the women contributors to this anthology. I note that women and men are not represented in anything like equal numbers, even in this radical text. There is still work to be done.

94 Marsha Prescod, 'Death by Self-Neglect', from *Land of Rope and Tory*, cited in Ngcobo, *Let It Be Told*, p. 117.

Afterword

An Old-Fashioned Politics

Take this nasty mess away, dear, and bring us some more wine.
Anna Livia, *Relatively Norma*

I am very aware that this book is out of step with the times. To many people
Sisters and Strangers will read like an old-fashioned book. I have written about
women and men, not femininity and masculinity, about sexual politics, not
gender theory, about male privilege, not sexual difference. And I have
questioned actual sexual practice, not celebrated an abstract desire. When I
have written about power I have not described a nebulous fog floating in the air,
which might descend upon anyone. Fiction usually reveals in whose hands it
lies; power, sexual, legal, educational, rhetorical. I have tried to write as if we
lived in kitchens, bedrooms, factories and the open fields, not in seminars. I do
not take the view that the more we have suffered the purer our ideas will be, but
I do believe that the liberation of women is about trying both to think differently
and to live differently. Having a degree in women's studies does not necessarily
involve being a feminist. The point of the struggle is not simply to understand
our oppression as women, but to end it; and that can only be achieved by a
strong, autonomous women's movement.

It is memory-time among the self-appointed historiographers of the women's
movement. Various retrospective collections of essays and memoirs have begun
to appear, charting our shifting concerns, priorities, enthusiasms. Elizabeth
Wilson's *Hidden Agendas: Theory, Politics and Experience in the Women's Movement*
might well have been subtitled 'The Rise and Fall of Socialist Feminism'. Her
novel *Prisons of Glass*, which tells the same tale in fiction, is saturated with the
valedictory, elegiac tones of a last farewell. This was the way we were, and are
not now. 'You know, I thought, it's not about women's lives exactly, and it's not
really about feminism either – really it's about the Movement, isn't it? What it
was. How we experienced it . . . We were all in it together.'[1] More libertarian
and energetic in style, Germaine Greer's *The Madwoman's Underclothes: Essays
and Occasional Writings 1968–1985* tells a slightly different story. Greer was one
of the anarchic sexual radicals of the sixties underground. The fresh air let in
through the holes in the shattered taboos still whistles through her prose.

> Revolutionary women may join Women's Liberation groups and curse and scream
> and fight the cops, but did you ever hear of one of them marching the public street
> with her skirt high crying 'Can you dig it? Cunt is beautiful!' The walled garden of

Eden was CUNT. The mandala of the beautiful saints was CUNT. The mystical rose is CUNT. The Ark of Gold, the Gate of Heaven . . . Once a woman throws a leg over her lover she has accepted responsibility for her own sexuality and recognised it as an integral part of her personality and her intelligence, and not merely a function of meat. Once she is poised over her lover, male or female, she is about not merely to claim the right of orgasm but espouse the sweet responsibility of giving pleasure.[2]

Sexuality is still very much on the agenda of the women's movement. But what is particularly refreshing about Greer is that she insists that women love themselves, feel good about their sex and about who they are. In a society where woman-hating is the rot within every structure it's still good to hear that 'Cunt is beautiful!' Greer and Wilson each write a very different history of feminism. This is neither surprising nor disturbing. For the writing of history is always a partisan affair. We take sides. Indeed, we must do so, because in how we construct our past we are trying to control and transform our present and our futures.

Greer has always ridden shotgun to the women's liberation movement. She is not a joiner and has never bothered with collective projects or party lines. Her valuable outrageousness and irreverence have always produced useful controversy. Her work has always opened new battlefields. *The Obstacle Race: The Fortunes of Women Painters and their Work* was the first salvo in a battery of books about women and art.[3] In the 1980s, Greer, as always in the vanguard, produced *Sex and Destiny: The Politics of Human Fertility*, a text marked by her romantic admiration of the extended Family.

Now, in developing the notion of the Family with a capital F I am striving for a description of an organic structure which can be shown in law, in genetic examination, in patterns of land ownership and parish records, but has its realm principally in hearts and minds . . . it is precisely in kinds of awareness, patterns of feeling, concepts of self, that the Family has its existence. Where Family is strong, individuals take first their friends, and then their lovers from inside its sphere of influence.[4]

In the beginning, we identified the family – and, indeed, the Family – as the cultural, economic and psychological structure, where the oppression of women was reproduced and enforced. The Family was, and is, one of the most effective institutions for the policing of women. Within the Family, role, identity and function become one. In her critique of 'pro-family feminism' Judith Stacey has this to say.

An attack on sexual politics is an attack on the radical core of feminist thought and practice – the recognition that the subordination of women to men is systemic and structural. Friedan, Elshtain, and Greer seek to avoid direct struggles to end this subordination . . . None of them support direct efforts to confront the domination of women by men.[5]

I think she is right. In the late 1960s, for white British feminists like myself who came out of the sexual liberation years, sexual practice – and direct efforts to

confront the domination of women by men – were the beginning. This was the
starting-point for an ever-deepening analysis of the sexual division of labour in
the home and in the workplace, in the field of representation, culture, ideology.
We could leave no stones unlifted, whatever was underneath them. And the
looking always involved seeing who was sitting on top of the stone clutching
their vested interests and the status quo. That analysis became even more
searching and, I hope, more self-critical. The Blackwomen's movement and the
international perspectives of feminism have transformed the emphases and
directions of the women's movement. We still have everything to fight for,
everything to gain.[6]

All of us within the women's liberation movement and those of us engaged
upon the feminist project of changing society are bound to history and to the
world we struggle to transform. Now, more than twenty years on a generation of
young women for whom feminism is a normative discourse, a moral ideology
full of 'shoulds', 'oughts', 'don'ts' and 'mustn'ts'. I find that feminists are
suspected of being against fornication, pleasure – whatever that means – sexy
jokes and revealing clothes. It is assumed that what we say is predictable. At the
'Homosexuality, Which Homosexuality?' Conference in Amsterdam in December 1987 Celia Kitzinger made a brief and rousing speech from the
platform on the theme of essentialism versus social constructivism in sexual
identity.[7] She suggested that the most pressing task was the deconstruction of
patriarchy and the heterosexual system. She declared that her understanding of
her Lesbianism was inseparable from her feminism. She was warmly applauded. But one of the first questioners in the hall prefaced her comments by
saying, 'I know what the feminist will say to this . . . ' She assumed that she
knew how Celia Kitzinger would respond when in fact she did not. Whenever
we assume that we know what someone will say, we are no longer talking to
them or engaging with their arguments. We can dismiss them outright.

The problem here is the way in which the women's liberation movement has,
in the popular mind at least, constructed WOMAN as an unproblematic and
unified category. Blackwomen have triumphantly exposed the fallacy embedded
in this assumption. We do not all define ourselves, and what it means to be a
woman, in the same way. How could we? Some of us see ourselves as mothers,
others do not. Some of us define ourselves as Lesbians and therefore as
something other than woman. Just as woman herself is a fractured identity, so
too feminism is a fractured politics. But male power too has many faces.
Feminism has acquired a rigid and dogmatic public face. However, my question
is not 'Is this really the case?' but 'In whose interests will it be if this appears to
be true?' It is not good news for us, but it is for our so-called masters. We need
to be wise virgins, flexible in our strategies, more imaginative than the
opposition. We have a great deal of work to do.

Our original aim was always the transformation of the world so that the
accident of sex was not oppressive to women. Thus, our goal was nothing less
than the destruction of the gender system which maintained men's power over
us. We all know that we are not safe in this world; we are not valued; we go
hungry, unpaid, our lives are cheap and at risk. The bodies at the bottom of the
pyramid of power will always be the bodies of women. And so we must insist

upon our rights and needs, as women; even when the obliteration of the invidious fact of sexual difference and all its works is at the core of our politics. The utopian impulse within the women's liberation movement must always be Mary Wollstonecraft's wild wish of feminism. 'A wild wish has just flown from my heart to my head, and I will not stifle it, though it may excite a horse-laugh. I do earnestly wish to see the distinction of sex confounded in society . . . '[8] But a political desire is not a belief. There is no core of feminist beliefs. That is the descent into faith. Feminism is not a morality, but a politics; not a credo, but an analysis.

What has been the place of feminist fiction within feminism? Well, it is there that we have worried away at the contradictions, imagined our radical solutions, tested theory against practice, re-visioned our lives. It is the place where we have spoken to each other, revealed our doubts and written our most disturbing warnings. One of the most terrifying books I have ever read, Margaret Atwood's *The Handmaid's Tale*, imagines a religious dystopia after the failure of feminism. Women are the absolute property of men and of the state. In the fundamentalist Christian republic of Gilead the reproductive capacity of the Lord's Handmaidens is their only value. The hierarchies and divisions between women, already neatly in place in our day, have now been systematized. Identity and role are fused; we are Aunts, Wives, Marthas, Handmaids, Whores. Women are now abused and murdered not only by individual men, but by the State. 'Women were not protected then . . . There is more than one kind of freedom, said Aunt Lydia. Freedom to and freedom from. In the days of anarchy, it was freedom to. Now you are being given freedom from. Don't underrate it.'[9] But of course, we the women, all the women, have never been free. Maybe some of us 'seemed to be able to choose' (p. 35). And, as in all dystopian fables, the most frightening aspects of *The Handmaid's Tale* are the details which are already true.

The balance of sexual power between women and men is carefully measured.

> To be a man, watched by women. It must be entirely strange. To have them watching him all the time. To have them wondering, What's he going to do next? To have them flinch when he moves, even if it's a harmless enough move, to reach for an ashtray perhaps . . .
> It must be just fine.
> It must be hell.
> It must be very silent. (pp. 98, 99)

This book began with my reflections upon women's silence. It is men who impose that silence and women who wonder and watch. Do men even notice that the women watch, in anger, indifference, fear? More crucially, do the women know that they watch – and why? Atwood writes against male power and against theocracy. She takes up the imaginative challenge of what happens to women in an extremist religious state. The reinforcement of patriarchy is achieved by reversing history. We fought for the right to own property, to cease to be property. In the Republic of Gilead all the women's computer cards are cancelled, all the women lose their jobs. They again become the property of men. When I heard Atwood speaking about her book in 1986, she pointed out how it had been done, smiled at us grimly and said: 'Resist the computerization of money.' In Atwood's text there are men who do not support the state. These are the dissidents who aid the women in revolt to escape. There will always be some members of an oppressor class who take sides with the oppressed; just as there are men now who say that they are supporters of the liberation of women; just as there were white folks who worked with the Black civil rights activists and said that they supported Black Power. But the question remains: how can we trust them?

Perhaps none of us can be trusted all of the time. On the fifth page of her spirited, intelligent defence of feminist literary history, a project with which I find myself wholly in sympathy, Janet Todd sold the pass to the enemy. She declared, 'I will start with the early days in the 1970s, often concentrating on Elaine Showalter . . . By doing so I am aware that I am omitting many other lines of development, especially those of black and lesbian critics whose work is at the moment among the richest and the most provocative in the socio-historical mode.'[10] In fact, while I was reading her book I let this pass. I said to myself – well, she can't write about everything, even if, by her own admission, her book would be richer and more provocative too, were she to have included work by Black and Lesbian critics. But as I read on, I realized that this was not space-saving, but open racism and anti-Lesbianism. Commenting on the early American feminist critics, Todd has this to say in their, and her own, defence. 'None the less the wholesale criticism seems excessive. Showalter, Moers, Spacks, Gilbert and Gubar may have been shortsighted or partially blind – clearly they were so in many different ways – but "homophobic" and "racist" do not appear helpful or appropriate adjectives for them' (p. 37). If you do not want to face the implications of an accusation, while acknowledging its justice, you can call it something different. Thus, racist and anti-Lesbian critics become 'short-sighted' or 'partially blind'. Needless to say, I searched Janet Todd's bibliography in vain for Meena Alexander, Barbara Christian, Gloria Joseph, Audre Lorde, Lauretta Ngcobo, Dorothea Smartt, Barbara Smith, Maud Sulter, Alice Walker. Alice Walker makes a footnote appearance, where she is accused of 'abuse' and 'attempted coercion' for pointing out that, in refusing to consider Black writing and Black experience, her colleague Patricia Spacks was being racist. Apparently, it is 'abusive' and 'coercive' to be angry if you are written out of history, silenced and ignored. The bitter truth of the matter is that, were Todd to have considered work by Blackwomen, Lesbians, Blacklesbians, it would have been quite impossible for her to write her book as she has done. All her emphases and terms of reference would have been different.

On the London streets I met a young woman I had known in a university feminist group. She was very smartly dressed. She was now working for a large publishing group. We talked for a while: 'Are you still a feminist?' I asked cautiously. She looked at me, astonished. 'You can't unsee things,' she said. 'You can't go back. You can only go on.' And she told me about her work in the local women's centre, her changed life. But what she said is not true. You can 'unsee things'. And – as I say – you can call them something different. So we can, most assuredly, go backwards. Michèle Roberts, in an interview with *The Guardian*, had this to say:

> ... As you get older you learn to receive. For me, the word passive used to have very negative connotations; associations of female masochism. Now I call it being accepting. You can be that, then at other times you can be very giving. Feminism has done lots of things for me. All my strength comes from it. Through it I have reclaimed being feminine after years with a crew cut and big boots.[11]

I wouldn't have thought that being 'passive' or 'feminine' had changed their political meanings within the context of our still resolutely patriarchal culture, however we choose to delude ourselves.

The notion of 'false consciousness' is now very unfashionable indeed in left-wing and feminist circles. Andrea Dworkin's collection of analytical essays *Right-Wing Women: The Politics of Domesticated Females* has, at its root, a brilliant political connection between radical feminists and domesticated women. The two groups of women share the same analysis of men and of patriarchy. One group chooses to get the best deal it can by conformism and flattery; the other group chooses the raw discomfort of liberty. Both are fully conscious of what they do. Both groups of women live at risk.

> Right-wing women see that within the system in which they live they cannot make their bodies their own, but they can agree to privatised male ownership: keep it one-on-one, as it were. They know that they are valued for their sex – their sex organs and their reproductive capacity – and so they try to up their value: through cooperation, manipulation, conformity; through displays of affection or attempts at friendship; through submission and obedience; and especially through the use of euphemism – 'femininity,' 'total woman,' 'good,' 'maternal instinct,' 'motherly love.'[12]

I have certainly met domesticated women whose cynicism is quite astonishing. But I do not believe that this is always the case. Many women are too brainwashed, broken-spirited, hungry and downtrodden to take action on their own behalf. Others sincerely believe that their oppression is joyfully chosen. Many more busily tell themselves comfortable lies, to be spared the pain of thinking. I am quite certain that at one time or another I have belonged to every category. For these are the realities of oppression and power; this is how oppression and suppression work within every subject group.

I do not believe that our analysis of the economic control men hold over women should ever be separated from our analysis of the heterosexual system. Women can never choose or define their relationship to men unless they are economically independent. This is not to deny the existence of other pressures and restraints that might make even a rich and financially autonomous woman subservient to men. But without direct access to and control over her own wealth no woman has any real choice at all. And as long as men rule women we shall never be economically free. As long as we are not in control of our own wealth, or paid justly for our labour, we will never be free of male rule. The circle is complete. 'Feminists appear to think that equal pay for equal work is a simple reform whereas it is not reform at all; it is revolution. Feminists have refused to face the fact that equal pay for equal work is impossible as long as men rule women, and right-wing women have refused to forget it.'[13] Dworkin is right. Feminist women and right-wing women are divided, not by their analysis of the heterosexual system, but by their methods of surviving in a world ruled by men in which women are exploited, brutalized and abused. This is not a counsel of despair. How can it be? We have analysed our situations, named our antagonists, begun our long revolution. But we must continue the struggle to see clearly, speak honestly, live differently.

I recently had a discussion with a married woman, a feminist, who fully understood the political meanings of her husband's objectional behaviour. 'But,' she said, as if this was the rock upon which our conversation must irrevocably founder, 'I love him.'

The parameters of our discussion had been limited by my friend so that my next question was out of court. 'How can you love him? If he behaves like that and won't change, why don't you leave him?' I was being rational. She was talking about her feelings. I was talking about her dignity as a human being. She was talking about her economic prospects in a nasty world. And so what do we do when we come to the end of the loving struggle with the men in our lives? Whether at work, in the kitchen, or in bed? What do we do when going on means giving in?

Women's love has always meant giving way, giving up, giving in – in fiction and in our lives. We need a new vision of love which involves saying and living a no which means no and a yes which is spoken from a position of strength and certainty – an assent that is not coerced, not by poverty, not by manipulation, not by fear. We are the only oppressed group who are actually required to be in love with our oppressors. We are the only group required to invite and enjoy aggression. The apparently natural connection between pleasure and pain, which is the hallmark of romantic love, is also the basis for the sado-masochistic construction of heterosexuality, the sadistic meanings of masculinity, and the masochistic meanings of femininity.[14] Pleasure, pain and love – in the largest sense, which includes the sexual – are and have always been the classic territory of feminist fiction. Can we imagine a world without force? A world based on mutual consent?

In dangerous times, when most of us are keeping quiet or backing away from our more radical proposals, I see little room for compromise. One of the danger signs which indicate that someone is about to begin compromising their feminist politics, or indicating that they never had any to begin with, is the moment when they declare that they are re-claiming something: marriage, the family, love, femininity or traditional religion. Re-claiming is not the same thing as challenging, transforming, confronting; an altogether less comfortable enterprise. For feminism will always be uncomfortable, unpopular, controversial and frightening. Feminism really is the politics which touches the parts of our lives no other politics will reach. This nasty mess of mixed motives, misery and joy, self-interest, self-deceit and liberating understanding is the stuff of sexual politics. This has been, and remains, our subject.

An older woman I know – she is in her mid-fifties – was telling me an appalling story of sexual harassment at work. It was high summer, and we stopped our bicycles in a cut wheat field. Suddenly she waved both her arms in the air, laughing. 'We must never lay down our arms!' she cried. 'We must never lay down our pens either!' I shouted back. But we laughed and laughed, because we were both on the same side of the barricades. We had talked for hours; we were very different women; I had understood her, she had understood me. I want a better life for all of us; fine prose, and more wine.

Notes

1 Elizabeth Wilson, *Prisons of Glass* (London, Methuen, 1986), pp. 250–1. *Hidden Agendas: Theory, Politics and Experience in the Women's Movement* (London, Tavistock, 1986). For an analysis of British feminism since the 1960s see Sheila Rowbottom, *The Past is Before Us* (1989; London, Penguin, 1990). For the American radical feminist version of how it was see Andrea Dworkin, *Letters from a War Zone: Writings 1976–1988* (London, Secker & Warburg, 1988).

2 Germaine Greer, 'The Politics of Sexuality', *The Madwoman's Underclothes: Essays and Occasional Writings 1968–1985* (London, Picador, 1986), pp. 37, 40 (first pubished in *Oz*, May 1970.

3 Germaine Greer, *The Obstacle Race: The Fortunes of Women Painters and Their Work* (London, Secker & Warburg, 1979. Here are a few initial suggestions for others: R. Parker and G. Pollock, *Old Mistresses: Women, Art and Ideology* (London, Routledge & Kegan Paul, 1981); Roszika Parker, *The Subversive Stitch: Embroidery and the Making of the Feminine* (London, Women's Press, 1984); Pamela Gerrish Nunn, *Victorian Women Artists* (London, Women's Press, 1987) – see also her collection of their writings, *Canvassing* (London, Camden, 1986); Jan Marsh, *The Pre-Raphaelite Sisterhood* (New York, St Martin's, 1985); Hilary Robinson (ed.), *Visibly Female: Feminism and Art. An Anthology* (London, Camden, 1987). Camden Press now runs a series 'Women on Art': write to Camden Press Ltd, 43 Camden Passage, London N1 8EB for their catalogue. I believe they are still trading, but in any case they should still have back stock.

4 Germaine Greer, *Sex and Destiny* (1984; London, Pan, 1985), pp. 223.

5 Judith Stacey, 'Are Feminists Afraid to Leave Home? The Challenge of Conservative Pro-Family Feminism', in Juliet Mitchell and Ann Oakley (eds), *What Is Feminism? A Re-examination* (Oxford, Blackwell, 1986), pp. 208–37, 221. See also Stacey's further thoughts: Deborah Rosenfelt and Judith Stacey, 'Review Essay: Second Thoughts on the Second Wave', *Feminist Review*, no. 27 (Autumn 1987), pp. 77–95.

6 Two useful starting-points on feminism outside Britain and the West are Kimari Jayawardena, *Feminism and Nationalism in the Third World* (London, Zed, 1986) and *Third World/Second Sex*, compiled by Miranda Davies, vol. 2 (London, Zed, 1987; vol. 1 was published in 1983). Both have excellent bibliographies for further reading.

7 See Celia Kitzinger, *The Social Construction of Lesbianism* (London, Sage, 1987).

8 Mary Wollstonecraft, *A Vindication of the Rights of Woman*, ed. Miriam Brody Kramnick (1792; London, Penguin, 1975), p. 147.

9 Margaret Atwood, *The Handmaid's Tale* (1985; London, Virago, 1987), p. 34.

10 Janet Todd, *Feminist Literary History: A Defence* (Cambridge, Polity, 1988), p. 5.

11 Michèle Roberts, interviewed in *The Guardian*, 27 May 1987.
12 Andrea Dworkin, *Right-Wing Women: The Politics of Domesticated Females* (London, Women's Press, 1983), p. 69.
13 Ibid., p. 67.
14 I have not engaged with the whole exhausting debate over Lesbian sado-masochism. Being a somewhat literal-minded believer in reading both sides of an argument, I sat down with SAMOIS (ed.), *Coming to Power: Writing and Graphics on Lesbian S/M* (Boston, Mass., Alyson, 1981, 1982) and Robin Ruth Linden (ed.), *Against Sadomasochism: A Radical Feminist Analysis* (California, Frog in the Well, 1982). Closer to home is the debate over the London Lesbian and Gay Centre in London. Should the S/M groups be allowed to use the centre – or should they be banned? See Susan Ardill and Sue O'Sullivan, 'Upsetting an Applecart: Difference, Desire and Lesbian Sadomasochism', *Feminist Review*, no. 23 (Summer 1986), special issue, 'Social Feminism: Out of the Blue', pp. 31–57. I have talked at length about the issue with various Lesbians, some of whom were all for S/M and some of whom were violently against. It seems to me that what S/M does is create a 'sexual theatre' where we can play roles, act out fantasies without asking where the roles and fantasies actually come from. And I could never be part of a performance where someone else had written the script. In short, I find myself in agreement with Ardill and O'Sullivan when they say:

> What we feel as women from a thousand different realities, as oppressed and oppressor, actor and object, is a vital *part* of what goes into our political analysis as feminists . . . But we don't base our understanding of women's continuing oppression and exploitation on it . . . Any of us must be able to develop politics which make us sensitive and open to learning from the experience of others *and* provide us with the tools and a framework for critically assessing theoretical analyses and daily political life. (p. 56)

A less tolerant but no less cogent and persuasive analysis of the implications of S/M can be found in the last chapter, 'The Murderer as Misogynist?' of Deborah Cameron and Elizabeth Frazer's study of sexual murder, *The Lust to Kill: A Feminist Investigation of Sexual Murder* (Cambridge, Polity, 1987). For those of us who emerged from the 1960s with our doubts about sexual liberation, the S/M debate has been a replay rather than foreplay. Nothing new under the sun, as the preacher says. For a brilliant, passionate and shrewd analysis of the debates surrounding the construction of sexuality in all its forms, see Sheila Jeffreys, *Anticlimax: A Feminist Perspective on the Sexual Revolution* (London, Women's Press, 1990).

Bibliography

All the books, articles, poems – and even cartoons – listed here have contributed to my thinking in substantial ways, and therefore to the making of this book. Detailed, annotated references to the books or writing cited in the text will be found in the notes at the end of each chapter. I hesitated for a long time before deciding to leave the books written by men alongside the books written by women in this bibliography. When I have hunted for women's books in men's bibliographies the numbers have been startlingly few. You will find that the reverse situation is reflected in this bibliography. Living and thinking differently from the heteropatriarchal world takes a great deal of emotional and intellectual effort; there are not many books written by men which offer any help whatsoever. The ones that do are fictional/poetical. But that is another story.

As the whole bibliography is quite extensive, I have divided it into three sections: the first including fictional/poetical books, the second books of a critical/theoretical/ historical nature and the third articles, journals and newsletters.

Fictional/Poetical/Autobiographical

Angelou, Maya, *I Know Why the Caged Bird Sings* (1969; London, Virago, 1984).
——*Gather Together in My Name* (1974; London, Virago, 1985).
——*Singin' and Swingin' and Getting' Merry Like Christmas* (1976, London, Virago, 1985).
——*The Heart of A Woman* (1981; London, Virago, 1986).
——*All God's Children Need Travelling Shoes* (1986; London, Virago, 1987).
Attic Press Fairytales for Feminists series, *Rapunzel's Revenge* (Dublin, Attic, 1985).
——*Ms [sic] Muffet and Others* (Dublin, Attic, 1986).
——*Mad and Bad Fairies* (Dublin, Attic, 1987).
——*Sweeping Beauties* (Dublin, Attic, 1989).
Atwood, Margaret, *The Handmaid's Tale* (1985; London, Virago, 1987).
Barton, Rachel (Sita), *The Scarlet Thread: An Indian Woman Speaks* (London, Virago, 1987).
Bennett, Arnold, *The Old Wives' Tale* (1908; London, Pan, 1964, 1975).
Birtha, Becky, *Lover's Choice* (1987; London, Women's Press, 1988).
Blackwomantalk (ed.), *Black Women Talk Poetry* (London, Black Womantalk Ltd, 1987).
Brown, Rita Mae, *Rubyfruit Jungle* (1973; New York, Bantam, 1977).
Burford, Barbara, *The Threshing Floor* (London, Sheba, 1986).

Clausen, Jan, *Sinking, Stealing* (London, Women's Press, 1985).
——*The Proserpine Papers* (1988, London, Women's Press, 1989).
Cobham, Rhonda and Collins, Merle (eds), *Watchers and Seekers: Creative Writing by Black Women in Britain* (London, Women's Press, 1987).
Coles, Diana, *The Clever Princess* (London, Sheba, 1983).
Collins, Merle, *Angel* (London, Women's Press, 1987).
——*Rain, Darling* (London, Women's Press, 1990).
Cruikshank, Margaret (ed.), *New Lesbian Writing: An Anthology* (San Francisco, Grey Fox, 1984).
Deming, Barbara, *A Humming Under My Feet: A Book of Travail* (London, Women's Press, 1985).
Devi, Mahasweta, 'Draupadi', from her collection *Agnigarbha* (Calcutta, 1978); and trans. by Gayatri Chekravorty Spivak, *In Other Worlds: Essays in Cultural Politics* (London, Methuen, 1987), pp. 179–96.
Dhingra, Leena, *Amritvela* (London, Women's Press, 1987).
Duffy, Maureen, *That's How It Was* (1962; London, Virago, 1983).
——*The Microcosm* (1986; London, Virago, 1989).
Duncker, Patricia (ed.), *In and Out of Time: Lesbian Feminist Fiction* (London, Onlywomen, 1990).
Dworkin, Andrea, *The New Woman's Broken Heart: Short Stories* (San Francisco, Frog in the Well, 1986).
——*Ice and Fire* (London, Secker & Warburg), 1986).
——*Mercy* (London, Secker & Warburg, 1990).
Edwards, Nicky, *Mud* (London, Women's Press, 1986).
——*Stealing Time* (London, Onlywomen, 1990).
Emecheta, Buchi, *Head Above Water* (London, Fontana, 1986).
Fairbairns, Zoë, *Stand We At Last* (1983; London, Pan, 1984).
Fairbairns, Zoë, Maitland, Sara, Miner, Valerie, Roberts, Michèle and Wandor, Michelene, *Tales I Tell My Mother: A Collection of Feminist Short Stories* (London, Journeyman, 1978).
Forbes, Caroline, *The Needle on Full: Lesbian Feminist Science Fiction* (London, Onlywomen, 1985).
Galford, Ellen, *Moll Cutpurse: Her True Story* (Edinburgh, Stramullion, 1984).
——*The Fires of Bride* (London, Women's Press, 1986).
——*Queendom Come* (London, Virago, 1990).
Green, Jen and Lefanu, Sarah (eds), *Despatches from the Frontiers of the Female Mind* (London, Women's Press, 1985).
Grewal, Shabnam, Kay, Jackie, Landor, Liliane, Lewis, Gail and Parmar, Pratibha (eds), *Charting the Journey: Writings by Black and Third World Women* (London, Sheba, 1988).
Haden Elgin, Suzette, *Native Tongue* (1984; London, Women's Press, 1985).
——*The Judas Rose* (1987; London, Women's Press, 1988).
Hall, Radclyffe, *The Well of Loneliness* (1928; London, Virago, 1983).
Hanscombe, Gillian and Namjoshi, Suniti, *Flesh and Paper* (Seaton, Devon, Jezebel, 1986).
Hazeley, Iyamidé, *Ripples and Jagged Edges* (London, Zora, n.d.).
Hemmings, Susan (ed.), *A Wealth of Experience: The Lives of Older Women* (London, Pandora, 1985).
Hensman, Savitri, *Flood at the Door* (London, Centerprise Trust, 1979).
Hurcombe, Linda (ed.), *Sex and God: Some Varieties of Women's Religious Experience* (London, Routledge & Kegan Paul, 1987).

Johnson, Amryl, *Sequins for a Ragged Hem* (London, Virago, 1988).
Jones, Jo, *Come Come* (London, Sheba, 1983).
La Tourette, Aileen, *Cry Wolf* (London, Virago, 1986).
——with Maitland, Sara, *Weddings and Funerals* (London, Brilliance, 1984).
Lawrence, D. H., 'The Man Who Died', *The Short Novels*, vol. 2 (London, Heinemann, 1972).
Le Guin, Ursula, *The Left Hand of Darkness* (1969; London, Futura, 1983).
Leduc, Violette, *La Bâtarde* (1964; London, Virago, 1985).
Levine, June, *Sisters: The Personal Story of an Irish Feminist* (Dublin, Hard River Press, 1982).
Livia, Anna, *Relatively Norma* (London, Onlywomen, 1982).
——*Accommodation Offered* (London, Women's Press, 1985).
——*Incidents Involving Warmth: Lesbian Feminist Love Stories* (London, Onlywomen, 1986).
——*Bulldozer Rising* (London, Onlywomen, 1988).
——*Saccharin Cyanide: Short Stories* (London, Onlywomen, 1990).
——(ed., with Lilian Mobin), *The Pied Piper: Lesbian Feminist Fiction* (London, Onlywomen, 1989).
Lorde, Audre, *The Cancer Journals* (San Francisco, Spinsters Ink, 1980).
——*Zami: A New Spelling of My Name* (1982; London, Sheba, 1984).
——*Our Dead Behind Us* (1986; London, Sheba, 1987).
McEwen, Christian (ed.), *Naming the Waves: Contemporary Lesbian Poetry* (London, Virago, 1988).
——(ed., with Sue O'Sullivan, *Out the Other Side: Contemporary Lesbian Writing* (London, Virago, 1988).
Maitland, Sara, *Daughter of Jerusalem* (1978; London, Sphere, 1981).
——*Telling Tales: Short Stories* (London: Journeyman, 1983).
——*Virgin Territory* (London, Michael Joseph, 1984).
——*A Book of Spells* (1987: Methuen: London, 1988).
——*Arky Types* with Michelene Wandor (Methuen: London, 1987).
Manning, Rosemary, *The Chinese Garden* (1962; London, Brilliance, 1984).
——*A Time and A Time: An Autobiography* (1971; London, Marion Boyars, 1986).
——*A Corridor of Mirrors* (London, Women's Press, 1987).
Maraini, Darcia, *Letters to Marina* (1981; London, Camden, 1987).
March, Caeia, *Three Ply Yarn* (London, Women's Press: 1986).
——*The Hide and Seek Files* (London, Women's Press, 1988).
Menchú, Rigoberta, *I . . . Rigoberta Menchú: An Indian Woman in Guatemala*, ed. and intr. by Elisabeth Burgos-Debray (1983; London, Verso Editions & NLB, 1984).
Meulenbelt, Anja, *The Shame is Over* (1976; London, Women's Press, 1980).
Miller, Isabel, *Patience and Sarah* (1969; London, Women's Press, 1979).
Miller, Jill, *Happy as a Dead Cat* (London, Women's Press, 1983).
Miller Gearhart, Sally, *The Wanderground* (1979; London, Women's Press, 1985).
Millett, Kate, *Flying* (1974, St Albans, Paladin, 1976).
Miner, Valerie, *Murder in the English Department* (London, Women's Press, 1982).
Mohin, Lilian, (ed.), *One Foot on the Mountain: British Feminist Poetry 1969–1979* (London, Onlywomen, 1979).
——(ed.), *Beautiful Barbarians: Lesbian Feminist Poetry* (London, Onlywomen, 1986).
——(ed.), with Sheila Shulman), *The Reach and Other Stories: Lesbian Feminist Fiction* (London, Onlywomen, 1984).
Molteno, Marion, *A Language in Common* (London, Women's Press, 1987).
Morgan, Claire (Patricia Highsmith), *The Price of Salt* (1952; republished as Patricia

Highsmith, *Carol*, Tallahassee, Fla, Naiad, 1984). (London, Bloomsbury, 1990).

Morrison, Toni, *Beloved* (London, Chatto & Windus, 1987).

Mukherjee, Bharati, *The Tiger's Daughter* (1971; Ontario, Penguin, 1987).

——*Wife* (1975; Ontario, Penguin, 1987).

——*Darkness: Short Fiction* (Ontario, Penguin, 1985).

——*The Middleman and Other Stories* (Ontario, Viking, 1988).

Namjoshi, Suniti, *Feminist Fables* (London, Sheba, 1981).

——*The Conversations of Cow* (London, Women's Press, 1985).

——*The Blue Donkey Fables* (London, Women's Press, 1988).

——*The Mothers of Maya Diip* (London, Women's Press, 1989).

——*Because of India* (London, Onlywomen, 1989).

——with Gillian Hanscombe, *Flesh and Paper* (Seaton, Devon, Jezebel, 1986).

Ngcobo, Loretta, *Let It Be Told: Black Women Writers in Britain* (London, Pluto, 1987).

Nichols, Grace, *i is a long-memoried woman* (London, Karnak House, 1983).

——*Whole of A Morning Sky* (London, Virago, 1986).

Oakley, Ann, *Taking It Like A Woman* (London, Cape, 1984).

O'Rourke, Rebecca, *Jumping the Cracks* (London, Virago, 1987).

Palmer, Jane, *The Planet Dweller* (London, Women's Press, 1985).

Perkins Gilman, Charlotte, *Herland* (1915; London, Women's Press, 1979).

Piercy, Marge, *Woman on the Edge of Time* (1976; London, Women's Press, 1979).

——*The High Cost of Living* (1978; London, Women's Press, 1979).

Prescod, Martha, *Land of Rope and Tory* (London, Akira, 1985).

Prince, Marcy, *The History of Mary Prince*, ed. Moira Ferguson (1831; London, Pandora, 1987).

Randhawa, Ravinder, *A Wicked Old Woman* (London, Women's Press, 1987).

Rich, Adrienne, *Of Woman Born: Motherhood as Experience and Institution* (1976; London, Virago, 1977).

——*On Lies, Secrets and Silence: Selected Prose 1966–1978* (New York, Norton, 1979).

——*The Fact of a Doorframe: Poems Selected and New 1950–1984* (New York, Norton, 1984).

——*Blood, Bread, and Poetry: Selected Prose 1979–1985* (New York, Norton, 1986).

Riley, Joan, *The Unbelonging* (London, Women's Press, 1985).

——*Waiting in the Twilight* (London, Women's Press, 1987).

——*Romance* (London, Women's Press, 1988).

Roberts, Michèle, *A Piece of the Night* (London, Women's Press, 1978).

——*The Visitation* (London, Women's Press, 1983).

——*The Wild Girl* (London, Methuen, 1984).

——*The Book of Mrs Noah* (London, Methuen, 1987, 1988).

Roche, Christine, *i'm not a feminist, but . . .* (London, Virago, 1985).

Rule, Jane, *Desert of the Heart* (1964; London, Pandora, 1986).

——*This Is Not For You* (1970; London, Pandora, 1987).

——*Against the Season* (1971; London, Pandora, 1988).

Russ, Joanna, *Extra(ordinary) People* (New York, St Martin's, 1984).

——*The Female Man* (1975; London, Women's Press, 1985).

——*The Two of Them* (1978; London, Women's Press, 1985).

Sarton, May, *Mrs. Stevens Hears The Mermaids Singing* (1965: W. W. Norton & Company: New York, 1975).

——*Journal of a Solitude* (1973; London, Women's Press, 1985).

——*As We Are Now* (1973; London, Women's Press, 1983).

——*A Reckoning* (1978; London, Women's Press, 1984).

——*Recovering: A Journal* (New York, Norton, 1980).

——*The Magnificent Spinster* (1985; London, Women's Press, 1986).
——*After the Stroke: A Journal* (London, Women's Press, 1988).
——*The Education of Harriet Hatfield* (1989; London, Women's Press, 1990).
Schneidermann, Stuart, *Jacques Lacan: The Death of an Intellectual Hero* (Cambridge, Mass., University Press, 1983).
The Seven Sisters: Selected Chinese Folk Tales (anon.) (Beijing, Foreign Languages Press, 1965).
Shan, Sharan-Jeet, *In My Own Name: An Autobiography* (London, Women's Press, 1986).
Shockley, Ann Allen, *Loving Her* (1974; Tallahassee, Fla, Naiad, 1987).
Sistren, *Lionheart Gal: Life Stories of Jamaican Women* (London, Women's Press, 1986).
Slovo, Gillian, *Death by Analysis* (London, Women's Press, 1986).
Steedman, Carolyn, *Landscape for a Good Woman: A Story of Two Lives* (London, Virago, 1986).
Stefan, Verena, *Shedding* (1975; London, Women's Press, 1979).
Swallow, Jean (ed.), *Out From Under: Sober Dykes and Our Friends* (San Francisco, Spinsters Ink, 1983).
Wakefield, Hannah, *The Price You Pay* (London, Women's Press, 1987).
Walker, Alice, *Meridian* (1976; London, Women's Press, 1982).
——*The Color Purple* (1982; London, Women's Press, 1983).
——*In Search of Our Mothers' Gardens: Womanist Prose* (1983; London, Women's Press, 1984).
Wandor, Michelene, *Gardens of Eden* (London, Journeyman, 1984).
Ward, Alison, *The Glass Boat* (London, Brilliance, 1983).
Warner-Vieyra, Myriam, *Juletane* (1982; London, Heinemann, 1987).
Wilson, Anna, *Cactus* (London, Onlywomen, 1980).
——*Altogether Elsewhere* (London, Onlywomen, 1985).
Wilson, Barbara, *Ambitious Women* (1982; London, Women's Press, 1983).
——*Murder in the Collective* (1984; London, Women's Press, 1984).
——*Sisters of the Road* (1986; London, Women's Press, 1987).
——*Cows and Horses* (1988; London, Virago, 1989).
——*The Dog Collar Murders* (London, Virago, 1989).
Wilson, Elizabeth, *Mirror Writing: An Autobiography* (London: Virago, 1982).
——*Prisons of Glass* (London, Methuen, 1986).
Wings, Mary, *She Came Too Late* (London, Women's Press, 1986).
——*She Came in A Flash* (London, Women's Press, 1988).
Winterson, Jeanette, *Oranges are not the Only Fruit* (London, Pandora, 1985).
——*The Passion* (London, Bloomsbury, 1987).
——*Sexing the Cherry* (London, Bloomsbury, 1989).
Wittig, Monique, *Les Guérillères* (1969; New York, Avon, 1973).
Wood, Elizabeth, *Mothers and Lovers* (London, Bloomsbury, 1988).
Wordsworth, Dorothy, *The Journals of Dorothy Wordsworth*, ed. Mary Moorman (Oxford, Oxford Paperbacks, 1971).

Critical/Theoretical/Historical

Anderson, Linda (ed.), *Plotting Change: Contemporary Women's Fiction* (London, Edward Arnold, 1990).
Armitt, Lucy (ed.), *Where No Man Has Gone Before: Women and Science Fiction* (London, Routledge, 1991).

Baker, Michael, *Our Three Selves: The Life of Radclyffe Hall* (London, Hamish Hamilton, 1985).

Bardsley, Barney, *Flowers in Hell: An Investigation into Women and Crime* (London, Pandora, 1987).

Barrett, Michèle and McIntosh, Mary, *The Anti-Social Family* (London, Verso, 1982).

Battersby, Christine, *Gender and Genius: Towards a Feminist Aesthetics* (London, Women's Press, 1989).

Benstock, Shari, *Women of the Left Bank: Paris 1900–1940* (London, Virago, 1987).

Brown, Wilmette, *Black Women and the Peace Movement* (International Women's Day Convention, funded by GLC Women's Committee; first edition July 1983).

Bryan, Beverley, Dadzie, Stella and Scafe, Suzanne, *The Heart of the Race: Black Women's Lives in Britain* (London, Virago, 1985).

Cady Stanton, Elizabeth, *The Women's Bible* (1895–8; Edinburgh, Polygon, 1985).

Cameron, Deborah, *Feminism and Linguistic Theory* (London, Macmillan, 1985).

——*The Feminist Critique of Language* (London, Routlege & Kegan Paul, 1990).

——with Elizabeth Frazer, *The Lust to Kill: A Feminist Investigation of Sexual Murder* (Cambridge, Polity, 1987).

Campbell, Beatrix, *Wigan Pier Revisited: Poverty and Politics in the 1980s* (London, Virago, 1984).

Caputi, Jane, *The Age of Sex Crime* (London, Women's Press, 1988).

Chapman, Rowena and Rutherford, Jonathan, *Male Order: Unwrapping Masculinity* (London, Lawrence & Wishart, 1988).

Chester, Gail and Nielsen, Sigrid, *In Other Words: Writing as a Feminist* (London, Century Hutchinson, 1987).

Christian, Barbara, *Black Women Novelists: The Development of a Tradition 1892–1976* (Westport, Conn., Greenwood Press, 1980).

Cline, Sally and Spender, Dale, *Reflecting Men at Twice their Natural Size: Why Women Work at Making Men Feel Good* (1987; Glasgow, Fontana, 1988).

Collins, Patricia Hill, *Black Feminist Thought: Knowledge, Consciousness and the Politics of Empowerment* (London, Unwin Hyman, 1990).

Corea, G. Duelli Klein, R., Hasmer, J., Holmes, H. B., Hoskins B., Kishwar, M., Raymond, J., Rowland, R., Steinbacker, R. *Man-Made Women: New Reproductive Technologies Affect Women* (London, Century Hutchinson, 1985).

Coveney, L. Jackson, M., Jeffrey, S., Kaye, L., Mahoney, D., *The Sexuality Papers: Male Sexuality and the Social Control of Women* (London, Hutchinson, 1984).

Cranny-Francis, Anne, *Feminist Fiction: Feminist Uses of Generic Fiction* (Cambridge, Polity, 1990).

Daly, Mary, *The Church and the Second Sex* (1968; Boston, Beacon, 1985).

——*Beyond God the Father: Towards a Philosophy of Women's Liberation* (1973; Boston, Beacon, 1974).

——*Gyn/Ecology: The Metaethics of Radical Feminism* (1978; London, Women's Press, 1979).

——*Pure Lust: Elemental Feminist Philosophy* (London, Women's Press, 1984).

Davies, Miranda (ed.), *Third World/Second Sex*, vol. 2 (London, Zed, 1987).

Dekker, Rudolf M. and Van De Pol, Lotte C., *The Tradition of Female Transvestism in Early Modern Europe* (Basingstoke, Macmillan, 1989).

Delphis, Morgan, *Caribbean and African Languages: Social History, Language Literature and Education* (London, Karia, 1985).

Deming, Barbara, *Remembering Who We Are* (Pagoda–Temple of Love, 1981; distributed by Naiad, Tallahassee, Fla).

Devonish, Hubert, *Language and Liberation: Creole Language Politics in the Caribbean* (London, Karia, 1986).

Dworkin, Andrea, *Woman Hating* (New York, Dutton, 1974).

——*Our Blood: Prophecies and Discourses on Sexual Politics* (1976; London, Women's Press, 1982).

——*Pornography: Men Possessing Women* (1981; London, Women's Press, 1981).

——*Right-Wing Women: The Politics of Domesticated Females* (London, Women's Press, 1983).

——*Intercourse* (London, Secker & Warburg, 1987).

——*Letters From A War Zone: Writings 1976–1987* (London, Secker & Warburg, 1988).

Ecker, Gisela (ed.), *Feminist Aesthetics* (London, Women's Press, 1985).

Ellis, Pat (ed.), *Women of the Caribbean* (London, Zed, 1986).

Evans, Mari (ed.), *Black Women Writers: Arguments and Interviews* (1984; London, Pluto, 1985).

Faderman, Lilian, *Surpassing the Love of Men: Romantic Friendship and Love Between Women from the Renaissance to the Present* (1981; London, Women's Press, 1985).

——*Scotch Verdict* (New York, Quill, 1983).

Feminist Anthology Collective, *No Turning Back: Writings from the Women's Liberation Movement 1975–80* (London, Women's Press, 1981).

Firestone, Shulamith, *The Dialectic of Sex* (1970; London, Women's Press, 1979).

Freer, Jean, *Raging Womyn: In Reply to* Breaching the Peace. *A Comment on the Women's Liberation Movement and the Common Womyn's Peace Camp at Greenham* (A Free Publication, 1984).

Frye, Marilyn, *The Politics of Reality: Essays in Feminist Theory* (Trumansberg, NY, Crossing Press, 1983).

Fuss, Diana, *Essentially Speaking: Feminism, Nature and Difference* (1989; London, Routledge, Chapman & Hall, 1990).

Garcia, Jo and Maitland, Sara, *Walking on the Water: Women Talk About Spirituality* (London, Virago, 1983).

Gerrard, Nikki, *Into the Mainstream: How Feminism has Changed Women's Writing* (London, Pandora, 1989).

Gerrish Nunn, Pamela, *Canvassing* (London, Camden, 1986).

——*Victorian Women Artists* (London, Women's Press, 1987).

Gilbert, Sandra M, and Gubar, Susan, *The Madwoman in the Attic: The Woman Writer and the Nineteenth Century Literary Imagination* (New Haven, Yale University Press, 1979).

Glen, Heather, *Vision and Disenchantment: Blake's Songs and Wordsworth's Lyrical Ballads* (Cambridge, Cambridge University Press, 1983).

Graves, Robert and Hodge, Allan, *The Long-Week End: A Social History of Great Britain 1918–1939* (1940; London, Faber, 1950).

Greene, Gayle and Kahn, Coppélia (eds), *Making a Difference: Feminist Literary Criticism* (London, Methuen, 1985).

Greer, Germaine, *The Female Eunuch* (London, MacGibbon & Kee, 1970).

——*The Obstacle Race: The Fortunes of Women Painters and Their Work* (London, Secker & Warburg, 1979).

——*Sex and Destiny: The Politics of Human Fertility* (1984; London, Picador, 1985).

——*The Madwoman's Underclothes: Essays and Occasional Writings 1968–1985* (London, Picador, 1986).

Hampson, Daphne, *Theology and Feminism* (Oxford, Blackwell, 1990).

Hanmer, Jalna and Saunders, Sheila, *Well-Founded Fear: A Community Study of Violence to Women* (London, Century Hutchinson, 1984).

Hanscombe, Gillian and Humphries, Martin (eds), *Heterosexuality* (London, GMP, 1987).

——and Smyers, Virginia, *Writing For Their Lives: The Modernist Women, 1910–1940*

(London, Women's Press, 1987).

Heilbron, Carolyn G., *Writing a Woman's Life* (London, Women's Press, 1989).

Hoagland, Sarah Lucia and Penelope, Julia (eds), *For Lesbians Only: A Separatist Anthology* (London, Onlywomen, 1988).

Hollis, Patricia, *Women in Public: The Women's Movement 1850–1900. Documents of the Victorian Women's Movement* (London, Allen & Unwin, 1979).

Humm, Maggie, *Feminist Criticism: Women as Contemporary Critics* (Brighton, Harvester, 1986).

Jacobus, Mary (ed.), *Women Writing and Writing about Women* (London, Croom Helm, 1979).

Jardine, Lisa, *Still Harping on Daughters: Women and Drama in the Age of Shakespeare* (Brighton, Harvester, 1983).

Jayawardena, Kumari, *Feminism and Nationalism in the Third World* (London, Zed, 1986).

Jeffreys, Sheila, *The Spinster and Her Enemies: Feminism and Sexuality 1880–1930* (London, Pandora, 1985).

——*Anticlimax: A Feminist Perspective on the Sexual Revolution* (London, Women's Press, 1990).

Johnston, Jill, *Lesbian Nation: The Feminist Solution* (New York, Simon & Schuster, 1973).

Joseph, Gloria I. and Lewis, Jill, *Common Differences: Conflicts in Black and White Feminist Perspectives* (New York, Anchor, 1981).

Kabbani, Rana, *Letter to Christendom* (London, Virago, 1989).

Kanter, Hannah, Lefanu, Sarah, Shah, Shaila and Spedding, Carole, *Sweeping Statements: Writings from the Women's Liberation Movement 1981–1983* (London, Women's Press, 1984).

Kappeler, Suzanne, *The Pornography of Representation* (Cambridge, Polity, 1986).

Kitzinger, Celia, *The Social Construction of Lesbianism* (London, Sage, 1987).

Kristeva, Julia, *Desire in Language: A Semiotic Approach to Literature and Art*, ed. Leon S. Roudiez (1980; Blackwell, 1981).

Le Guin, Ursula, *The Language of the Night: Essays on Fantasy and Science Fiction* (1979; rev. edn London, Women's Press, 1989).

Lefanu, Sarah, *In the Chinks of the World Machine: Feminism and Science Fiction* (London, Women's Press, 1988).

Lerner, Gerda, *The Creation of Patriarchy* (Oxford, Oxford University Press, 1986).

Linden, Robin Ruth, Pagano, D. R., Russell, Diana E. H. and Leigh Stur, Susan, *Against Sadomasochism: A Radical Feminist Analysis* (California, Frog in the Well, 1982).

London Rape Crisis Centre, *Sexual Violence: The Reality for Women* (London, Women's Press, 1984).

Lorde, Audre, *Sister/Outsider: Essays and Speeches* (Trumanberg, NY, Crossing Press, 1984).

——*A Burst of Light* (Ithaca, NY, Firebrand, 1988).

Macdonald, Barbara with Rich, Cynthia, *Look Me in the Eye: Old Women, Aging and Ageism* (London, Women's Press, 1984).

Maitland, Sara, *A Map of the New Country: Women and Christianity* (London, Routledge & Kegan Paul, 1983).

Marks, Elaine and de Courtivron, Isabelle (eds), *New French Feminisms: An Anthology* (Brighton, Harvester, 1981).

Marsh, Jan, *The Pre-Raphaelite Sisterhood* (New York, St Martin's, 1985).

Masson, Jeffrey, *The Assault on Truth: Freud's Suppression of the Seduction Theory* (1984; Harmondsworth, Middx, Penguin, 1985).

——*Against Therapy* (1988; London, Fontana, 1990).
Mavor, Elizabeth, *The Ladies of Llangollen: A Study in Romantic Friendship* (1971; Harmondsworth, Middx, Penguin, 1985).
Miller, Jane, *Women Writing About Men* (London, Virago, 1986).
Millett, Kate, *Sexual Politics* (1970; London, Virago, 1977).
Modleski, Tania, *Loving With A Vengeance: Mass-Produced Fantasies for Women* (1982; London, Methuen, 1984).
Moi, Toril, *Sexual/Textual Politics: Feminist Literary Theory* (London, Methuen, 1985).
——(ed.), *The Kristeva Reader* (Oxford, Blackwell, 1986).
Montefiore, Jane, *Feminism and Poetry: Language, Experience and Identity in Women's Writing* (London, Pandora, 1987).
Monteith, Moira (ed.), *Women's Writing: A Challenge to Theory* (Brighton, Harvester, 1986).
Morley, Dave and Worpole, Ken, *The Republic of Letters: Working Class Writing and Local Publishing* (London, Comedia, 1982).
Mulford, Wendy, *This Narrow Place: Sylvia Townsend Warner and Valentine Ackland, Life, Letters and Politics 1930–1951* (London, Pandora, 1988).
Olsen, Tillie, *Silences* (London, Virago, 1980).
Onlywomen Press Collective, *Love Your Enemy? The Debate between Heterosexual Feminism and Political Lesbianism* (London, Onlywomen, 1981).
——*Breaching the Peace: A Collection of Radical Feminist Papers* (London, Onlywomen, 1983).
O'Rourke, Rebecca, *Reflecting on the Well of Loneliness* (London, Routledge & Kegan Paul, 1989).
Owusu, Kwesi (ed.), *Storm of the Heart: An Anthology of Black Arts and Culture* (London, Camden, 1988).
Oxford University Student Union Women's Committee, *'The Ones Who Just Patronise Seem Genial by Comparison . . . ': Enquiry into Sexual Harassment of Women in Oxford University*, a survey published by the Oxford University Student Union Women's Committee, April 1984.
Pagels, Elaine, *The Gnostic Gospels* (1979; New York, Vintage, 1981).
Palmer, Paulina, *Contemporary Women's Fiction: Narrative Practice and Feminist Theory* (Hemel Hempstead, Harvester, 1989).
Parker, Rozsika, *The Subversive Stitch: Embroidery and the Making of the Feminine* (London, Women's Press, 1984).
——and Pollock, Griselda, *Old Mistresses: Women, Art and Ideology* (London, Routledge & Kegan Paul, 1981).
Poole, Roger, *The Unknown Virginia Woolf* (1978; Brighton, Harvester, 1982).
Radstone, Susannah (ed.), *Sweet Dreams: Sexuality, Gender and Popular Fiction* (London, Lawrence & Wishart, 1988).
Raymond, Janice G., *A Passion for Friends: Towards A Philosophy of Female Affection* (London, Women's Press, 1986).
——*The Transsexual Empire* (1979; Women's Press, 1980).
Rhodes, Dusty and McNeill, Sandra (eds), *Women Against Violence Against Women* (London, Onlywomen, 1985).
Robinson, Hilary, *Visibly Female: Feminism and Art – An Anthology* (London, Camden, 1987).
Roe, Sue (ed.), *Women Reading Women's Writing* (Brighton, Harvester, 1987).
Rowbotham, Sheila, *The Past Is Before Us: Feminism in Action since the 1960s* (1989; London, Penguin, 1990).
Rule, Jane, *Lesbian Images* (1975; Trumansberg, NY, Crossing Press, 1982).
Russ, Joanna, *How To Suppress Women's Writing* (1983; London, Women's Press, 1984).

Russell, Letty M., *Feminist Interpretation of the Bible* (Oxford, Blackwell, 1985).

Samois (ed.), *Coming to Power: Writing and Graphics on Lesbian S/M* (Boston,   Alyson, 1981, 1982).

Sargent, Lydia (ed.), *Women and Revolution: The Unhappy Marriage of Marxism and Feminism* (London, Pluto, 1981).

Saunders, Lesley (ed.), *Glancing Fires: An Investigation into Women's Creativity* (London, Women's Press, 1987).

Schüssler Fiorenza, Elisabeth, *In Memory of Her: A Feminist Theological Reconstruction of Christian Origins* (London, SCM, 1983).

Segal, Lynne (ed.), *What Is To Be Done About The Family? Crisis in the Eighties* (Harmondsworth, Middx, 1983).

——*Is the Future Female? Troubled Thoughts on Contemporary Feminism* (London, Virago, 1987).

Semple, Linda, *An Unsuitable Job for a Woman: A History of Women Crime Writers* (London, Pandora, 1988).

Shepherd, Simon (ed), *The Women's Sharp Revenge: Five Women's Pamphlets from the Renaissance* (London, Fourth Estate, 1985).

Showalter, Elaine, *A Literature of Their Own: British Women Novelists from Brontë to Lessing* (1987; London, Virago, 1978).

——*The Female Malady: Women, Madness and English Culture, 1830–1980* (1985; London, Virago, 1987).

——(ed.), *The New Feminist Criticism: Essays on Women, Literature and Theory* (1985; London, Virago, 1986).

Smith, Barbara, *Towards a Black Feminist Criticism* (1977: Out and Out Books, Pamphlet No 5: Th Crossing Press: Trumansberg, New York, 1980).

Snitow, Ann with Stansell, Christine and Thompson, Sharon (eds), *Desire: The Politics of Sexuality* (1983; London, Virago, 1984).

Spencer, Jane, *The Rise of the Woman Novelist: From Aphra Behn to Jane Austen* (Oxford, Blackwell, 1986).

Spivak, Gayatri Chakravorty, *In Other Worlds: Essays in Cultural Politics* (London, Methuen, 1987).

Tate, Claudia (ed.), *Black Women Writers at Work* (1983; Herts, Oldcastle, 1985).

Taylor, Barbara, *Eve and the New Jerusalem: Socialism and Feminism in the Nineteenth Century* (London, Virago, 1983).

Teish, Luisah, *Jambalaya: The Natural Woman's Book of Personal Charms and Practical Rituals* (San Francisco, Harper & Row, 1985).

Todd, Janet, *Feminist Literary History: A Defence* (Cambridge, Polity, 1988).

——*The Sign of Angellica: Women Writing and Fiction 1660 –1800* (London, Virago, 1989).

Valverde, Mariana, *Sex, Power and Pleasure* (Toronto, Women's Press, 1986).

Ward Jouve, Nicole, *The Streetcleaner: The Yorkshire Ripper Case on Trial* (London, Marion Boyars, 1986).

——*White Woman Speaks with Forked Tongue: Criticism as Autobiography* (London, Routledge, 1991).

Wheelwright, Julie, *Amazons and Military Maids: Women who Dressed as Men in Pursuit of Life, Liberty and Happiness* (London, Pandora, 1989).

Williams, Raymond, *The Country and the City* (1973; St Albans, Paladin, 1975).

Wilson, Amrit, *Finding a Voice: Asian Women in Britain* (1979; London, Virago, 1984).

Wilson, Elizabeth, *Hidden Agendas: Theory, Politics and Experience in the Women's Movement* (London, Tavistock, 1986).

Wollstonecraft, Mary, *A Vindication of the Rights of Woman*, ed. Miriam Brody Kramnick (1792; Harmondsworth, Middx, Penguin, 1975).

Woolf, Virginia, *A Room of One's Own* (1928; Harmondsworth, Middx, Penguin, 1972).
Zipes, Jack (ed.), *Don't Bet on the Prince* (Aldershot, Hants, Gower, 1986).

Articles/Journals/Newsletters

Abraham, Susan and Desai, Nishtha, 'Letter: Giving Details of the Case of Vanita Khera' *Manushi: A Journal About Women and Society*, no. 47, 1988, p. 23.
Amos, Valerie and Pamar, Pratibha, 'Challenging Imperialist Feminism', *Feminist Review*, no. 17 (Autumn 1984), *Many Voices: One Chant: Black Feminist Perspectives*, pp. 3–19.
Anderson, Linda, 'At the Threshold of the Self: Women and Autobiography' in Maria Monteith (ed.), *Women's Writing: A Challenge to Theory* (Brighton, Harvester, 1986), pp. 54–71.
Ardill, Susan and O'Sullivan, Sue, 'Upsetting an Applecart: Difference, Desire and Lesbian Sadomasochism', *Feminist Review*, no. 23 (Summer 1986), Special Issue: 'Socialist Feminism: Out of the Blue', pp. 31–57.
Ahmad, Rukhsana, 'What's Happening to the Women's Presses?', *Spare Rib*, no. 223 (May 1991), pp. 10–13.
Benn, Melissa 'Isn't Sexual Harassment Really About Masculinity?' *Spare Rib*, no. 156 (July 1985), pp. 6–8.
Burford, Barbara, 'The Landscapes Painted on the Inside of my Skin', *Spare Rib*, no. 179 (June 1987), pp. 36–8.
Cameron, Deborah, 'Sex With Your Tutor? It's his Fringe Benefit', *Spare Rib*, no. 99 (November 1980), pp. 23–5. A briefer, edited version is reprinted in Marsha Rowe (ed.), *Spare Rib Reader* (Harmondsworth, Middx, Penguin, 1982), pp. 257–8).
Campbell, Beatrix, 'Sex – A Family Affair', in Lynne Segal (ed.), *What Is To Be Done About The Family? Crisis in The Eighties* (Harmondsworth, Middx, Penguin, 1983), pp. 157–67.
Carmen, Gail, Shaila and Pratibha (participants' first names), 'Becoming Visible: Black Lesbian Discussions', *Feminist Review*, no. 17 (Autumn, 1984), pp. 53–72.
Chandler, Raymond, 'The Simple Art of Murder', in *The Chandler Collection*, vol. 3 (London, Pan, 1980), pp. 175–92.
Cixous, Hélène, 'The Laugh of the Medusa', in Elaine Marks and Isabelle de Courtivron (eds), *New French Feminisms: An Anthology* (Brighton, Harvester, 1981), pp. 245–64).
Coffey, Irene, 'Lesbian Sleuths', *Spare Rib*, no. 217 (October 1990), pp. 34–5.
Collins, Merle, 'Women Writers from the Caribbean', *Spare Rib*, no. 194 (September 1988), pp. 18–22.
Douglas, Carol Anne, 'Passages: Lesbians Aging', Report on the Washington Conference, 23 January 1988, *Off Our Backs*, vol. 18, no. 4 (April 1988), pp. 16–17.
Duncker, Patricia, 'The Sexual Politics of Fairy Tales'. *Lilith: Oxford's Women's Paper*, no. 14 (January 1984), pp. 4–5.
——'Re-imagining the Fairy Tales: Angela Carter's Bloody Chambers', in Peter Humm, Paul Stigant and Peter Widdowson (eds), *Popular Fictions: Essays in Literature and History* (London, Methuen, 1986), pp. 222–36.
Dworkin, Andrea, 'The Rape Atrocity and the Boy Next Door', in *Our Blood: Prophecies and Discourses on Sexual Politics* (1976; London, Women's Press, 1982), pp. 22–49.
Fairbairns, Zoë, 'I Was a Teenage Novelist', *Women's Review*, no. 8 (June 1986), pp. 8–11.
Feminist Review Collective, 'Feminism and Class Politics: A Round-Table Discussion', *Feminist Review*, no. 23 (Summer 1986), pp. 13–30.

Fetterley, Judith, 'Writes of Passing', *Gay Studies Newsletter*, vol. 14, no. 1 (March 1987); reprinted in *Gossip: A Journal of Lesbian Feminist Ethics*, no. 5 (Autumn 1987), pp. 21–8.

Ford Smith, Honor, 'Sistren Women's Theatre, Organizing and Conscientization', in Pat Ellis (ed.), *Women of the Caribbean* (London, Zed, 1986).

Furman, Nelly, 'The Politics of Language: Beyond the Gender Principle?' in Gayle Green and Coppélia Kahn (eds), *Making a Difference: Feminist Literary Criticism* (London, Methuen, 1985), pp. 59–79.

Gowens, Pat, 'Womb Oppression and Sex as Power', *Off Our Backs*, vol. 17, no. 8 (August–September 1987), p. 24.

Greene, Gayle and Kahn, Coppélia, 'Feminist Scholarship and the Social Construction of Woman', *Making a Difference: Feminist Literary Criticism* (London, Methuen, 1985), pp. 1–36.

Grundberg, Sibyl, 'Deserted Hearts: Lesbians Making it in the Movies', *Gossip: A Journal of Lesbian Feminist Ethics*, no. 4 (Spring 1987), pp. 27–39.

Hennegan, Alison, 'What Lesbian Novel?' *Women's Review*, no. 1 (November 1985), pp. 10–12.

Heresies: A Feminist Publication on Art and Politics, 'Racism is the Issue', Collective Editorial Statement, vol. 4, no. 3, issue 15, 21 October 1982.

Jacobus, Mary, 'Is there a Woman in this Text?' *New Literary History*, vol. 14, no. 1 (1982), pp. 117–41.

Jeffreys, Sheila, 'Does it Matter if they Did it? Lilian Fadermann and Lesbian History', *Trouble and Strife*, no. 3 (Summer 1984), pp. 25–9.

——'Butch and Femme: Now and Then', *Gossip: A Journal of Lesbian Feminist Ethics*, no. 5 (Autumn 1987), pp. 65–95; reprinted in Lesbian History Group, *Not A Passing Phrase: Reclaiming Lesbians in History 1840–1895* (London, Women's Press, 1989), pp. 158–87.

Jones, Gwyneth, 'Imagining Things Differently', *Women's Review*, no. 3 (January 1986), pp. 10–11.

Joseph, Gloria I., 'The Incompatible Menage à Trois: Marxism, Feminism and Racism', in Lydia Sargent (ed.), *Women and Revolution: The Unhappy Marriage of Marxism and Feminism* (London, PLuto, 1981), pp. 91–107.

Kanter, Hannah and Swirsky, Ruth, 'Jewish Women in London', *SHIFRA: A Jewish Feminist Magazine*, nos. 3, 4 (Chanukkah 5747/December 1986), pp. 4–7.

Kaplan, Cora, 'Pandora's Box: Subjectivity, Class and Sexuality in Socialist Feminist Criticism', in Gayle Green and Coppélia Kahn (eds), *Making a Difference: Feminist Literary Criticism* (London, Methuen, 1985), pp. 146–76.

Kappeler, Suzanne, 'What is a Feminist Publishing Policy?' in Gail Chester and Julienne Dickey (eds), *Feminism and Censorship: The Current Debate* (Bridport, Dorset, Prism, 1988), pp. 233–7.

Karimjee, Mumtaz, 'Black and Asian: Definitions and Redefinitions', *Mukti*, no. 6 (Spring 1987), special issue on 'Racism and Prejudice'.

Kris, 'Another Kind of Coming Out', *Gossip: A Journal of Lesbian Feminist Ethics*, no. 2(1986), pp. 80–9.

Krut, Riva and Otto, Elaine, 'Danger! Male Bonding at Work', *Trouble and Strife*, no. 4 (Winter 1984), pp. 41–7.

Lamont, Juliet, 'Many of Those Burned as Witches were Weavers', *Women for Life On Earth*, no. 14 (Summer 1986), p. 17.

Lefanu, Sarah, 'Robots and Romance: The Science Fiction and Fantasy of Tanith Lee' in Susannah Radstone (ed.), *Sweet Dreams: Sexuality, Gender and Popular Fiction* (London, Lawrence & Wishart, 1988), pp. 121–36.

Lindner, Elsbeth, 'An Editor's View . . . ', *Women's Review*, no. 8 (June 1986), p. 11.

Livia, Anna, 'I Would Rather have been Dead than Gone Forever: Butch and Femme as Responses to Patriarchy', *Gossip: A Journal of Lesbian Feminist Ethics*, no. 5 (Autumn 1987), pp. 53–64.

——with Lilian Mohin, 'Editorial: Notes from the Desk of the Many-Headed Hydra', *Gossip: A Journal of Lesbian Feminist Ethics*, no. 6 (1988), pp. 5–6.

Lorde, Audre, 'No, We Never Go Out of Fashion . . . For Each Other', Audre Lorde interviewed by Dorothea, Jackie Kay and Uma, *Spare Rib*, no 149 (November 1984), pp. 26–9.

Maitland, Sara, 'Passionate Prayer: Masochistic Images in Women's Experience', in Linda Hurcombe (ed.), *Sex and God: Some Varieties of Women's Religious Experience* (Routledge & Kegan Paul, 1987), pp. 125–40.

Minsky, Rosalind, 'The Trouble is it's Ahistorical: The Problem of the Unconscious in Modern Feminist Theory', *Feminist Review*, no. 36 (Autumn 1990), pp. 4–14.

Molina, Papusa, 'Building Alliances Against Racism: An Interview with Becky Thompson', *Sojourner: The Women's Forum* (Cambridge, Mass.), vol. 14, no. 3 (November 1988), pp. 16–18.

Morrison, Toni, 'Rootedness: The Ancestor as Foundation', in Mari Evans (ed.), *Black Women Writers: 1950–1980* (1984; London, Pluto, 1985), pp. 339–45.

Mulhern, Francis, 'Writing for the Future: The Politics of Literature', *New Statesman*, 22 March 1985, pp. 24–6.

Munt, Sally, 'The Investigators: Lesbian Crime Fiction', in Susannah Radstone (ed.), *Sweet Dreams: Sexuality, Gender and Popular Fiction*, (London, Lawrence & Wishart, 1988), pp. 91–119.

Newton, Esther, 'The Mythic Mannish Lesbian: Radclyffe Hall and the New Woman', in Estelle B. Freeman et al. (eds), *The Lesbian Issue: Essays from* Signs (Chicago, University of Chicago Press, 1985), pp. 7–25.

Norden, Barbara, 'Utopia is Dead', *Spare Rib*, no. 174 (January 1987), pp. 40–3.

O'Donoghue, Noreen, 'The Fate of *Out for Ourselves: The Lives of Irish Lesbians and Gay Men*, in G. Chester and J. Dickey (eds), *Feminism and Censorship: The Current Debate* (Bridport, Dorset, Prism, 1988).

Ogunyemi, Chikwenye Okonjo, 'Womanism: The Dynamics of the Contemporary Black Novel in English', *Signs*, vol. 11, no. 1 (Autumn 1985), pp. 63–80.

Packwood, Marlene, 'The Colonel's Lady and Judy O'Grady – Sisters under the Skin?' *Trouble and Strife*, no. 1 (Winter 1983), pp. 7–12.

Palmer, Paulina, 'Contemporary Lesbian Feminist Fiction: Texts for Everywoman', in Linda Anderson (ed.), *Plotting Change: Contemporary Women's Fiction* (London, Edward Arnold, 1990), pp. 42–62.

——'The Representation of Lesbianism in Contemporary Women's Fiction: The Division between "Politics" and "Psychoanalysis" ', in Jane Aaron and Sylvia Walby (eds), *Out of the Margins: Women's Studies in the Nineties* (Basingstoke, Falmer, 1991).

Payne, Tracey and Scott, Sara, 'Underneath We're All Lovable', *Trouble and Strife*, no. 3 (Summer 1984), pp. 21–4.

Penelope, Julia, 'The Mystery of Lesbians', three-part article, *Gossip: A Journal of Lesbian Feminist Ethics*, nos 1, 2, 3 (London, Onlywomen, 1986).

Raymond, Janice, 'The Politics of Passion', interview with Suzanne Kappeler, Liz Kelly and Kathy Parker, *Trouble and Strife*, no. 11 (Summer 1987), pp. 38–42.

Reyes, Elma, 'Women in Calypso', in Pat Ellis (ed.), *Women of the Caribbean* (London, Zed, 1986), pp. 119–21.

Rule, Jane, 'Lesbian and Writer: Making the Real Visible', in M Cruikshank (ed.), *New Lesbian Writing* (San Francisco, Grey Fox, 1984), pp. 96–9.

Semple, Linda, 'Lesbians in Detective Fiction', *Gossip: A Journal of Lesbian Feminist Ethics*, no. 5 (Autumn 1987), pp. 47–52.
——Review of Elizabeth Woods' *Mothers and Lovers* (1988), *Silver Moon Quarterly*, no. 6 (Spring 1988).
Sheba Feminist Publishers Collective, 'Can Black and White Women Work Together?' *Spare Rib*, no. 168 (July 1986), pp. 18–20.
Showalter, Elaine, 'Towards a Feminist Poetics', in Mary Jacobus (ed.), *Women Writing and Writing About Women* (London, Croom Helm, 1979), pp. 22–41.
Shulman, Sheila, 'Some Thoughts on Biblical Prophecy and Feminist Vision', *Gossip: A Journal of Lesbian Feminist Ethics*, vol. 6 (1988), pp. 68–79.
——'Versions of a Story' (unpublished essay, 1988).
Smartt, Dorothea and Mason-John, Val, 'Black Feminists Organising on Both Sides of the Atlantic', *Spare Rib*, no. 171 (October 1986), pp. 20–4.
Stacy, Judith, 'Are Feminists Afraid to Leave Home? The Challenge of Conservative Pro-Family Feminism', in Juliet Mitchell and Ann Oakley (eds), *What is Feminism? A Re-Examination* (Oxford, Blackwell, 1986), pp. 208–37.
Stimpson, Catharine R., 'Zero Degree Deviancy: The Lesbian Novel in English', in E. Abel (ed.), *Writing and Sexual Difference* (Brighton, Harvester, 1982), pp. 243–59.
Sulter, Maud, 'Black Codes: The Misrepresentation of Black Lesbians in Film', *Gossip: A Journal of Lesbian Feminist Ethics*, no. 5 (Autumn 1987), pp. 29–36.
Thomas, Elean, 'Lionhearted Women', *Spare Rib*, no. 172 (November 1986), pp. 14–19.
Tivedi, Parita, 'To Deny our Fullness: Asian Women in the Making of History', *Feminist Review*, no. 17 (Autumn 1984), pp. 37–50.
Toynbee, Polly, Review article of Mary Wibberley's *To Writers With Love – On Writing Romantic Novels* (Buchan & Enright, 1985), *The Guardian*, 22 July 1985.
——'More Deadly than the Male': profile of P. D. James, *The Guardian*, 2 June 1986.
Trouble and Strife: The Radical Feminist Magazine, Editorial, No. 1 (Winter 1983).
Vlasta: fiction/utopies/amazoniennes, no. 4 (Mai 1985), Special issue on Monique Wittig (available from Collectif Memoires/Utopies, B.P. 130, 75663 Paris, Cédex 14).
Wallsgrove, Ruth, 'The Four Lives of Joanna', *Trouble and Strife*, no. 5 (Spring 1985), pp. 30–3.
Weigel, Sigrid, 'Double Focus: On the History of Women's Writing', in Gisela Ecker (ed.), *Feminist Aesthetics* (London, Women's Press, 1985), pp. 59–80.
Williams, Claudette, 'Feature/Review of Video Film and Radio Play based on the poetry of Grace Nichols, 'i is a long-memoried woman': by Leda Serene Productions', *Spare Rib*, no. 218 (November 1990), pp. 20–2.
Wilson, Anna, 'On Being a Lesbian Writer: Writing Your Way out of the Paper Bag', in Lesley Saunders (ed.), *Glancing Fires: An Investigation into Women's Creativity* (London, Women's Press, 1987), pp. 141–5.
Wilson, Elizabeth and Weir, Angela, 'The British Women's Movement' (first published 1984 in *New Left Review*), in Elizabeth Wilson with Angela Weir, *Hidden Agenda: Theory, Politics and Experience in the Women's Movement* (London, Tavistock, 1986), pp. 93–133.
——'Tell It Like It Is: Women and Confessional Writing', in Susannah Radstone (ed.), *Sweet Dreams: Sexuality, Gender and Popular Fiction* (London, Lawrence & Wishart, 1988), pp. 21–45.
Woolf, Virginia, 'Women and Fiction' (1929), in *Women and Writing*, essays by Virginia Woolf selected and introduced by Michèle Barrett (London, Women's Press, 1979), pp. 43–52.

Index